A structured approach to

FORTRAN 77
Programming

INTERNATIONAL COMPUTER SCIENCE SERIES

Consulting editors **A D McGettrick**
University of Strathclyde

J van Leeuwen
State University of Utrecht

A structured approach to
FORTRAN 77
Programming

T M R ELLIS (University of Sheffield)

ADDISON-WESLEY PUBLISHING COMPANY
London · Reading, Massachusetts · Menlo Park, California
Amsterdam · Don Mills, Ontario · Manilla · Singapore
Sydney · Tokyo

Phototypesetting in Times and OCRB by Parkway Illustrated Press, London and Abingdon

Printed in the United States of America.

Library of Congress Cataloging in Publication Data
Ellis, T. M. R., 1942–
    A structured approach to Fortran 77 programming.

    (International computer science series)
    Includes index.
    1. FORTRAN (Computer program language) 2. Structured
    programming. I. Title. II. Series.
    QA76.73.F25E44   001.64'24   81-20563
    ISBN 0-201-13790-9 (pbk.)   AACR2

British Library Cataloguing in Publication Data
Ellis, T. M. R.
    A structured approach to Fortran 77 programming.
    —International computer science series; 3)
    1. FORTRAN (Computer programming language)
    I. Title   II. Series
    001.64'Z4   QA76.73.F25

    ISBN 0-201-13790-9

ABCDEFGHIJ-HA-89876543

Preface

The ability to utilise the power of a computer is an increasingly important part of the education of scientists, technologists and, indeed, students of most other disciplines. However it is vital that this power is used to best effect, and this, in turn, implies that computer programs are written in such a way as to maximise the efforts of both the computer and the programmer. The key to this is *planning* and an orderly method of working.

This book has been written for those with little or no previous computing experience and endeavours to teach the reader how to plan and write good, well-structured, programs using the latest version of the Fortran language – commonly referred to as Fortran 77. The book is particularly suitable for undergraduate programming courses in the pure and applied sciences, as well as in many social sciences, and will also be found appropriate for anyone who is interested in learning how to write computer programs for scientific, technical, or other, primarily numerical, applications.

The Fortran language can, in fact, trace its origins back to the mid-1950s, although the developments in computing since then have led to enormous changes not only in the details of the language, but also in the whole philosophy of programming. In 1966 the Fortran language was the subject of an American National Standard (ANSI X3.9-1966), and this 'Standard Fortran' (or Fortran IV as it was frequently called, after the IBM Fortran IV language on which the standard was based) was subsequently the starting-point for many substantial developments by computer manufacturers and others. In 1978 a new standard was issued (ANSI X3.9-1978), partly to rationalise the many slightly different Fortran dialects that had grown up, and partly to lead the way towards better Fortran programming through the inclusion of a number of new features – notably the Block IF structure. With these new features Fortran 77 (as the new Standard Fortran is usually called) can be used to write well-structured and efficient programs in a way which was difficult, if not impossible, with earlier versions of the language. Thus Fortran, which is by far the most widely used programming language in the world for scientific and technological programming, is likely to retain its pre-eminent position in these areas for many years to come.

The impetus for this book came primarily from the production, in 1980, of a Fortran 77 videotape teaching course which has met with considerable success in both Great Britain and other countries throughout the world. This book follows the same broad principles as the videotape course, but is not directly based upon it. The approach used is pedagogic in nature, and the various features of the Fortran 77 language are introduced at appropriate stages of the development of the reader's programming skills. A comprehensive index enables the book to be used as a source of reference – a mode of use which is enhanced by a complete specification of the syntax of the language in the form of 'railroad charts' in Appendix B.

Great emphasis is laid on the planning and the structure of programs as well as on the detailed Fortran instructions and their syntax. The 'top-down' approach to problem analysis and program design has for many years been accepted as a desirable aim, and in this book I use it extensively in the form of 'structure plans'. My experience in the classroom has shown that the use of these structure plans as a design aid both assists in the reduction of the problem to its constituent steps and leads to well-structured programs in a way that is not possible with the traditional use of flow-charts. This approach also lends itself quite naturally to the early introduction of the concept of modularisation, although the full realisation of that concept by the writing of private procedures (subroutines or functions) is left until after the fundamental features of Fortran 77 (assignment, repetition, decision-making and input/output) have been introduced.

The book consists of two parts, each of which contains six chapters. The first part introduces the fundamental principles of programming and good program design, and covers the main control structures and input/output facilities of Fortran 77 using only non-subscripted real and integer variables. This takes the reader to the point at which he can use the computer to solve quite sophisticated problems, despite the absence of several powerful and/or useful features such as arrays, file-handling and character variables. It is my experience that at about this stage the student frequently needs to slow down his rate of acquisition of knowledge. The second part of the book, which covers all those further features which are essential for *real* programs, will therefore usually be taken at a more gentle pace than the first part. This change, which is often quite abrupt, is partly due to the fact that the programs being written start to become more complex than those written in the early stages. The major reason, however, is that the use of characters, arrays, subroutines, files, etc. frequently emphasises any misconceptions remaining or any lack of comprehension of fundamental principles, and *always* highlights any poor program design practices that may have developed. Another problem which often becomes apparent at this stage is a lack of structure in the development and testing of programs, and there is, therefore, a short discussion of this subject immediately before the second part of the book.

The first three chapters explain the basic principles of program design and Fortran 77 programming utilising simple (list-directed) input and output together with the various arithmetic facilities, including the use of standard (intrinsic) functions. The next two chapters build on this foundation to add first repetition (using DO-loops) and then decision-making (using IF statements), in order to provide the capability to solve quite sophisticated numerical problems, and Chapter 6 shows how the power of Fortran formatted input and output can be used to give total control over the layout of data and results in a way which is not possible with the simple forms of input and output that were used in the earlier chapters.

This leads naturally to a discussion of characters and other types of data as well as to the concept of an array of variables. The ways in which these can be used to improve the flexibility and structure of a program are dealt with in some detail. Chapter 10 is concerned with how to write functions and subroutines, and the implications which these have upon the design of programs, with particular reference to the advantages of modularity when developing and testing larger programs. Finally, the last two chapters describe the use of global storage (i.e. COMMON blocks) and the various facilities for file handling, including both formatted and unformatted files which may be accessed in either a sequential or a random fashion.

The book contains a considerable number of examples but, nevertheless, one of the most important factors in learning how to write computer programs is practice. In order to help the reader to develop his skills and to eliminate his faults there are a number of exercises at the end of each chapter, most of which involve the writing of a program. *It is essential that the reader should both write as many as possible of these programs and test them on a computer.* If necessary (and it usually will be!) they should then be corrected and tested again, until such time as they work correctly. At the end of the book are the answers to the non-programming exercises and sample solutions for a number of the programming ones. It is recommended that the latter are not consulted until *after* a working solution has been obtained.

This book has developed from my experience in teaching and using various dialects of Fortran over the past 15 years, during which time I have received advice, assistance and encouragement from a great many people. I cannot attempt to identify them all, but I do wish to acknowledge a particular debt of gratitude to two people who in very different ways have had a profound influence upon what success I may have had. The first of these is Art Pfeiffer of the Illinois Institute of Technology Research Institute in Chicago, from whom I learned a great deal about good programming practice during a four-month secondment in 1966. The second is Herbert Deas, whose words of praise and encouragement after my first lecture course at Sheffield gave me the confidence that every new lecturer needs. To them both I offer my grateful thanks.

I must also thank Andrew McGettrick and Jan van Leeuwen for their constructive comments on the first draft of this book, which have, I hope, enabled me to tidy up a few loose ends and to produce a better end result. The text of the book was typed by Sandra Bissatt, and I am extremely grateful for the many long hours she has spent alone with her typewriter and my almost illegible handwritten manuscript.

All the programming examples were tested on the University of Sheffield's Prime 750 computer and then transferred to a word-processor. I am grateful for being allowed to use these facilities in this way. Finally I must thank my wife, Margaret, and my children, David, Sarah and Richard, for their patience and forbearance during many evenings and weekends while this book was being written when they might reasonably have expected to have rather more of my time than proved possible.

On a lighter note, I feel that I should say a few words about the cover of this book. It is based on a suggestion made by my wife, and shows the Iron Bridge at Ironbridge in Staffordshire – the first such structure in the world to be entirely built using cast-iron. You can read whatever you like into this – building bridges, developing structures, elegance, style, permanence, etc. – but at least it makes a change from abstract patterns and punched cards!

Sheffield   T. M. R. Ellis
June, 1982

Contents

Part I

FUNDAMENTAL PRINCIPLES

1 Introduction

1.1 Computers, programs and high-level languages

What is a computer? This is a question which is frequently asked by those who come into contact with computers and computing, and yet it is a question which is extremely difficult to answer. To an electronics engineer a computer may be just a collection of transistors, resistors, capacitors, integrated circuits and many other basic elements of electronic hardware. On the other hand to a computer scientist it may be an electro-mechanical realisation of a complex logical design, to a businessman it may be a 'black box' which provides him with accurate details of his business and projections into the future for different hypothetical scenarios, and to a child it may be a magic box which provides him with an almost infinite variety of 'electronic games'. All of these, and many more, are perfectly valid answers to the question posed above, for a computer is an extremely powerful tool which, chameleon-like, can appear in almost any guise that its users require it to.

Nevertheless at heart a computer is merely an inanimate collection of electronic circuits and devices with, usually, a considerable amount of electromechanical equipment attached to it. What sets a computer apart from other machines which may be built from similar (or even identical) component parts is its ability to 'remember' a sequence of instructions and to 'obey' these instructions at a predetermined point in time. Such a sequence of instructions is called a *program*, and what we usually refer to as a computer is more correctly called a *stored-program computer*. How we write a program to instruct the computer to perform the task(s) that we require of it is the subject of this book.

The very first stored program computer was designed by Charles Babbage in England in the 19th century; however the complexity of its construction and the extreme accuracy required in its many hundreds of gear-wheels meant that it was not practicable to build such a computer of the size necessary for most real-life calculations. One was built (the 'Difference Engine') and can be seen in the Science Museum in London, but its more sophisticated successor (the 'Analytical Engine') proved too complex to build. It was not until the early 1940's that the ideas were to be once more taken up, but this time using thermionic valves and other electrical devices as the basic components.

The programming of these early machines (i.e. the writing of the instructions which would form the program for the solution of a particular problem) was a highly complex task since the instructions were represented by strings of 0's and 1's known as *machine code* and were unique to a particular type of computer

3

> 0010100011 010 0 010111

It was not long, therefore, before a more compact form was devised in which each group of three 'binary digits' (or *bits*) was replaced by a single number in the range 0–7 (the 'octal' equivalent of the 3-bit binary number)

> 243 2 0 27

This was still a matter for a specialist, although, as there were only a handful of computers in the world, that in itself was of no great importance. Even for a specialist, however, it was difficult to remember which code number represented which operation, and where each data value was kept in the computer's 'memory'. The next development was the creation of a mnemonic form for the instructions, and the use of names to identify memory locations. For example

> LDA 2 X

meant 'load a special location (register 2) with the contents of location X'. This is known as *assembly language* programming, and the principles have survived almost unchanged to the present day.

Note that this way of programming requires a detailed understanding of the computer's instructions and their effects, and each type of computer has its own, quite distinct, form of assembly language. During the early and mid-1950's a great deal of effort was expended in finding a method which would enable the program to be formulated in the *user's* terms and not in those of the computer. The approach adopted, by most of the workers in this field, was to use an algebraic method of expressing formulae and a 'pidgin English' method of describing the other (non-mathematical) operations. The resulting program was said to use a 'high-level' language, since the method enabled a programmer to write programs without needing to know much about the details of the computer itself. One of the earliest of these languages (see Section 1.3) was known as FORTRAN.

Since that time the concept has been considerably refined, and today virtually all programs are now written in some form of high-level language (Algol, PL/I, Cobol, etc.). All such languages have several common features and we must establish these before we proceed further. First, almost invariably, English-like expressions are used to define what operations are to be carried out. The problem is expressed in a way that does not demand that the programmer is familiar with the internal working of the computer. Second, the organisation of the storage of both program and data is almost completely outside the control of the programmer – he merely gives a name of his own choice to abstract storage locations and these are automatically (through the computer's own operational software) related to some real locations within the computer's memory. Most importantly, the same program may usually be submitted to many different types of computers without the need for any significant changes.

As was mentioned earlier, the computer can only understand its own machine code and, therefore, before a high-level program can be obeyed by the computer it must be *translated* into the appropriate machine code. A special program (the *compiler*) is used to translate the high-level language program into a machine code program, for a particular computer, in such a way that the machine code may be kept for use on subsequent occasions. Since the compiler can only translate correct high-level program statements, an important part of its task is to check the syntax of each statement and to produce *diagnostic* information to help the programmer to correct any errors. Thus the statement

A = B + C

(which means that the location called A is to have placed in it the sum of the values currently stored in the locations called B and C) might be compiled into the three instructions

    011000000000011001010000 (LDX 3 B)
    011000000100011001010010 (ADX 3 C)
    011000100000011001001110 (STO 3 A)

On a different type of computer, however, the same statement would be translated into a totally different set of instructions, for example

    110000010010101111   (B)
    110000010010110000   (C)
    010001   (+)
    110001010010101110   (= A)

Thus the same high-level program can be run on two completely different types of computers simply by compiling it using two compilers which take the same input but produce quite different output. It was the development of this concept that enabled the use of computers to spread from the research laboratory into industry, commerce, government, education and (more recently) even into the home. A high-level program can, therefore, be transported from one place to another, can be developed by programmers who neither know nor care about the computer(s) on which it is to run, and can outlive the relatively short life of the computer itself in a period of rapid technological change.

1.2   What is a computer?

We can now return to the question posed earlier and define a model of a computer which will enable us to understand more easily exactly what we are doing when we write a program. We have already referred to the computer's *memory* – a set of electronic or magnetic devices in which information may be stored. That information may be either *program* – instructions which the computer is to obey – or *data* – values (numbers, words, etc.) which the computer is to process in a way defined by a program.

This processing is carried out by the *central processing unit* (C.P.U.) which consists of (at least) two quite separate parts – a *control unit* which fetches instructions, decodes them, and initiates appropriate action, and an *arithmetic unit* which carries out arithmetic and other types of operation on items of data.

These two parts – the C.P.U. and the memory – could be said to constitute the computer, but there are other essential parts of the system still to be discussed. To be of any practical use a computer must be able to communicate its results to the outside world, and this calls for some form of *output device* such as a display, a printer or a graph plotter. Similarly, there must be some way of getting both the program and any variable data it requires into the computer and therefore an *input device* is needed such as a keyboard, card reader or paper tape reader. One particular device, known as a *terminal*, has both a keyboard and either a display or some form of printer, and can therefore act as both an input and an output device.

Finally there is the question of large and/or long-term data storage. The devices used to form the memory of a computer are normally transient devices – when the power is switched off they lose the information stored in them and are thus of no use for storage of information other than during the running of a program. In addition, if the computer is to be able to access the information in the memory rapidly it can only be of a relatively small size (typically of the order of a few million characters). A memory of more than this size would place unacceptable burdens on both power requirements and physical space. Magnetic media, however, such as tapes or disks coated with a fine magnetic oxide (similar to that used on tapes for domestic cassette or videotape recorders) can be used to store very large amounts of information easily and economically, although at the cost of slower access time. Virtually all computers use magnetic media as a *backing store* enabling programs and data to be stored in a permanent fashion within the overall computer system. A single unit of program, data, or both together, is called a *file*.

Thus a computer can be represented by a simple diagram as shown in Fig. 1.1. The memory and central processor are usually electronic; however, the input, output and backing store devices also contain mechanical components, with the result that the speed of transfer of information between them and the central processor is many times slower than that between the memory and the central processor. For example, on a large ICL 2900 series computer, data can be input from cards at a rate of 160 000 characters per minute (c.p.m.), sent for printing at a rate of 240 000 c.p.m., and transferred to or

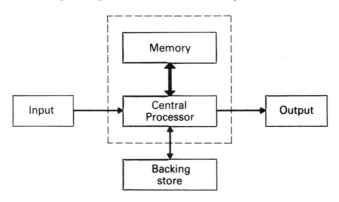

Fig. 1.1 An idealised computer

from backing store (on disks) at a rate of 70 million c.p.m. However items can be transferred between the memory and the central processor in 0.000001 seconds, which is equivalent to a rate of 500 million c.p.m. Because of this disparity in speed, most computers arrange for transfers between the central processor and input, output and backing store devices to proceed semi-autonomously – and in many cases bypass the central processor and transfer information directly to or from the memory. As a result of this, and because they are usually physically separated from the C.P.U., these types of device are referred to as *peripheral devices* – a distinction which has been emphasised in Fig. 1.1 by enclosing the memory and central processor in a dashed box.

Let us consider the memory and its mode of operation. Conceptually we can use an analogy with a large number of glass boxes, each containing a single ball on which is written a number, or a word, or any other single item that we may wish to store. To distinguish one box from another each has a label attached with an identifying name (see Fig. 1.2). Clearly we can find out what is in any of the boxes simply by looking at it, as long as we have the name of the box. Equally clearly, if we wish to put another value in a box we shall first have to remove (or otherwise get rid of) the ball which is already there so as to leave room for the new one. This is exactly the way the computer's memory works – if we wish to find out what is stored in a particular location the process does not affect what is stored there, whereas if we store a new value in some location then whatever was stored there is destroyed and lost.

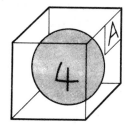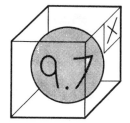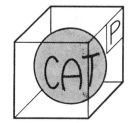

Fig. 1.2 A storage model

Now consider the names on the boxes, A, X and P, in Fig. 1.2. It is quite clear that these are the names of the *boxes* and not their contents, for if we were to store a new ball with the value 6 in box A we would not alter its name, and if we now looked at box A we would find that it contained the value 6 (Fig. 1.3).

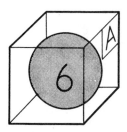

Fig. 1.3 An altered storage model

We shall come back to this when we start to write programs, but it is important to realise from the outset that the *names* that are used to refer to storage locations in the memory always identify the *location* and not the value that is stored there.

The boxes have, by implication, been open so that the current value may be removed and a new one inserted. To complete the analogy with the computer's memory we must have a rule that says that a box is never left empty; every box must contain a ball, even if it is a blank one or one with the value zero. Because such boxes, or rather the corresponding storage locations in the memory, can have their contents changed at will they are referred to as variable storage locations, or *variables*. Boxes which are identical with these except that they have a sealed lid can have their contents looked at, but it is not possible to replace the contents by a new value. Such storage locations are called constant storage locations, or *constants*.

1.3   What is Fortran?

Towards the end of 1953 John Backus proposed to his employers, the International Business Machines Corporation (IBM), that it would be beneficial if a small research group were to be set up to develop a more efficient and economical method of programming their 704 computer than the assembly language used at that time. The proposal was accepted and the group started work almost at once. By mid-1954 an initial specification had been produced for a 'programming language' of considerable power and flexibility. This language was to be called 'the IBM Mathematical FORmula TRANslation System, FORTRAN'. The project was initially intended purely for use by IBM on a single computer; however, soon after the preliminary report of the language was produced word got out to some of IBM's customers, with the result that the decision was made to make it available to anyone purchasing a 704 computer.

The first 'Programmer's Reference Manual' for the FORTRAN language was released in October 1956 and the compiler was finally delivered to customers in April 1957. This was followed twelve months later by Fortran II – an improved version of the system with a considerably enhanced diagnostic capability and a number of significant extensions to the language. Despite initial resistance on the grounds that the compiled programs were not as efficient as hand-coded ones, the language soon caught on, and by 1960 IBM had released versions of Fortran for their 709, 650, 1620 and 7070 computers. The most important development however was that other manufacturers started to write compilers for Fortran and by 1963 there were over 40 different Fortran compilers in existence!

One problem though was that the 704 Fortran (and Fortran II) had used certain specific features of the instruction set of the 704 computer and therefore the other Fortran compilers tended to do likewise. In addition, the advantages to be gained by having a standard language had not been fully appreciated and there were incompatibilities between different compilers, even between those written by the same manufacturer. As a result of pressure from their users as early as 1961, IBM set about developing a still further improved Fortran which did away with the machine-dependent features of Fortran II. This new system, Fortran IV, was released for the IBM 7030 (Stretch) computer in 1962, and later for the IBM 7090/7094 machines.

The most significant development of all, however, was the decision of the American Standards Association (now the American National Standards Institute) in May 1962 to set up a committee to develop an American Standard Fortran. This committee defined two languages – FORTRAN, based largely on Fortran IV, and Basic FORTRAN, which was based on Fortran II but without the machine dependent features. These standards were ratified in March 1966.

The existence of an officially defined standard (which was also effectively an international standard) meant that further development of the language had a firm and well-defined base from which to work. The 1960s and early 1970s saw computers become established in all areas of society, and this dramatic growth led, amongst other things, to a proliferation of different programming languages. Many of these were oriented towards specific application areas, but a substantial proportion were intended to be 'general-purpose' languages. Most noteworthy amongst these were Algol 60, Algol 68, Basic, Cobol, Pascal and PL/I.

In the midst of all this language research and development Fortran did not remain static. Computer manufacturers wrote compilers which accepted considerable extensions to the 'Standard Fortran', while in 1969 the American National Standards Institute (ANSI) set up a working committee to revise the 1966 standard. Partly because of the many changes in the philosophy and practice of programming during this period, a draft standard did not appear until some seven years had elapsed. During 1977 this draft was the subject of world-wide discussion and comment before a revised version was approved as the new Standard in April 1978.

The new (1977) Standard FORTRAN replaces both the older (1966) FORTRAN and Basic FORTRAN Standards, although included within the Standard defining document is a definition of a smaller, more restricted, Subset FORTRAN. In order to distinguish the new standard language from the old one, the Standard suggests that the new language should be called 'Fortran 77'.

1.4   Why learn Fortran 77?

Fortran is not, of course, the only computer language. There are a very great many languages available throughout the world, some widely, some not so widely, and some only in one place. However two languages stand head and shoulders above the others in terms of their total usage. These languages are Cobol (first released in 1960) and Fortran (first released in 1957).

Fortran was originally designed with scientific and engineering users in mind, and during its first 25 years it has completely dominated this area of programming. For example, most of the body structure of a Boeing 747 airliner or a NASA lunar capsule have been manufactured using machine tools whose movements are controlled by means of a Fortran program. The dies which are used in pressing the bodyshells of virtually all British or American mass-produced motor cars are also made by machines controlled by Fortran programs. The structural analysis of bridges or skyscrapers, the calculation of stresses in chemical plant piping systems, the design of electric generators, and the analysis of the flow of molten glass are all usually carried out using computer programs written in Fortran.

Fortran has also been the dominant language in academic circles and has been widely used in other, less obvious, areas. One of the most widely used programs in both British and American Universities is SPSS (Statistical Package for the Social Sciences) which enables social scientists to analyse survey or other research data; SPSS is written in Fortran. Indeed, because of the extremely widespread use of Fortran in higher education and industry, many standard 'libraries' have been written in Fortran in order to enable programmers to utilise the experience and expertise of others when writing their own Fortran programs. Two notable examples of such libraries are NAG (a large, and extremely comprehensive, collection of 'subprograms' for numerical analysis applications) and GINO (a highly sophisticated graphics package). Thus, because of the widespread use of Fortran over a period of more than 20 years, a vast body of experience is available in the form of existing Fortran programs. Fortran 77 allows access to all this experience, while adding new and more powerful facilities to the Fortran language.

Unlike Fortran, Cobol is designed primarily for business data processing use and does not purport to be suitable for scientific or technical programming; Fortran, on the other hand until the advent of Fortran 77, was notoriously weak on character handling and is still not the most appropriate language for business data processing. Other high-level languages in widespread use such as Algol 60, Algol 68, Basic, Pascal, PL/I and Simula all have both advantages and disadvantages for their particular field of use.

This book introduces the Fortran 77 language in a way that will encourage the embryo programmer to develop a good style of programming and a sound approach to the design of his programs. It must, however, be emphasised that programming is a practical skill, and that to develop this skill it is essential that as many programs as possible are written and tested on a computer. The exercises at the end of each chapter will help here, but it should always be realised that to write fluent, precise and well-structured programs requires both planning and experience. Fortran has evolved over a quarter of a century in what has often been a pragmatic fashion, but always with the emphasis on efficiency and ease of use. Fortran 77 provides a number of powerful features which were not available in earlier versions; these enable Fortran programmers to write more elegant and well-structured programs and to carry out activities (such as character manipulation) which were previously difficult or impossible. The next Standard version of Fortran is due around 1986 and will incorporate *all* of Fortran 77. Thus programs written in Fortran 77 will have life well into the twenty-first century.

Bibliography

American National Standard Programming Language FORTRAN. (ANSI X3.9–1978). American National Standards Institute, New York, 1978.

SPSS — Statistical Package for the Social Sciences (2nd Edition). (Nie, Norman H., Hadlai Hull, C., Jenkins, Jean G., Steinbrenner, Karin, and Bent, Dale H.). McGraw-Hill, New York, 1975.

GINO-F User Manual (Issue 2). Computer Aided Design Centre, Cambridge, 1979.

NAG Fortran User Manual (Mark 8). Numerical Algorithms Group, Oxford, 1981.

A Simple Program

2.1 Our first program

Fig. 2.1 is a complete Fortran 77 program. It appears to use a number of English words in a fairly understandable way. The program will 'read' two numbers, add them together, and print them with their sum and some text. There are a lot of important principles to be learned from this simple program, so we shall examine each line in turn to establish exactly what it means and how it is used.

```
      PROGRAM FIRST
C THIS IS OUR FIRST PROGRAM
      READ *,A,B
      SUM = A+B
      PRINT *,'THE SUM OF',A,' AND',B,' IS',SUM
      STOP
      END
```

Fig. 2.1   A Fortran program

The format in which a Fortran program must be typed is very important. Remember that Fortran was developed in the mid-1950's for internal use (initially) on an IBM 704 computer. The only form of input to that computer was a punched card – that is a card which is marked with 80 columns and 12 rows and which can have small rectangular holes punched in any of the 960 resulting positions. Each column represents one character (a letter, a digit, a space, or one of several special characters such as +,.* etc.) which is punched as a coded combination of one, two or three holes. Thus a single card can contain 80 characters. The first Fortran system therefore limited the length of a line to 80 characters.

However the influence of the card went further than that, for the designers of the first Fortran system decided that, in order to speed up processing, they would use certain parts of the card for specific purposes. To this day, a Fortran statement has to follow certain rules of layout even if, as is very likely, it is being typed directly into the computer from a keyboard without any cards being involved at all. We shall not introduce all these rules at this point but will simply mention two main and two minor ones.

The first rule is that the last 8 columns (73–80) are not used at all! Or, to be more accurate, they are not treated as part of the program but can be used for other, identifying purposes. When large programs were punched on cards and submitted to the computer many times, it was a sensible precaution to punch sequence numbers on the cards in case they should get dropped or otherwise out of order! Nowadays programs are almost invariably either typed directly into the computer or else punched on cards which are then read *once* by the computer and stored in a file on backing store. In practice, therefore, columns 73–80 are rarely, if ever, used.

The second rule is that the first 6 columns are used for special purposes and that as a result the Fortran statements always begin at (or after) column 7.

One of the special purposes for which the first 6 columns may be used is shown in the above program. If the first column contains a C or an asterisk (*) then the whole line is treated as a *comment* and ignored when the program is being compiled into machine code. It will, however, be listed with all the other lines and is used to add explanatory comments so that the program is easy to understand.

Thus our simple program contains seven lines, of which six start in column 7, while the second line has a C in column 1 and is therefore a comment line whose format is of no concern.

A second, special, use of the first six columns is to specify a *continuation line*. If column 6 of a line contains any character other than a space or a zero then the line is treated as a continuation of the previous line. In this case columns 1–5 of the continuation line must be blank, and column 7 is treated as though it came immediately after column 72 of the previous line. There can be up to 19 continuation lines following any initial line, although it is unusual to need more than one or two.

We can now return to our program and examine the first few lines.

        PROGRAM FIRST

This line gives a name to our program and consists of the word PROGRAM followed by a name which we can choose. This name must satisfy the basic rules for Fortran names and must

- start with a letter
- contain only letters and digits
- be at most six characters long

In practice many computer systems will allow more than six characters in a name, but the Standard specifies a maximum of six and so it is advisable to observe this limit. We shall do so throughout this book.

Thus our program is called FIRST, which satisfies the above rules. One point to note is that spaces have no significance in general and may be used, as in ordinary English, to improve the layout. Thus we could equally well have written

        PROGRAMFIRST

which is not very clear to the human reader, although perfectly acceptable to the Fortran compiler, or

        P R O G R A M F I R S T

or even

```
PRO GRA MFI RST
```

However since it makes no difference to the computer it is sensible to make the layout easy for the human reader to follow by including spaces in the natural places, i.e. between words and/or numbers

```
PROGRAM FIRST
```

We may choose any name we like for the program (as long as it is a valid Fortran name), but having once chosen a name we cannot use the same name for another purpose (e.g. a storage location) in the same program. If we were to do so, it would be confusing for both us and the computer and this is something that must always be avoided.

If we do not want to give our program a name at all then the PROGRAM statement can be omitted altogether. There is no particular advantage to be gained by so doing, and some compilers may insist on it being present, so it is strongly recommended that every program should start properly with a PROGRAM statement.

The next line

```
C  THIS IS OUR FIRST PROGRAM
```

is a comment and merely confirms what we already know, namely that this is our first program. It will be listed and otherwise ignored by the compiler.

The third line of the program is where things really start to happen

```
READ *,A,B
```

This apparently simple statement disguises a very complex situation. The input of data (and the output of results) is always the most complicated part of any programming language, and Fortran is no exception. The problem is that we see numbers, words, or anything else in quite a different manner to the way in which they are stored within the computer.

For example Fig. 2.2 shows how a hypothetical computer might store several numbers and names and it can easily be seen how two apparently similar numbers (123 and 123.0) are stored totally differently, while on the other hand three completely different items (−3.1324, −3946591 and the word PLAY) are stored identically. However, even this disguises the true magnitude of the problem because what we write cannot be read directly by the computer (as a general rule) and must be typed in at a keyboard, or punched on to cards, or coded in some other way for the computer. In addition there is the question of layout. For example, what does the card shown in Fig. 2.3 represent? It could be the number 123456789, or it could be the nine numbers 1,2,3,4,5,6,7,8,9 punched without any intervening spaces, or it could even be the number 12345.6789 with the convention that the decimal point is not punched but will be assumed to fall between the fifth and sixth digits. All of these are pefectly valid interpretations of the contents of the card.

Us	Computer
123	00000000000000001111011
123.0	01000111111011000000000
0.123	00111101111101111100111
−1.23	11000001100110101110000
−123	11111111111111110000101
−3.1324	11000010110010000111001
−3946 591	11000010110010000111001
PLAY	11000010110010000111001

Fig. 2.2   How we and the computer see data items

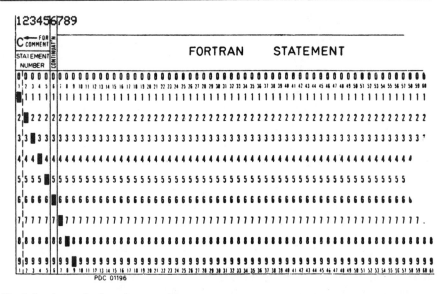

Fig. 2.3   A punched card

We shall see in Chapter 6 how to resolve most of these problems; however, fortunately Fortran 77 comes to our aid with a special, simplified form of input/output which avoids the necessity for any consideration of most of the problems, although at the cost of a slight loss of flexibility. This special type of input/output is called *list-directed input/output*.

For the input of data this takes the form

```
READ *, input-list
```

where 'input-list' is a list of one or more variable names (into which the data is to be placed) separated by commas. Thus the statement

```
READ *,A,B
```

tells the computer that it is to read (or input) two data items and store them in the locations A and B respectively. But what are these data items? The answer here is that unless otherwise instructed (as we shall see in Chapters 7 and 8) all data is assumed to be numeric. Furthermore, if the first letter of the name of a storage location begins with one of the letters I, J, K, L, M or N the number will be stored as an *integer* (or whole number), while if it begins with one of the remaining 20 letters (A–H, O–Z) the number will be stored as a *real* number (with a fractional, or decimal, part).

The above statement therefore also tells the computer that the two data items are *real numbers* and must be stored as such. However there still remains the question of how the data is to be typed (or punched) – in other words what *format* it is in – and where it is to be read from (terminal, card reader, etc.). The format is defined largely as a result of the input-list – this is the meaning of list-directed – and quite simply means that the first number starts with the first non-blank character and then continues until either a comma, or a blank, or a blank (or blanks) followed by a comma, or the end of a line is reached. The second number (if any) then starts with the next non-blank character, and so on. Notice that this means that the number is not allowed to contain any blank characters. The data for the above READ statement could, therefore, be typed in any of the following ways

(a) `123.45,67.89`
(b) `123.45 67.89`
(c) `        123.45 , 67.89`
(d) `        123.45`
     `67.89`
(e) `123.45,`
     `67.89`

If the name of the variable (location) in which the data is to be stored is a real name (i.e. it starts with one of the letters A–H or O–Z) then the number may have a decimal point and/or sign as required and, for example, 123 will be treated as 123.0. However if the name is an integer name then the data must be a whole number, optionally preceded by a sign, and may not contain a decimal point.

When using the simple form of input statement described above, the READ statement will take its data from the 'standard input unit'. This will be defined for the computer system being used and will typically be the keyboard in an interactive system (i.e. one where the user types his program at a terminal and receives his results there). In a batch system, where jobs are submitted on cards, it will normally be the card reader. A READ statement will input as many lines of data as are necessary to obtain values for all the variable names in the input-list, but a new READ statement will always start a new line of data. If a / character is input it is treated as a terminator for the current number (like a space or a comma) *and also for the whole statement*; any variables in the input-list which have not yet had values input and stored will be set to a null value (i.e. in practice will normally be left unchanged).

Thus our input statement reads two real numbers from the standard input unit and stores them in the variables A and B.

The next statement is easier

`SUM=A+B`

This is called an *assignment statement* because it assigns a value for storage in a variable. The equals sign (=) is misleading because what the statement means is 'take the values stored in A and B, add them together, and store the result in a variable called SUM'. There is, therefore, a sense of direction about the statement and a form such as

    SUM←A+B

would be rather clearer. It is very important to understand this and not to confuse it with an algebraic equation which might look the same. Thus the two statements

    B=C

and

    C=B

are totally different. The first takes the contents of C and stores the same value in B; the second stores the value of B in C. If, initially, B contains 1.0 and C contains 2.0 then the first statement leaves B *and* C both containing the value 2.0, while the second one would leave them both containing the value 1.0.

The next statement

    PRINT *,'THE SUM OF',A,' AND',B,' IS',SUM

is a list-directed output statement. This is very similar to the list-directed input statement discussed earlier and takes the form

    PRINT *, output-list

It causes the items in the output-list to be sent to the 'standard output unit' in a format which is determined by the output-list itself. The standard output unit will usually be the display or printer on the terminal for an interactive system, or the computer's printer for a batch system. The output-list and the output formats are, however, rather more complicated than for input.

The most obvious difference in the output-list is that it is not restricted to variable names, but may also contain constants or expressions (expressions are dealt with in Chapter 3). If a name (of a variable) appears in the output-list then the value which is stored in the location with that name is output in a format which depends upon the type of the variable. If a constant appears in the output-list then it is output in a format which depends upon the type of the constant.

There are three types of constant which may concern us at present – real, integer and character

- A *real* constant is a number which contains a decimal point, and which may (optionally) be preceded by a sign,
  e.g. 4.7 −0.01 +3.14159 17. −.1

- An *integer* constant is a number which does not contain any decimal point, and which may (optionally) be preceded by a sign, e.g. 4 −1 +275

- A *character* constant is a sequence of characters enclosed in single quotes (or apostrophes), and is often referred to as a string, e.g. 'MILES ELLIS' 'H2SO4'
  If it is required to include an apostrophe in a string then two consecutive apostrophes are written (but only a single apostrophe is stored within the computer),
  e.g. 'TODAY''S LUCKY NUMBER'
  The apostrophes which enclose the string are not part of the string, and are not stored in the computer.

The format that is used to output the required values is a 'reasonable' one according to the defining Standard. This means that integers will be printed preceded by one or more spaces, that real numbers (unless they are very large or very small) will be preceded by one or more spaces and limited to a certain number of decimal places (typically 4 or 5), and characters will be printed exactly as they are stored in the computer's memory. It is possible for numbers (but *not* characters) to be followed by a comma, but this is unusual. Each PRINT statement will start to print on a new line and continue over as many lines as are necessary.

Thus the PRINT statement in our program sends a line of output to the standard output channel consisting of the words THE SUM OF, followed by the value of A, the word AND, the value of B, the word IS, and finally the value stored in SUM (which has, of course been already assigned the value of A+B). If A was 7.0 and B was 12.0 it would therefore take the following form (or something like it)

```
THE SUM OF    7.0000 AND    12.0000 IS    19.0000
```

The layout here could do with some improvement, but that will need to wait until the full Fortran input/output capability is discussed in Chapter 6. It will be noted, however, that whereas each number is preceded by several spaces it is only followed by one. This is because a character constant is not preceded by spaces during output and, in fact, the space before AND and the one before IS are part of the string. If the program had read

```
PRINT *,'THE SUM OF',A, 'AND',B,'IS',SUM
```

then the result would have been

```
THE SUM OF    7.0000AND    12.0000IS    19.0000
```

We can also see that because A and B are real numbers the output format is appropriate to such numbers, and has caused the numbers to be printed with four decimal places (all zero!).

The next statement

```
STOP
```

has fairly obvious meaning – it tells the computer to stop. This is where the difference between the logic of a computer and that of a human is once again apparent. *We* know that we have finished (it's obvious) but the computer doesn't know anything – it has to be told. The STOP statement therefore instructs the computer to finish obeying (or *executing*) this program, and to return to the state it normally is in when not obeying such a program.

There is, however, one final statement

    END

This indicates that there are no more lines of program to come and marks, therefore, the physical end of the program (or rather, as we shall see in Chapter 10, of this program unit). In Fortran 77 (although not in earlier versions of Fortran) this also has the effect of terminating the execution of the program if it is obeyed and therefore the STOP statement could be omitted. This is not good practice, however, as the purpose of the two statements is quite different – STOP marks the *logical* end of the program (which as we shall see later need not be at the last line) while END merely signifies its *physical* end, and is therefore primarily an instruction to the compiler, informing it that it may now proceed with translating (or compiling) the Fortran program into machine code prior to its execution.

2.2   A word about numbers

We should now examine the differences between the two types of numbers, real and integer, in some detail before learning any more about their use.

An integer is a whole number and is therefore stored in the computer's memory without any decimal (or fractional) part. However because of the way in which information is stored there are limits to its size. These limits vary from one computer to another and depend upon the physical design of the computer's memory. We can illustrate this by considering a hypothetical computer which (for ease of comprehension!) stores its data in decimal form instead of the binary (base 2) system used by all normal computers. This means that a single digit will be recorded by means of some device which has 10 states (corresponding to the 10 digits) instead of one with two states (e.g. on and off) as required for binary numbers. Each location in the memory used for storing integers will consist of a fixed number of these devices, say 8, which will impose a limit on the size of the number – in this case up to 99 999 999. There remains the question of the sign of the numbers.

Suppose that the device which stored the integer was an electronic equivalent of a mileometer, such as that fitted to a car (see Fig. 2.4). If the reading is 00 000 000 and the car moves forward 2 miles (i.e. adds 2) the mileometer will read 00 000 002. However if the car now reverses for 3 miles (i.e. subtracts 3) the reading will successively go to 00 000 001, 00 000 000 and finally 99 999 999. Thus the same reading is obtained for a value of -1 as for $+99\,999\,999$, and adding 1 to 99 999 999 will give zero. We could therefore adopt a convention which says that readings from 1 to 49 999 999 will be considered to be positive, whereas 50 000 000 to 99 999 999 will be considered to be negative, and equivalent to $-50\,000\,000$ to -1 respectively. Almost all computers work like this, although when using the binary system the effect is

(a) | 0 | 0 | 0 | 0 | 0 | 0 | 0 | 0 | initial mileometer reading

(b) | 0 | 0 | 0 | 0 | 0 | 0 | 0 | 2 | after two miles

(c) | 0 | 0 | 0 | 0 | 0 | 0 | 0 | 1 | after reversing one mile

(d) | 0 | 0 | 0 | 0 | 0 | 0 | 0 | 0 | after reversing one more mile

(e) | 9 | 9 | 9 | 9 | 9 | 9 | 9 | 9 | after reversing one more mile

Fig. 2.4   Mileometer readings during travel

that if the first 'binary digit' (or bit) is a one then the number is negative, while if it is zero the number is positive.

Using the convention just described our eight-digit memory location can hold a whole number in the range $-50\,000\,000$ to $+49\,999\,999$, as shown in Fig. 2.5.

(a) | 5 | 0 | 0 | 0 | 0 | 0 | 0 | 0 | represents $-50\,000\,000$

(b) | 9 | 9 | 9 | 9 | 9 | 9 | 9 | 9 | represents -1

(c) | 0 | 0 | 0 | 0 | 0 | 0 | 0 | 0 | represents 0

(d) | 0 | 0 | 0 | 0 | 0 | 0 | 0 | 1 | represents $+1$

(e) | 4 | 9 | 9 | 9 | 9 | 9 | 9 | 9 | represents $+49\,999\,999$

Fig. 2.5   Storage of 8-digit integers

Now let us consider real numbers. These have a fractional part and clearly one way would be to assume that, for example, the first four digits come before the decimal point and the second four after it. However this would mean that the numbers could only lie between -5000.0 and $+4999.9999$ and that all numbers would be stored with exactly four decimal places. Clearly this is ridiculous and another way must be found. One solution might be to allow more digits, but the problem with this approach is that a large number of them will be wasted on many occasions. For example if 16 digits were allowed, so as to give a range as for integers but with eight places of decimals then, on the one hand, a number such as 100 000 000.0 cannot be stored because it needs 9 digits before the decimal place, even though all of those after it are not needed, while on the other a number such as 0.000 000 004 would have to be treated as zero because it needs 9 decimal places even though all 8 before the decimal point are not needed.

The solution is to consider a real number as a fraction lying between 0.1 and 1.0 which is multiplied or divided by 10 a certain number of times. Thus

$$100\,000\,000.0 \text{ is the same as } 0.1 \times 10^9$$
$$0.000\,000\,004 \text{ is the same as } \frac{0.4}{10^8} \text{ or } 0.4 \times 10^{-8}$$

We can now define a method of storage which says that the first six digits represent a fraction to six decimal places (with the first being non-zero), while the last two represent the number of times that the fraction is to be multiplied or divided by 10. Fig. 2.6 illustrates this method, which is known as *floating point* storage.

(a) 4 1 3 7 0 2 0 3   represents 0.413702×10^3
                           $= 413.702$

(b) 6 8 4 9 1 5 0 4   represents -0.315085×10^4
                           $= -3150.85$

(c) 4 1 3 7 0 2 9 7   represents 0.413702×10^{-3}
                           $= 0.000413702$

(d) 6 8 4 9 1 5 9 8   represents -0.315085×10^{-2}
                           $= -0.003\,150\,85$

Fig. 2.6 Floating-point numbers

This method of storage has two main implications. The first is that all numbers, whatever their size, are held to the same degree of accuracy. In the example being used they will all be stored to an accuracy of six significant digits. Thus the problem of wasted digits does not arise. The second implication is that the limits for the size of the numbers are very much greater than was the case for integers. In our hypothetical computer, for example, real numbers can lie anywhere in the range from -5×10^{48} to $+4.999\,99 \times 10^{48}$, and at the same time the smallest number that can be differentiated from zero is 0.1×10^{-50} (i.e. 10^{-51}).

In our hypothetical computer, therefore, the number 41370203 represents the real value 413.702 or the integer value 41370203, depending upon which storage method is being used. It is clearly of vital importance that both we and the computer know which of the two possibilities is required.

In a real computer exactly the same situation arises and it is essential that the two methods of storage are clearly defined. As has already been mentioned, if the name of a variable starts with one of the letters I, J, K, L, M or N then it refers to an integer; the computer therefore uses the integer storage method. If the name starts with one of the other letters then it refers to a real value and the computer uses the floating point storage method.

It is important that the difference between an integer and a real number is thoroughly appreciated. An integer is a whole number, is always held exactly in the computer's memory, and has a (relatively) limited range (e.g. between about -2×10^9 and $+2 \times 10^9$ on a typical 32-bit computer). A real number, on the other hand, is stored as a floating-point number, is held as an approximation to a fixed number of significant digits and has a very large range (e.g. between about -10^{38} and $+10^{38}$ to 7 or 8 significant digits on the same 32-bit computer). Where necessary, numbers are converted from one system to the other (see Chapter 3).

2.3 Running Fortran programs on a computer

Up to now we have considered the Fortran program in isolation with little reference to the method whereby the program is input to the computer, compiled, executed, and the results returned to the user. This omission is deliberate and is due to the fact that whereas the Fortran language is standardised the computer *operating system* is not. We shall digress slightly and look at the broad principles of the overall computer system.

In the early days of computing the programmer had to do everything himself. He would load his program (probably written in an assembly language or even machine code) and press the appropriate buttons on the machine to get it to work. When the program required data he would either type it in or, more probably, load some data cards. When the program wanted to print results he would ensure that the printer (or other output device) was ready. Before long the computers developed in two directions – first, magnetic tapes (and later disks) were added to provide backing store, and second, high-level languages such as Fortran became available. Now he had to load the compiler first and get it to input his program as data. The compiled program (possibly on 'binary' punched cards produced by the compiler) would then be input as before. In addition if any backing storage was required he had to load the correct tapes. In some cases a full-time operator was employed to carry out all these tasks, but this of course meant that detailed instructions were required to ensure that the job was processed correctly and so many programmers still preferred (if they were allowed) to run their programs themselves.

The major change was heralded by the development at Manchester University of the *multiprogramming* system for the Atlas computer. This took advantage of the high speed of a computer's arithmetic and logical functions compared with its input/output functions to process several programs apparently simultaneously. The effect is similar to that experienced by 'amateur' chess-players when facing a Chess-Master in a simultaneous match, where the Master plays against a number of opponents at the same time. In fact, of course, he moves from one board to another, but because of his much greater ability and speed in assessing the board position he appears to each of his oppenents to be devoting most, if not all, of his time to them. The Atlas system took advantage of the (relatively) long delays during input or output of even a single number to leave that program (whose input/output could proceed autonomously) and start to process another.

A further development at the Massachusetts Institute of Technology led to the concept of *time-sharing* which placed the user at a terminal through which most input/output took place, with each user having a small *slice* of time in turn. The much slower speed of a terminal allowed more programs to run at once, but because the user was communicating directly with the computer his work was processed much more quickly in this new *interactive* mode of operation than was possible with *batch* working.

However the advent of first multiprogramming and then time-sharing meant that it was no longer possible for the programmer, or even a full-time operator, to carry out all the routine tasks associated with loading and executing a program; too many things were happening in different jobs at the same time. Since the computer was now doing several things at once it was natural that it should be given the additional task of organising its own work. Special programs were therefore written, called *operating systems*, which enabled the programmer to define what he wanted to be done and caused the computer to carry out these instructions. What gradually emerged were new languages (*job control* languages, or JCL's) with which the programmer instructed the computer how to run his jobs.

Unfortunately, job control languages are a very long way from being standardised, and in order to run a Fortran program on a particular computer it is almost always necessary to learn (at least a little) about the JCL for that computer. Fig. 2.7 and 2.8 show examples of how the program discussed above would be run on two totally different computers.

In the example of Fig. 2.7 the program and data are submitted on cards for processing in a batch mode; the results will be printed and returned later. The details of this job are not important, but it can be seen that both program and data are there, together with several other lines of JCL.

```
JOB FIRSTPROG,:CS1TMRE,JD(UR E)
FORTRAN77
      PROGRAM FIRST
C  THIS IS OUR FIRST PROGRAM
      READ *,A,B
      SUM = A+B
      PRINT *,'THE SUM OF',A,' AND',B,' IS',SUM
      STOP
      END
      FINISH
7,12
****
```

Fig. 2.7 A Fortran 77 job for an ICL 1906S

The example of Fig. 2.8 is rather different and shows a (slightly edited) record of an interactive session during which the same program was typed at a terminal, stored in a file, compiled and then executed with the results appearing on the same terminal. Because this happens to be an interactive process, those items typed by the computer have been underlined to distinguish them from those typed by the programmer. Once again the details are not important; it is sufficient to observe that there are very substantial differences between the two sets of JCL commands.

```
OK, LOGIN CS1TMRE

OK, ED
INPUT
        PROGRAM FIRST
C   THIS IS OUR FIRST PROGRAM
        READ *,A,B
        SUM = A+B
        PRINT *,'THE SUM OF',A,' AND',B,' IS',SUM
        STOP
        END

EDIT
FILE FIRSTPROG. F77
OK, COMPILE FIRSTPROG

        several lines of system output

OK, EXECUTE FIRSTPROG

Executing "FIRSTPROG.F77"

7,12
    THE SUM OF      7.00000 AND      12.0000 IS      19.0000
****STOP

OK, LOGOUT

OK,
```

Fig. 2.8   A Fortran 77 interactive job on a Prime 750

Throughout the rest of this book we shall ignore this aspect of running programs, and concentrate on the programs themselves. However before any programs are actually compiled and executed it will be necessary for the reader to establish the essential features of the JCL that he will be using on his particular computer.

2.4 Errors in programs

It is an unfortunate fact that programs often (one might even say usually) contain errors. These fall into two distinct groups – syntactic (or grammatical) errors and semantic (or logical) errors. An example of the first type of error would be the omission of the asterisk in the READ statement of our first program

```
        READ A,B
```

When the compiler is translating this statement it finds that it does not match with any of the valid forms of READ statement (there are several more, as we shall see in Chapters 6 and 12), and the appropriate machine code cannot be generated. It will therefore produce an error message such as

**** SYNTAX ERROR

or possibly a more helpful one such as

**** READ NOT FOLLOWED BY ASTERISK, FORMAT REFERENCE
      OR LEFT PARENTHESIS

Since the program may contain more than one error the compiler will usually continue to check the rest of the program (in some cases other apparent errors may be caused which will disappear when the first one is corrected). However no machine code will be produced, and no loading or execution will take place (if these would otherwise have been automatically initiated).

Errors detected by the compiler (called *compilation errors*) are no great problem. That they are there indicates a degree of carelessness on the part of the programmer, but they can be easily corrected and the program recompiled. Far more serious is an error in the logic of the program. Occasionally this may lead to a compilation error, but usually it will lead either to an error during the execution of the program leading to an abnormal end (such as would occur if one number was accidentally divided by zero leading to a theoretical answer of infinity, which is too big for any computer!), or to the program producing incorrect answers. For example if the fourth line of our program had inadvertently been written as

SUM=A−B

then its execution would have led to the result printed being

THE SUM   7.0000 AND   12.0000 IS   −5.0000

This is a type of error which the computer can give no help with – the program is syntactically correct and runs without causing a failure. It produces an incorrect answer because the logic was incorrect and only the programmer or some other thinking human being can correct it.

Because errors in the logic of a program are often quite difficult to find (the trivial error in a very simple program shown above is hardly typical!) it is very important that programs are planned carefully in advance and not rushed. This discussion of errors seems to stress the importance of a planned structure to programs and programming and we shall begin to develop a useful approach to good program design in the next chapter.

Summary

- A Fortran program is written using a maximum of 80 characters per line, of which the last eight are purely for identification purposes.

- Each statement uses only columns 7–72, with columns 1–6 being reserved for special purposes.

- C or * in column 1 causes the remainder of the line to be treated as a comment.

- Any character other than a space or a zero in column 6 causes columns 7–72 to be treated as a continuation of the previous line.

- Fortran names for programs and/or variables are defined as consisting of up to six letters and/or digits, of which the first must be a letter.

- Every program will normally begin with a PROGRAM statement. This is optional and may be omitted.

- Every program must end with an END statement.

- List-directed READ and PRINT statements are used for simple input of data from the standard input unit and output of results to the standard output unit.

- The arithmetic assignment statement is a means of evaluating an arithmetic expression and storing it in a user-defined variable.

- Variables are named so that their initial letter defines their type (A–H and O–Z means real, I–N means integer).

Initial statement	PROGRAM name
List-directed input and output	READ *,list of names
	PRINT *,list of names and/or values
Assignment statement	name = expression
STOP *statement*	STOP
END *statement*	END

Fig. 2.9 Fortran 77 statements introduced in Chapter 2

Exercises

2.1 What are each of the following (real constants, integer constants, character constants, none of these)?

17	17.0	'17.0'	−124
−'124'	A	A17	'A17'
2.413	24.196	14+23	+93.715
SEVEN	12	0.0001	−0
9.4 3	4 .	'A'B'	'A''B'

2.2 Which of the following are valid Fortran names?

FRED	JACOB	F17A	P119H2R
ALPHA	6F19A	SIXTH	SEVENTH
R17.4	X9–4A	PQ4 AX	4A M62
$N	'JACK'	N$	F62 BX9

2.3 What will be printed by the following program if it reads the data shown
below it?

```
PROGRAM TEST23
READ *,A,B,C
READ *,P,Q,R
READ *,X,Y,Z
READ *,A,B,C
READ *,X,Y,Z
PRINT *,P,Q,R,X,Y,Z,A,B,C
STOP
END
```

```
   A     B    C
 1.23 4.56 7
 0.9,8
 76 54
 x1      ,     2
 345.6/
 9.8/
 1.23/4.56/7.89
```

2.4 Which of the following are integer variable names, which are real
variable names, and which are something else?

A	BCD	NAME	NUMBER
AVERAGE	MEAN	JOKE	TABLE
F17D	LIST	SEX	NINE
DIGIT	H12P4	4P12	CHARACTER

2.5 What is the difference between a floating-point number and an integer?
What is a real number?

2.6 How do you submit a simple Fortran 77 program to your computer?
How do you supply the data?

2.7 Write and run a program to read 10 numbers and to find their sum. Run
the program with various sets of data, including the following
1,5,17.3,9,−23.7142,12.9647,0.0005
−2974,3951.44899,−1000
In all cases work out by hand what the answer should be before you run
the program.

2.8 Write and run a program to read four integers and print the *difference*
between the sum of the first two and the sum of the last two.

Arithmetic, Expressions and Assignment

3.1 The assignment statement

The assignment statement

    SUM=A+B

means 'take the values stored in the real variables **A** and **B**, add them together, and store the result in a real variable called **SUM**'. The assignment statement is an extremely important type of statement since it is the only way in which a value can be stored in a particular storage location (other than by means of a **READ**, or input, statement). It takes the general form

    name = expression

where the *name* on the left of the equals sign is the name of the storage location to which will be *assigned* the value of the *expression* on the right of the equals sign. Fig. 3.1 illustrates this by reference to the storage model we used in Chapter 1.

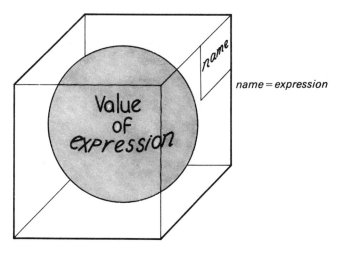

Fig. 3.1 Assignment in the storage model

There are three types of assignment statement corresponding to the three major types of storage location, namely arithmetic assignment, logical assignment and character assignment. The most widely used is the arithmetic assignment statement, and we shall therefore only consider this type for the present (the other two types will be discussed in Chapters 7 and 8).

3.2 Arithmetic expressions

An arithmetic expression is used to express a numeric computation, and evaluation of an arithmetic expression produces a numeric value. Thus A+B is an arithmetic expression whose evaluation leads to the value of the sum of the two numbers (or values) stored in the real variables A and B.

The simplest form of an arithmetic expression is an unsigned constant (e.g. 25) or a variable name (e.g. A). More complex expressions can be formed by use of arithmetic operators, of which there are five, shown in Fig. 3.2.

+   means addition
−   means subtraction
*   means multiplication
/   means division
**   means exponentiation

Fig. 3.2   Arithmetic operators

Thus, as we have already seen

    A+B

represents 'A plus B' and is evaluated to give the sum of the real values stored in A and B. In a similar way

    X−Y
    P*Q
    D/E
    U**V

represent subtraction, multiplication, division and exponentiation, respectively.

The above operators have all been defined in a *diadic* sense – that is they have been used between two operands. The + and − operators can also be used as *monadic* operators with only one operand. Thus

    −G

represents the negated value stored in G and has the same value as 0.0−G, while

    +T

has the same as T (or 0.0 + T).

The above examples have all used variable names, but constants can, of course, be used as well

```
A+5
6.7-X
Q*1.42
S/3
12.5**D
-4.7
+0.13
```

Of course we frequently want more complex expressions than these and we can therefore extend this principle to include as many operators as we wish. This can be expressed as

expression ≡ expression [operator expression]

where [. . .] implies that this is optional. Thus we may write expressions such as

```
A+B/C-12*D**E
```

However the question which then arises concerns the order of evaluation. For example what is the value of the following expression?

```
4.0+6.0*2.0
```

There could be two possibilities: 20 and 16. The first is obtained by working from left to right and the second from right to left. And consider the following expression

```
3.0+4.0**2.0-8.0/4.0+2.0
```

The rules in Fortran are the same as the normal arithmetic priority rules, as shown in Fig. 3.3, with the proviso that within any one priority level

Operator	Priority
**	High
* and /	Medium
+ and -	Low

Fig. 3.3 Arithmetic operator priorities

evaluation is carried out from left to right. Thus, in the expression above, the exponentiation will be carried out first, causing the expression to reduce to

```
3.0+16.0-8.0/4.0+2.0
```

and then any multiplication or division, leading to

```
3.0+16.0-2.0+2.0
```

Finally the addition and subtraction is carried out, leading to a value of **19.0**.

There is one more aspect of an arithmetic expression left to consider, namely the use of parentheses (or brackets). Consider for example the algebraic expression

$$\frac{A+B}{C}$$

Clearly in order to evaluate this correctly the sub-expression $A+B$ must be evaluated first, and the resulting sum then divided by C. This means that addition is carried out before division, contrary to the priority rules already established above. However if we write (in Fortran)

(A+B)/C

then all is well because *any expression enclosed in parentheses is evaluated first*. Once again, this is the same as normal arithmetic or algebraic practice. If one pair of parentheses is enclosed within another pair then, as one would expect, the inner pair is evaluated first. Thus in the following expression

A*((B+C)**D-E)

the order of evaluation is as follows

(a) Calculate B+C, because this is enclosed in an inner pair of parentheses.
(b) Evaluate the contents of the outer parentheses in the usual order, i.e. first calculate (B+C) raised to the power of D, and then subtract E.
(c) Finally, multiply A by the result of the above evaluation (at step b).

If we replace A, B, C, D and E by the numbers 2.0, 3.0, 4.0, 5.0 and 6.0 we can follow this through

2.0*((3.0+4.0)**5.0-6.0)

becomes

2.0*(7.0**5.0-6.0)

then

2.0*(15827.0-6.0)

then

2.0*15821.0

and then

31642.0

We can now use our present knowledge of arithmetic expressions (and assignment statements) to solve some simple examples.

Example 3.1

Write a program to read a Centigrade temperature and convert it to Fahrenheit, using the formula

$$F = \frac{9C}{5} + 32$$

This is a simple program and can probably be written down without much thought

```
PROGRAM CONVRT
READ *,TEMPC
TEMPF = 9.0*TEMPC/5.0+32.0
PRINT *,TEMPC,'C =',TEMPF,'F'
STOP
END
```

Notice that the program name (CONVRT) and the names of the two variables used (TEMPC and TEMPF) have been chosen to give an indication of their purpose within the limit of six characters for a name.

The names used for variables (and program names) are purely for the writer's convenience – they have no special meaning to the compiler. Thus instead of TEMPC and TEMPF we could have written C and F, or X and Y, or A17 and B49! However in order to make the program understandable to the reader (who will often, though not always, be the writer) meaningful names should be used wherever possible. Note that the names used in the above program (and the alternatives just discussed) are all names of real variables. Since we shall be carrying out a division it would not be sensible to use only whole numbers (or integers), and indeed variables used for any form of calculation are almost invariably real variables. Section 3.3 discusses the use of integer variables and expressions in detail.

Since we are using *real* variables to calculate a *real* expression we have written the expression in the third line of the above program using *real* constants

```
TEMPF = 9.0*TEMPC/5.0+32.0
```

This is not strictly necessary as one of the rules concerned with evaluating arithmetic expressions states that when evaluating an expression of the form

   operand operator operand

both operands must be of the same type (other than in expressions of the form X**2). If one is an integer and the other is real then the integer operand will be converted to its real equivalent before the evaluation takes place. The result of the evaluation will be of the same type as the operands.

This means that if the expression was written in the form

```
9*TEMPC/5
```

then, when it is evaluated, the rules of evaluation will cause the following steps to take place

(a) As there are no exponentiations (or parentheses), evaluate multiplications and divisions from left to right.
(b) Evaluate `9*TEMPC`. This is a 'mixed-mode' expression (i.e. 9 is integer, `TEMPC` is real); therefore first convert 9 to real (which we shall write as `9.0`). Now evaluate `9.0*TEMPC` to give a real result.
(c) Evaluate `(9.0*TEMPC)/5`. Again this is a mixed-mode expression since the result of the previous step, `(9.0*TEMPC)`, is real and 5 is integer. Before the evaluation of `(9.0*TEMP)/5.0` is carried out, 5 is therefore converted to real.
(d) All multiplication and division is now complete so evaluate additions and subtractions, i.e. `(9.0*TEMPC/5.0)+32`. Once again the same thing happens and 32 is converted to real before the final evaluation takes place.
(e) The real result is now available for storing in a suitable location.

One minor point concerning this expression is that since the order of multiplication and division is immaterial we could have written

```
9.0/5.0*TEMPC+32.0
```

which will clearly be the same as

```
1.8*TEMPC+32.0
```

This is one of those cases where personal style enters into things. This form of the expression avoids the unnecessary extra division, but at the cost of a loss of clarity in the program. A compromise might be to add a comment line

```
C   USE FORMULA F=9C/5+32 (=1.8C+32)
      TEMPF=1.8*TEMPC+32.0
```

Finally notice that the `PRINT` statement has identified the meaning of the results. If we had written

```
PRINT *,TEMPF,TEMPC
```

it is not obvious from the results printed (just two numbers) what they mean.

Example 3.2
Write a program to calculate the nett pay of a British worker who pays 5% of his gross pay towards his superannuation, 25% of what is left as income tax, and also has fixed deductions for health insurance etc. amounting to £14.50 per week. Print a payslip showing gross pay, nett pay and all deductions.

This is a fairly straightforward program and introduces no new problems

```
PROGRAM PAY
READ *,GROSS
SUPER = 0.06*GROSS
XPAY = GROSS-SUPER
TAX = 0.25*XPAY
PAYNET = XPAY-TAX-14.5
PRINT *,'GROSS PAY:',GROSS
PRINT *,'SUPERANNUATION:',SUPER
PRINT *,'TAX:',TAX
PRINT *,'INSURANCE:',14.5
PRINT *,' '
PRINT *,'NETT PAY:',PAYNET
STOP
END
```

Notice that in line 6 the nett pay has been stored in a variable called PAYNET, because NETPAY (the obvious name) would have been integer. Notice also that lines 10 and 11 print only constants. Line 10 prints the insurance details (which are a constant deduction of £14.50), while line 11 prints a single space thus causing a blank line to be printed. The results might therefore look as shown in Fig. 3.4. The layout of these results leaves a lot to be desired and could be improved by the inclusion of additional spaces in the character constants, e.g.

```
PRINT *,'GROSS PAY:      ',GROSS
```

However the list-directed PRINT statement is essentially a simple form of output statement and is not intended for use where the detailed layout of results is important. For that we need the full power of Fortran formatting discussed later in Chapter 6.

```
GROSS PAY:      173.5000
SUPERANNUATION:      10.41000
TAX:     40.77250
INSURANCE:      14.50000

NETT PAY:     107.8175
```

Fig. 3.4   Results produced by Example 3.2

3.3 Integer expressions

The above discussion of arithmetic expressions has assumed that all the operands are either real or are converted to a real value before evaluation. However what about the situation where both operands are integer? The five arithmetic operators can all be used with integers (Fig. 3.5). There is, however, one problem.

```
I+J
N-6
K*L
4/M
N**4
J*(K/(N+4)-L)**(N-M)
```

Fig. 3.5   Integer expressions

As long as the operator is +, −, * or ** the evaluation of the expression proceeds without any difficulty, but division is another matter. For example in the fourth line of Fig. 3.5 what is the value of the expression if M has the value 3? The expression reduces to 4/3 which is 1.3333...; but the rule introduced in Example 3.1 stated that 'the result of the evaluation will be of the same type as the operands'. In this case, therefore, the result will be an integer and thus can have no fractional part! The solution is to ignore the fractional part of the result and to treat it as 1; thus 4/3 is evaluated to give 1. Similarly if M was 5 the result would be 0.

The rule is that when integer division is carried out the result is obtained by ignoring any fractional part that would exist had the evaluation been mathematically accurate. Fig. 3.6 shows the results obtained by evaluating several integer expressions which contain integer divisions.

Expression	Value	
17/5	3	
99/100	0	
−12/7	−1	
4/(5−8)	−1	(4/(−3))
17/4*4	16	(4*4)
17/4*4/17	0	(16/17)
17*4/4/17	1	(68/4/17 = 17/17)

Fig. 3.6   Examples of integer division

The last three examples in Fig. 3.6 show how, due to the loss of fractional parts, the order of multiplication and division is important when using integers. However integer division is normally only used deliberately for certain specific purposes and is not used at all in most programs. It can however be a cause of errors in programs if care is not taken. Consider, for example, the program written in Example 3.1 to convert a Centigrade temperature to Fahrenheit.

This used the formula

$$F = \frac{9C}{5} + 32$$

which appreared in the original program as

```
TEMPF = 9.0*TEMPC/5.0+32.0
```

or, more succinctly, as we saw later

```
TEMPF = 9*TEMPC/5+32
```

Now consider what might have happened if the formula had been written (equally correctly) as

$$F = \frac{9}{5} C + 32$$

If the programmer had followed this and written

```
TEMPF = 9/5*TEMPC+32
```

the wrong results would have been obtained! This is because when the expression is evaluated the process works from left to right. Thus the first sub-expression to be evaluated is 9/5. Here both operands are integer and so an integer division is carried out, leading to a value of 1.

The next step is to evaluate (9/5)*C, that is 1*C. This is a mixed-mode expression and so 1 is converted to its real equivalent – but it is clearly too late. The expression has effectively been reduced to TEMPC+32.

The ideal solution is never to write mixed-mode expressions, and then there will be no chance of this error occurring. In practice, however, mixed-mode expressions are no problem as long as care is taken to ensure that no integer division takes place where it is not intended.

Example 3.3
Work out what will be printed by the following program

```
PROGRAM EX33
X1 = 5
N1 = 5
X2 = -9
N2 = -9
X3 = 4
N3 = 4
A1 = X1*X2/X3
M1 = N1*N2/N3
A2 = X2/X3*X1
M2 = N2/N3*N1
A3 = X1/X3*X2
M3 = N1/N3*N2
PRINT *,A1,A2,A3
PRINT *,M1,M2,M3
STOP
END
```

A glance at the program shows that each pair of lines is the same except that

X1, X2, X3, A1, A2, A3 are replaced by N1, N2, N3, M1, M2, M3 respectively. The calculation of A1 in line 8 thus leads to the value −11.25 (5.0*(−9.0)/4.0). In a similar manner line 10 leads to a value of −11.25 for A2 (−9.0/4.0*5.0), and line 12 stores −11.25 (5.0/4.0*(−9.0)) in A3.

The first integer calculation in line 9 causes the value −11 (5*(−9)/4→ −45/4) to be stored in M1. However line 11 sets M2 to the value −10 (−9/4*5 → −2*5), while line 13 stores −9 in M3 (5/4*(−9)→ 1*(−9))!

The results produced are therefore

```
−11.25    −11.25    −11.25
−11    −10    −9
```

Thus we see that although the order of evaluation of multiplication and division makes no difference when using real operands, it can make a significant difference when using integers.

Example 3.4
Write a program which reads the number of apples that can be packed in a carton and the number of apples that need to be packed. Print the number of cartons which the apples will fill and the number which will be left over.

This problem is an example of the use of integer division to find a whole number quotient and remainder

```
PROGRAM APPLES
READ *,NBOX,NAPPLS
N = NAPPLS/NBOX
NLEFT = NAPPLS−N*NBOX
PRINT *,N,' FULL CARTONS'
PRINT *,NLEFT,' APPLES LEFT OVER'
STOP
END
```

In this program the integer division in line 3 will set N to the largest integer which is not greater than the (mathematical) number of boxes. Thus if each box would take 72 apples and there were 450 apples in all, the value of N would be 6 (since 450/72 is 6.25). Line 4 then finds the remainder by multiplying this by the divisor (the number per box) and subtracting the result from the total number of apples. Thus with the figures above the remainder would be 18.

If only the number left over (the remainder) had been required it could have been calculated in a single expression

```
NLEFT = NAPPLS−NAPPLS/NBOX*NBOX
```

3.4 Arithmetic assignment

We have not considered any implications that the different types of expressions, real, integer and 'mixed-mode', may have on the rest of the assignment statement. The result of the evaluation of an arithmetic expression will be integer if *all* the operands are integer and will be real if *any* of the operands are real. (Since a mixed-mode expression has the integer operand converted to real and has a real result, it follows that if any operand is real there will be a mixed-mode expression at some point in the evaluation and all subsequent sub-expressions will be mixed-mode, leading to a real result.) In all the examples we have used so far we have ensured that a real result is stored in a real variable, and an integer result is stored in an integer variable. But what will happen in the following cases?

```
X=I*J-K*L
N=P*Q/R
M=I+4*J/K-A
```

In the first case the expression to the right of the equals sign is integer whereas the variable on the left is real. Here there is no problem and the real equivalent of the integer value is assigned to X. Thus if I, J, K and L have the values 3, 5, 6 and 2 respectively, the value of the expression is 3 (3*5−6*2) and so the *real* representation of 3 (which we shall write as 3.0) is stored in X.

In the second case all the items in the expression are real and so a real result is obtained, which is to be assigned to the integer variable N. In this case the real value is converted to integer and, in a similar way to integer division, the fractional part (if any) is lost. Thus if P, Q and R have the values 6.0, 7.0 and 9.0, the value of the expression is 4.6666... and so the value 4 is assigned to N. Notice in particular that the real value is *truncated* and not rounded. This can lead to problems if care is not taken. For example, if P, Q and R have values 2.0, 3.0 and 6.0 then the expression reduces to 6.0/6.0, which clearly should cause N to take the value 1; however, the calculation might lead to a value (before truncation) of 0.9999..., which although close enough to 1.0 for most purposes will lead to N taking the value 0! The solution to this difficulty is to add a small value before truncation, e.g. N=P*Q/R+0.001.

The third case shows an expression which is almost entirely integer except for one operand. If I, J and K are assumed to have the same values as before (3, 5 and 6) and A is 4.1 then the evaluation of the expression proceeds as follows

(a)   I+4*5/K−A → I+20/K−A
(b)   I+20/6−A → I+3−A
(c)   3+3−A → 6−A
(d)   6−4.1 → 6.0−4.1 → 1.9

Finally the value 1.9 must be assigned to M, which therefore takes the value 1, due to truncation.

Example 3.5
During a journey a driver stops to fill up with petrol several times. Each time he stops he always puts in exactly 8 gallons. At the end of the journey he fills up the tank until it is full (as it was at the start) and notes the total distance travelled in miles (the mileometer does not show fractions of a mile). Write a program to read the number of miles travelled, the number of stops for petrol and the amount of petrol put in at the end of the journey, and then to print

the average fuel consumption in miles per gallon *to the nearest whole number*.
(Round up for 0.5 upwards, round down for less than 0.5).

This is a fairly straightforward exercise apart from the question of rounding

```
PROGRAM FUEL
READ *,MILES,NSTOPS,TOPUP
MPG = MILES/(8.0*NSTOPS+TOPUP)+0.5
PRINT *,'AVERAGE MPG WAS',MPG
STOP
END
```

Let us examine the assignment statement in line 3 more closely. The first
step will be to evaluate the expression in parentheses which will calculate the
amount of petrol used. Notice that this is a mixed-mode expression and will
cause the result to be real. The number of miles travelled is then divided by
this figure in another mixed-mode expression thus leading to a real result for
the miles per gallon. However if this were then assigned to the integer
variable MPG it would be truncated and, for example, 35.9 would be stored as
35 which is not what is required. The constant 0.5 is therefore added to the
calculated mpg before it is assigned. Fig. 3.7 shows the effect of this in some
specific instances and it can easily be seen that it causes rounding to take place
exactly as required.

Calculated mpg	'+0.5'	*Value stored in* MPG
34.0	34.5	34
34.49	34.99	34
34.5	35.0	35
34.99	35.49	35

Fig. 3.7   Rounding in Example 3.5

3.5   Procedures, subprograms and functions

All the programs that we have written so far have consisted of a number of
lines of instructions such that if they are all obeyed in sequence the required
actions will take place. However this is not always the way we do things in real
life. For example, look at Fig. 3.8. This is a note such as the author's wife
might leave to tell him how to cook a meal. It is a sequence of instructions but
with one important difference – *not all the instructions are there*. The main
part of the preparation is covered in one of her cookery books, so instead of
writing it all down she simply referred him to the appropriate page of the
book. There was no point in her either copying it out or describing what to do
in her own words; it was much easier to make use of what had already been
written by the author of the book.

Miles,

Can you make the Hot Pot? I'll be back around 1.30.

Peel half-a-dozen potatoes. Then cut them into thickish slices. Do the same with a large onion.

The lamb is in the fridge – chop it into smallish chunks (about 1½ inches).

Details are in Mary Berry's Cookbook, but ignore the bit about kidneys and mushrooms.

Put it on at 11.00 – DON'T FORGET

Love

Margaret

Fig. 3.8   An example of the use of a standard cooking procedure

In a rather different vein, Fig. 3.9 shows an extract from a car maintenance manual. In this case there is a lot of cross-referencing to other sections of the manual which describe how to carry out certain basic procedures. This is done to avoid duplication and to keep the structure of the manual fairly simple and logical. For example, in this manual Chapter 9 is concerned with

4.4 ~~belt tension~~
1/37:14.
4.5   Check for tightness all body bolts, engine mountings, door
locks and hinges etc.

RM 8 The ignition tir
C = TDC.

---
5   Every 18,000 miles (30,000 km)

Do all shorter mileage tasks, and also:
5.1   Change the generator 'V' belt. See Chapter 1/40. See also
task 5.3 or 6.2.
5.2   Remove the starter motor. Clean the commutator, renew
the brushes, and relubricate the bearings and drive. See Chapter
9/19 and 9/20.
5.3   If the generator is a dynamo, remove it, and clean the
commutator, renew the brushes, and relubricate the bearings.
See Chapter 9/9 and 9/10.
5.4   If fitted with fuel vapour control, replace the absorption
canister filter. See Chapter 3/12.
5.5   Clean the fuel pump filter on cars with mechanical
pumps. On cars so equipped change the fuel line filter. (In the
supply pipe just short of the carburettor). See Chapter 3/4.

---
6   Every 36,000 miles (60,000 km)

RM 9 The t

Do all shorter mileage tasks, and also:
6.1   Change the camshaft cogged timing belt. See Chapter 1/9
for removing the old one and 1/37 for fitting the new one. Never
turn the engine over with the belt removed unless the camshaft is
at i~~~~ position, with the camshaft p~~~~ ~~~~ming
~~~~ on the bearin~~~~

Fig. 3.9 Using cross-referencing to avoid duplication (Reproduced with permission
from *Fiat 128 Owners Workshop Manual*, published by J. H. Haynes & Co. Ltd.,
1974)

the car's electrical system and, therefore, throughout the rest of the manual
any electrical work required is dealt with by a reference to the appropriate
part of Chapter 9 (cf. steps 5.2 and 5.3).

Both of these situations (use of standard procedures and avoidance of
duplication with consequent structural improvements) appear in programming as well. In Fortran a special section of program which is in some way
referred to whenever required is known as a *procedure*, and is one type of
subprogram.

Procedures (or subprograms) fall into two broad categories, namely
those which are written by the programmer (or by some other person who
then allows the programmer to use them) and those which are part of the
Fortran language. There is a further categorisation, based upon their mode of
use, into what are called *subroutines* and *functions*.

All the procedures which are part of the Fortran language are functions and are referred to as *intrinsic functions*. The purpose of a function is to take one or more values (or *arguments*) and create a single result, thus

SIN(X)   produces the value of sin X (where X is in radians)
LOG(X)   produces the value of log$_e$X
SQRT(X) produces the value of $\sqrt{X}$

As can be seen from these examples a function reference takes the general form

name(argument)

or, where there are two or more arguments

name(arg1,arg2,...)

A function is used simply by referring to it in an expression in place of a variable or constant. Thus

A+B*LOG(C)

will first calculate B*log$_e$C and then add this to A. Similarly

−B+SQRT(4*A*C)

will first calculate 4*A*C, then use the function to find its square root, and finally add this to −B.

There are over 40 intrinsic functions available in Fortran 77, mainly concerned with standard mathematical functions such as those illustrated above, but some dealing with other matters. A full list will be found in Appendix A. Many of these functions can have arguments of more than one type, in which case the type of the result will usually (though not always) be of the same type as the arguments. Thus

ABS(X)

will produce the absolute value of the real variable X (that is the value ignoring the sign) as a real quantity, whereas

ABS(N)

will produce the absolute value of the integer variable N as an integer quantity.

The functions which exhibit this quality are referred to as *generic* functions since the name really refers to a group of functions, the appropriate one of which will be selected by the compiler depending upon the type of the arguments. It is also possible to refer directly to the actual function instead of using its generic name (e.g. IABS(N)), although this is only to provide compatibility with earlier versions of Fortran which had no generic capability and is not normally recommended.

Example 3.6

A farmer has a triangular field which he wishes to sow with wheat. Write a program that reads the lengths of the three sides of the field (in metres), and the sowing density (in grams per square metre). Print the number of 10 kilo bags of wheat he must purchase in order to sow the whole field.

The crux here is the equation

$$\text{area} = \sqrt{s(s-a)(s-b)(s-c)}$$

for the area of a triangle whose sides have lengths a, b and c, where $2s = a+b+c$.

```
PROGRAM WHEAT
READ *A,B,C
READ *,DENSTY
S = 0.5*(A+B+C)
AREA = SQRT(S*(S-A)*(S-B)*(S-C))
QTY = DENSTY*AREA
NBAGS = (QTY+9999)/10000
PRINT *,'AREA OF FIELD IS',AREA
PRINT *,NBAGS,' 10 KILO BAGS REQUIRED'
STOP
END
```

The program uses the SQRT function to calculate the area of the field, and then calculates the number of grams of wheat that are required. The expression (QTY+9999)/10000 is used to calculate the number of 10 kilo bags required. If QTY is an exact multiple of 10000 then the addition of 9999 will have no effect due to the subsequent truncation. However, if there would have been a remainder of one or more after dividing QTY by 10000 (i.e. one gram or more of wheat) then the addition of 9999 will cause an extra bag to be specified, from which the extra amount can be taken.

3.6 Expressions in output lists

In Chapter 2 we mentioned that the output list for a PRINT statement can consist of variables, constants and expressions. We have now examined arithmetic expressions in some detail and can see how an expression could be used directly in a PRINT statement. There are however two points to beware of. The first of these is that if an expression appears in an output list then clearly the value of that expression cannot be preserved for future use. For example, Fig. 3.10 shows an alternative solution to Example 3.4 which uses no assignment statements. However, as a result of this the expression NAPPLS/NBOX appears, and is evaluated, twice on consecutive lines.

```
PROGRAM APPLES
READ *,NBOX,NAPPLS
PRINT *,NAPPLS/NBOX,' FULL CARTONS'
PRINT *,NAPPLS-(NAPPLS/NBOX)*NBOX,' APPLES LEFT OVER'
STOP
END
```

Fig. 3.10   Alternative solution to Example 3.4

The second point concerns type conversion, specifically the truncation that takes place when a real quantity is stored in an integer variable. For instance in Example 3.6 the variable NBAGS is only used to store a value prior to being printed. However if the assignment to NBAGS was eliminated and the arithmetic expression included in the PRINT statement no conversion to integer would take place. This can easily be dealt with by use of the intrinsic function INT which converts its argument to integer form in the usual way. Fig. 3.11 shows the modified program, which eliminates all reference to both QTY and NBAGS.

```
PROGRAM WHEAT
READ *,A,B,C
READ *,DENSTY
S = 0.5*(A+B+C)
AREA = SQRT(S*(S-A)*(S-B)*(S-C))
PRINT *,'AREA OF FIELD IS',AREA
PRINT *,INT((DENSTY*AREA+9999)/10000),' 10 KILO BAGS',
* ' REQUIRED'
STOP
END
```

Fig. 3.11   Alternative solution to Example 3.6

As long as the value of an expression will not be required elsewhere it can be evaluated as part of the output list; if it is required elsewhere it is preferable to assign it to a variable to avoid the need for subsequently re-evaluating it.

Example 3.7
Write a program that reads 10 observations (real numbers) and prints their average value and the values of the highest and lowest observations.

This is a simple program, but one which uses two new intrinsic functions – MAX and MIN. These are unlike all other intrinsic functions in that they have a variable number of arguments (all of the same type) and return as their value the largest and smallest of these respectively.

```
PROGRAM EX37
READ *,A,B,C,D,E,F,W,X,Y,Z
PRINT *,'AVERAGE IS',(A+B+C+D+E+F+W+X+Y+Z)/10
PRINT *,'LARGEST IS',MAX(A,B,C,D,E,F,W,X,Y,Z)
PRINT *,'SMALLEST IS',MIN(A,B,C,D,E,F,W,X,Y,Z)
STOP
END
```

3.7   Structure plans

The overall logic and structure of our programs so far have been quite straightforward and it has been easy to write the programs without any additional planning. In general, this will not be the case and some form of additional planning or *analysis* is essential. This is particularly true once we start to instruct the computer how to take decisions and to repeat parts of the program a number of times. One traditional way of planning programs is by use of flowcharts; however these, by their nature, tend to encourage badly structured programs and modern programming practice frowns on their use.

Probably the best approach to program design is first to list the major objectives and then to expand each of these objectives to a (slightly) greater level of detail. Further expansions lead to more detailed objectives, and so on. Eventually a level of detail is reached which can easily be directly converted to a program. Exactly what this final level of detail is will depend upon the problem and the skill and experience of the programmer. This broad approach is called *top-down analysis* and the method of developing a final design is called *stepwise refinement*.

Exactly how the various levels of the design plan are written is a matter of personal preference and may be influenced partly by the language in which the final program will be written. The approach evolved by the author is particularly well suited for Fortran programs and is called a *structure plan*.

The approach can best be illustrated by developing a structure plan for one of the examples used earlier in this chapter, namely Example 3.6, which was concerned with calculating the number of bags of wheat required to sow a triangular field. The first level plan might be simply a statement of the problem

   1   Read lengths of sides of field and sowing density
   2   Calculate and print number of bags needed

Notice that each line has been numbered. This is not strictly necessary at this stage but will be very useful later.

Now the first step is fairly straightforward but the second needs elaboration, so we can go to a greater level of detail

   2.1   Calculate area of field
   2.2   Calculate weight of seed required
   2.3   Calculate the number of bags, including any partly used one
   2.4   Print number of bags

If we wished we could put more information in these steps, such as the formulae to be used

2.1 Calculate area of field $(=\sqrt{s(s-a)(s-b)(s-c)})$
2.2 Calculate weight of seed required (= area × density)
2.3 Calculate number of bags (= (wt + 9999)/1000 to allow for a partly used bag)
2.4 Print results

There are no hard and fast rules about structure plans (or any other design aid) as they are intended to assist in the development of a particular individual's programs and will therefore reflect his particular skills (and weaknesses!). The important point is that the development of the structure plan should enable the programmer to get the logic of his program clear and well-defined before bothering with detailed coding. At the same time the final plan should contain enough detail for the coding to be carried out directly without any further analysis. The top-down approach means that the details are only brought in after the overall structure for (part of) the program has been thought out, and the two, slightly conflicting, aspects of program design are kept apart as far as possible.

It is essential, when writing most programs, to plan the structure before starting to write the code as otherwise errors in the logic are almost inevitable.

Summary

- The order of evaluation of an arithmetic expression is: ** first, then * and /, finally + and −. Expressions in parentheses are evaluated first.

- Integer division involves truncation of the result.

- Real values are truncated before being assigned to integer variables.

- Integer values are automatically converted to real in a mixed-mode expression.

- Procedures clarify the structure of a program and utilise the experience of others.

Assignment statement	name = expression
	e.g. X = A+B
	N = I−J
	P = Q*R
	W = D/E
	L = K**M
	H = I+J*X**(N−B)
Function references	function name(argl,arg2,....)
	e.g. X = SIN(Y)
	A = B+ABS(P−Q)
	N = MAX(I,J,K,L,M)
	P = MAX(A,B,C,D,E,F)

Fig. 3.12 Fortran 77 statements introduced in Chapter 3

- Intrinsic functions are a special class of 'built-in' procedures.

- Generic functions enable the same intrinsic functions to be used with different types of arguments.

- Expressions can be used in the output list of a PRINT statement as an alternative to first assigning the value of the expression to a variable.

- An English-language structure plan provides a means for (i) top-down analysis of the problem and (ii) step-wise refinement down to a level of detail which can easily be coded.

Exercises

3.1 What are the values of the following expressions?

```
17-12*4              9.5+23/2
4-6+18.0/3/3         9.5+2.3/.2
4-(6+18.0/3)/3       45/4*4
19-ABS(7-9)          19-(7-9)

SQRT(ABS(SQRT(256.0)-SQRT(625.0)))
```

3.2 What is the most obvious difference between the way in which the intrinsic functions MAX and LOG are used?

3.3 Write a structure plan for Example 3.4

3.4 Write a structure plan for Example 3.5

3.5 Write a program which reads up to 10 examination marks and calculates their average. (Hint: you will need to read the number of marks first and utilise one of the features of list-directed input.)

3.6 If the input statement

```
    READ *,A,B,C,I,J,K
```

is used to input the following data

```
    19,26,-12,19,26,-12
```

what will be the value calculated by the following expressions?
(a)   A+C+B/K
(b)   I+K+J/C
(c)   A+C+J/K
(d)   A+(C+J)/K
Check your answers with the computer.

3.7 A man wishes to build a wall 4 ft high along one side of his garden. Each row of bricks is 3 in high and the mortar between each row is ½ in thick. Each brick is 9 in long and there is ½ in of mortar between them. If the wall is to be exactly 23 ft 6 in long, how many bricks will be required?

Write a program to solve this problem and then use it to calculate the number of bricks for other combinations of heights and lengths.

3.8 A small business wishes to use a computer program to calculate how to make up the pay packets for its employees. The program should read the total amount to be paid and print the number of £10, £5 and £1 notes required and the number of 50p, 10p, 5p, 2p and 1p coins needed. It is a requirement of the problem that every pay packet should contain at least 25p in coins and at least one £1 note. Subject to this restriction the program must use as few coins and notes as possible.

4 Loops

4.1 Program repetition

So far most of our programs have taken rather longer to write than it would have taken to solve the problem by hand! This is because they have consisted of a series of instructions which are obeyed in sequence *once only*. In many cases the programs would be much more useful if they could be repeated with different sets of data. For instance Example 3.1 converted a single Centigrade temperature to Fahrenheit and Example 3.2 calculated one worker's pay. They would be much more useful if they could convert 50 temperatures or calculate 100 workers' pay details.

Before we see how we can do this in Fortran let us look at a structure plan. The structure plan for Example 3.1 would look like this

1 Read Centigrade temperature
2 Calculate Fahrenheit equivalent
3 Print both temperatures

We could alter this in two ways to allow a larger number of conversions. The first, and most obvious way is to write

1 Repeat the following 50 times
   1.1 Read Centigrade temperature
   1.2 Calculate Fahrenheit equivalent
   1.3 Print both temperatures

which quite clearly states that we wish to repeat the whole process 50 times. Thus a total of 50 Centigrade temperatures must be supplied as data and a total of 50 conversions will be carried out and printed.

This is perfectly acceptable and is clearly the sort of requirement which will appear frequently. However, if a large number of temperatures were to be converted a more useful way would surely be as follows

1 Repeat the following for each Centigrade temperature from 0 to 100 in steps of 5
   1.1 Calculate Fahrenheit equivalent
   1.2 Print both temperatures

Clearly this will produce a table of equivalent temperatures at 5°C intervals from 0°C to 100°C without the need for any data to be prepared at all.

We could rewrite step 1 of the earlier version in this same style by introducing a 'counter'

1 Repeat the following for each value of a 'counter' from 1 to 50 (in steps of 1)

The counter in this case is a variable whose only purpose is to record a count of how many times the statements have been repeated.

4.2 DO-loops

The repetition of a number of statements a predetermined number of times is so important that Fortran contains a special statement with exactly the features that are required. It is called a DO-*statement* and takes the form

DO label, var = e1,e2,e3

The statement starts with the word DO, which like PROGRAM, READ, PRINT, STOP and END is a word with a special meaning in Fortran. The rest of the statement consists of two parts separated by a comma (although this comma can be omitted for compatibility with earlier versions of Fortran).

The first part is a statement label. This identifies the last statement in the group which is to be repeated and consists of a whole number in the range 1 to 99999.

The second part consists of the name of a variable (var) followed by an equals sign and then either two or three arithmetic expressions separated by commas

var = e1,e2   or   var = e1,e2,e3

The variable is usually an integer variable but it can be real if required (although this can lead to problems, see section 4.3). It is called the DO-*variable*. The two or three expressions define the number of times that the statements are to be obeyed.

Note that if we follow each of the steps in one of the structure plans introduced above we find ourselves back at the beginning (see Fig. 4.1). It can be clearly seen that a loop will be traced during this process. For this reason this type of program structure is called a *program loop*, or loop, and a loop which is controlled by a DO-statement is called a DO-*loop*.

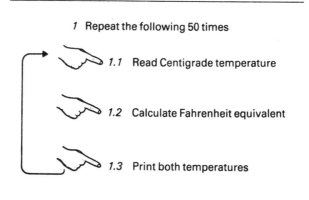

1 Repeat the following 50 times

1.1 Read Centigrade temperature

1.2 Calculate Fahrenheit equivalent

1.3 Print both temperatures

Fig. 4.1 A loop

When a DO-statement is first encountered the three expressions e1, e2 and e3 are evaluated to give three values m1, m2 and m3 of the same type as the variable, var. Informally we can consider these three values to be the initial value of the variable var (m1), the amount it is to be incremented by each time the loop is repeated (m3), and the final value (m2) – although the last will not always be the case.

The number of times the loop is to be obeyed (the *trip count*) is calculated using the following formula

$$\text{MAX} \left(0, \; \text{INT} \left(\frac{m2 - m1 + m3}{m3}\right)\right)$$

Thus the statement

    DO 100,I=0,100,5

leads to a trip count of 21, i.e. $\left(\dfrac{100 - 0 + 5}{5}\right)$. On the other hand the statement

    DO 50,J=0,100,9

leads to a trip count of 12, i.e. $\left(\text{INT}\left(\dfrac{100 - 0 + 9}{9}\right)\right)$, while the statement

    DO 999,K=100,0,10

leads to a trip count of 0, i.e. $\left(\text{MAX}\left(0, \; \text{INT}\left(\dfrac{0 - 100 + 10}{10}\right)\right)\right)$.

If the trip count is zero then the statements in the loop will be ignored. However, if it is greater than zero (it cannot be less) the DO-variable is set to the value m1 and the statements in the loop obeyed. When the last statement in the loop has been obeyed the DO-variable is incremented by m3 and the loop obeyed again if the trip count is greater than one. The process is repeated until the loop has been obeyed the required number of times.

DO-*statement*	*Trip count*	DO-*variable values*
DO 10,I=1,10,1	10	1,2,3,4,5,6,7,8,9,10
DO 25,J=20,50,5	7	20,25,30,35,40,45,50
DO 99,L=7,19,4	4	7,11,15,19
DO 1,K=4,17,5	3	4,9,14
DO 5,I=-20,20,6	7	-20,-14,-8,-2,4,10,16
DO 30,N=25,0,-5	6	25,20,15,10,5,0
DO 100,M=20,-20,-6	7	20,14,8,2,-4,-10,-16

Fig. 4.2 DO-statement evaluation

This may sound complicated, but in practice it is really very simple. For example in Fig. 4.2 it can be seen that where an integer variable is used with a positive increment the three expressions can be thought of as initial value, final (or maximum) value, and increment. The loop will continue to be obeyed until another pass through the loop would cause the DO-variable to become greater than the value of the second expression (m2). If the increment is negative then m2 represents a minimum value.

In a great many cases the DO variable is only being used as a counter so that a loop of the type 'repeat the following *n* times' can be set up. In this case the increment (m3) will be one, and if desired may be omitted altogether. Thus the statements

      DO label,var=e1,e2

and

      DO label,var=e1,e2,1

are identical in their effect.

There is however, still one aspect of the DO-statement unresolved, namely the label. We have so far seen how a C in column 1 indicates that the line is a comment, but have made no other use of the first six columns. A further use is to identify a particular line by means of a *label*.

A label is a whole number written (typed or punched) in columns 1–5. It follows, therefore, that the number must lie in the range 1–99999. One of the reasons for labelling a line is to identify the last statement of a DO-loop. The number chosen can be any whole number in the specified range as long as it is unique, i.e. used once only.

There are some restrictions on the statements which may appear as the last line of a DO-loop. For obvious reasons the following are not permitted.

- PROGRAM – since this is the first statement it is clearly not possible in any case.
- STOP – as this would prevent any looping.
- END – as this would prevent any looping.

We shall meet several other forbidden terminating statements in the next chapter.

In order to avoid any problems many programmers always finish a DO-loop with a special statement

      CONTINUE

This does absolutely nothing! It can however be labelled and it can appear as the last statement in a DO-loop.

Example 4.1

Write a program to read 100 exam marks and to calculate the average mark.

This problem requires us to use a loop to read the marks and accumulate a sum of all the marks. We must remember to set the sum to zero before starting. The structure plan is

   1 Initialise sum (to zero)
   2 Repeat 100 times
      2.1 Read a mark
      2.2 Add it to the cumulative sum
   3 Calculate and print average mark

Indenting the steps in the loop helps to emphasise the structure; we shall do this in the program also.

```
      PROGRAM MARKS
      MKSUM = 0
      DO 10, I=1,100
         READ *,MARK
         MKSUM = MKSUM+MARK
10       CONTINUE
      PRINT *,'AVERAGE MARK IS',MKSUM/100.0
      STOP
      END
```

Notice that the average is calculated using the real constant 100.0, thus causing real division to be used to give a real value for the average.

Example 4.2
Write a program which first reads the number of people sitting an exam. Then read their marks and print the highest and lowest marks, followed by the average mark.

This is a variation of Example 4.1 which uses a variable to control the number of times the loop is repeated. It also will need the use of the MAX and MIN intrinsic functions.

   1 Initialise sum and maximum mark to zero, minimum mark to a large value
   2 Read number of examinees (N)
   3 Repeat N times
      3.1 Read a mark
      3.2 Add it to cumulative sum
      3.3 Set maximum to maximum mark so far
      3.4 Set minimum to minimum mark so far
   4 Calculate average
   5 Print maximum, minimum and average marks

Initialisation of variables must always be handled carefully. In this case the cumulative sum must obviously start at zero, but what about the maximum and minimum marks? What we shall do (at steps 3.3 and 3.4) is to compare each mark with the highest (or lowest) read previously and store the higher (or lower) as the new maximum (or minimum). It follows therefore that initially the maximum must be set to a lower value than any marks are likely to take, and the minimum must be set to a higher value than is likely as a mark. If marks are to lie in the range 0–100 then the two extremes could be used. The program then follows easily

```
PROGRAM EXAMS
MKSUM = 0
MAXMK = 0
MINMK = 100
READ *,N
DO 10, I=1,N
   READ *,MARK
   MKSUM = MKSUM+MARK
   MAXMK = MAX(MAXMK,MARK)
   MINMK = MIN(MINMK,MARK)
10   CONTINUE
AV = REAL(MKSUM)/N
PRINT *,'HIGHEST MARK IS',MAXMK
PRINT *,'LOWEST MARK IS',MINMK
PRINT *,'AVERAGE MARK IS',AV
STOP
END
```

Notice particularly the line after the end of the loop in which the average is calculated. Since both MKSUM and N are integer the expression MKSUM/N would cause integer division to take place. The intrinsic function REAL converts an integer to its real equivalent, thus forcing a real division to take place.

4.3   DO-loops with real DO-variables

The DO-variable is normally used to cause the loop to be obeyed a fixed number of times and it is therefore usually more appropriate for it to be an integer; indeed in earlier versions of Fortran it had to be an integer. Fortran 77 however allows the use of a real variable for this purpose if so desired, which can be useful in certain circumstances. For example consider the situation postulated earlier in which a table of equivalent temperatures between two limits is required

1 Repeat for each Centigrade temperature from 0 to 100 in steps of 5
   1.1 Calculate Fahrenheit equivalent
   1.2 Print both temperatures

At first sight this is quite straightforward and will use a DO-statement of the form

```
DO 20,C=0,100,5
```

However it is not so simple as it appears!

Remember that an integer is a whole number and is always held exactly. A real number may contain a fractional part and is stored to a fixed degree of accuracy (see section 2.2). It is never safe to assume that it is held *exactly*, but rather it is an *approximation*. Consider now how the trip count is calculated.

First, the three expressions are evaluated and if necessary converted to the same type as the DO-variable. In this case, therefore, m1, m2 and m3 will have the values 0.0, 100.0 and 5.0 respectively. The trip count is then calculated using the formula

$$\text{MAX } (0, \text{ INT } \left(\frac{m2 - m1 + m3}{m3} \right))$$

This is where the problem lies for since m1, m2 and m3 are all real values the expression (m2 − m1 + m3)/m3 will be calculated using real arithmetic. The result will therefore be an *approximation* (albeit a very accurate one). However whereas *we* should expect a value of exactly 21 from this evaluation, the computer might produce a value of 21.000001 or 20.999999. For most purposes this does not matter but in this case it does, because the next thing that happens is that the integer equivalent is produced. If the value was 21.000001 the value 21 will result, but it it was 20.999999 the truncation process will lead to a trip count of 20!

This can be dealt with quite easily by ensuring that the calculated value of (m2 − m1 + m3)/m3 should not be a whole number but slightly larger. For example, if we write

```
DO 20,C=0,101,5
```

then the correct value of the expression will be 21.2 which will be truncated to 21 as required. The size of the potential rounding error in this calculation will be very small and will certainly affect no more than the last significant digit, and so a statement such as

```
DO 20,C=0,100.001,5
```

which would lead to a value of 21.0002 would still leave room for considerably larger rounding errors than will in fact occur.

A similar rounding error will, of course, occur in the incrementing of the DO-variable. However in this case it will not be significant (unless the loop is being repeated millions of times!) as the value is being used in a real calculation to produce a real result.

Example 4.3
Produce a table of Centigrade and Fahrenheit equivalent temperatures, where the limits and increment are provided as data. The table should have the highest temperature at the top.

This is essentially a generalisation of the problem discussed above. An interesting point is that the table must start with the highest temperature but nothing is said about the data order. We shall allow for both 'min, max, increment', which is the natural way, and 'max, min, increment'.

   1 Read limits and increment
   2 Establish max, min and (negative) increment
   3 Repeat for C from max to min in (negative) steps of increment
      3.1 Calculate Fahrenheit equivalent
      3.2 Print both temperatures

The program is as follows

```
      PROGRAM TEMPS
      READ *,C1,C2,CINC
C  SET CINC TO NEGATIVE VALUE
      CINC = -ABS(CINC)
      CMAX = MAX(C1,C2)
      CMIN = MIN(C1,C2)+0.1*CINC
      DO 1, C=CMAX,CMIN,CINC
        F = 1.8*C+32.0
        PRINT *,C,'C =',F,'F'
    1   CONTINUE
      STOP
      END
```

Notice here that `CINC` is first set to its negated absolute value. Therefore regardless of whether it is supplied as a positive or negative value it is set negative. `CMAX` is set to the larger of `C1` and `C2`, and `CMIN` to the smaller *less* a small amount. Since `CINC` is negative, `0.1*CINC` is a small negative amount which will deal with any rounding errors by increasing the value of $(m2-m1+m3)/m3$ by approximately 0.1. The rest is then as before.

4.4 Restrictions on DO-loops

Unlike most other statements in Fortran a `DO`-statement affects one or more following statements, and the whole 'range' of the loop (from the `DO`-statement to the terminal statement of the loop) is necessarily governed by certain rules. These rules do not in any way intrude or restrict what would normally be carried out in the loop.

A brief consideration of the mechanism necessary for a `DO`-loop to operate will show the reasons for the few restrictions that do exist. Fig. 4.3

Program		Action
DO label, var=e1,e2,e3	1	Calculate trip count
	2	Set var to initial value (m1)
	3	Leave loop if trip count = 0
		(go to step n+3)
'First statement'	4	'First statement'
.		
.		
.		
label 'Terminal statement'	n	'Terminal statement'
	n+1	Add m3 to var
	n+2	Subtract 1 from trip count
	n+2	Go back to step 3
'Next statement'	n+3	'Next statement'

Fig. 4.3 Actions taken during DO-loop processing

shows the processes that are required at the start of the loop to calculate the trip count and initialise the DO-variable, and at the end to increment the DO-variable and decide whether another pass through the loop is required. There are two key points to note. The first is that the DO-variable is set to its initial value *before* the decision is made whether to obey the loop at all. The second is that *after* the last (terminal) statement of the loop some extra statements will be inserted to increment the DO-variable, decrement the trip count and return to the start of the loop to decide whether another pass is required.

It is clear therefore that there are three situations which could conflict with this structure, namely altering the DO-variable within the body of the loop, obeying statements within the loop (and hence the 'housekeeping' at the end) without first obeying the DO-statement which sets up various values and variables, and having as the terminal statement of the loop some statement which affects the following statement(s) and which will be disrupted by the extra housekeeping statements. (Since the trip count is stored in a location which is known only to the compiler it is not possible for the Fortran program to access it directly, and it therefore cannot be changed other than by the DO-loop housekeeping statements.)

These three possible conflict situations are covered by the three restrictions on DO-loops

- The DO-variable must not be altered within the DO-loop although its value may be used in an expression.

- It is not permitted to enter the range of a DO-loop except by obeying the initial DO-statement.

- The terminal statement of a DO-loop must be one which is complete in itself and which will always allow processing to continue at the next statement. Of the statements we have met so far this rules out PROGRAM, STOP, END and DO. If you are in any doubt you can always finish the loop with a CONTINUE statement.

4.5   Nested DO-loops

Apart from the restrictions mentioned above concerning the last statement of a DO-loop, there are no restrictions concerning the type of statements which can appear within the body of such a loop. In particular there may be another DO-statement, as long as the range of this DO-loop is totally within the first one. Fig. 4.4 illustrates examples of valid and invalid structures. A few moments thought will confirm this, since the end of the first loop (at label 1) will cause a return to the start of the second loop during the next pass, even though it was never completed, while once the first loop is completed the end of the second loop will cause an (illegal) return to the middle of the first loop (i.e. the start of the second one). If the loops are indented as shown it is perfectly obvious what is legal and what is not without any further thought.

The one point to remember about nested loops is that since the DO-variable may not be altered during the loop, the inner loop must use a different DO-variable from that used by the outer one.

Permitted	Not permitted
DO 1,...	DO 1,...
.	.
.	.
.	.
DO 2,...	DO 2,...
.	.
.	.
.	.
2 CONTINUE	1 CONTINUE
.	.
.	.
.	.
1 CONTINUE	2 CONTINUE

Fig. 4.4 Valid and invalid DO-loop nesting

There are innumerable examples of the usefulness of nested DO-loops, based on structure plans such as the following

Repeat for each street
  Repeat for each house
    Repeat for each occupant
      Process personal details

or

Repeat for each experiment
  Repeat for each reading
    Process experimental reading

etc.

Many of these examples are most appropriate when used in conjunction with *arrays* of values, and will be introduced in Chapter 9. However a good example of the power of DO-loops when used together is given in Example 4.4.

Finally, there is no limit to the number of loops that may be nested within each other, although it is not easy to imagine a situation requiring more than two or three levels. Since the number of times the innermost loop is obeyed increases alarmingly with each extra level of nesting, it is not practical to try to do too much at once on the grounds of time and cost.

Example 4.4

Write a program to print a set of multiplication tables from 2 times up to 12 times.

We can see from the structure plan that this will be a short, yet powerful, program

1 Repeat for I from 2 to 12
   1.1 Print heading
   1.2 Repeat for J from 1 to 12
      1.2.1 Print 'I times J is I*J'

The program is equally simple

```
      PROGRAM TABLES
      DO 10, I=2,12
        PRINT *,I,' TIMES TABLE'
        DO 20, J=1,12
 20       PRINT *,I,' TIMES',J,' IS',I*J
 10     CONTINUE
      STOP
      END
```

```
      PROGRAM TABLES
      DO 10, I=2,12
        PRINT *,I,' TIMES TABLE'
        DO 10, J=1,12
 10       PRINT *,I,' TIMES',J, IS',I*J
      STOP
      END
```

Fig. 4.5   A program to print multiplication tables

.	.	.
.	.	.
.	.	.
3 TIMES	9 IS	27
3 TIMES	10 IS	30
3 TIMES	11 IS	33
3 TIMES	12 IS	36
4 TIMES TABLE		
4 TIMES	1 IS	4
4 TIMES	2 IS	8
4 TIMES	3 IS	12
4 TIMES	4 IS	16
4 TIMES	5 IS	20
4 TIMES	6 IS	24
4 TIMES	7 IS	28
4 TIMES	8 IS	32
4 TIMES	9 IS	36
4 TIMES	10 IS	40
.	.	.
.	.	.
.	.	.

Fig. 4.6   Results produced by TABLES program

In this instance we have finished the inner loop with a PRINT statement instead of a CONTINUE; however as there is nothing else to do in the outer loop a CONTINUE has been used as the terminal statement so that it can be labelled. This is not strictly necessary, as Fortran allows two loops to be terminated by the same statement. Since the rule is that an inner loop must be totally within an outer one there is no confusion and the compiler generates the code in such a way that the inner loop is finished before any attempt is made to return for another pass through the outer loop. The program can therefore be modified to take account of this. Fig. 4.5 shows the modified program and Fig. 4.6 shows part of the results produced by running it.

4.6   The DO-variable on exit from the loop

One problem area concerns the value of the DO-variable after leaving the loop. There are two situations here and both can easily be resolved by considering the sequence of operations, as shown in Fig. 4.3. This shows that:

(a) The DO-variable is set to its initial value *before* any decision is made whether to obey the loop.
(b) The DO-variable is updated at the end of each pass through the loop, but *before* a decision is made about another pass.
(c) The DO-variable is not altered anywhere else.

It follows that if an exit is made from the loop before it has been completed (as we shall see in Chapter 5) then the DO-variable has the value that it had during the last pass (i.e. its 'current' value). On the other hand, if the loop is fully completed the DO-variable is incremented before the decision is made and will thus have the value it would have had on the next pass. An example will illustrate this.

Example 4.5
What is printed by the following program?

```
        PROGRAM EX45
        DO 1, I=1,10
          DO 1, J=I,I**2
            DO 1, K=J+1,I*10
1             L = I+J+K
        PRINT *,I,J,K,L
        STOP
        END
```

Initially I is set to 1 and then the second DO-statement has initial and terminal values of 1 and 1. This gives a trip count of 1 so the next DO-statement is obeyed for K taking values from J+1 (i.e. 2) to 10. On the last pass K is 10 and L is set to 12. K is then increased to 11 prior to the completion of the innermost loop. J is then incremented to 2 and the middle loop is also complete. Finally I is increased to 2 and the process repeated.

On the last pass through the outer loop I is 10 and the middle loop is obeyed for J taking values from 10 to 100. On the last but one pass J is 99 and the inner loop is to be obeyed for K taking values from J+1 (i.e. 100) to I*10 (i.e. 100). K therefore becomes 100 and L is set to 209 (10 + 99 + 100).

K is now incremented to 101 at the completion of the loop and J incremented to 100 for another pass through the middle loop. This leads to the inner DO-statement stipulating that K is to run from 101 to 100. K is therefore set to 101 but the trip-count calculated is zero and therefore the loop is not obeyed. It is therefore the end of the inner loop and so J is increased to 101. This is, however the end of the middle loop so I is incremented to 11. This is now the end of the outer loop, and so the values printed are

    11   101   101   209

Summary

- The DO-loop is a means of repeating a block of statements a given number of times (the trip count).

- A zero trip count means that the loop is not obeyed at all.

- A statement label is a whole number in the range 1–99999 written in columns 1–5.

- Some statements (e.g. PROGRAM, STOP, END, DO) cannot appear as the terminal statement of a DO-loop.

- The CONTINUE statement (which does nothing, but can be labelled) can terminate a DO-loop.

- The DO-variable can be real but in this case care must be taken to deal with any rounding errors.

- Nested DO-loops may share the same terminal statement.

- After normal completion of a DO-loop, the DO-variable has the value it would have had on the next pass through the loop.

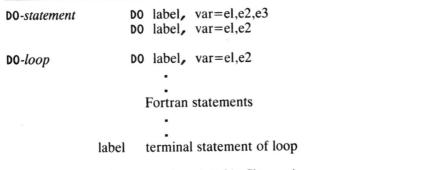

| DO-*statement* | DO label, var=el,e2,e3 |
| | DO label, var=el,e2 |

DO-*loop*	DO label, var=el,e2
	.
	.
	Fortran statements
	.
	.
label	terminal statement of loop

Fig. 4.7   Fortran 77 statements introduced in Chapter 4

Exercises

4.1 How many times will the loops controlled by the following DO-statements be obeyed?
  (a) DO 10, I=−5,5
  (b) DO 20, X=1.2,4.5,1.4
  (c) DO. 30, K=1.2,4.5,1.4
  (d) DO 40, L=17,15,−1
  (e) DO 50, L=17,15
  (f) DO 60, J=4,29,3

4.2 Write a program to print a table of squares, cubes, square roots and cube roots of whole numbers from 1 to 100 inclusive.

4.3 The students in a class each take several examinations (not more than 6). Write a program which reads all the marks and prints the average mark obtained by each student, the average mark for each examination, and the overall average mark. (Hint: you will need to utilise one of the features of list-directed input to deal with the unknown number of examinations (when writing the program); the numbers of examinations and students will form part of the data.)

4.4 The small business referred to in Exercise 3.8 identifies its employees by numbers running consecutively from 101 upwards. Modify the program written for Exercise 3.8 so that it calculates the cash requirements for each employee (in order), prints the identity of the employee with the cash breakdown, and finally prints the total requirements for each value of note and coin. (The program will require initially the number of employees.)

4.5 A cricketer's batting average is calculated by dividing the total number of runs he has scored by the number of times he has been out; thus a 'not out' score is added to his total runs without affecting the number of times he has been out. Write a program which first reads the number of players in a cricket club and then, for each player, reads the number of innings followed by the score in each innings. A 'not out' score will be preceded by a minus sign to distinguish it from other scores. The program should calculate the average for each player and print his batting statistics in the following form

PLAYER:n INNINGS:ni NOT OUT:nn TOTAL:t AVERAGE:a

(Hint: the counting of 'not out' innings will require some clever use of intrinsic functions or DO-loops; a much easier way will be introduced later.)

4.6 The length (L) of a bar of metal at a temperature T °C is given by the equation

$L=L_0+E*T*L_0$

where L_o is the length at $0\,°C$ and E is the coefficient of expansion. Write a program that will produce a set of tables showing the lengths of 10 bars at various temperatures if each is exactly 1 m long at $20\,°C$. The program should read 10 sets of data (one for each bar) consisting of the coefficient of expansion and the range of temperatures to be covered.

5 Decisions

5.1 Choice and decision-making

In everyday life we frequently come up against a situation which involves several possible alternative courses of action, requiring us to choose one of them based on some decision-making criteria. Fig. 5.1 shows a hypothetical discussion about how to get from Vienna to Budapest. Clearly there are several answers based upon the preferred method of travel and the time available. If we eliminate the details of the answer we see that it has a definite structure, as shown in Fig. 5.2. Each of the various alternative forms of transport (or 'actions') is preceded by a condition or test of the form '*if* some criterion holds *then*', apart from the last form (travel by road) which is

---

Q: How do I get to Budapest from Vienna?

A: It depends how you want to travel.
  If you are in a hurry *then*
      you should fly from Schwechat airport in Vienna
      to Ferihegy airport in Budapest;
  but if you are a romantic or like trains *then*
      you should take the Orient Express from the
      Sudbanhof to Budapest's Keleti palyudvar;
  but if you have plenty of time *then*
      you can travel on one of the boats which ply on
      the Danube;
  otherwise
      you can always go by road.

Fig. 5.1 An example of decisions in English

If criterion *then*
    action
but if criterion *then*
    action
but if criterion *then*
    action
otherwise
    action

Fig. 5.2 English language alternatives

---

included as a final alternative if none of the others are suitable and is preceded by the word 'otherwise'.

Fortran 77 has a very similar construction, shown in Fig. 5.3, which uses the words IF and THEN exactly as they were used in the English language example, the words ELSE IF where the English used 'but if', and the word ELSE instead of 'otherwise'. In addition, so that there is no doubt about the end of the final 'action', the words END IF are placed at the very end. The only other difference is that the criterion on which the decision will be based is enclosed in parentheses. This structure is known as a Block IF structure and the initial 'IF (criterion) THEN' is called a Block IF statement.

```
IF (criterion) THEN
    action
ELSE IF (criterion) THEN
    action
ELSE IF (criterion) THEN
    action
ELSE
    action
END IF
```

Fig. 5.3   Fortran 77 alternatives

The way a Block IF works is that each decision criterion is examined in turn. If it is true then the following action or 'block' of Fortran statements is obeyed. If it is not true then the next criterion (if any) is examined. If none of the criteria are found to be true then the block of statements following the ELSE (if there is one) is obeyed; if there is no ELSE statement, as in Fig. 5.4, then no action is taken and the computer moves on to the next statement, i.e. the one following the END IF statement. There must always be an IF statement (and a corresponding block of statements) and an END IF statement, but ELSE IF and ELSE statements are optional.

```
IF (criterion) THEN
    action
END IF
```

Fig. 5.4   A minimal block IF

Before we can start to use this facility for taking one of several alternative courses of action we must define the criteria on which the decisions will be based. These all consist of a new type of expression – a *logical expression*.

5.2 Logical expressions

In the English language discussion about how to get from Vienna to Budapest the decision depended upon the truth or otherwise of certain assertions. Thus '*if* you are in a hurry *then* travel by plane' could be expressed (rather quaintly) as '*if* it is true that you are in a hurry *then* travel by plane', and similarly for the other decision criteria. We see therefore that each decision depends upon whether some assertion is true or false.

The Fortran decision criterion is also an assertion which is true or false, and because this is a new concept, and not to be confused with numbers or character strings, the values 'true' and 'false' are called *logical values*, and an assertion (or expression) which can take one of these two values is called a *logical expression*. The simplest forms of logical expressions are those expressing the relationship between two numeric values, thus

    A.GT.B

is true if the value of A is greater than the value of B, and

    I.EQ.J

is true if the value of I is equal to the value of J.

Notice that in these two cases the names A and B, and I and J, are separated by a composite item consisting in each case of two letters enclosed in full-stops. This is because when Fortran was first defined it was not possible to punch signs such as $<$, $>$, etc. and therefore all *logical operators* consist of two, three or four letters enclosed in full stops.

The two expressions shown above, which express a relationship between two values, are a special form of logical expression called a *relational expression* and the operators are called *relational operators*. Fig. 5.5 shows the six relational operators which exist in Fortran, and a few moments thought

---

A.LT.B is *true* if A$<$B
P.LE.Q is *true* if P$\leq$Q
X.GT.Y is *true* if X$>$Y
I.GE.J is *true* if I$\geq$J
S.EQ.T is *true* if S$=$T
U.NE.V is *true* if U$\neq$V

Fig. 5.5   Relational operators and expressions

---

will show that they define all possible relationships between two arithmetic values. Indeed there is a certain amount of redundancy which leads to the possibility of expressing the same condition in several different ways; for example, the following four relational expressions are identical in their effect and will always give the same results

    B**2.GE.4*A*C
    B**2−4*A*C.GE.0
    4*A*C.LE.B**2
    4*A*C−B**2.LE.0

(The mathematically-oriented reader will recognise them as expressing the condition for a quadratic equation to have two real roots.)

This variety means that each programmer is free to choose his own way of expressing such conditions. For example, the author would always use the first one above, as it is the way in which he always thinks of the condition (i.e. $b^2 \geq 4ac$).

Notice that in these examples the values being compared are not necessarily expressed as variables or constants but as arithmetic expressions. All arithmetic operators have a higher priority than any logical operator and the arithmetic expression, or expressions, are therefore evaluated *before* any comparisons take place. The formal definition of a relational expression is thus

> expression   relational operator   expression

Example 5.1
Example 3.6 calculated the number of bags of wheat that were required to sow a triangular field. Modify this program to deal with the situation in which an exact number of full bags is required in a more aesthetically pleasing manner (and one which is easier to follow).

In Example 3.6 we added 9999 to the quantity of seed required before dividing by 10000. This uses the truncation mechanism to specify an extra bag (which will only be partially used) if the true quantity is not an exact multiple of 10000. A much better way would be to use a block IF. A revised structure plan could then read

> *1*   Read lengths of sides of field and sowing density
> *2*   Calculate area of field and weight of seeds
> *3*   Calculate number of full bags needed
> *4*   If any more seed needed then
>   *4.1*   Add one to number of bags
> *5*   Print size of field and number of bags

We can find out if any more is needed by testing if the amount required is greater than the amount in the bags

```
PROGRAM WHEAT
READ *,A,B,C
READ *,DENSTY
S=0.5*(A+B+C)
AREA=SQRT(S*(S-A)*(S-B)*(S-C))
QTY=DENSTY*AREA
NBAGS=QTY/10000
IF (QTY.GT.10000*NBAGS) THEN
  NBAGS=NBAGS+1
END IF
PRINT *,'AREA OF FIELD IS ',AREA
PRINT *,NBAGS,' 10 KILO BAGS REQUIRED'
STOP
END
```

There are two important points to note here. The first is that the relational expression is comparing a real value (**QTY**) with an integer one (**10000*NBAGS**). In this case the expression is evaluated by comparing the difference between the two arguments and zero; thus the expression

QTY.GT.10000*NBAGS

is evaluated as

(QTY-10000*NBAGS).GT.0.0

It is thus clear that **10000*NBAGS** will be converted to its real equivalent and a real subtraction then performed.

The second point concerns the accuracy of real arithmetic. Real numbers are stored in the computer as an approximation, to a defined degree of accuracy and, therefore, when such numbers are used in arithmetic expressions the least significant digits may get lost. Fig. 5.6 illustrates this in the context of hand calculation to six digits of accuracy, where the product of two four digit numbers requires seven digits to be accurate; the answer is therefore expressed as a six digit number after rounding the sixth digit. The normal rule is that if the first digit to be omitted (i.e. the seventh in this case) is in the range 0–4 then it (and any subsequent ones) are simply dropped, but if it is in the range 5–9 (as in this case) then the last significant digit is increased by one (from 7 to 8 in this case) before the remainder are dropped.

Multiply 25.39 by 17.25 to six significant figures

$$
\begin{array}{r}
25.39 \text{ x} \\
\underline{17.25} \\
2539 \\
17773 \\
5078 \\
\underline{12695} \\
437.9775
\end{array}
$$

Answer is 437.978

Fig. 5.6 An example of rounding errors in hand calculations

A computer operates in exactly the same way and therefore any real arithmetic operation, especially multiplication or division, is liable to introduce such a rounding error. Usually this is of no consequence as the computer is working to a greater accuracy than required for the problem. However there are three cases where it does matter. One of these is where a great deal of numerical calculation is being carried out and in this case the accuracy can be increased as we shall see in Chapter 8. The second case is where the calculated real number is to be truncated before being stored as an integer, as, for example, in the calculation of a **DO**-loop trip count (see section 4.3). The third case is where we wish to compare or subtract two real numbers which are almost exactly the same. We can illustrate this easily with an example.

Let us suppose that the sides of the field are 130 m, 100 m and 130 m, and that the sowing density is 25 g/m². A few moments calculation shows that the area of the field is 6000 m², and hence that 150 kg of seed are required. NBAGS should therefore be 15 and the test should find that these contain exactly enough seed. In practice, it probably won't be like that. For example, the calculation of the area could lead to a value such as 5999.999999 (to 10 significant figures) or to 6000.000001. The subsequent calculation of the quantity of seed and its division by 10000 will give further possible rounding errors leading to a (real) value for QTY/10000 of perhaps 14.99999999 or 15.00000001.

Although for all practical purposes these two values are the same as the true value of 15, when they are truncated to calculate NBAGS they will lead to integer values of 14 and 15 respectively. In the first case QTY will clearly be greater than NBAGS*10000 and so the situation will be compensated for. In the second case, however, it is possible that QTY is fractionally more than 150000 (e.g. 150000.0001) and that the relational expression will be true, leading to a calculation of 16 bags!

We can deal with this by *never* testing whether two real values are equal (which is essentially what we are doing here in the borderline case) but rather by testing whether their difference is acceptably small. In this case, therefore, we could say that since the grain is sown at 25 g/m², a shortfall of 1 g will not be noticeable. However any error in calculating the quantity will be far less than this as we have seen, and so we can alter the test to read

```
IF (QTY.GT.10000*NBAGS+1) THEN
   NBAGS=NBAGS+1
END IF
```

In practice, of course the farmer would accept a considerably larger shortfall and the 'error factor' could be increased to perhaps 100 (i.e. 1% of a full bag) or even more.

Example 5.2
Write a program to read the coefficients of a quadratic equation and print its roots.

This program will use the formula

$$x = \frac{-b \pm \sqrt{b^2 - 4ac}}{2a}$$

where

$$ax^2 + bx + c = 0.$$

There are several potential problems so we start with a structure plan

1 Read coefficients
2 If $b^2 > 4ac$ then
    2.1 calculate the two roots
    but if $b^2 = 4ac$ then
    2.2 calculate two equal roots
    otherwise
    2.3 there are no roots
3 Print results

There are three possible cases, namely two (unequal) roots, two identical roots, and no (real) roots, which correspond to $b^2 > 4ac$, $b^2 = 4ac$ and $b^2 < 4ac$ respectively. However before starting to write the program we should have a more detailed look at this plan.

First we notice that there are two tests comparing b^2 and $4ac$ and, in addition, the value of $b^2 - 4ac$ will be required at step 2.1. A lot of unnecessary calculation can therefore be avoided if we calculate $b^2 - 4ac$ once only, before carrying out any tests.

The second point concerns mathematical rounding, as discussed above. The problem here is particularly acute because if, for example, $b^2 - 4ac$ is calculated to be 0.000 000 0001 (instead of zero) an unnecessarily complicated calculation will ensue, while if it should be calculated to be $-0.000 000 0001$ the program will assume that there are no real roots when there are, in fact, two equal ones. We deal with this by comparing $b^2 - 4ac$ with a very small number, but one which is large enough to be larger than any likely rounding error, for example 10 times the smallest positive real number that can be stored on the computer.

The third point is that step 2.3 has a different effect from steps 2.1 and 2.2 in that it does not produce any results for step 3 to print. It would be easier, therefore, to print the roots in steps 2.1 and 2.2 and a message in step 2.3. Our structure plan is now as follows

1 Set e to a very small value
2 Read coefficients
3 Calculate $b^2 - 4ac$
4 If $b^2 - 4ac > e$ then
    4.1 Calculate and print two roots
    but if $b^2 - 4ac > -e$ then
    4.2 Calculate and print two equal roots
    otherwise
    4.3 Print message 'no roots'

Notice the way the test now works. First we test whether $b^2 - 4ac$ is greater than a very small value (e). If it is not then it is zero (for our purpose) or negative. We now test whether it is greater than a very small negative value ($-e$). If it is then, since it is also less than or equal to a very small positive value, it can be considered to be zero. We can now write the program – a trivial task now that it has been properly thought out and planned

```
        PROGRAM QUAD
C  E IS A VERY SMALL NUMBER, BUT GREATER THAN LIKELY
C  ROUNDING ERRORS
        E = 1E-9
        READ *,A,B,C
        S = B**2-4*A*C
        IF (S.GT.E) THEN
           D = SQRT(S)
           X1 = (-B+D)/(2*A)
           X2 = (-B-D)/(2*A)
           PRINT *,'ROOTS ARE',X1,X2
        ELSE IF (S.GT.-E) THEN
           X = -B/(2*A)
           PRINT *,'ROOTS ARE',X,X
        ELSE
           PRINT *,'THERE ARE NO REAL ROOTS'
        END IF
        STOP
        END
```

Notice the constant 1E−9 in the initial assignment statement. This is a particularly convenient way of writing very large or very small real constants. In its general form the constant

$n\mathrm{E}m$

is interpreted as the *real* value

$n*10^m$

and thus 1E−9 is equal to $1*10^{-9}$ (or simply 10^{-9}).

If the program was being run from a terminal, this is all that is needed. However if it was to be run in any form of batch system, with the results being printed on a printer, it is highly desirable to include an extra statement to print the data – the three coefficients in this case. The following statement, just after the READ statement, is all that is required

```
        PRINT *,'COEFFICIENTS ARE',A,B,C
```

5.3   The block IF structure

Examples 5.1 and 5.2 have shown the block IF structure in operation, and it is now appropriate to define formally the way it works. Fig. 5.7 shows in diagrammatic form the basic structure, and it can be seen that it starts with a block IF statement and ends with an END IF. Between these statements there may be one or more 'blocks' of Fortran statements. Each such block is preceded by an IF (in the case of the first one), ELSE IF or ELSE statement, and is followed by an ELSE IF, ELSE or (in the case of the last one) END IF statement. There may be any number of ELSE IF statements, or none at all, and there may be one ELSE statement, or none at all. If there is an ELSE

```
IF (logical expression) THEN
    block of Fortran statements
ELSE IF (logical expression) THEN
    block of Fortran statements
ELSE IF (logical expression) THEN
        .
        .
        .
ELSE
    block of Fortran statements
END IF
```

Fig. 5.7 Block IF structure

statement then it must, of course, immediately precede the last block of statements.

There are no restrictions concerning the statements which constitute a block other than the obvious one that any DO or block IF statements must have all their controlled statements within the same block. (Any other course would clearly be impossible.) Thus the final statement of a DO-loop must be in the same block as the initial DO-statement, and the END IF statement of a block IF must be in the same block as its initial block IF statement. In the latter case the 'nested' block IF structure is said to be at a lower level, see Fig. 5.8. In order to clarify the structure the author always indents each level, as shown, in a similar way to the indenting of DO-loops in Chapter 4.

```
IF (logical expression) THEN
    block of Fortran statements
ELSE IF (logical expression) THEN
    Fortran statements
    IF (logical expression) THEN
        block of Fortran statements
            .
            .
            .
    END IF
    Fortran statements
ELSE IF (logical expression) THEN
        .
        .
        .
END IF
```

Fig. 5.8 Nested block IF structure

The block IF is a very powerful structure as it reflects the way in which real-life decisions usually arise. It also has the added advantage that its use encourages a well-formulated structure to the program. Fortran 77 , however, contains a number of other types of statement which can be used to cause the computer to take decisions and/or to alter the normal sequential execution of program statements. These exist in Fortran 77 mainly for historical reasons and to retain compatibility with earlier versions of the language. One of these can be useful in certain situations, as described in the next section, but the others are not recommended other than in a particular construction which is described in Sections 5.7 and 5.8; they are described briefly in Section 5.6.

5.4   The logical IF statement

Until the advent of Fortran 77, the most powerful decision-making statement in Fortran took the form

IF (logical expression) Fortran statement

This is exactly equivalent to the minimum block IF with a block consisting of a single statement

IF (logical expression) THEN
        Fortran statement
END IF

Because the second part of the logical IF statement is only a single statement, however, there are some restrictions on its type. Thus it is not permissible to have a DO-statement or a block IF statement (or, of course, an ELSE IF, ELSE or END IF statement), nor is it permissible to have another logical IF statement.

On its own, therefore, the logical IF statement has limited usefulness. Essentially it is a means of making the execution of a single statement conditional upon the value of a logical expression. Although it is the chronological ancestor of the block IF it should be considered as merely a 'shorthand' version of the minimum block IF with a single-statement block. Nevertheless, because it is more compact, it can be used in a number of situations without any loss of clarity or efficiency.

Example 5.3
Write a program which reads 100 sets of data, each consisting of two co-ordinates and a code. Plot an X at every point and surround it with a circle if the code is negative.

This example requires us to plot a series of points on a graph plotter or graphic screen. The first question, therefore, is how do we do that? This is, in fact, a specific example of a general problem – namely, how do we carry out complex actions which are common to large numbers of computer users? (Examples are statistical analysis, numerical analysis and graphics as well as a number of more application-oriented activities.) In Chapter 3 we first met the idea of a *function* subprogram as a way of carrying out standard operations (usually, though not always, mathematical) on one or more values so as to give a single value as the result. A more general form of subprogram is called a *subroutine*.

Unlike a function a subroutine does not produce a single result; instead it may take any number of values (or none) and may produce any number of results (or none). It is, in effect, an extension of the program with a defined number of links between it and the original program, and with no restrictions upon what actions it may take. A subroutine is accessed by a statement of the form

CALL name(arg1,arg2,...argn)

where there may be any number of arguments enclosed in parentheses after the name of the subroutine, or none at all in which case the parentheses are also omitted

CALL name

The subroutine may use the arguments (if any) to obtain information from the 'calling' program, or to return information to it.

A subroutine is the main way in which useful computing procedures written by one person can be made available for use by others; in addition (as we shall see in Chapter 10), they help to make the writing and testing of non-trivial programs considerably easier. A subroutine is an independent piece of program whose only link with other parts of the whole program is through a clearly defined interface (e.g. its arguments), and it is therefore possible to build up a 'library' of useful subroutines. For example a graphical library might contain a subroutine called BOX which draws a rectangular box whose sides are defined by co-ordinates supplied as arguments. Anyone could then use this without having to bother about the details of using the graph plotter or other graphic devices (and those details are extremely complex!). Similarly a subroutine called GAUSS might solve a set of simultaneous linear equations using the Gaussian elimination method, without requiring the programmer to even understand the method used (let alone how to program it!).

Returning to our problem we shall assume the existence of a suitable library of graphical routines, and we shall further assume that it contains two subroutines, defined in Fig. 5.9, which we can use without formality.

CROSS(X,Y,W)   draws a cross whose centre is at the point (X, Y) and whose width (i.e. the length of its arms) is W.

CIRCLE(X,Y,R)   draws a circle of radius R whose centre is at the point (X, Y).

Fig. 5.9 Two hypothetical graphical subroutines

We can now develop a structure plan for our problem, and write the corresponding program.

1 Repeat the following 100 times
    2 Read a set of data
    3 Draw a cross
    4 If the code is negative then
        4.1 Draw a circle

```
      PROGRAM POINTS
      DO 10, I=1,10
        READ *,X,Y,N
        CALL CROSS(X,Y,0.25)
        IF (N.LT.0) CALL CIRCLE(X,Y,0.125)
  10    CONTINUE
      STOP
      END
```

Notice that because the two subroutines require three arguments, the last of which defines the size of the cross or circle, we have used an appropriate constant so as to give a cross of width 0.25 inch and a circle of the same diameter (so as to exactly surround it). A logical IF statement has been used since it is much neater than the block IF alternative

```
      IF (N.LT.0) THEN
        CALL CIRCLE(X,Y,0.125)
      END IF
```

The DO-loop ends on a CONTINUE because, as might be expected, an IF statement (or an END IF) cannot be the last statement of a DO-loop.

5.5   More about logical expressions

We have seen how the block IF and logical IF use the value of a logical expression to determine their course of action, and the six relational operators have been used to create such a logical expression. However, this is often not enough. For example in Fig. 5.1, which discussed the alternative ways of travelling from Vienna to Budapest, the second decision took the following form

> '*but if* you are a romantic *or* like trains *then*'

Here we have not one decision criterion but two criteria, only one of which needs to be satisfied for the appropriate action to be taken

> you should take the Orient Express from the Sudbanhof to Budapest's Keleti palyudvar.

A similar double criterion could have been used to cater for the fact that some people are afraid of flying

> *If* you are in a hurry *and* you are not afraid of flying *then* you should fly from Schwechat airport in Vienna to Ferihegy airport in Budapest.

In this case the use of the word 'and' indicates that both the criteria must be satisfied for the specified action to be carried out.

In Fortran we use the same two words to form composite logical expressions, but written as .OR. and .AND. in a similar way to that used for the relational operators `.GT.`, `.EQ.`, etc. They are called *logical operators* and are used to combine two logical expressions

     logical expression   logical operator   logical expression

Thus we could write

    `(A.LT.B).OR.(C.LT.D)`

or

    `(X.LE.Y).AND.(Y.LE.Z)`

In fact the parentheses shown in these examples are not strictly necessary because the relational expressions will always be evaluated first, but to human eyes expressions such as

    `A.LT.B.OR.C.LT.D`

and

    `X.LE.Y.AND.Y.LE.Z`

are not immediately clear and can cause some confusion. The effect of the `.OR.` and `.AND.` operators is as one would expect. `.OR.` gives a true result if either of its operands is true whereas `.AND.` gives a true result only if both are true. Fig. 5.10 illustrates this.

L1	L2	L1.OR.L2	L1.AND.L2
true	true	true	true
true	false	true	false
false	true	true	false
false	false	false	false

Fig. 5.10 The logical operators `.OR.` and `.AND.`

Two other logical operators exist which do not have an exact equivalent in normal English usage, namely `.EQV.` and `.NEQV.`. The first of these (`.EQV.`) gives a true result if both its operands have the same value (i.e. both are true or both are false), while the other (`.NEQV.`) is the opposite and gives a true result if they have opposite values. Fig. 5.11 illustrates this.

L1	L2	L1.EQV.L2	L1.NEQV.L2
true	true	true	false
true	false	false	true
false	true	false	true
false	false	true	false

Fig. 5.11 The logical operators `.EQV.` and `.NEQV.`

Essentially these operators are used in complex logical expressions to simplify their structure. Thus the following two expressions are equivalent in their effect

```
(A.LT.B.AND.X.LT.Y).OR.(A.GE.B.AND.X.GE.Y)
         A.LT.B.EQV.X.LT.Y
```

There is one further logical operator – .NOT. Unlike all the other relational and logical operators this only has a single operand, whose value it inverts. Thus if the logical expression L is true then .NOT.L is false, and vice versa. As with some of the relational operators the effect of the .NOT. operator on an expression can always be obtained in some other way, for example the following expressions are equivalent in their effect

```
.NOT.(A.LT.B.AND.B.LT.C)
    A.GE.B.OR.B.GE.C
```

anu, of course

```
.NOT.(A.LT.B.EQV.X.LT.Y)
    A.LT.B.NEQV.X.LT.Y
```

However, in some circumstances (especially when logical values are stored in special variables as we shall see in Chapter 8) the .NOT. operator can make a logical expression clearer.

If logical operators are used to build up a complicated logical expression then it is clearly important that we understand the priority rules which are used in its evaluation (just as in an arithmetic expression where * and / have a higher priority than + or −). Fig. 5.12 shows the priority order, and it should be noted that, as with arithmetic operators, parentheses can be used to change this order. It should also be noted that any arithmetic operators or relational operators (*in that order*) have a higher priority than any logical operators.

Operator	Priority
.NOT.	highest
.AND.	
.OR.	
.EQV. and .NEQV.	lowest

Fig. 5.12   Logical operator priorities

An interesting point concerning the evaluation of a logical expression is that frequently the computer will not need to evaluate it all, but will establish the final value at an early stage in the evaluation and then omit any remaining work. Consider, for example, the expression

```
A.LT.B.AND.C.LT.D.OR.X.EQ.Y
```

Let us suppose that the variables A, B, C, D, X and Y have the values 4, 8, 5, 9,

4 and 3 respectively. The computer will normally first evaluate `A.LT.B` (which is true) and will then proceed to evaluate `C.LT.D` (which is also true). The expression now reduces to

    true .AND. true .OR.X.EQ.Y

which, because of the priority rules, reduces further to

    true .OR.X.EQ.Y

which is, of course, true. It was not, therefore necessary to evaluate `X.EQ.Y` (which would have been false). Now, if `B` was 3 instead of 8 the value of `A.LT.B` would be false and so the expression woud reduce to

    false .AND.C.LT.D.OR.X.EQ.Y

which further reduces to

    false   .OR.X.EQ.Y

without the need to evaluate `C.LT.D`. If the expression had been

    A.LT.B.AND.(C.LT.D.OR.X.EQ.Y)

then it would reduce to

    false .AND.(C.LT.D.OR.X.EQ.Y)

and hence to a final value of false without evaluating either `C.LT.D` or `X.EQ.Y`.

Example 5.4

A set of survey data contains the age and weight of the respondents together with a code to indicate their sex (0 = male, 1 = female). Write a program which reads the number of people in the survey and then calculates the average weight of the men between the ages of 21 and 35 (inclusive).

This is a common type of problem and should not cause us much difficulty. Our structure plan will be as follows

   1 Read number of people (`N`)
   2 Initialise sums of weights and people to zero
   3 Repeat `N` times
      3.1 Read age, weight and sex code
      3.2 If male *and* aged between 21 and 35 then
            3.2.1 Add weight to sum of weights
            3.2.2 Add one to sum or people
   4 Calculate and print average weight

Note that in order to calculate the average weight we shall need to calculate the sum of the weights of the people concerned (step *3.2.1*) and also to count them (3.2.2), and that we must therefore ensure that they are both set to zero at the start (step 2). The program is now straightforward

```
      PROGRAM AVWT
      READ *,N
      NUM = 0
      SUMWT = 0.0
      DO 5, I = 1,N
         READ *,NAGE,WT,ISEX
         IF (ISEX.EQ.0 .AND. NAGE.GE.21 .AND. NAGE.LE.35) THEN
            SUMWT = SUMWT+WT
            NUM = NUM+1
         END IF
    5    CONTINUE
      IF (NUM.GT.0) THEN
         PRINT *,'AVERAGE WEIGHT IS',SUMWT/NUM
      ELSE
         PRINT *,'THERE ARE NO MEN AGED BETWEEN 21 AND 35'
      END IF
      STOP
      END
```

Notice the order of the three relational expressions which are used in the block IF statement in the DO-loop. Since, if the survey is a random one, approximately 50% of the respondents will be male, whereas probably rather more will be over 21 or under 35, the test for sex has the greatest chance of being false. By placing it first we ensure that the minimum number of expressions are evaluated.

Note also the block IF at the end of the program. Just because the problem asks for the average weight of males between 21 and 35 it does not mean that there will necessarily be any such people in the survey data. If there were none and the program always calculated the average, then it would fail because it would try to divide by zero – an impossible action and one which on a computer will cause a failure known as 'overflow' due to its efforts to calculate an infinitely large number (which is too large to store in a finite storage location!). The block IF at the end of the program detects this situation and prints a suitable message.

5.6   Some other control statements

The block IF (and in some situations the logical IF) provide a powerful decision-making capability, and one which can be used while still retaining a good overall structure for the program. Fortran 77, however, also contains several other types of statement which can be used to control the execution of statements or blocks of statements, but whose use encourages badly structured programs leading to errors of several types. They are included within the Fortran 77 language purely for compatibility with earlier versions of Fortran and, with one exception which is discussed in sections 5.7 and 5.8, *they should never be used*.

They all have one thing in common, namely the identification of one or more statements by means of a statement label followed by the transfer of control to that statement (or one of those statements) depending upon some condition. Potentially this may lead to a total breakdown of any ordered structure (at the very least a partial breakdown is inevitable). It makes their use dangerous, and since they provide no capability which does not already exist there is, in the author's view, no reason to use them. Nevertheless they will be mentioned, briefly, for the sake of completeness.

The first is another type of IF statement – the *arithmetic* IF – which allows a three-way choice depending uon the value of an *arithmetic* expression. It takes the form

IF (arithmetic expression) label1,label2,label3

and causes control to be transferred to the statement labelled label1 if the value of the arithmetic expression is negative, to the one labelled label2 if it is zero, and to the one labelled label3 if it is positive.

The second allows for a multi-way decision based upon the value of an integer expression, and takes the form

GOTO (label1,label2,...,labeln), integer expression

This is called a *computed* GOTO and causes control to be transferred to the statement labelled label1 if the value of the integer expression is 1, to the one labelled label2 if it is 2, and so on. If the value of the integer expression is negative or zero, or if it is greater than the number of labels specified, then the computed GOTO has no effect and the next statement is obeyed.

The third is the worst of all and is known as an *assigned* GOTO. It will not be described at all.

Because of the lack of any structure in these statements a fourth type is required to sort things out again, although it can be very valuable in its own right in certain situations. This statement is the *unconditional* GOTO which simply transfers control to a specified statement

GOTO label

To see why it is needed, consider a variation of Example 5.4 in which we merely require the number of men and the number of women to be counted. Using a block IF the DO-loop would be as shown in Fig. 5.13, while the

```
      DO 5, I=1,N
        IF (ISEX.EQ.0) THEN
          NM = NM+1
        ELSE
          NF = NF+1
        END IF
    5   CONTINUE
```

Fig. 5.13 Counting sexes using a block IF

corresponding loops for an arithmetic IF and a computed GOTO are given in Figs. 5.14 and 5.15. Since the block IF has assumed that any non-zero code represents a female, the same assumption has been made for the other two versions.

```
      DO 5, I=1,N
        IF (ISEX) 4,3,4
  3     NM = NM+1
        GOTO 5
  4     NF = NF+1
  5     CONTINUE
```

Fig. 5.14 Counting sexes using an arithmetic IF

```
      DO 5, I=1,N
        GOTO (4,3),ISEX+1
  3     NF = NF+1
        GOTO 5
  4     NM = NM+1
  5     CONTINUE
```

Fig. 5.15 Counting sexes using a computed GOTO

A glance shows that even for this very simple problem all sense of structure has been lost in the arithmetic IF and computed GOTO versions. In both of these it has been necessary to include an unconditional GOTO in order to avoid counting each individual as both male *and* female! In the case of the computed GOTO it has been necessary to reverse the order of the updating statements so that the (unexpected) cases in which ISEX is some value other than 0 or 1 are dealt with correctly.

The unconditional GOTO statement (or simply the GOTO statement), however, can be very useful particularly in conjunction with a logical IF statement. One such use is to exit from a DO-loop before it has been completed the specified number of times, while another is to create another type of loop which is controlled by some external condition instead of by a count.

5.7 IF-controlled loops

All the loops we have used so far have been controlled by a DO-statement and have, therefore, been of the form

Repeat the following 'n' times
    Block of statements

However there are two other ways in which we frequently may wish to define a loop, as shown below

(i)   Repeat the following while some condition is true
        Block of statements
(ii) Repeat the following until some condition is true
        Block of statements

Some languages have special statements for these types of loops, but in Fortran we can use a logical IF statement together with one or two GOTO statements, as shown in Fig. 5.16 and 5.17.

```
label1 IF (.NOT.condition) GOTO label2
       block of Fortran statements
       GOTO label1
label2 next statement
```

Fig. 5.16   The repeat…while…loop structure

```
label1 first statement
       block of Fortran statements
       IF (.NOT.condition) GOTO label1
```

Fig. 5.17   The repeat…until…loop structure

In the first case the loop is to be repeated as long as some condition is true. We start the loop with an IF statement which will GOTO the statement immediately after the end of the loop if the condition is not true, and terminate the loop with an unconditional GOTO which returns to the start of the loop. As long as the condition is true, therefore, the block of statements in the loop is obeyed and control is then returned to the beginning; once it becomes false the first GOTO is obeyed and control is passed to the statement immediately after the loop.

The second case is even simpler. Here the first statement of the block which is to be repeated is labelled and a logical IF added at the end, which causes a return to the beginning if the condition is false. Once it becomes true then the IF statement does not obey the GOTO and execution continues from the statement following the loop.

The major difference between these two types of loop is that the first (repeat . . . while) need not be obeyed at all (in the case where the condition is initially false), whereas the second (repeat . . . until) will always be obeyed at least once. This is quite obvious when we look at Figs. 5.16 and 5.17, where the placing of the IF statement means that the 'repeat . . . while' form need not be obeyed since the test is before the start of the loop, while the test for the 'repeat . . . until' form of loop comes at the end. We can see how both of these can be used by modifying Examples 5.3 and 5.2.

Example 5.5

Write a program which reads a series of sets of data, each consisting of two co-ordinates and a code. Plot an X at every point and surround it with a circle if the code is negative. A zero code means that this is the last point.

This is the same as Example 5.3 except that instead of having a fixed number of points the number is determined by a special (zero) code for the last one. The structure plan is therefore only a minor variation on the one we used earlier

> *1* Repeat until a zero code is read
> >   *2* Read a set of data
> >   *3* Draw a cross
> >   *4* If the code is negative then
> >   >   *4.1* Draw a circle

Notice that because we wish to draw a cross for every point, including the last one, we shall always obey the loop at least once and the second type of loop is appropriate. The program then follows

```
      PROGRAM PNTS2
   1  READ *,X,Y,N
      CALL CROSS(X,Y,0.25)
      IF (N.LT.0) CALL CIRCLE(X,Y,0.125)
      IF (N.NE.0) GOTO 1
      STOP
      END
```

Here we see that since the condition for ending the loop was N.EQ.0, the condition to be used in the IF statement should be .NOT.N.EQ.0 or, more succinctly, N.NE.0.

Example 5.6

Write a program to read a series of sets of coefficients of quadratic equations and to print their roots. The data is terminated by a zero set (i.e. $A = B = C = 0$).

This is an extension of Example 5.2 which solves a number of equations instead of just one. Unlike the situation in Example 5.4, however, the final data set is not part of the data but is purely a terminator. If we attempted to solve the equation using the formula

$$x = \frac{-b \pm \sqrt{b^2 - 4ac}}{2a}$$

when a, b and c were all zero we would cause a program failure when we attempted to evaluate 0/0. In this case, therefore, the 'repeat . . . while' structure is appropriate, and our structure plan will be

1   Set e to a very small value
2   Read first set of coefficients
3   Repeat while a, b and c are non-zero
    3.1   Calculate $b^2 - 4ac$
    3.2   If $b^2 - 4ac > e$ then
        3.2.1   Calculate and print two roots
        but if $b^2 - 4ac > -e$ then
        3.2.2   Calculate and print two equal roots
        otherwise
        3.2.3.   Print message 'no roots'
    3.3   Read next set of coefficients

Notice that we need to read the first set of coefficients before we enter the loop and then always to read the next set after we have solved the equation. This is because the form of the condition requires that we have the coefficients at the very start of the loop. Once again the program is quite straightforward

```
      PROGRAM QUAD2
C E IS A VERY SMALL NUMBER, BUT GREATER THAN LIKELY
C ROUNDING ERRORS
      E = 1E-9
      READ *,A,B,C
    1 IF (A.EQ.0 .AND. B.EQ.0 .AND. C.EQ.0) GOTO 2
      S = B**2-4*A*C
      IF (S.GT.E) THEN
         D = SQRT(S)
         X1 = (-B+D)/(2*A)
         X2 = (-B-D)/(2*A)
         PRINT *,A,'X**2 +',B,'X +',C,' = 0 HAS ROOTS',
     *       X1,' AND',X2
      ELSE IF (S.GT.-E) THEN
         X = -B/(2*A)
         PRINT *,A,'X**2 +',B,'X +',C,' = 0 HAS ROOTS',
     *       X,' AND',X
      ELSE
         PRINT *,A,'X**2 +',B,'X +',C,' = 0 HAS NO ROOTS'
      END IF
      READ *,A,B,C
      GOTO 1
    2 STOP
      END
```

The initial test could probably have been abbreviated to a test for A alone, because if A.EQ.0 then the equation is not a quadratic and the division by 2*A will cause an error. It would seem reasonable, therefore, to assume that if A.EQ.0, this is the special terminator. However the order of evaluation means that if A.NE.0 then the whole condition is false and so no time is wasted in comparing B and C with zero; the only time they will be checked is for the case when A *is* zero, i.e. for the terminator data set.

5.8 Conditional DO-loops

The one great danger in the forms of a loop described above is the situation that can result if the condition for ending the loop never arises. In the two examples just discussed this would mean that the programs attempt to read more data, and in its absence might fail. However, consider the common situation in which no data is being read in the loop, but in which successive calculations are being made until further iterations produce no significant change in the result. Examples in the form of structure plans might be

    (a)   Repeat while error factor is greater than a very small value
          Calculate next value
          Calculate error factor between this and the last value
or (b)   Repeat until the error factor is less than a very small value
          Calculate next value
          Calculate error factor between this and the last value

It is well known to mathematicians that some types of series approximations will converge rapidly to a point where further terms in the series have a negligible effect, that others will do so more slowly, and that others will never do so but will oscillate around the 'true' value. If an attempt was made to evaluate a series approximation of the third type, using either of the types of loop above, then it would never terminate and we would have what is called an *infinite loop*, i.e. a loop from which the program can never exit.

An infinite loop is just one of the dangers implicit in the use of any form of GOTO statement. It is often more advisable to use a combination of a DO-loop and a logical IF to create other types of loop, in order that a 'fail-safe' structure is created. We can express these in the following ways

    (a)   Repeat the following up to 'n' times while some condition is true
          Block of statements
    (b)   Repeat the following 'n' times or until some condition is true
          Block of statements

The Fortran implementations of these two loop structures are shown in Figs. 5.18 and 5.19. It can be seen that both of them now have a very similar structure with a single *forward* GOTO controlled by a logical IF statement. The absence of any backward GOTOs means that there is no danger of creating an infinite loop and also restores a well-defined structure to the program. In fact we can generalise these two structures to form what we shall henceforth call a *conditional* DO-*loop*.

```
          DO labell, var=1,n
              IF (.NOT.condition) GOTO label2
              block of Fortran statements
      labell    CONTINUE
      label2 next statement
```

Fig. 5.18 The improved repeat…while…loop structure

```
                DO  label1, var=1,n
                    block of Fortran statements
                    IF (condition) GOTO label2
        label1      CONTINUE
        label2 next statement
```

Fig. 5.19   The improved repeat...until...loop structure

This is, quite simply, a DO-loop which contains one or more conditions upon which an exit is made from the loop

Repeat the following 'n' times
    If some condition is true then exit
    Block of statements
    If some condition is true then exit
    Block of statements

    .
    .
    .

    If some condition is true then exit
exit point next statement

where any (or all) of the tests may be omitted. Fig. 5.20 shows the Fortran implementation of this. The most important thing to notice about this is that regardless of the number of tests within the body of the loop *they should all exit to the same place*. Only in this way can we avoid the development of an unstructured and potentially dangerous situation.

```
                DO  label1, var=1,n
                    IF (condition1) GOTO label2
                    block of Fortran statements
                    IF (condition2) GOTO label2
                    block of Fortran statements

                        .
                        .
                        .

                    IF (conditionm) GOTO label2
        label1      CONTINUE
        label2 next statement
```

Fig. 5.20   The general form of a conditional DO-loop

It will be seen that the three types of loops used earlier are all special cases of this general form:

- A DO-loop is a conditional DO-loop with *no* tests.
- A 'repeat . . . while' loop is a conditional DO-loop with a single test at the beginning.
- A 'repeat . . . until' loop is a conditional DO-loop with a single test at the end.

Example 5.7

A set of exam marks is provided together with a code (0 = male, 1 = female) to indicate the sex of the examinee. The data is terminated by a record containing a negative code. It is required to calculate the average mark for the class, and also the average mark for the boys and girls separately.

The program for this problem needs to produce a sum of all the marks and to count the examinees in order to calculate the class average, and also needs to do the same for the boys and the girls separately. With the total figures and those for the boys we can easily calculate the girls' figures without the need to accumulate them. Our structure plan is therefore as follows

1 Initialise sums for marks and pupils
2 Repeat the following
   2.1 Read a mark and code
   2.2 If code is negative then exit
   2.3 Update sum of marks
   2.4 If code is male (=0) then
      2.4.1 Update sum of boy's marks
      2.4.2 Add 1 to count of boys
3 Calculate number of girls and their total mark
4 Calculate and print required averages

Remember that a conditional DO-loop is counting how many times it is obeyed. This value is available after exit from the loop, thus avoiding the need to count the total number of pupils. The program can now be written from the structure plan, although we must first decide on the maximum number of times we shall allow the loop to be repeated. Since the problem refers to a class a maximum of 100 should be more than sufficient.

```
      PROGRAM EXAMS
      MARKS = 0
      MARKSB = 0
      NBOYS = 0
      DO 10, I=1,100
        READ *,MARK,ISEX
        IF (ISEX.LT.0) GOTO 20
        MARKS = MARKS+MARK
        IF (ISEX.EQ.0) THEN
          MARKSB = MARKSB+MARK
          NBOYS = NBOYS+1
        END IF
 10     CONTINUE
 20 N = I-1
      MARKSG = MARKS-MARKSB
      NGIRLS = N-NBOYS
      IF (N.GT.0) THEN
        PRINT *,'AVERAGE MARK IS',REAL(MARKS)/N
        IF (NBOYS.GT.0) THEN
          PRINT *,'AVERAGE BOY''S MARK IS',REAL(MARKSB)/
     *      NBOYS
```

```
          ELSE
            PRINT *,'THERE ARE NO BOYS IN THE CLASS'
          END IF
          IF (NGIRLS.GT.0) THEN
            PRINT *,'AVERAGE GIRL''S MARK IS',REAL(MARKSG)/
     *      NGIRLS
          ELSE
            PRINT *,'THERE ARE NO GIRLS IN THE CLASS'
          END IF
        ELSE
          PRINT *,'THERE ARE NO MARKS!'
        END IF
        STOP
        END
```

Notice that at the exit from the loop we set N to the value I−1. There are two cases – either the special terminator data is read or 100 sets of marks are read with no terminator. Let us look at each of these cases separately.

Assume that the class has 35 pupils. On the first pass through the loop I is 1 and the first pupil's mark is read. On the next pass I is 2 and the second pupil's mark is read. On the 35th pass I is 35 and the 35th, and last, pupil's mark is read. On the next pass I is therefore 36 and the terminator data is read. On exit from the loop I is thus one more than the number of pupils.

If no terminator is read, then after 100 pupil's marks have been read the loop will finish. In Chapter 4 we saw that if a DO-loop completes its defined number of passes then the DO-variable will have the value *it would have had on the next pass*. In our case it will be 101 – one more than the number of pupils whose marks were read.

In both cases therefore the number of pupils is I−1, although it might be desirable to include an extra statement between those labelled 10 and 20

```
        PRINT *,'NO TERMINATOR – ONLY 100 MARKS READ'
```

This will draw attention to the omission of some marks if the 'fail-safe' action of the DO-loop came into effect too soon.

There are two points to note about the calculation and printing of the averages. The first is that a test is made to see if there are any pupils in each category (so as to avoid dividing by zero) and a suitable message printed if there are not. The second concerns the calculation of the average. The program has assumed that the marks are integers, and of course the number of pupils is an integer. The expression MARKS/N would therefore lead to an integer division being carried out and the average given in integer form (truncated not even rounded). This is not suitable and so steps must be taken to force a real division.

For example, the sums of marks could be kept in real variables such as SUM, SUMB and SUMG. The ensuing expressions, such as SUM/N, would be mixed-mode and would therefore be evaluated using real arithmetic. Alternatively, the sums can be converted to real form. The easiest way to do this is to use the intrinsic function REAL which simply produces as its result the real equivalent of its argument, thus once again leading to a mixed-mode expression.

Summary

- The block IF statement is the major method of introducing the concept of choice and decision-making into a program.

- The logical IF statement is used where only a single statement is to be the subject of a logical decision.

- The combination of logical IF statements and a DO-loop can be used to create a powerful, general-purpose conditional DO-loop.

- The CALL statement is a means whereby a subroutine subprogram may be accessed.

Relational expressions   e.g. A.LT.B
                                 I.EQ.J
                                 etc.

Logical expressions   e.g. X.LT.Y .AND. P.GE.Q
                                 I.NE.J .OR. (A.GT.B .EQV. C.LE.D)

Block IF   IF (logical expression) THEN
                                Fortran statements
                            ELSE IF (logical expression) THEN
                                Fortran statements
                            ELSE
                                Fortran statements
                            END IF

Logical IF   IF (logical expression) Fortran statement

Subroutine call   CALL subroutine name(argl,arg2,....)
                            CALL subroutine name

Unconditional GOTO   GOTO label
(to be used with care!)

Conditional DO-loop   DO label1, var=1,max
                                   .
                                   .
                                IF (logical expression) GOTO label2
                                   .
                                   .
                                IF (logical expression) GOTO label2
                                   .
                                   .

                            label1   terminal statement of loop
                            label2 next statement

Fig. 5.21   (Recommended) Fortran 77 statements introduced in Chapter 5

Exercises

5.1 What are the values of the following logical expressions?
(a) `1.GT.2`
(b) `(1+3).GE.4`
(c) `(1+3).LE.4`
(d) `2.GT.1.AND.3.LT.4`
(e) `3.GT.2.AND.(1+2).LT.3.OR.4.LE.3`
(f) `3.GT.2.OR.(1+2).LT.3.AND.4.LE.3`
(g) `3.GT.2.AND.(1+2).LT.3.OR..NOT.4.LE.3`
(h) `(4−1).GT.3.EQV.(1+2).LT.3`

5.2 The number of entries for a cycle race is so large that it is decided to divide them into two separate races, based upon an initial time trial. Write a program which reads data for each rider consisting of the rider's number and his time, and prints a list giving the number and the race (A or B) to which he has been allocated. If his time is less than 1 minute 50 seconds for the trial he should be in race A, otherwise in race B. The data will be terminated by a rider with a negative time.

5.3 Students in an exam are awarded a pass if they average over 50% for the three papers and a distinction if they average more than 75%. Write a program to read the three marks for each student (who will be identified by his position in the data) and to print his result (i.e. distinction, pass or fail). Finally, print the average mark for all students and the average for each group (i.e. those with distinctions, those with passes, and those who failed). You may choose your own way of terminating the data.

5.4 Rewrite question 4.5 (calculation of batting averages) using logical expressions as a means of dealing with 'not out' innings.

5.5 The value of $\sin X$ (where X is in radians) can be expressed by the infinite series

$$\sin X = X - \frac{X^3}{3!} + \frac{X^5}{5!} - \frac{X^7}{7!} + \frac{X^9}{9!} - \ldots$$

(where $n! = n*(n-1)*(n-2)*\ldots*2*1$)

Write a program that reads a value of X and uses the above series to calculate $\sin X$ to an accuracy that is also read as part of the data. (Hint: $\sin(X+2\pi) = \sin(X)$ where $\pi = 3.1415926536$; therefore we may use a value of X which lies between $-\pi$ and $+\pi$ to reduce the size of the expressions. Once this has been done, every term after the second is smaller than its predecessor and so it is easy to know when to stop the loop.)

5.6 Modify the previous program (question 5.5) so that it produces a table showing the value of $\sin X$ for X taking values from 0 to 90 degrees in steps of 1 degree, where 360 degrees $= 2\pi$ radians. Each line of the results should show the angle (in degrees), $\sin X$ (as calculated) and a further value of $\sin X$ produced by the intrinsic function `SIN`.

Simple Input/Output

6.1 The interface with the computer

We can now instruct the computer to manipulate information, repeat sequences of instructions and take alternative courses of action depending upon decisions which are only made during the execution of the program. Compared with the sophistication of which we are capable in these areas, our control over the interpretation of data and the presentation of results is woefully primitive. The problem arises because it is in this area that the world of the computer (where everything is stored as an electric or magnetic signal in one of only two states) comes face-to-face with the world of the human computer user (where there are an almost infinite number of ways of storing or presenting information). It is the interface between these two worlds that we must now examine.

Fig. 6.1 A punched card

A graphic example of this problem can be seen in the punched card shown in Fig. 6.1, which has the digits 1 to 9 punched in the first nine columns. What does this represent?

It could be the number 123 456 789.

Or it could be the nine numbers 1, 2, 3, 4, 5, 6, 7, 8 and 9.

Or it could be the three numbers 123, 456, 789.

Or it could even be the number 12 345.6789.

Or it could be the four numbers 1.23, 0.45, 67 and 8900.

Or it could be one of hundreds of other valid interpretations of these nine digits.

The output of results presents even greater difficulties. If, for example, we wished to print the character string `THE ANSWERS ARE` followed by the values stored in two real variables `X` and `Y` we should have a vast choice of ways in which to arrange our results. They could all be on one line like this

```
THE ANSWERS ARE   12.34   -7.89
```

or they could be on three lines

```
THE ANSWERS ARE

12.34      -7.89
```

or

```
THE ANSWERS ARE
12.34
-7.89
```

or a number of other variations. They could also be printed immediately below the last item, or separated from it by one or more blank lines, or at the top of a new page, or in the middle of one. The numbers might be printed with two decimal places, or with five, or with any other number. The possibilities are enormous.

There is a further problem concerned with where the data comes from and where the results are to go to. Is the data on cards, or paper tape, or is it typed directly at a terminal, or perhaps stored on backing store – and if so, where? Are the results to be printed on a printer, or at a terminal, or sent to backing store? And in any of these cases is the peripheral device a 'local' one (i.e. one which is more or less directly attached to the computer) or is it at some remote site, possibly many miles away?

So far we have used two simple 'list-directed' statements for input and output. For input we write

```
READ *, input-list
```

and for output

```
PRINT *, output-list
```

If we consider the READ statement first, we find that the source of the data is dealt with by a neat piece of sleight-of-hand. Input is taken, we said in Chapter 2, from the 'standard input unit', which is defined by the particular computer system being used; typically it will be the terminal keyboard or a card reader. The interpretation of the data is dealt with primarily by treating a space or a comma (or a /) as a separator between items of data.

In a similar way, the PRINT statement sends its results to the 'standard output unit' which is also processor dependent, but which will usually be the terminal screen (or printer) or the computer's printer. The layout of the results is less satisfactory since each PRINT statement starts at the beginning of the next line and prints the various items in a 'reasonable' format. This varies according to the type (and size) of the values to be output, and is defined by the writer of the Fortran compiler and not by the standard. In effect, the results will always be clearly printed, but the programmer has virtually no control over their layout.

These two 'list-directed' input/output statements are thus severely restricted in their ability to define both the format of the information and its source or destination; nevertheless they can be extremely useful, especially for input, in a great many cases.

The remainder of this chapter will examine how we can provide the flexibility needed in many cases for both input and output. We shall restrict ourselves to the input of numbers and the output of numbers and titles for the present. Subsequently new types of information (such as characters) will be introduced and the input/output facilities will be extended as and when necessary.

6.2   The FORMAT concept

An input statement must contain (at least) three types of information – where the data is to be found, where it is to be stored, and how it is to be interpreted. Similarly an output statement must define where the results are stored, where they are to be sent, and in what form they are to be displayed. These three types of information are not all dealt with in the same way. In English language terms a READ instruction says 'read some information from unit "n" (e.g. a terminal or a card reader) and store it in the variables X, Y and Z'. This cannot (usually) be fully achieved without defining the layout of the data and so some supplementary information is usually supplied. Fig. 6.2 shows a variation of the instructions for cooking the lunch which were used earlier (see Fig. 3.8), and it can be seen that a footnote refers to the cookery book to be used and the page on which to find the recipe. The body of the instructions are thus of the form 'do this . . .', while the footnote provides extra information which is necessary if the instructions are to be obeyed satisfactorily.

The Fortran input/output statements operate exactly like this, and indeed we have been using exactly the same convention without realising it in all the programs we have written. When we wrote

```
READ *,X,Y,Z
```

or

Miles,

Can you make the Hot Pot? I'll be back around 1.30.

Peel half-a-dozen potatoes. Then cut them into thickish slices. Do the same with a large onion.

The lamb is in the fridge — chop it into smallish chunks (about 1½ inches).

Follow the instructions in the book,* but ignore the bit about kidneys and mushrooms.

Put it on at 11.00 – DON'T FORGET

Love

Margaret

* Mary Berry's Cookbook, page 78. You'll find it in the top drawer.

Fig. 6.2   More cooking instructions

```
PRINT *,'RESULT IS',FRED
```

the asterisk (*) was actually referring to a format for the data or results. This format, supplied by the system, is called a *list-directed* format, and is defined by reference to the input or output list. If we wished we could define our own format and refer to it by writing

READ label, input-list

or

PRINT label, output-list

where 'label' is the number of a statement label which will appear elsewhere in the program attached to a special FORMAT statement which will define the layout of the data or results, as appropriate. Thus our input statement could take either of the forms

READ *, input-list
READ label, input-list

and our output statement could do likewise

PRINT *, output-list
PRINT label, output-list

The facilities available in Fortran 77 for defining the format of data and results are extremely powerful, and provide enormous flexibility to the programmer. Before we consider them, we should examine the basic input/output statements in more detail. Once we have seen the variations that are possible we shall return to examine the FORMAT statement and to see how it is used in conjunction with both input and output statements.

6.3   The READ statement

The two variants of the READ statement, that we have met, take their input from the 'standard input unit'. In order to vary this, and to allow the possibility of monitoring the success or otherwise of the reading process, we must use a more general form of READ statement. This takes the form

READ (cilist) input-list

where 'cilist' represents a control information list consisting of (normally) two or more items (known as *specifiers*) separated by commas. Fig. 6.3 shows a list of these specifiers, all of which take the same basic form

keyword = value

although the keyword may, in certain circumstances, be omitted in two cases.

These specifiers, or rather those which are used in a particular case, may appear in any order as long as the full form (with keyword) is used.

```
UNIT   = u (or u)
FMT    = f (or f)
REC    = rn
ERR    = s
END    = s
IOSTAT = ios
```

Fig. 6.3 Control information list items

There must always be one unit specifier in the control information list, which takes the form

UNIT = u

where 'u' is the peripheral unit from which input is to be taken (or the name of an *internal file* – see Chapter 12). It takes either the form of an integer expression whose value is zero or positive, or it may be an asterisk to indicate that the 'standard input unit' is to be used. The way in which the unit number is related to a particular peripheral device is, to a large extent, dependent upon the computer system being used. Normally several units will be *preconnected* and will automatically be available to all programs. The 'standard input unit' and the 'standard output unit' will be preconnected in this way, but a particular Fortran 77 implementation may well have others. Any other peripheral devices or files (see Chapter 12) which are required must be given a unit number by the program and *connected* to that program by an OPEN statement.

The standard input unit will usually be preconnected either as unit 1 or as unit 5. (This is purely for historical reasons since while many early Fortran systems used unit 1 for the card reader and unit 2 for the printer, IBM and several other manufacturers used units 5 and 6 for these units, respectively. A great many programs written in earlier versions thus expect their input from unit 1 or 5 and send their results to unit 2 or 6, depending upon the type of computer being used. For compatibility, a new Fortran 77 system is likely to preserve the convention in use at a particular site.) We shall assume that it is unit 1, but it must be emphasised that *this is only an assumption*; a particular implementation may use any positive number or zero for the standard input unit.

With this assumption we may write

UNIT = 1

or

UNIT = *

to identify the standard input unit. If, and only if, the unit specifier is the first item in the control information list we may omit the keyword and = sign, and simply write

    1

or

    *

Normally the input will need to be converted from some 'external' form such as holes in a card, signals sent by a terminal, etc. to an 'internal' form suitable for storing in the computer's memory, although in some circumstances (see Chapter 12) this is not necessary. To carry out this conversion we need a FORMAT statement, and this is identified by a format specifier which takes the form

    FMT = f

where 'f' is the statement label of the appropriate FORMAT statement, or an asterisk to indicate list-directed formatting, or an embedded format (see Section 6.9). If the format specifier is the second item in the control information list and the first item is a unit specifier without any keyword (i.e. 'u') then the keyword and = sign may also be omitted from the format specifier. Thus the following are all acceptable alternatives

```
READ (UNIT = 1, FMT = 100) X,Y,Z
READ (FMT = 100, UNIT = 1) X,Y,Z
READ (1, FMT = 100) X,Y,Z
READ (1, 100) X,Y,Z
```

The last, and shortest, form is the only form that was acceptable before the advent of Fortran 77.

We can also see that the statement

```
READ (*,*) A,B,C
```

is identical to the earlier list-directed input statement

```
READ *,A,B,C
```

as is the statement

```
READ (1,*) A,B,C
```

if, and only if, unit 1 is also the standard input unit.

The next input specifier (REC = rn) does not concern us at this stage. It is used for 'direct access' input and is discussed in detail in Chapter 12.

The remaining three specifiers are concerned with monitoring the reading process. The first of them

    ERR = s

takes special action if an error should occur. This might be one of several types such as misreading of data, running out of data, etc. Normally if this happens execution of the program is terminated; however if an error specifier is included in the control information list of the READ statement which caused the error, processing will continue from a statement in the program which has a statement label 's'. Thus if an error occurs during the statement

```
READ (UNIT=1,FMT=100,ERR=999) A,B,C
```

the program will continue from the statement with label 999. In this event the items in the input list become 'undefined' – in other words it is not known what value they contain – as does the position in the input data. It is, in most cases therefore, impossible to continue, but the program can take such action as the programmer may deem appropriate (such as printing intermediate results) before it finishes.

A special type of error concerns the situation in which a program tries to read more data than is available. There are actually two situations here. One concerns the use of files (see Chapter 12) in which a special 'marker', called an end-of-file record, may come after all the data; the other concerns simple input such as we are considering. In the former case, and *in some implementations* when dealing with simple input, we can take special notice of running out of data by use of the end-of-file specifier

```
END = s
```

This is similar to the error specifier and causes processing to continue from the statement labelled 's' if the READ statement encounters an end-of-file marker or, otherwise sets an end-of-file condition. More details are given in Chapter 12, but if a particular Fortran 77 implementation sets an end-of-file condition and not an error, when it runs out of data, this can be used as an easy way of detecting the end of the data for a program. (As an example of this we may cite one widely used Fortran 77 compiler. If data is supplied on cards or typed in at the terminal then the absence of any more data will cause an error. However if this data is first stored in a file and then read from there *as though from cards* (which is the normal mode of operation) then an end-of-file condition, and not an error, will arise if there is no more data.)

The final specifier enables more information to be made available to the program in the event of an error. It takes the form

```
IOSTAT = ios
```

where 'ios' is an integer variable. When the READ statement is obeyed the variable will be set to a value which indicates the result of the input operation, as shown in Fig. 6.4. If no error occurred and there was no end-of-file then the variable is set to zero. If there was no error but an end-of-file condition did occur, then it will be set to a negative value. This value is processor-dependent, but the fact that it is negative is really all that matters. If there was an error, however, the variable will be set to a positive value. In this last case there will probably be several possible (positive) values used to indicate different types of errors; what these values are, and what they mean is, however, dependent upon the particular computer system. It does, though, provide a means whereby the program can decide upon what action to take in the event of different types of errors, for example if running out of data does not set an end-of-file condition it will almost certainly be identifiable by means of a unique error number.

---

ios = 0   if there was no error and no end-of-file
   > 0   if an error occurred
   < 0   if an end-of-file condition occurred, but no error

Fig. 6.4   Input/output status values (IOSTAT = *ios*)

The input/output status specifier can either be used on its own, in which case a test must be included after the READ statement

```
          .
          .
          .
      READ (*,50,IOSTAT=I) A,B,C
      IF (I.LT.0) THEN
C    END OF FILE
          .
          .
      ELSE IF (I.GT.0) THEN
C    ERROR
          .
          .
      END IF
C  CONTINUE NORMAL PROCESSING
          .
          .
```

or it can be used in combination with the error and/or end-of-file specifiers

```
      READ (*,50,IOSTAT=I,ERR=300,END=250) A,B,C
```

in which case these will take care of the branching away from the normal sequence of processing. In both cases the value of I may be inspected to find out the exact cause of the error.

6.4   The WRITE and PRINT statements

Output is essentially the reverse of input, so far as the transfer of information is concerned, and as one would expect, the facilities available are essentially the same. The most obvious difference is that for input the word READ is used in all cases, but for output we have two words. We have used the PRINT statement for list-directed output and the same form of statement could be used for user-formatted output to the standard output unit. To take advantage of the full range of facilities, however, we use a different word, WRITE , in a form of statement which is almost identical to that used for input

```
WRITE (cilist) output-list
```

Exactly the same specifiers are available as was the case for the READ statement although, other than a special situation (see Chapter 12), it will not normally be possible to encounter an end-of-file condition during output. The only other difference is the obvious one that an asterisk as a unit identifier refers to the standard output unit. Thus the following statements have an identical effect

```
WRITE (UNIT=*,FMT=*) P,Q,R
WRITE (FMT=*,UNIT=*) P,Q,R
WRITE (*,FMT=*) P,Q,R
WRITE (*,*) P,Q,R
PRINT *,P,Q,R
```

The choice of a unit number for the standard output unit is dependent upon the particular implementation. It will usually be 2 (when 1 is used for input) or 6 (when 5 is used for input), although some interactive systems may use the same number for both the keyboard and the display of a terminal. In this book *we shall assume that the standard output unit is* 2 and that, therefore, the following statements are equivalent

```
WRITE (2,75) D,E,F
WRITE (*,75) D,E,F
```

6.5   The FORMAT statement

In the above variations of READ, WRITE and PRINT statements we have defined the format of the data or results by a format specifier of the form

```
FMT = f
```

where f is either a statement label or an asterisk (to indicate list-directed formatting), or simply by writing

```
READ f, input list
PRINT f, output list
```

where f is defined in the same way. We are now ready to examine the FORMAT statement.
   This takes the form

```
label FORMAT (ed1,ed2,...,edn)
```

where ed1,...,edn are *edit descriptors*. These will be used to convert (or edit) the data in one form (e.g. as holes in a card or values in a memory location) into another form (e.g. values in a memory location or characters on a printed sheet). Notice that a FORMAT statement will *always* have a statement label because it is not the same as the other statements, but is more like a footnote (see Section 6.2). In computer terminology it is *non-executable* and is always used by another statement, which identifies it by its label.

Fig. 6.5 shows some of the edit descriptors used for input, and we shall examine these in turn. Other edit descriptors will be introduced later. The first two edit descriptors in Fig. 6.5 are concerned with reading input characters and converting them into either integer or real numbers, while the remainder are concerned with altering the order in which these characters are read.

Descriptor	Meaning
Iw	Read the next w characters as an integer
F$w.d$.	Read the next w characters as a real number with d digits after the decimal place if no decimal point is present
nX	Ignore the next n characters
Tc	Next character to be read is at position c
TLn ⎫ TRn ⎭	Next character to be read is n characters before (TL) or after (TR) the current position

Fig. 6.5 Some edit descriptors for input

The first, and simplest, edit descriptor is used for inputting whole numbers which are to be stored in an *integer* variable, and consists of the letter 'I' followed by a number 'w'. This indicates that the next w characters are to be read and interpreted as an integer. Thus if we wished to read the card shown in Fig. 6.1 (which had the digits 1 to 9 punched in columns 1 to 9) as a single integer we could write

```
      READ 101,N
  101 FORMAT (I9)
```

although the resulting number (123456789) would be too large to hold as an integer on most computers and would probably lead to an error. The READ statement could also be written in one of several other ways, e.g.

```
      READ (UNIT=1,FMT=101) I
      READ (1,101) I
      READ (*,101) I
      READ (FMT=101,UNIT=*) I
      etc
```

In future examples we shall use only one of the various alternatives without any further comment.

If we wished to read the same card as nine separate integers (1,2,3,....,9) then we could write

```
      READ (1,102) N1,N2,N3,N4,N5,N6,N7,N8,N9
  102 FORMAT (I1,I1,I1,I1,I1,I1,I1,I1,I1)
```

This format interacts with the READ statement in the following way.

First the READ statement recognises that it requires an integer to store in N1; the FORMAT statement indicates that the first item to be read is an integer occupying one column (I1). The character '1' is therefore read and converted to the internal form of an integer before being stored in N1. The READ statement then requires another integer and the FORMAT indicates that this is to come from the *next* column (I1). And so the process is repeated until the ninth column is read and the value 9 stored in N9. The READ statement is now satisfied and so input of this card is complete.

Notice that there is an implied concept of a 'pointer' which is always indicating which is the next character of the input record to be read. Normally this pointer is moved through the record as characters are read; however the X and T edit specifiers allow the pointer to be moved without any characters being read. The X edit descriptor takes the form of a whole number 'n' followed by an 'X' and causes the pointer to be moved forward across n characters. The next character to be read will be n positions to the right of the current position and the effect is to ignore the next n characters. Thus, using the same data card, the statements

```
      READ (*,103) K
103 FORMAT (4X,I5)
```

will ignore the first four columns and then read the next five as an integer; the value 56789 will therefore be stored in K. Similarly

```
      READ (1,104) I,J
104 FORMAT (I2,3X,I3)
```

will cause the value 12 to be stored in I and 678 in J. Notice that in this case the 9 punched in column 9 is not read because the format only specifies the first eight columns.

The T (for Tab) edit descriptor comes in three variations. The first consists of the letter 'T' followed by a whole number 'c' and causes a 'tab' to character position 'c'; in other words the next character to be read will be from position 'c'. Thus the statements

```
      READ (UNIT=1,FMT=105) I,J,K
105 FORMAT (T4,I2,T8,I2,T2,I4)
```

will first move the pointer to position 4 and read the number 45 into I, then move it to position 8 before reading 89 into J, and then move it to position 2 before reading the number 2345 into K. The T edit descriptor thus provides a means of not only skipping over unwanted characters, but also of going back in the record and reading it (or parts of it) again.

The T edit descriptor moves to a character position which is defined *absolutely* by its position in the record. The TL and TR edit descriptors, on the other hand, specify a *relative* tab – that is a move to a character position which is defined relative to the current position. The letters 'TR' followed by a number 'n' indicate that the next character is to be n positions to the right of the current position; it is thus identical in its effect to nX. The letters 'TL' followed by a number 'n' specify a tab to the left and cause the next character to be n positions to the left of (or before) the current position. If 'TLn' would cause the next position to be before the first character of the record then the pointer is positioned at the start of the record; 'TL' followed by a large number can therefore always be used to return to the beginning of the record (as can T1).

Example 6.1
If an input record (e.g. card or line of tape) consists of the ten digits 1,2,3,4,5,6,7,8,9,0 repeated five times, what is stored in the variables I,J,K,L,M and N after the following statements?

```
110 FORMAT(T5,I4,21X,I3,TL7,I2,TR13,I3,TL45,TR7,I5,TL5,I5)
    READ 110,I,J,K,L,M,N
```

The READ statement requires six integers and will therefore use the FORMAT labelled 110 to obtain them. The T5 descriptor causes the following I4 to start at position 5 and read 5678 into I, leaving the pointer at position 9. The 21X descriptor moves the pointer 21 positions to the right and the following I3 descriptor thus starts at position 30 and reads the characters 012, i.e. 12, leaving the pointer at position 33.

TL7 then moves the pointer back 7 positions to position 26 and the number 67 is read and stored in K. The pointer is then moved 13 positions to the right, i.e. to position 41, and the number 123 read into the variable L, leaving the pointer at position 44. The next edit descriptor is TL45 which will attempt to move the pointer 45 characters to the left; however as this would move it to before the start of the record, it is positioned at the first character position. The following TR7 therefore moves the pointer to position 8 and the value 89012 is read into M due to the I5 descriptor.

The last two edit descriptors cause the pointer to be moved back five characters and then five characters to be read as an integer. This causes the same characters to be read for N as for M. The final state of the six variables is therefore

```
I = 5678
J = 12
K = 67
L = 123
M = 89012
N = 89012
```

Finally the F edit descriptor is used for reading real values. This consists of the letter 'F' followed by a number 'w', a decimal point '.', and a second number 'd'. It can be used in two rather different ways, depending upon the format of the data.

If the data is typed (or punched) with a decimal point in the appropriate position then the edit descriptor causes the next 'w' characters to be read and converted into a real number. The value of 'd' is irrelevant (although it must be included in the format).

On the other hand if the 'w' columns, which are to be read as a real number, do not contain any decimal point then the 'd' indicates where one may be assumed to have been omitted, by specifying that the number has 'd' decimal places. Thus (assuming our usual input record as shown in Fig. 6.1) the following statements

```
      READ  121,X
121 FORMAT (F9.4)
```

will cause the first nine characters to be read as a real number with four decimal places. The variable X will therefore have the number 12345.6789 stored in it. In a similar way

```
      READ  122,A,B,CD
122 FORMAT (F3.1,F2.2,F3.5,TL6,F4.0)
```

will cause the value 12.3 to be stored in A, 0.45 in B, 0.00678 in C, and 3456.0 in D. Notice especially that the third edit descriptor (F3.5) causes three characters to be read (678) and treated as a real number with five decimal places. This requires the implied insertion of two leading zeros to give the value 0.00678.

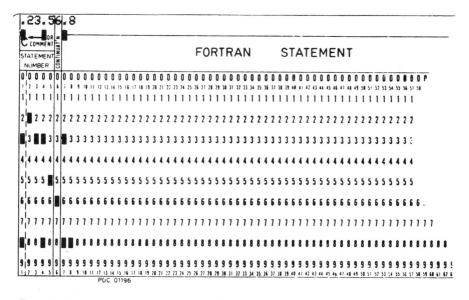

Fig. 6.6   Another punched card

Consider now the same program statements used to read a card punched as shown in Fig. 6.6. The first descriptor requires three columns to be read, and since these (.23) contain a decimal point the second part of the edit descriptor is ignored and the value 0.23 stored in A. In a similar way the F2.2 descriptor causes the characters '.5' to be read, and B is therefore given the value 0.5. The F3.5 edit descriptor also has its second part over-ridden by the decimal point in 6.8 and so this is the value stored in C. Finally 'TL6,F4.0' cause the characters '3.56' to be read and so this value is stored in D

```
A = 0.23
B = 0.5
C = 6.8
D = 3.56
```

As a general rule, data which is to be stored as real values will be presented to the computer with the decimal points in their correct places. However sometimes, especially when the data has been collected independently from the programmer, it is presented as whole numbers which need to be processed by the computer as real numbers.

Example 6.2

A survey, consisting of a maximum of 1000 respondents, has recorded the names, ages, sexes, heights and weights of a number of people. The information has been punched onto cards as follows

Name	in columns 1–20
Sex	coded in column 23
	0 = male
	1 = female
Age (yr)	in columns 27, 28
Height (cm)	in columns 31–33
Weight (kg)	in columns 36–41 in the form *nnn.dd*

The data is terminated by a card which has a 9 punched in column 23 (the sex code). Write a program to calculate the average height of female respondents between the ages of 21 and 35 (inclusive) and the average weight of those in this group who are over 1.7 m in height.

First we must write a structure plan

    1 Initialise variables
    2 Repeat the following up to 1000 times
        2.1 Read sex, age, height and weight
        2.2 If sex code is 9 then exit
        2.3 If female and between 21 and 35 then
            2.3.1 Add height to sum of heights
            2.3.2 Add 1 to sum of people
            2.3.3 If height is more than 1.7
                2.3.3.1 Add weight to sum of weights
                2.3.3.2 Add 1 to sum of tall people
    3 Calculate and print averages

The program is then quite straightforward

```
PROGRAM SURVEY
SUMHT = 0
SUMWT = 0
NH = 0
NW = 0
```

```
C  THERE ARE A MAXIMUM OF 1000 PEOPLE
      DO 10, I=1,1000
         READ (5,101) ISEX,NAGE,HT,WT
         IF (ISEX.EQ.9) GOTO 11
         IF (ISEX.EQ.1 .AND. NAGE.GE.21 .AND. NAGE.LE.35) THEN
            SUMHT = SUMHT+HT
            NH = NH+1
            IF (HT.GT.1.7) THEN
               SUMWT = SUMWT+WT
               NW = NW+1
            END IF
         END IF
   10    CONTINUE
      PRINT *,'NO TERMINATOR READ'
      PRINT *,'ONLY THE FIRST 1000 RECORDS PROCESSED'
   11 IF (NH.GT.0) THEN
         PRINT *,'AVERAGE HEIGHT IS',SUMHT/NH
         IF (NW.GT.0) THEN
            PRINT *,'AVERAGE WEIGHT IS',SUMWT/NW
         ELSE
            PRINT *,'NO 21-35 YEAR OLD FEMALES OVER 1.7 METRES'
         END IF
      ELSE
         PRINT *,'NO 21-35 YEAR OLD FEMALES'
      END IF
      STOP
  101 FORMAT(T23,I1,3X,I2,2X,F3.2,2X,F6.0)
      END
```

Notice that the FORMAT statement does not need to be placed next to the READ statement. Many programmers place all their FORMATs together at the end of the program (before the END of course) as has been done here, as this enables them to be easily found and checked when necessary. In this case we see that 'T23,I1' will cause the first item read to be an integer taken from column 23; this is where the sex code is punched. '3X,I2' then causes the next item to be read as an integer from columns 27 and 28 (having ignored columns 24–26); this is where the age is punched.

The height was to be punched in columns 31–33 in centimetres; however it is more convenient for it to be stored internally as a real value and in metres. The edit descriptors '2X,F3.2' will cause columns 31–33 to be read as a real number with two decimal places; thus if the data is punched as 172 (i.e. 172 cm) it will be stored in the variable HT as 1.72 (i.e. 1.72 m = 172 cm). The edit descriptor therefore automatically converts an integer height in centimetres to a real height in metres.

The fourth item to be read is the weight, and this is punched in columns 36–41 as a real number in kilograms and fractions of a kilogram. The edit descriptors '2X,F6.0' will deal with this; the decimal point in the data will mean that the second part of the F edit descriptor (0) is ignored.

The program uses a conditional DO-loop to read a maximum of 1000 records and prints an error message if 1000 records are read without a terminator. Two nested IF blocks accumulate the required sums in accordance with the structure plan, while two more nested IF blocks are used to print the averages and/or messages stating that there are no heights or weights to average.

We now come to the use of the FORMAT statement for output. Fig. 6.7 shows some of the edit descriptors used for this purpose, most of which are similar to those used for input. Thus the I edit descriptor (Iw) causes an integer to be output in such a way as to utilise the next w character positions. These w positions will consist of (if necessary) one or more spaces, followed by a minus sign if the number is negative, followed by the value of the number. Thus the statements

```
    I = 23
    J = 715
    K = -12
    PRINT 201,I,J,K
201 FORMAT(I5,I5,I5)
```

will produce a line of output as follows (where the symbol ▽ represents a space)

▽▽▽23▽▽715▽▽-12

If the output is to go to the computer's *printer* then the results which actually appear will probably be very slightly different; this is discussed in Section 6.6. If it is sent to a terminal or most other peripheral devices, however, the layout will be exactly as defined.

Descriptor	Meaning
Iw	Output an integer in the next w character positions
Fw.d	Output a real number in the next w character positions with d decimal places
nX	Ignore the next n character positions
Tc	Output the next item starting at character position c
TLn ⎱ TRn ⎰	Output next item starting n character positions before (TL) or after (TR) the current position
'$h_1 h_2 h_3 .. h_n$'	Output the string of characters $h_1 h_2 h_3 .. h_n$ starting at the next character position
$nHh_1 h_2 .. h_n$	Output the n characters following the H in the next n character positions

Fig. 6.7   Some edit descriptors for output

The F edit descriptor operates in a similar way and 'Fw.d' indicates that a real number is to be output occupying w characters of which the last d are to follow the decimal point. The real value is *rounded* (not truncated) to d places of decimals before being output. Rounding is carried out in the usual arithmetic way. Thus the statements

```
       X = 3.14159
       Y = -275.3024
       Z = 12.9999
       PRINT 202,X,Y,Z
   202 FORMAT (F10.3,F10.3,F10.3)
```

will produce the following line of output

vvvvv3.142v−275.302vvvv13.000

Notice that, because the edit descriptor specifies only three places of decimals, the value of X is printed as 3.142 (rounded up), the value of Y as −275.302 (rounded down), and the value of Z as 13.000 (rounded up).

It is important to realise that if the number does not require the full 'field width', w, it will be preceded by one or more spaces. By allowing more room than is necessary, several numbers may be spaced across the page and the printing of tables becomes very easy, as can be seen in Fig. 6.8. In this case the FORMAT statement specifies that the three items to be printed $(X, \sqrt{X}, \sqrt[3]{X})$ are all to use an edit descriptor of F10.4. The three numbers are therefore spread evenly across the page, with the next three directly below them, and so on.

```
       PROGRAM FIG68
       THIRD = 1.0/3.0
C  AVOID ROUNDING ERRORS IN DO-STATEMENT
       DO 10, X=1.0,10.5
   10    WRITE (2,201) X,SQRT(X),X**THIRD
       STOP
  201 FORMAT(F10.4,F10.4,F10.4)
       END
```

```
    1.0000     1.0000     1.0000
    2.0000     1.4142     1.2599
    3.0000     1.7321     1.4422
    4.0000     2.0000     1.5874
    5.0000     2.2361     1.7100
    6.0000     2.4495     1.8171
    7.0000     2.6458     1.9129
    8.0000     2.8284     2.0000
    9.0000     3.0000     2.0801
   10.0000     3.1623     2.1544
```

Fig. 6.8   An example of tabular printing

In the example shown in Fig. 6.8, as in several other programs in this section, the same edit descriptor has been repeated several times. A number, called a *repeat count*, may be placed *before* the I and F edit descriptors to indicate how many times they are to be repeated. Thus

```
201 FORMAT (3I5,4F6.2)
```

is identical to

```
201 FORMAT (I5,I5,I5,F6.2,F6.2,F6.2,F6.2)
```

The first version, using a repeat count, is both easier to write and, more importantly, easier to read than the full version. A repeat count may be used in formats for both input and output to cause repetition of an edit descriptor which is used in conjunction with an input or output list item; it cannot be used to repeat the other edit descriptors.

The X edit descriptor is used on output to ignore, or skip over, the next n character positions. If no output has yet been sent to these positions the effect is to insert *n* spaces; if some output has already been sent to these positions however the X edit descriptor merely moves the pointer. The effect of *n*X is best appreciated by assuming that an output record always consists of spaces before the start of a WRITE or PRINT statement, and that *n*X moves the pointer n character positions.

T, TL and TC also operate in the same way as for input, if we assume the output record initially consists of spaces, and enable items to be positioned in an exact place in the record (or line).

There are two additional edit descriptors which can only be used for output; both of these cause a (constant) string of characters to be output, starting at the next character position. The first of these is the *apostrophe edit descriptor* and consists of a string of characters enclosed between apostrophes. This is exactly the same form as the character strings that we have used in PRINT statements to identify the meaning of our results. Thus, if we write

```
202 FORMAT ('THE SUM OF',I4,' AND',I4,' IS',I5)
    WRITE (*,202) I,J,I+J
```

we shall get the results printed as follows

```
THE SUM OF  74 AND 149 IS   223
```

Notice that the last two apostrophe edit descriptors start with a space to separate the string from the preceding number.

The second edit descriptor is older and is not recommended (except for one situation, see Section 6.6). It does exactly the same as the apostrophe descriptor, but in a more clumsy and error-prone manner. This is the H edit descriptor and consists of a number 'n' followed by 'H' and then 'n' characters. The n characters will be output starting at the next character position. Thus the FORMAT shown above could also be written

```
202 FORMAT(10HTHE SUM OF,I4,4H AND,I4,3H IS,I5)
```

This edit descriptor is only included in Fortran 77 for compatibility with earlier versions of Fortran.

Example 6.3

A piece of experimental apparatus is monitoring the radioactive decay of a specimen. At approximately regular intervals it records the time since the start of the experiment (in hundredths of a second), the number of α-particles emitted during the interval, the number of β-particles emitted and the amount of γ-radiation in the same period. These are output as an eight digit number (for the time) and three six digit numbers. There are five spaces between each number. Write a program to read this data and to print a table containing the following information: a sequence number for each interval, the length of the interval, the three readings obtained and the average emission of α-particles, β-particles and γ-rays (per second) during the interval. After 1000 time intervals print the time interval which had the highest rate of emission of γ-radiation.

As usual we shall start with a structure plan

    1 Initialise maximum radiation and interval
    2 Print column headings
    3 Repeat 1000 times
        3.1 Read next set of data
        3.2 Calculate length of interval and average emissions
        3.3 Print details
        3.4 If γ-radiation > max γ-radiation then
                3.4.1 Save maximum γ-radiation and interval number
    4 Print details of maximum γ-radiation

This is fairly straightforward except for step 2. We shall be printing a table with eight columns and it is sensible to identify these by headings. We can do this by means of a WRITE statement which has no output list, but which uses a FORMAT consisting solely of apostrophe (or H) edit descriptors together with any necessary positioning descriptors.

We also need to consider the formats for both input and output. As is often the case, the format of the data is already defined and our FORMAT statement must therefore reflect it. In this case it is quite simple

```
101 FORMAT (F8.2,5X,I6,5X,I6,5X,I6)
```

The time is provided in hundredths of a second so the easiest approach is to read it as a real number in seconds with an implied decimal point before the last two digits. The other items are all integers. Notice that on this occasion we have a repeated sequence (5X,I6). We can shorten the FORMAT in two ways, either by enclosing this sequence in parentheses and preceding it by a repeat count, or by including the leading spaces as part of the numeric field (but see section 6.8), thus

```
101 FORMAT (F8.2,3(5X,I6))
```

or

```
101 FORMAT (F8.2,3I11)
```

Notice in the first case that the X edit descriptor can be repeated when it is part of a repeated sequence which contains at least one repeatable edit descriptor.

Output is rather different because usually, though not always, we have complete control over its format. In this case we have a table of eight items – a sequence number, a time interval (to one hundredth of a second), three integer values and three averages. A suitable format might be

```
202 FORMAT(I4,F6.2,3I8,3F8.2)
```

Here all the edit descriptors have a field width wider than is necessary in order to space the columns across the page, and also to leave room for column titles. We can now write the program

```
      PROGRAM DECAY
      GMAX = 0
      MAXINT = 0
      TLAST = 0
      WRITE (2,201)
      DO 10, I=1,1000
         READ (1,101) T,NALPHA,NBETA,NGAMMA
         TIME = T-TLAST
         AVA = NALPHA/TIME
         AVB = NBETA/TIME
         AVG = NGAMMA/TIME
         WRITE (2,202) I,TIME,NALPHA,NBETA,NGAMMA,
     *                 AVA,AVB,AVG
C  SET TLAST TO TIME OF LAST READINGS
         TLAST = T
         IF (AVG.GT.GMAX) THEN
            GMAX = AVG
            MAXINT = I
         END IF
   10    CONTINUE
      WRITE (2,203) GMAX,MAXINT
      STOP
  101 FORMAT(F8.2,3(5X,I6))
  201 FORMAT(T2,'INT',T7,'TIME',T14,'ALPHA',T23,'BETA',
     *  T30,'GAMMA',T38,'AV. A',T46,'AV. B',T54,'AV. G')
  202 FORMAT(I4,F6.2,3I8,3F8.2)
  203 FORMAT('MAXIMUM AVERAGE GAMMA RADIATION OF',F7.2,
     *  ' WAS IN INTERVAL NUMBER',I5)
      END
```

Notice the use of continuation lines in both WRITE and FORMAT statements in this program – a character in column 6 being used to indicate a continuation line as mentioned in Chapter 2. FORMAT statements frequently require more than 66 characters (i.e. columns 7–72) and we shall need to use this facility quite regularly.

An example of part of the results produced by this program can be seen in Fig. 6.9.

INT	TIME	ALPHA	BETA	GAMMA	AV. A	AV. B	AV. G
.	.	.	.	.	.	.	.
.	.	.	.	.	.	.	.
.	.	.	.	.	.	.	.
990	2.56	175	23	401	68.36	8.98	156.64
991	2.59	168	22	395	64.86	8.49	152.51
992	2.48	181	27	412	72.98	10.89	166.13
993	2.51	177	25	410	70.52	9.96	163.35
994	2.48	166	29	391	66.94	11.69	157.66
995	2.54	181	25	397	71.26	9.84	156.30
996	2.51	169	28	407	67.33	11.16	162.15
997	2.58	159	23	388	61.63	8.91	150.39
998	2.51	177	26	401	70.52	10.36	159.76
999	2.47	173	24	398	70.04	9.72	161.13
1000	2.52	183	28	403	72.62	11.11	159.92

MAXIMUM AVERAGE GAMMA RADIATION OF 174.28 IN INTERVAL NUMBER   741

Fig. 6.9   Results produced by DECAY program

6.6   Printer control characters

We have seen how a FORMAT statement can be used to define the layout of data or results. However, when the results are being output on a 'lineprinter' – the main, high-speed, form of producing printed output on most large and medium-sized computers – there is one further level of control possible. This is a (limited) control of the vertical spacing of the printed output.

When a line of output is sent to the *printer* it is not all printed. Instead, the first character of the line is removed and treated as a *printer control character* which determines how much the paper is to be moved up before the remainder of the line is printed. There are four characters which have a particular significance in this regard, as shown in Fig. 6.10. If the first character is not one of these four then the effect on the printer is undefined; in practice, however, any other character will usually have the same effect as does a space, i.e. printing will take place on the *next* line.

Character	Vertical spacing before printing
space	one line
0 (zero)	two lines
1 (one)	first line of next page
+	no paper advance

Fig. 6.10   Printer control characters

Because the first character is removed and not printed it is important that we insert an extra 'control' character at the start of each record that is to be output to the printer; Fig. 6.11 shows what can happen if we do not. Because the edit descriptor in format 200 (F5.2) only allowed room for two digits

```
      PROGRAM DEMO
      X = 3.0
      Y = 4.0
      WRITE (2,200) X
      WRITE (2,200) Y
      WRITE (2,200) X*Y
      WRITE (2,201) X/Y
  200 FORMAT(F5.2)
  201 FORMAT(F5.3)
      STOP
      END
```

3.00
4.00
— _ —
2.00

.750

Fig. 6.11   An example of printer control errors

before the decimal point, and format 201 only allowed room for one, the records produced were as follows

3.00
4.00
12.00
0.750

The printer, however, needs the first character. In the first two lines this merely means that the leading space is removed, causing the correct number to be printed on the next line. The third line, however, starts with a one. This is removed and the remainder of the record (2.00) is printed at the top of the *next page*, as defined by the (apparent) control character (1). A similar thing happens with the next line, where the leading zero causes double spacing (i.e. a blank line before printing).

There are several ways in which a control character can be inserted at the start of a line, especially if it is a space (as is usually the case). The author always uses the H edit descriptor for this purpose, *and for no other*, so that it stands out as not being part of the format proper. The two formats in Fig. 6.11 could therefore be rewritten as

```
  200 FORMAT (1H ,F5.2)
  201 FORMAT (1H ,F5.3)
```

Note that this only applies to the printer; other output devices, including those which produce printed output such as a terminal, do not need a control character and will print the complete record. Note also that the PRINT statement automatically inserts a (space) control character at the start of each line if the standard output unit is the printer.

6.7 More sophisticated FORMAT statements

The foregoing has provided the means whereby a program may define formats for both input and output of considerable complexity. However a number of other facilities are available to enable still more aspects of input and output to be defined. Probably the most important of these concern multi-record formats and repetition of formats.

Let us consider a hypothetical program that wishes to read 12 real numbers, typed 4 to a line. With our present knowledge we could write

```
      READ 100,A,B,C,D
      READ 100,E,F,G,H
      READ 100,P,Q,R,S
100 FORMAT (4F12.3)
```

However consider what would happen if we wrote

```
      READ 100,A,B,C,D,E,F,G,H,P,Q,R,S
100 FORMAT (4F12.3)
```

After the READ statement has used the FORMAT to input four real numbers (which are placed in A,B,C and D) it finds that the input list is not yet exhausted, and that another real number is required. The format is, however, completed and it therefore follows that this input record contains no more (useful) information.

There is only one sensible thing to do, namely, to read a new record and interpret its contents using the same FORMAT. This is exactly what happens.

Whenever a FORMAT is fully used up and there are still items in the input (or output) list awaiting processing the FORMAT will be repeated. The rule governing the point from which it will be repeated is rather complicated

- If there are no nested parentheses then the format is repeated from the beginning.

- If the format contains any nested parentheses then it is repeated from the left parenthesis corresponding to the last right parenthesis.

- If the left parenthesis defined above is preceded by a repeat count then the format is repeated from immediately before the repeat count.

The following examples should make this clear; an arrow is shown below the point from which repetition (if any) will take place

```
1  FORMAT (I6,10X,I5,3F10.2)
```

```
2  FORMAT (I6,10X,I5,(3F10.2))
```

```
3  FORMAT (I6,(10X,I5),3F10.2)
```

```
4  FORMAT (F6.2,(2F4.1,2X,I4,4(I7,F7.2)))
```

```
5  FORMAT (F6.2,2(2F4.1,2X,I4),4(I7,F7.2))
```

```
6  FORMAT (F6.2,(2(2F4.1,2X,I4),4(I7,F7.2)))
```

The repetition of a format can be extremely useful; however in many cases it is desirable to be able to define a format which consists of two or more separate lines, or (more accurately) *records*. This is achieved by the / edit descriptor (which need not be separated from any preceding or succeeding descriptor by a comma). This indicates the end of the current record.

On input a / causes the rest of the current record to be ignored and causes the next input item to be the first item of the next record. On output a / terminates the current record and starts a new one. Thus the statements

```
      READ (1,101) A,B,C,I,J,K
  101 FORMAT (2F10.2,F12.3/I6,2I10)
```

will read three real numbers from the first record and three integers from a second. The statements

```
      WRITE (2,201) A,B,A+B,A*B
  201 FORMAT (1H1,T10,'MULTI-RECORD EXAMPLE'/
     *  1H0,'THE SUM OF',F5.2,' AND',F5.2,' IS',F6.2/
     *  1H ,'THEIR PRODUCT IS',F8.2)
```

will cause a title to be placed at the top of a new page, the sum of A and B to be printed after leaving a blank line, and their product to be printed on the next line.

Several / descriptors in succession cause several input records to be skipped or several null (blank) records to be output. Thus

```
      READ (1,102) A,B,C,I,J,K
  102 FORMAT (2F10.2,F12.3//I6,2I10)
```

will cause the real numbers to be read from the first record and the integers from the third. Multiple / descriptors are particularly useful on output as we see below

```
      WRITE (2,202) A,B,A+B,A*B
  202 FORMAT (1H1////1H ,T10,'MULTI-RECORD EXAMPLE'///
     *  1H ,'THE SUM OF',F5.2,' AND',F5.2,' IS',F6.2//
     *  1H ,'THEIR PRODUCT IS',F8.2////)
```

This will print four blank lines at the top of a new page before the title, two blank lines before the first line of results, a further blank line before the second, and three blank lines after the last line (thus separating it from any results printed later in the program).

The combination of a / edit descriptor and a repeated format can provide a very powerful degree of flexibility; thus the following format

```
  110 FORMAT (I6/(I4,3F12.2))
```

specifies that the first record consists of a single integer and the following ones of an integer followed by three real numbers.

Fig. 6.12 shows most of the remaining edit descriptors, none of which are used very often. A brief description of each is, however, appropriate.

Descriptor	Meaning
/	Terminate current record
:	Terminate format if no more list items
SP	Print + signs before positive numbers
SS	Do not print + signs before positive numbers
S	Processor decision whether to print + signs before positive numbers
kP	Apply scale factor of k to numeric input or output
BN	Ignore blanks in numeric input fields
BZ	Treat blanks in numeric input fields as zeros
I$w.m$.	Output integer with at least m digits
E$w.d$ E$w.d$Ee D$w.d$ G$w.d$ G$w.d$Ee	Input or output real or double-precision values (see text for details)

Fig. 6.12 Further edit descriptors

The : edit descriptor is used to terminate a format if there are no more list items. This is not usually necessary as the format will terminate in any case at the next edit descriptor which requires a list item. In an output format, however, this could cause some unnecessary printing to occur. Fig. 6.13 shows the effect of the : edit descriptor on output.

```
       PROGRAM COLON
       A = 3.5
       B = 7.2
       WRITE (2,201) A,B,A+B
       WRITE (2,202) A,B,A+B
       STOP
   201 FORMAT(1H1,'THE SUM OF',F5.2,' AND',F5.2,' IS',F6.2/
      *  1H ,'THEIR PRODUCT IS',F8.2)
   202 FORMAT(1H0,'THE SUM OF',F5.2,' AND',F5.2,' IS',F6.2:/
      *  1H ,'THEIR PRODUCT IS',F8.2)
       END
```

```
THE SUM OF 3.50 AND 7.20 IS 10.70
THEIR PRODUCT IS

THE SUM OF 3.50 AND 7.20 IS 10.70
```

Fig. 6.13 An example of : editing

The SP edit descriptor effects any numbers output by any following edit descriptors in this format, and causes a + sign to be placed before positive numbers (just as a − sign is placed before negative ones). SS has the opposite effect and prevents a + sign being placed before positive numbers. S restores the normal (default) situation which, for most systems, will usually be to omit + signs.

BN and BZ are discussed in Section 6.8, while the P edit descriptor is dealt with at the end of this section after the introduction of the D, E and G edit descriptors.

Iw.m is an extended form of the I edit descriptor which only affects the output of integers; if used for input it is treated as though it were Iw. On output it specifies the minimum number of digits which are to be printed, including if necessary one or more leading zeros. The value of m must not be greater than w, while if it is zero and the value of the integer is also zero only blanks are output. Fig. 6.14 gives an example of its use.

```
      PROGRAM IWM
      DO 10, I=-10,10,5
  10    WRITE (2,220) I,I,I
 220 FORMAT(I5,I5.2,I5.0)
      STOP
      END

  -10  -10  -10
   -5  -05   -5
    0   00
    5   05    5
   10   10   10
```

Fig. 6.14 An example of Iw.m editing

As well as the F edit descriptor there are a number of other ways of inputting and outputting real numbers which provide slight variations on the standard 'F' method. Before discussing these, however, we must extend our understanding of the format of real numbers.

We have seen already (see Section 5.2) that a real constant may be written followed by an exponent (e.g. 1.5E−6) and a similar extension is allowed in the format of numbers being input. In this case the exponent may take one of three forms

● a signed integer constant

● E followed by an optionally signed constant

● D followed by an optionally signed constant

In the latter two cases the letter (D or E) may be followed by one or more spaces.

Thus the number 231.436 may be presented in any of the following ways

```
231.436
2.31436+2
231436-3
23.1436E1
2314.36D-1
2.31436E +2
etc.
```

For *input* all the following edit descriptors have the identical effect

```
Fw.d
Ew.d
Dw.d
Gw.d
Ew.dEe
Gw.dEe
```

where e may have any value (and is ignored).

For output however there are significant differences. As we have already seen, Fw.d will output a real number rounded to d decimal places with an external field of width w.

The E edit descriptor, however, produces a representation of a real number consisting of a decimal fraction of *d* digits in the range 0.1 to 0.9999 . . ., followed by a four character exponent; the whole number occupies a field width of w characters. It is therefore much more flexible, and will cater more easily than the F edit descriptor with very large or very small numbers. Thus the number 0.0000231436 will be output as shown below with various edit descriptors

```
E10.4   0.2314E-04
E12.3     0.231E-04
E12.5   0.23144E-04
```

In some implementations the exponent may consist of a + or − sign followed by three digits

```
E11.3    0.231-004
```

If the Ew.d is followed by Ee then the exponent consists of e digits

```
E12.5E3  0.23144E-004
E12.6E1  0.231436E-4
```

The D edit descriptor (Dw.d) is the same as the Ew.d descriptor except that the letter E on output may be replaced by a letter D. It exists mainly for compatibility with earlier versions of Fortran.

Finally the G edit descriptor attempts to provide the best of both worlds. On input it is the same as Fw.d, but on output it uses either the Fw.d, Ew.d or

Ew.dEe formats depending upon the magnitude of the number being output. The layout produced by the F edit descriptor is much clearer for us to read than that produced by the E edit descriptor. The latter will cover a far wider range of numbers. The G format is used when the programmer is not sure how large or small his results may be, or when they may vary very widely.

If the magnitude (i.e. absolute value) of the number to be output lies between 0.1 and 10^d (i.e. the exponent in E format would lie between 0 and d inclusive) then F format is used; otherwise E formatting takes place. If F formatting is used the field width is reduced by four for Gw.d and by e+2 for Gw.dEe and the number is followed by four spaces or e+2 spaces, respectively. In all cases the number is printed, therefore, with d significant digits. Fig. 6.15 shows a comparison of F, E and G editing, and the advantage of the G format when a wide range of numbers is possible is readily apparent. Notice in particular the −132651.0 has proved to be too large for the F format (and has been printed as a row of asterisks), while 0.00010471 has lost all semblence of accuracy in the F format.

Internal value	External representation		
	(F12.5)	(E12.5)	(G12.5)
132651.0	132651.00000	0.13265E+06	0.13265E+06
−132651.0	************	−0.13265E+06	−0.13265E+06
13265.1	13265.10000	0.13265E+05	13265.
−12.43	−12.43000	−0.12430E+02	−12.43
0.10471	0.10471	0.10471E+00	0.10471
0.010471	0.01047	0.10471E−01	0.10471E−01
0.00010471	0.00010	0.10471E−03	0.10471E−03

Fig. 6.15   A comparison of F, E and G editing

The effect of the F, D, E and G edit descriptors can be altered by use of a *scale factor*. This is applied by means of a P edit descriptor (kP), which causes a scale factor of k to be applied to all F, D, E or G edit descriptors following it in a format.

On input, as long as the input data does not contain an exponent, it has an effect as though the data were followed by an exponent of −k. Thus if an input record contains the three numbers 17.5, 2410 and 9.3E6, the following statements

```
     READ (*,111) X,Y,Z
 111 FORMAT (3P,3F10.2)
```

will cause the variables X, Y and Z to take the values 0.0175, 0.0241 and 9300000.0. Let us examine this in detail.

The first number read is 17.5 and the scale factor therefore causes this to be multiplied by 10^{-3}, with the result that 0.0175 is stored in X. The next number is 2410 which (assuming that it is at the right of the input field) will therefore have a decimal point implied before the last two digits; the resulting value of 24.1 becomes 0.0241 after the scale factor of 10^{-3} has been applied. The third number is 9.3E6 and since an exponent is specified the scale factor does not apply and this is the value stored.

On *output* with F editing a similar process operates, but in reverse; thus the number output is the internal value multiplied by 10^k.

When a scale factor is used for output with D or E editing, however, it does not affect the value output, but only its representation. In this case the exponent is reduced by k and the mantissa (the preceding real part) is multiplied by 10^k.

When a scale factor is used with a G edit descriptor for output it has no effect when F formatting is being used. It has the same effect as for E editing when E formatting is in operation.

Fig. 6.16 shows the effect of this, and it can be seen very clearly that the '3P' scale factor causes the values in the first column (printed using an F12.4 edit descriptor) to be multiplied by 1000 (10^3). The values output in the remaining columns (printed using E12.4 and G12.4 descriptors) are not changed – only their format is.

```
      PROGRAM FIG616
      X = 147.903
      Y = 0.0147903
      WRITE (2,201) X,X,X,Y,Y,Y
  201 FORMAT(1H ,3P,F12.4,E12.4,G12.4)
      STOP
      END

147903.0000  147.90E+00   147.9
    14.7903  147.90E-04  147.90E-04
```

Fig. 6.16 An example of a scale factor on output

6.8   The inputting of blanks in numbers

We have already seen that data may be read from a number of different sources, one of which will be defined as the 'standard input unit'. We shall see in Chapter 12 how we can establish a link between our program and any input or output device by a process known as *connecting*. The standard input and output devices, however, are *preconnected* and are automatically available to all programs. This has an important implication when we are reading numbers.

When a *file* of information is first connected to a program it is possible to specify that any blanks (or spaces) within a number are to be treated either as blanks (and ignored) or as zeros. If no action is taken they are assumed (by default) to be blanks. However in the case of preconnected files (or devices) the situation is slightly different.

In all earlier versions of Fortran, blank characters in data which were being input from cards (or some other 'standard input device') were treated as zeros. Thus if the card in Fig. 6.17 was read by the statements shown the variables X and L would have the values 320.0 and 90 respectively. This is because the field for X is treated as 00032000 and that for L as 000090.

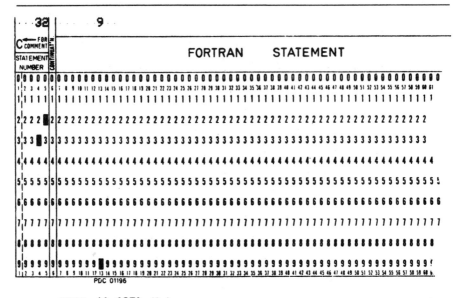

```
      READ (1,123) X,L
  123 FORMAT (F8.2,I6)
```

Fig. 6.17   Reading a card with blanks in numbers

Unfortunately the committee, who drew up the standard definition of Fortran 77, found themselves unable to decide whether Fortran 77 should follow earlier custom and practice with preconnected files or, whether it should follow the same pattern as with files which are connected by the program. In the latter case blanks are ignored and so the effect of the statements in Fig. 6.17 would be to set X to 0.32 and L to 9, since with all blanks ignored the input fields have the digits moved to the right and so become ▽▽▽▽▽▽32 and ▽▽▽▽▽9 respectively.

The Standard passes this decision back to the compiler writer. At a stroke the whole concept of standardisation in an extremely important area is destroyed and there is a distinct possibility that a program will not transfer correctly to another computer system! Fortunately there is a remedy which enables the programmer to over-ride the default (either treat blanks as zeros, or ignore them) used by a particular compiler.

The BZ edit descriptor specifies that blanks are to be treated as zeros for all numeric input edited by I, F, E, D or G edit descriptors in the remainder of the format. By placing BZ at the start of a format we can ensure that all blanks in numbers are treated as zeros, regardless of the default used by any particular system.

The BN edit descriptor, on the other hand, causes all blanks in numeric input fields to be treated as *null* characters – in other words they are ignored. BN at the start of an input format ensures that all blanks in numbers are ignored, regardless of the default used by any particular system. However if *all* the characters in a numeric input field are blank the number is treated as zero.

It is the author's view that the BZ option can be very useful when reading large amounts of real data as it avoids the necessity of typing all trailing zeros when decimal points are omitted. This is a personal view, however, and a more important point is that all programs written for earlier versions of Fortran will assume the BZ option.

There is the possibility that a program which works correctly on one computer may fail on another because a different default is used. It is highly desirable, therefore, that *all* formats used for input from the standard input unit (or any other preconnected file) should start with BZ or BN in order to ensure that the program has a known and fixed mode of operation. We shall do this in all future programs and examples.

The input statements in Fig. 6.17 should now become

```
    READ (1,123) X,L
123 FORMAT (BZ,F8.2,I6)
```

The BZ and BN edit descriptors have no effect on any input editing other than that carried out by I, F, E, D or G edit descriptors; they have no effect at all during output.

6.9 Embedded formats

We have considered a format as a 'footnote', appearing in a labelled FORMAT statement, which is referenced as and when required by an input or output statement. This is normally the most convenient method, since the format defines the layout (or format) of the data or results on some external medium. It may then be referred to, if necessary, by READ or WRITE statements in several places in a program.

Sometimes, however, a format is only referred to once and it may seem more appropriate to include the format with the input/output statement. This is called an *embedded format*, and may either be constant or vary. Chapter 7 is concerned with the handling of variable character data, and Section 7.5 describes how a variable format may be created and embedded in an input or output statement. We shall restrict ourselves at this stage to constant formats.

In any READ, WRITE or PRINT statement we may include an embedded format by replacing the label of a FORMAT statement with a character constant which consists of a format specification (as used in a FORMAT statement after the word FORMAT). The format specification therefore begins with a left parenthesis and ends with a right parenthesis, and we may write

```
    READ (1,'(BZ,F8.2,I6)') X,L
```

as an alternative to

```
    READ (1,123) X,L
123 FORMAT (BZ,F8.2,I6)
```

122   FORTRAN 77 PROGRAMMING

Naturally all the variations which were discussed in Section 6.3 are also allowed

```
READ (FMT='(BZ,F8.2,I6)',UNIT=*) X,L
READ '(BZ,F8.2,I6)',X,L
etc.
```

One important point to note here concerns a format which contains an apostrophe edit descriptor, e.g.

```
201 FORMAT (1H1,'RESULTS OF PRIMARY ANALYSIS'////)
```

Since the apostrophe edit descriptor takes the form of a character constant it cannot be included directly within another character constant because the multiple apostrophes would create errors. Remember that an apostrophe is included within a character constant by representing it by two consecutive apostrophes. If the above format were to be embedded in a WRITE statement it would, therefore, take the following form

```
WRITE (2,'(1H1, ''RESULTS OF PRIMARY ANALYSIS''////)')
```

An even worse case is where the title itself includes an apostrophe, as shown in Fig. 6.18. It can be seen that the apostrophe in the title is represented by no less than four consecutive apostrophes!

Title required	DUMKOPF'S RESULTS
(a) *With* FORMAT *statement*	WRITE (2,200) 200 FORMAT (1H1,'DUMKOPF''S RESULTS')
(b) *With embedded format*	WRITE (2,'(1H1,''DUMKOPF''''S RESULTS'')'

Fig. 6.18 Embedded formats containing apostrophes

Example 6.4

A survey has been carried out to obtain statistics concerning the occupation of people in a certain area. The results of the survey are available for input to the computer in the following format

columns 1–20 Name
column 23   Sex = 0 if male
              = 1 if female
column 25   Job status = 1 if in full-time education
                         = 2 if in full-time employment
                         = 3 if in part-time employment
                         = 4 if temporarily unemployed
                         = 5 if not working or seeking a job

This is followed by one or more items depending upon the job status of the respondent

job status = 1   columns 28,29   Age
     = 2   columns 28–31   Monthly salary (£)
     = 3   columns 28–31   Monthly salary (£)
        columns 34–37   Other monthly income (£)
     = 4   columns 28,29   Age
        columns 32–34   No. of months unemployed
     = 5   columns 28,29   Age
        column 31   Code = 1 if looking after children
                = 2 if looking after other relatives
                = 3 for any other reason

The data is terminated by a record that is blank apart from column 23, which contains a 9.

Write a program to read the data and print the percentage of each sex in full-time education who are 18 or over, the average length of unemployment for those under 18 and those over 45, and the percentage of men who are not in full-time education who stay at home to look after the children.

The major problem here is the variable format of the data. We shall see, in Chapter 12, how an *internal file* can be used to simplify this, but we can tackle it with what we know by reading parts of the record more than once. On examining the details we see that there are two possibilities

(a) columns 28,29 contain age
   column 31   blank or code
   columns 32–34 blank or no. of months unemployed
(b) columns 28–31 monthly salary
   columns 34–37 other monthly income or blank

Since all these items are integer qualities it will be easy to define a format to convert the data into all these values and then use the job status code to determine which are meaningful. We cannot wait until we have read the job status code and then read the rest of the record, because that would start a new record! A suitable format specification is

   (BZ,T23,I1,1X,I1,2X,I2,1X,I1,I3,T28,I4,2X,I4)

We can now write a structure plan

  1 Initialise totals, etc.
  2 Repeat the following
   2.1 Read next record
   2.2 If sex = 9 then exit
   2.3 If job = education then
    2.3.1 Increment total (male or female)
    2.3.2 If age ≥ 18 then increment 'old total' (male or female) otherwise
    2.3.3 If sex = male then
     2.3.3.1 Increment no. of males not in full-time education
     2.3.3.2 If job = looking after children increment no. of full-time fathers

> *2.3.4* If job = unemployed then
> > *2.3.4.1* If age < 18 update number and sum of periods
> > *2.3.4.2* If age > 45 update number and sum of periods
> *3* Calculate and print averages and percentages

Notice the logic in step *2.3*. First we see if the person is in full-time employment and, if so, then appropriate totals are incremented. If the person is not in full-time education there are two possibilities in which we are interested; however these are not exclusive and so they will not form part of a single IF block but will be nested IF blocks.

We can write the program from this structure plan quite easily

```
      PROGRAM JOBS
      NEDM = 0
      NEDF = 0
      NEDM18 = 0
      NEDF18 = 0
      MNOTED = 0
      NDADS = 0
      NOJOBY = 0
      NOJOBO = 0
      LENY = 0
      LENO = 0
      DO 10, I=1,1000
C PROGRAM ONLY ALLOWS 1000 RESPONDENTS
      READ 100,ISEX,JOBTYP,NAGE,IHOME,LEN,MONSAL,MONINC
      IF (ISEX.EQ.9) GOTO 11
      IF (JOBTYP.EQ.1) THEN
C RESPONDENT IS IN FULL-TIME EDUCATION
         IF (ISEX.EQ.0) THEN
            NEDM = NEDM+1
            IF (NAGE.GE.18) NEDM18 = NEDM18+1
         ELSE
            NEDF = NEDF+1
            IF (NAGE.GE.18) NEDF18 = NEDF18+1
         END IF
      ELSE
         IF (ISEX.EQ.0) THEN
C RESPONDENT IS MALE
            MNOTED = MNOTED+1
            IF (JOBTYP.EQ.5.AND.IHOME.EQ.1) NDADS = NDADS+1
         END IF
         IF (JOBTYP.EQ.4) THEN
```

```
C   RESPONDENT IS UNEMPLOYED
                IF (NAGE.LT.18) THEN
                    NOJOBY = NOJOBY+1
                    LENY = LENY+LEN
                ELSE IF (NAGE.GT.45) THEN
                    NOJOBO = NOJOBO+1
                    LENO = LENO+LEN
                END IF
              END IF
            END IF
    10    CONTINUE
C   1000 RECORDS READ AND NO TERMINATOR
          PRINT *,'WARNING — NO TERMINATOR FOUND IN 1000 RECORDS'
C   PRINT MAIN TITLE AND NUMBER OF RECORDS READ
    11 WRITE (2,'(1H1,20X,''RESULTS OF JOB SURVEY''///
       *  1H ,20X,I4,'' RECORDS READ''//)') I-1
C   CALCULATE PERCENTAGE OF OVER-17S IN FULL-TIME EDUCATION
          ED18M = 100.0*NEDM18/NEDM
          ED18F = 100.0*NEDF18/NEDF
          WRITE (2,201) ED18M,ED18F
   201 FORMAT(1H0,20X,F4.1,' PER CENT OF BOYS, AND'/
       *         1H ,20X,F4.1,' PER CENT OF GIRLS'/
       *         1H ,20X,'IN FULL-TIME EDUCATION ARE 18 OR OVER')
C   CALCULATE AVERAGE LENGTHS OF UNEMPLOYMENT
          AVY = REAL(LENY)/NOJOBY
          AVO = REAL(LENO)/NOJOBO
          WRITE (2,202) AVY,AVO
   202 FORMAT(1H0,20X,'AVERAGE LENGTH OF UNEMPLOYMENT IS:'/
       *         1H ,20X,F5.1,' MONTHS FOR THOSE UNDER 18'/
       *         1H ,20X,F5.1,' MONTHS FOR THOSE OVER 45')
C   CALCULATE PERCENTAGE OF FULL-TIME FATHERS
          IF (NDADS.EQ.0) THEN
             WRITE (2,'(1H0,20X,''THERE ARE NO MEN WHO STAY'',
       *      '' AT HOME TO LOOK AFTER THE CHILDREN'')')
          ELSE
             FTDADS = 100.0*NDADS/MNOTED
             WRITE (2,203) FTDADS
   203 FORMAT(1H0,20X,F4.1,' PER CENT OF MEN NOT IN FULL-TIME'
       *  ' EDUCATION STAY AT HOME WITH THEIR CHILDREN')
          END IF
          STOP
   100 FORMAT(BZ,T23,I1,1X,I1,2X,I2,1X,I1,I3,T28,I4,2X,I4)
          END
```

Notice that the part of the main loop which deals with over-18's in education has a slightly different structure from that in the plan (*2.3.1* and *2.3.2*). The use of a logical IF clarifies the structure in this case. Also notice that it is not enough to test (for the males) whether IHOME is 1. If JOBTYP was not 5 the value of IHOME might be anything, so JOBTYP must be checked as well.

Finally it should be pointed out that apart from the case of 'full-time fathers' the program has not checked to see if there were no respondents in a particular category. This is purely to shorten an already lengthy example. In real life the program should include checks of the form

```
IF (NEDM.GT.O) THEN ...
```

Fig. 6.19 shows the results obtained by running the program on a sample set of data.

```
RESULTS OF JOB SURVEY


  23 RECORDS READ



57.1 PER CENT OF BOYS, AND
33.3 PER CENT OF GIRLS
IN FULL-TIME EDUCATION ARE 18 OR OVER

AVERAGE LENGTH OF UNEMPLOYMENT IS:
  2.3 MONTHS FOR THOSE UNDER 18
  12.5 MONTHS FOR THOSE OVER 45

THERE ARE NO MEN WHO STAY AT HOME TO LOOK AFTER THE CHILDREN
```

Fig. 6.19 Results produced by **JOBS** program

Summary

- A unit number is used to identify a particular input or output unit.

- Every Fortran 77 implementation has preconnected standard input and output units.

- List directed **READ** and **PRINT** statements use the standard input and output units.

- Extended **READ** and **WRITE** statements use a control information list to define units, formats and exception action.

- **FORMAT** statements define the layout of data or results.

- A format may be embedded in an input or output statement.

- A printer control character is required to control vertical paper movement for output to the printer.

Input and output	READ *,input list
	READ label,input list
	READ format,input list
	READ (control information list) input list
	PRINT *,output list
	PRINT label,output list
	PRINT format,output list
	WRITE (control information list) output list

FORMAT statement   label FORMAT(list of edit descriptors)

Embedded format   ' (list of edit descriptors) '

Fig. 6.20   Fortran 77 statements introduced in Chapter 6

Exercises

6.1 If a card is punched with the nine digits 1 to 9 in the first 9 columns, what is printed by the following?

```
    READ (*,101) I,J,X,Y
    PRINT 200,Y—I,J—X,I/J*Y—X,I—J
101 FORMAT (BZ,I4,3X,I3,TL4,F3.1,TL10,F6.2)
200 FORMAT (1H1,2F8.1,10X,F8.2,I6)
```

6.2 Write formats and associated input or output statements to read or print the dimensions of a box as follows
   (a) Read dimensions in metres and centimetres provided in the form

   m.cc * m.cc * m.cc

   where all sides are thus less than 10 metres.
   (b) Read the dimensions in feet and inches provided in the form

   ffFT iiINS BY ffFT iiINS BY ffFT iiINS

   where all sides are less than 30 feet.
   (c) Print the dimensions and volume of the box in the form

   $a * b * c$ (v cubic feet)

   where a, b, c are the three dimensions (in feet).
6.3 Find out which are the standard input and output units for the computer you are using. Also find out if any other units are preconnected. Establish what is the default interpretation of blank characters in numeric fields input from the standard input unit or any other preconnected input unit.

6.4 A bank wishes to write a simple program to produce monthly statements. The input for the program is to be as follows

(i)   An initial record containing the date in columns 1–8 in the form dd.mm.yy, followed by an eight-digit account number in columns 13–20 and the previous balance in columns 22–30 in the form ±lllll.pp

(ii) A series of transaction records consisting of

columns 1–8   account number (as above)
         11–18   date of transaction (as above)
         21–28   cheque number (for a debit) or blank (for a credit)
         31–38   the amount of the debit or credit in the form lllll.pp (Note that this amount has no sign.)

The series is terminated by a blank record.

The program is required to print the statement in four columns (headed by the date and account number). The first column should contain the date of the transaction, the second column the cheque number (or blank), the third column the value of the transaction proceded by a + for a credit and a − for a debit, and the fourth column the cumulative balance (again preceded by + or − as appropriate).

6.5 Write a program which produces a 'multiplication square' of the form shown below

	1	2	3	4 . . .	10	11	12
1	1	2	3	4	10	11	12
2	2	4	6	8	20	22	24
3	3	6	9	12	30	33	36
.							
.							
.							
10	10	20	30	40	100	110	120
11	11	22	33	44	110	121	132
12	12	24	36	48	120	132	144

6.6 The data collected in a survey on drinking habits has been coded in the following way

column   1   Sex (0 = male, 1 = female)
columns   3–5   Age
columns   9,10 Social class (A,B,C1,C2,D or E)
column   14   Usual main drink
                (1 = beer, 2 = wine, 3 = whisky, 4 = gin, 5 = other spirits, 6 = sherry, 7 = soft drinks, 8 = cider, 9 = other)
column   17   = 1 if most drinking carried out at home
                = 2 if most drinking carried out in a public house
                = 3 if most drinking carried out elsewhere
For those who mainly drink in a pub
column   19   No. of evenings/week at the pub
columns 23,24 Average no. of drinks per visit

For those who mainly drink at home
column 19   = 0 if only drink when with guests
                   = 1 otherwise
columns 23,24   Average no. of drinks when with guests
columns 27,28   Average no. of drinks otherwise
For those who mainly drink elsewhere
column 19   Usual drinking place
                   (1 = while staying at a hotel, 2 = while travelling, 3 =
                   at a friend's house, 4 = elsewhere)
columns 23,24   Average no. of drinks per week
The data is terminated by a blank record

Write a program which uses this data to calculate
(a) The proportion of respondents (by sex) who visit a pub more than
     three times a week on average.
(b) The most popular drink (by sex) in a pub, at home and while
     travelling.
(c) The average beer consumption per night of all men who drink their
     beer mainly in a pub.
(d) The average sherry consumption (by sex) in a pub, at home (both
     with and without guests), and in a hotel at which the drinker is
     resident.

6.7 Rewrite the programs written for questions 5.2, 5.3 and 5.4 using
formats for both input and output.

Intermission – Developing and Testing Programs

Developing and Testing Programs

The first part of this book has covered the fundamental principles of programming and of most of the major concepts of Fortran 77. The second part will develop from this basic framework until the full power of the language is available to solve even the most complex problems. It is appropriate at this stage, however, to pause and consider the way in which we actually develop and test our programs.

Anyone who has ever been involved with helping others to get their programs to work correctly has come across the 'last bug' syndrome. A 'bug' is the programmer's expression for an error in a program, and it appears that almost every program 'is working perfectly except for one *last* bug'. The trouble is that when you have found and corrected it there always seems to be *another* 'last bug'! Many of the errors that cause this problem could have been eliminated by better program design, and still more could be eliminated by a planned approach to *testing*.

This book is about programming in Fortran 77, and as such it naturally concentrates on the design of well-structured programs and the coding techniques that are used to implement that design. However we should never lose sight of the fact that the object of writing a program is to instruct a computer to carry out some action or to solve some problem; the program is not an end in itself. Our job is not finished, therefore, until the program works correctly and deals in an appropriate manner with any reasonable (or even unreasonable) exception situations. Indeed, it is usually the exceptions which cause the most trouble. For example, it is relatively easy to write a compiler which will process an absolutely correct Fortran 77 program and produce a correct machine-code program. It is, however, far more difficult to make that compiler deal in a sensible way with any myriad syntactic or other errors made when writing a Fortran 77 program, however unlikely or far-fetched they may be. The logical complexity of most programs means that it is unlikely that any method will ever be devised to *prove* them to be totally correct. We must therefore rely on good design to minimise the likelihood of errors, together with well-structured and comprehensive testing to search out any that have managed to slip into our programs.

Program testing is both a negative and a destructive process. Its purpose is to use data which is similar to the real data on which the program is designed to execute in order to discover any errors or omissions in the program. This means that, although program testing can establish the presence of errors in a program, it cannot prove their absence. It is thus an essentially negative process.

130

The destructive aspect of program testing arises because it attempts to cause the program to fail or to produce incorrect results. It is psychologically difficult to attempt to destroy what one has just created, and it is therefore highly desirable that the testing should either partially or largely be carried out by someone other than the programmer.

The *testing* of a program should never be confused with the *debugging* of that program. The former process is the systematic execution of the program with specially prepared data with the intention of establishing the presence of any errors that may exist. The debugging of the program, on the other hand, is the process of establishing the cause of these errors, and then correcting the program so as to eliminate them. Although these two processes are closely related it is important to realise that they are quite distinct and must be approached from rather different viewpoints.

It is appropriate here to outline some of the most important aspects of testing in the context of an actual example. The best methods of debugging will depend upon the computer system being used, as most systems will contain facilities for producing 'dumps' of variables and other stored values, for stopping at pre-defined 'breakpoints' to investigate the current state of any required aspect of the program and its data, for 'single stepping' through the program statement by statement, etc. In addition, the inclusion of extra PRINT statements at key places can often provide the information needed for debugging.

In order to illustrate the main principles of planned program testing we shall consider Example 6.4 in Chapter 6 which was concerned with the analysis of a set of survey data detailing the job(s) or other activities of the respondents.

Probably the single most important rule about program testing is to progress in stages in an incremental fashion. A program of any significant size will, almost inevitably, contain a number of errors when it is first written. (This may appear to be an admission of failure, but it is a fact of life and must not be ignored.) If the complete program is written before any testing takes place then it can be extremely difficult, if not impossible, to debug the program because the testing will show the presence of errors but it will not usually be apparent in which part of the program the trouble lies. We therefore *always* adopt a stage-by-stage, or *incremental* approach to program development and testing.

We shall see in Chapter 10 how we can develop a program as a series of subprograms, which are individually tested before being linked together to form the complete program. This process is known as *bottom-up* development and testing, and contrasts with the *top-down* design process that we have been using. Occasionally it may be appropriate to carry out a form of top-down testing, but this is usually more cumbersome and only relevant in the case of very large and complex systems.

We can develop and test our programs in a bottom-up fashion even without the use of subprograms, by ensuring that at each stage we only add one further element of the program. In this way the new code at each stage is clearly identified, and the identification of the cause of any errors becomes a much easier task.

Returning to Example 6.4 we find that a simplified structure plan is as follows

1   Initialise totals, etc.
2   Repeat the following
    2.1   Read next record
    2.2   If sex = 9 then exit
    2.3   If job = education then
        2.3.1   Update appropriate totals
        otherwise
        2.3.2   If sex = male then
            2.3.2.1   Update appropriate totals
        2.3.3   If job = unemployed then
            2.3.3.1   Update appropriate totals
3   Calculate and print results

The first part of the program to be written is, logically, that part which deals with the input of the data and the recognition of the end of the data. In order to check this part it would seem sensible to print the data as it is read. A structure plan for this stage is

1   Repeat the following
    1.1   Read next record
    1.2   Print record
    1.3   If sex = 9 then exit
2   Print heading and number of records read

It is often desirable to reduce various program limits during testing. For example, in the sample solution to Example 6.4 a maximum of 1000 sets of data was assumed. It is sensible to reduce this to a more manageable number during testing (e.g. 50) so that the effect of too much data can be properly tested.

A program can now be written according to the above plan and then tested with suitable test data. When preparing test data it is essential to test particularly thoroughly those cases which are on, or close to, the border-line between different cases. The following list shows what is required in order to thoroughly test this simple input loop
(a)   valid data, less than maximum number, correctly terminated
(b)   valid data, exactly maximum number, correctly terminated
(c)   valid data, more than maximum number, correctly terminated
(d)   no data other than terminator
(e)   valid data, less than maximum number, no terminator
(f)   valid data, exactly maximum number, no terminator
(g)   valid data, more than maximum number, no terminator
(h)   no data
(i)   invalid data, less than maximum number, correctly terminated

    .
    .
    .

Thus cases (a)–(d) test what happens with different amounts of otherwise valid data, while cases (e)–(h) repeat these tests for data without the special terminating record. The program should deal with all these cases in a sensible and predictable fashion. (Note that the sample solution in Chapter 6 could be improved to check for the presence of a terminator in cases (b) and (f); it will fail in cases (e) and (h). It might be possible to detect the absence of any more data in cases (e), (f) and (h) by use of the IOSTAT specifier, but this would depend upon the use of an implementation-dependent error number to indicate this situation).

Once these eight cases have been dealt with successfully, further tests can be carried out to ensure that all valid combinations of data items are read correctly, and that invalid data is recognised and processed appropriately. Invalid data falls into two distinct groups – correctly formatted but meaningless data, and incorrectly formatted data. Examples of the former are a sex code other than 0,1 or 9 (terminator), job status outside the range 1–5, etc. How many checks are inserted in the program for these types of errors depends very much on the source of the data; for example if it was computer-generated, or has already been checked by some other program, then it can be normally assumed to be correct in this respect. (The sample solution in Chapter 6 omits all such checks – mainly for reasons of economy of space in this book, but also to improve the clarity of the program.)

Incorrectly formatted data (e.g. characters where numbers are expected) will usually cause a catastrophic failure and there is relatively little that can be done other than recognising the cause of the failure (again by the use of IOSTAT and an implementation-dependent error number), ignoring the input record, and continuing execution.

Once this program has been fully tested we should be confident that the data will be read correctly. This is always a very important step because until we know that the data is being input in the way that we intend it to be, any testing of later stages of the program is difficult and potentially error-prone.

The next stage in building up the complete program might be to analyse those aged 18 or over who are still in full-time education

1 Initialise totals
2 Repeat the following
   2.1 Read next record
   2.2 Print items read
   2.3 If sex = 9 then exit
   2.4 If job = education then
      2.4.1 Increment total (male or female)
      2.4.2 If age ≥ 18 then increment 'old total' (m/f)
3 Print totals and percentages

Since we have already written and tested steps *2*, *2.1*, *2.2* and *2.3* we need only supply data which will test the new parts of the program. This does not mean that only data in which 'job status' is 'full-time education' should be supplied, but that each data set can lie within the maximum data limits and be properly terminated. Examples of suitable test data sets are
(a) one record, job status = full-time education
(b) one record, job status ≠ full-time education
(c) more than one record, job status = full-time education in all records
(d) more than one record, job status = full-time education in some records
(e) more than one record, job status ≠ full-time education in all records

In cases (a), (c) and (d) appropriate combinations of sex (all male, all female, mixed sexes) and age (all under 18, all exactly 18, all over 18, etc.) should be included.

One point which is often overlooked is that when testing a program we must always ensure that we know *exactly* what the answers should be. It is quite easy for a program to contain some (minor) error which leads to the answer calculated being similar to the correct answer, and yet not correct. If the programmer has not worked out in advance exactly what results he is expecting then this type of error may slip through unnoticed.

The process of gradually extending the program can then be continued until eventually the full program is working correctly. Because at each step we only add a relatively small amount of extra code we do not have far to look if errors do occur and there is much less chance of any mistakes being missed.

Finally never make the mistake of thinking that some section of the program 'is bound to work and doesn't need testing'. It is a chastening experience to realise how easy it is to miss even the most obvious error in one's own programs.

The features and concepts which we shall be discovering during the second part of this book will enable and encourage us to develop larger and more sophisticated programs than were appropriate in the first part. It is, therefore, a matter of increasing importance that programs are not only well-designed but also developed and tested in a planned and well-structured manner.

Part II

TOWARDS REAL PROGRAMS

7 Character Handling

7.1 Characters and character storage units

So far all our variables have been either integer or real. We can now consider the storage of characters in variables. There is however one very great difference between the storage of numbers and the storage of characters. A typical modern computer might use 32 *bits* (0's or 1's) to store a number of either type in what is formally called a *numeric storage unit*. Such a numeric storage unit might be able to hold integers in the range from about $-2*10^9$ to $+2*10^9$, or it might hold real numbers in the range -10^{38} to $+10^{38}$ with an accuracy of about seven significant figures. However the same storage unit would probably only hold *four* characters in coded form. This is because each character normally requires either 6 or 8 bits (depending on the code being used). Characters are therefore dealt with in a rather different way.

A *character storage unit* is a location in the memory which will hold exactly *one* character (or rather the code for one character), and a *character variable* will consist of one or more character storage units. There is no assumption about the relationship, if any, between numeric and character storage units although, in practice, most computers will use the same physical memory devices for both types, so that, for example, four 8-bit character storage units may be kept together in what would otherwise be a single 32-bit numeric storage unit.

Programs in the Fortran language are written using only 49 different characters, which are known as the 'Fortran Character Set' and are shown in Fig. 7.1. However, any particular implementation will almost certainly have codes for other characters, since a 6-bit code gives 64 different codes and an 8-bit code can deal with 256 different characters. Appendix C gives some examples of widely used coding systems, although the actual codes should not

```
A  B  C  D  E  F  G  H  I  J
K  L  M  N  O  P  Q  R  S  T
U  V  W  X  Y  Z

0  1  2  3  4  5  6  7  8  9

▽  =  +  -  *  /  (  )        (▽ = space)
,  .  $  '  :
```

Fig. 7.1 The Fortran character set

normally be of any concern to the programmer (but see Section 7.4). Any character which can be coded by a particular implementation can be stored as part of a character constant or character variable.

7.2   CHARACTER **variables and expressions**

Before we can store characters in a variable we must inform the compiler that we wish to do so, because otherwise it will be assumed that the variable is to contain either integers or real numbers (depending on the first letter of its name). We inform the compiler by a process called *declaration*, and, as we shall see in Chapter 8, we can declare that a variable is to contain values of any one of six different types. The declaration statement for a character variable takes one of several, closely related, forms

```
CHARACTER   name1,name2, . . .
CHARACTER* len name1,name2, . . .
CHARACTER   name1*len1,name2*len2, . . .
CHARACTER* len name1*len1, name2*len2, . . .
```

The first form states that the variables called name1,name2, etc. are to be CHARACTER variables, and that each such variable is to consist of *one* character storage unit, i.e. each will contain exactly one character.

The second form states that each of the variables is to consist of 'len' character storage units, and that each will therefore contain exactly 'len' characters.

The third form specifies a (different) *length* for each variable; thus name1 contains 'len1' characters, name2 contains 'len2' characters, and so on. If any name is not followed by a length (*len) then it is given a single character storage unit, i.e. a length of one.

Finally the fourth variation states that unless otherwise specified each variable has a length of 'len', thus

```
CHARACTER*4 A,B*6,C
```

gives A and C four character storage units, and B six storage units.

The length ('len') may be specified either as a positive integer constant or as an integer constant expression enclosed in parentheses. Thus the following declarations both have an identical effect

```
CHARACTER*6  A,B,C
CHARACTER*(8-2) A,B,C
```

The declaration statement is what Fortran calls a *specification statement*; we shall meet several more in the remaining chapters. A specification statement, as its name implies, is a statement which specifies some condition (such as the type of a variable) that the compiler needs to know about because it is different from the standard, or default, condition. One of the fundamental rules of Fortran 77 is that such a specification must come before the main body of the (executable) program statements.

A **CHARACTER** declaration must, therefore appear before *any* executable statements in the program.

Once we have declared a character variable we can, of course, use it in character expressions and assignment statements in a similar way to numeric variables. There are, however, a number of very important differences, of which the most obvious concerns the length of a character variable or expression. We can see these most readily by means of an example (see Fig. 7.2). Here we have three character variables declared, two of length four, and one (**A**) of length three. The first assignment statement assigns the character constant ' END ' to **A**. We can readily see that the value to be assigned (i.e. the constant) has a length of three and so it exactly occupies the three storage units which constitute the variable **A**, and all is well.

```
PROGRAM CHAREX
CHARACTER*4 A*3,B,C
A  =  'END'
B  =  A
C  =  'FINAL'
STOP
END
```

Fig. 7.2 Character assignment

The next assignment statement (**B** = **A**) is, however, more of a problem. **A** has a length of 3 and contains the three characters **END**; **B**, however, has a length of 4 so what will be stored in the four storage units? The answer is that if a character string has a shorter length than the variable to which it is to be assigned then it is extended to the right with blank (or space) characters until it is the correct length. In this case therefore it will have a single, blank, character added after the **D**, thus making its length four.

The third assignment statement poses the opposite problem. Here the character constant to be assigned has a length of 5 whereas the variable, **C**, only has one of 4. In this case the string is truncated to the correct length before assignment.

At the end of this program therefore the three variables **A**, **B** and **C** contain the character strings ' END ', ' END ' and ' FINA ', respectively.

The importance of this extension and truncation makes it desirable that we restate these rules more formally

> When assigning a character string to a character variable whose length is not the same as that of the string, the string is extended on the right with blanks, or truncated from the right, so as to make its length the same as that of the character variable to which it is being assigned.

However the ability to assign a character constant, or the string stored in a character variable, does not in itself take us very far. Just as we have had arithmetic expressions and logical expressions, we can also create character expressions. The major difference between character expressions and the other types of expressions is that there are very few things we can actually do with strings of characters. One thing that we can do, though, is combine two strings to form a third, composite, string. This process is called *concatenation*, and is carried out by means of a *concatenation operator* (/ /)

```
'FRED'//'DIE'
```

The composite string will, of course, have a length equal to the sum of the lengths of the two strings which were concatenated to form it.

There are no other meaningful things that we can do with two strings in order to produce a third string. One further operation is possible on a single character string, namely the identification and extraction of a *part* of the string. A part of a string which is identified in this way is called a *substring* and is defined by following the string, or the name of the variable containing the string, by one or two integer expressions separated by a colon and enclosed in parentheses

```
'RHUBARB'(2:4)
ALPHA(5:7)
BETA(4:)
GAMMA(:6)
DELTA(I:J+K)
```

The first of the two integer expressions defines the position in the string of the first character of the substring, while the second defines the position of the last character of the substring. The positions within a character string are numbered from 1 up to the length of the string, and it follows, therefore, that the values of both integer expressions must lie in this range and that the first must be less than or equal to the second. If the first expression is omitted then the substring starts at the beginning of the string; if the second is omitted then it continues to the end. Fig. 7.3 shows an illustration of this, in which a substring consisting of the first five characters of A (i.e. 'ALPHA') is assigned to B, and the concatenation of two substrings ('BET' and 'A') causes the string 'BETA ' to be assigned to C. Notice that in the latter case the two substrings have lengths of 3 and 1, resulting in a length of 4 for the composite string; this is extended to a length of 5 before it is assigned to C.

```
PROGRAM CHARS
CHARACTER*5 A*8,B,C
A = 'ALPHABET'
B = A(:5)                  ALPHA
C = A(6:)//A(5:5)          BET//A
STOP
END
```

Fig. 7.3 Character expressions

It is also possible to assign to a substring without altering the rest of the contents of the variable. Thus if we added an extra statement

```
A(4:) = 'INE'
```

after the assignment to C in the program shown in Fig. 7.3 the string stored in A would become 'ALPINE '. It is instructive to examine this in detail.

The substring A(4:) is the substring from character 4 to the end of A – a total of 5 characters. The string ' INE ' only has a length of 3 so it is extended by adding two blank characters before being assigned to A(4:). The assignment means that the old substring value ('HABET ') is replaced by the new value (' INE ') leaving the rest of A unchanged. The final result, therefore, is that A contains 'ALPINE '.

There is one very important restriction concerning the assignment of character expressions. *None of the character positions to which a value is being assigned may appear in the character expression on the right-hand side of the equals sign.* The assignment of a character string will normally take place in several steps (and not all at once as is the case with numbers), and therefore, if this rule did not exist, part of the string might be altered before it had been assigned. Thus the expression

```
A(4:6) = A(2:4)
```

is *not* allowed, while the expression

```
A(4:6) = A(1:3)
```

is allowed since none of the character positions on the left-hand side appear on the right-hand side.

Example 7.1

Write a program which, with apologies to Neil Armstrong, uses 'A KINDLY GIANT' to convert 'A SMALL STEP FOR A MAN' into 'A GIANT LEAP FOR MANKIND '.

This program will be purely concerned with character manipulation and so does not need a structure plan

```
      PROGRAM MOON
      CHARACTER*24 A,B,C
      A = 'A KINDLY GIANT'
      B = 'A SMALL STEP FOR A MAN'
C  CREATE 'LEA' IN C
      C = B(6:6)//B(11:11)//B(:1)
C  CHANGE WORDS IN B
      B(3:11) = A(10:15)//C
      C = B(20:)
      B(18:) = C
      B(21:) = A(3:6)
      PRINT *,B
      STOP
      END
```

The program first extracts the letters L, E and A from the string stored in B and combines them to form the string ' LEA ' in C. The substring ' SMALL STE in B is then replaced by the string ' GIANT LEA ' (formed by concatenating a substring of A and C). Next the last few characters of B are stored in C before being replaced in B two places to the left (to avoid breaking the rule about having the same character position on both sides of the equals sign). This removes the A before MAN, and finally the substring ' KIND ' is inserted immediately after ' MAN '.

The variable B now contains the required string ' A GIANT LEAP FOR MANKIND '.

Notice, incidentally, that the first and last assignment statements could have been written

```
C = B(6:6)//B(11:11)//B
B(21:) = A(3:)
```

In both cases this would have led to the string to be assigned being too long (' LEA SMALL STEP FOR A MAN ' and ' KINDLY GIANT ' respectively), and they would have been truncated to three and four characters respectively (' LEA ' and ' KIND '). This is wasteful and badly written and is *not* to be recommended, although it does further illustrate the way in which character assignment operates.

7.3   Input and output of character variables

Now that we have seen how to declare and manipulate character variables, it is clearly desirable that we establish how to read characters into such variables and write characters from them. To do this we need a new edit descriptor – the A edit descriptor – as shown in Fig. 7.4 and 7.5.

Descriptor	Meaning
A*w*	input *w* characters
A	input sufficient characters to fill the input list item

Fig. 7.4   Edit descriptors for inputting characters

Descriptor	Meaning
A*w*	output characters in the next *w* character positions
A	output the contents of the output list item with no leading or trailing blanks

Fig. 7.5   Edit descriptors for outputting characters

The A edit descriptor can be used in two ways – with or without a field width, w. To fully understand the way in which it operates we need to consider input and output separately.

On input the edit descriptor Aw refers to the next w characters (much as Iw and Fw.d refer to w characters). However, a character variable has a defined length and any string which is to be stored in it must be made to have the same length. Let us assume that the length of the input list item is 'len'

(a) If w is less than len then extra blank characters will be added at the end so as to extend the length of the input character string to w. This is similar to the procedure with assignment.
(b) If w is greater than len, however, the *right-most* len characters of the input character string will be stored in the input list item. This is the opposite of what happens with assignment.

The reason for the apparent contradiction, whereby on input the right-most len characters are stored while during assignment the left-most len characters are assigned, can be understood if we consider the output of characters. In this case, Aw will cause characters to be output to the next w character positions of the output record, and once again we need to establish exactly what happens if the length of the output list item is not w

(a) If w is greater than len then the character string will be right-justified within the output field, and will be preceded by one or more blanks. This is similar to the procedure with the I, F, E, D and G descriptors.
(b) If w is less than len then the *left-most* w characters will be output.

A comparison of the two sets of rules shows that they are compatible with each other. Thus if characters are written using a particular format then, if the results produced could be subsequently read using an identical format, the values stored would be the same as those originally output, see Fig. 7.6. A few moments' thought shows that if output added blanks at the beginning, as it must logically do for w > len, and input truncated at the right, then there would be a major incompatibility. The rules elaborated above are, therefore, the only ones which make real sense, despite the apparent difference between the treatment of over-long strings. Fig. 7.7 demonstrates this difference.

Both A and C are read using an A6 edit descriptor. In the first case, therefore, only the right-most four characters are stored. C is now assigned to B, and in this case the left-most four characters are stored. The printed result confirms this difference between direct input to A and 'indirect' input to B via C (whose length is the same as the field width).

For both input and output the field width need not be specified, in which case a field width is used which is equal to the length of the input/output list item. This can be particularly useful on output since it can enable the same basic format to be used with character variables of different lengths, but it should only be used on input with extreme caution. When reading characters they should normally either occupy a known field width, in which case Aw can be used, or be read in such a way that the *data* controls the input.

There is one further way of reading and writing character information, namely the use of list-directed formatting. This can be useful for output (subject to the limitations of list-directed formatting regarding overall layout), but is of less use for input.

```
      PROGRAM CHEX1
      CHARACTER*4 A,B
      A = 'DAFT'
      B = 'DOG'
      WRITE (2,201) A,B
  201 FORMAT(1H ,A6,3X,A3)
      STOP
      END
```

DAFT   DOG

```
      PROGRAM CHEX2
      CHARACTER*4 A,B
      READ (1,101) A,B
  101 FORMAT(A6,3X,A3)
      STOP
      END
```

A contains 'DAFT', B contains 'DOG'

Fig. 7.6 Input and output of characters

```
      PROGRAM CHEX3
      CHARACTER*4 A,B,C*6
C  DATA IS 'ABCDEFABCDEF'
      READ (1,101) A,C
  101 FORMAT(2A6)
      B = C
      WRITE (2,201) A,B,C
  201 FORMAT(1H ,3A8)
      STOP
      END
```

   CDEF   ABCD   ABCDEF

Fig. 7.7 Character input and assignment

If a character variable or expression appears in the output list of a WRITE or PRINT statement, which is using list-directed formatting, the effect is the same as if an A edit descriptor had been used, i.e. the full character string is output using as many character positions as are necessary. We have used this form of output in most of our earlier programs when writing statements such as

```
      PRINT *,'THIS IS A STRING'
```

The only item in the output list here is a character constant, which is, after all, a very simple form of character expression. We could equally well have written

```
STRING = 'THIS IS A STRING'
PRINT *,STRING
```

where STRING is a character variable of length 16.

Input is, however, rather different. We have seen, in connection with numbers, that a data item for list-directed input is terminated by a space, a comma, a 'slash' (/) or the end of a record. Since spaces (in particular) often occur in character data there would clearly be a problem if character data was not identified in some other way. In Fortran 77 the character data must be enclosed between apostrophes (as for a character constant). Thus if a character variable appears in the input list of a READ statement, which is using list-directed formatting, the corresponding data item must consist of a string of one or more characters enclosed between apostrophes. If the data contains an apostrophe then this must be represented by two consecutive apostrophes. A character string which is input in this way may be continued onto a second or subsequent record. However, it is not usually convenient to provide character data in this form, and so list-directed formatting is of less use with character data than it is with numeric data.

Example 7.2

The 4-round scores in a golf tournament are typed into the computer in the following way

Columns 1–12   player's name
        14,15 ⎫
        17,18 ⎬
        20,21 ⎬ player's scores
        23,24 ⎭

The data is terminated by typing END OF DATA in columns 1–11. Assuming that the total scores for all the players are different, write a program to print the names of the winner and the runner-up, together with their scores for each round. (*Note* for non-golfers: the player with the lowest total score is the winner.)

There is one slight problem here concerning the recognition of the terminator; however, as we shall see in the next section, the six relational operators which were introduced in Chapter 5 can be used to compare characters as well as numbers. In this case we are only comparing for equality, and we need only state here that if the two strings being compared are of unequal length then the shorter one is extended on the right with spaces before the two strings are compared.

We can now produce a structure plan

1 Initialise details for first two places
2 Repeat the following
   2.1 Read name and scores

    2.2   If name = ʹ END OF DATA ʹ then exit
    2.3   Calculate total score
    2.4   If total < current leader then
         2.4.1   Move current leader to 2nd place
         2.4.2   Insert this player as new leader
         but if total < current 2nd player then
         2.4.3   Insert this player as new 2nd player
  3   Print details of first two players.

Note here the logic for checking the player's score against the best so far and for moving the details down the list. We can now write the program

```
      PROGRAM GOLF
      CHARACTER*12 PLAYER,FIRST,SECOND
      FIRST = ' '
      SECOND = ' '
      N11 = 500
      N12 = 500
      N13 = 500
      N14 = 500
      N21 = 500
      N22 = 500
      N23 = 500
      N24 = 500
      NT1 = 2000
      NT2 = 2000
      DO 10, I=1,100
C PROGRAM ASSUMES NO MORE THAN 100 PLAYERS
         READ (1,101) PLAYER,N1,N2,N3,N4
         IF (PLAYER.EQ.'END OF DATA') GOTO 11
         NT = N1+N2+N3+N4
         IF (NT.LT.NT1) THEN
           SECOND = FIRST
           N21 = N11
           N22 = N12
           N23 = N13
           N24 = N14
           NT2 = NT1
           FIRST = PLAYER
           N11 = N1
           N12 = N2
           N13 = N3
           N14 = N4
           NT1 = NT
         ELSE IF (NT.LT.NT2) THEN
           SECOND = PLAYER
           N21 = N1
           N22 = N2
           N23 = N3
           N24 = N4
           NT2 = NT
```

```
      END IF
10    CONTINUE
11 WRITE (2,201) FIRST,NT1,N11,N12,N13,N14,SECOND,NT2,N21,
   *  N22,N23,N24
   STOP
101 FORMAT(BZ,A12,4(1X,I2))
201 FORMAT(1H1,'FORTRAN77 GOLF TOURNAMENT'///
  1 1H ,'THE WINNER AND RUNNER-UP (IN ORDER) WERE:'//
  2 (1H ,A12,2X,'TOTAL:',I4,' (',3(I2,','),I2,')'))
    END
```

When we exchange players' names and scores we must take care of the order in which we do it. If we were to put the new player's details in first position before moving the previous leader's details to second position we should find that we had destroyed values that we wished to keep.

Another point concerns the formats (101 and 201). The input format is the easier so we shall examine this first. It consists of an A12 edit descriptor, followed by 1X,I2 repeated four times. This corresponds to character data in columns 1–12 and four integers in columns 14–15, 17–18, 20–21 and 23–24, which is exactly how the data was specified.

The output format is much more interesting. The first two lines start a new page, print an overall title and then print a heading for the actual results. The last line of the format is complicated and we note that it consists of a nested format expression

```
(1H ,A12,2X,'TOTAL:',I4,' (',3(I2,','),I2,')')
```

If any repetition of the format occurs the repetition will therefore start from the beginning of this nested expression. This starts by outputting a printer control character followed by a 12-character value (which will be a player's name). After two spaces TOTAL: is printed followed by an integer occupying 4 characters. A look at the WRITE statement shows us that the total score is output after the name, and since this cannot require more than three digits (because it is the sum of four 2-digit scores) there will be a space after the colon, before the score.

This is followed by a space and a left parenthesis enclosed in apostrophes, and then a three-times repeated sequence I2,' , ' which will output three 2-digit integers followed by commas. Finally another two-digit integer is output followed by a right parenthesis. The complete sequence when printed would therefore look like this

```
MILES ELLIS    TOTAL: 321 (84,77,91,69)
```

If we now examine the WRITE statement we see that the names and scores of both the winner and the runner-up are included in the same output list. When the winner's details have been printed, therefore, the format will be exhausted and will repeat from the beginning of the nested expression, thus printing the second player's results in the same format. Fig. 7.8 shows the results of running the program.

```
FORTRAN77 GOLF TOURNAMENT


THE WINNER AND RUNNER-UP (IN ORDER) WERE:

NICKLAUS      TOTAL: 278 (71,69,68,70)
PLAYER        TOTAL: 279 (73,66,71,69)
```

Fig. 7.8   Results produced by GOLF program

7.4   Comparing character strings

In the last example we used a character string as a terminator for the data and checked for it with the statement

```
IF (PLAYER.EQ.'END OF DATA') GOTO 11
```

As might be expected, we can use all six relational operators (.GT., .GE., .EQ., .NE., .LE., .LT.) to compare character strings; what is not so obvious, however, is how we define the relationship between two strings.

The key to this is the *collating sequence* of letters, digits and other characters. Fortran 77 lays down four rules for this, as shown in Fig. 7.9, which cover letters, digits and the space or blank character. The other 12 special characters, and any others which may be available on a particular computer system, do not have any defined position in the collating sequence. In practice they will usually be ordered according to the internal code used by the computer as long as this code satisfies the four rules laid down in Fig. 7.9. Appendix D shows two of the more widely used internal codes.

---

1   The 26 upper case letters are collated in the following order:

ABCDEFGHIJKLMNOPQRSTUVWXYZ

2   The 10 digits are collated in the following order:

0123456789

3   Digits are either all collated before the letter A, or all after the letter Z

4   A space (or blank) is collated before both letters and digits

Fig. 7.9   The Fortran 77 rules for collating characters

When two character operands are being compared there are three distinct stages in the process

(a)   If the two operands are not the same length the shorter one is extended on the right with blanks until it is the same length as the longer one.

(b) The two operands are compared character by character, starting with the left-most character, until a difference is found or the end of the operands is reached.

(c) If a difference is found then the relationship between these two different characters defines the relationship between the two operands.

The result of this process is that the relational expression always has the value we would instinctively expect it to have. Thus

'ADAM'.GT.'EVE' is false

because 'A' comes before 'E' and therefore 'A'.GT.'E' is false

'ADAM'.LE.'ADAMANT' is true

because after 'ADAM' has been extended the relationship reduces to ' '.LE.'A' after the first four characters have been found to be the same. Since a blank comes before a letter, this is true.

'120'.LT.'1201' is true

because, once again, the first difference in the strings leads to an evaluation of ' '.LT.'1', which is true since a blank also comes before a digit.

Notice, however, that the value of the expressions

'XA'.LT.'X4'

and

'VAR-1'.LT.'VAR.1'

are not defined. In the first case the standard does not define whether letters are to be before or after digits and so the value of 'A'.LT.'4' will depend upon the particular computer system being used. In the second case the special characters are not defined at all, so that, once again, the value of '-'.LT.'.' depends upon the computer system.

These undefined areas are not, in practice, any problem. It is unlikely that any normal application would expect to compare character strings (other than for equality) in which the order was to be determined by characters other than letters, digits or blanks. The concepts of alphabetic or numeric ordering are natural ones, as is the concept of shorter strings coming before longer ones which start with the shorter one (i.e. John comes before Johnson, alpha before alphabet). The only practical area of doubt concerns the question of whether digits come before or after letters.

If, for reasons of portability, it is required to define, within the program and independent of the computer system, the ordering of *all* characters then another way of comparing them is available. This uses one of four intrinsic functions shown in Fig. 7.10. These functions return the value true or false after a comparison which uses the ordering of characters defined in the American National Standard Code for Information Interchange (ANSI X3.4

1977), which is usually referred to as ASCII. This code, which is widely used as an internal code, is shown in Appendix D.1.

LGE(C1,C2) is the same as C1.GE.C2 using ASCII ordering
LGT(C1,C2) is the same as C1.GT.C2 using ASCII ordering
LLE(C1,C2) is the same as C1.LE.C2 using ASCII ordering
LLT(C1,C2) is the same as C1.LT.C2 using ASCII ordering

Fig. 7.10 Intrinsic functions for lexical comparison

Since the four lexical comparison functions return a logical value they can be used in logical expression in the same way as a relational or logical expression. For example, the following block IF structure will only obey the block of statements if the characters in the variable NAME start with one of the characters <, = or > (see Appendix D.1)

```
IF (LGE(NAME,'<').AND.LLT(NAME,'?')) THEN
    block of statements
END IF
```

Example 7.3
A hospital has a library of subprograms which are used to update various medical records, arrange appointments and provide statistics. In particular, the subroutine ADMIT is used to plan admittances for surgical operations and requires three character arguments – the patient's name, the surgeon and the type of operation. The proposed date of admission (as an 11 character string – dd mmm yyyy) and the expected length of stay in days (as an integer) are returned through two further arguments. In order to avoid any accusations of bias the hospital has decided that the surgeon to operate on a particular patient will be chosen according to the following rules

(a) The patient is given a number based on his or her name. If it starts with
        A–D the number is 1
        E–J the number is 2
        K–P the number is 3
        R–T the number is 4
        U–Z the number is 5
(b) This number is multiplied by the patient's age (in years).
(c) The resulting number is divided by 17 and the remainder taken.
(d) If the patient is female, one is added.
(e) The remainder after dividing by 4 is taken and the patient allocated to
        Mr. Awful   if it is 3
        Mr. Brilliant   if it is 2
        Mr. Careless   if it is 1
  and Mr. Dreadful if it is 0 (i.e. there is no remainder)

Write a program that reads a patient's details and prints a list of names surgeons, dates of admission and anticipated length of stay in hospital. The data is typed as follows

Columns 1–20 Patient's name
Column 23   Sex (M or F)
Columns 26–28 Age (in years)
Columns 31–40 Operation required

The data is terminated by a line which consists solely of the word END in columns 1–3.

As usual we start with a structure plan, although in this case (unless we wish to include the details of calculating the surgeon) it is a very simple one

> *1*   Repeat the following
>   *1.1* Read the next patient's details
>   *1.2* If name = END then exit
>   *1.3* Calculate surgeon's name
>   *1.4* Use ADMIT to arrange operation
>   *1.5* Print details

The calculation of the surgeon at step 1.3 could be described in more detail, but since we already have this in the description of the problem there seems little point. We can therefore proceed to the program

```
      PROGRAM HOSP
      CHARACTER*20 NAME,OP,SEX*1,SRGEON*9,DATE*11
      DO 10, I=1,1000
         READ (1,100) NAME,SEX,NAGE,OP
      IF (NAME.EQ.'END') GOTO 11
      IF (NAME.LT.'E') THEN
         N = 1
      ELSE IF (NAME.LT.'K') THEN
         N = 2
      ELSE IF (NAME.LT.'R') THEN
         N = 3
      ELSE IF (NAME.LT.'U') THEN
         N = 4
      ELSE
         N = 5
      END IF
      N = MOD(N*NAGE,17)
      IF (SEX.EQ.'F') N = N+1
      N = MOD(N,4)
      IF (N.EQ.3) THEN
         SRGEON = 'AWFUL'
      ELSE IF (N.EQ.2) THEN
         SRGEON = 'BRILLIANT'
      ELSE IF (N.EQ.1) THEN
         SRGEON = 'CARELESS'
      ELSE
         SRGEON = 'DREADFUL'
      END IF
         CALL ADMIT(NAME,SRGEON,OP,DATE,LENGTH)
   10    WRITE(2,200) NAME,DATE,OP,SRGEON,LENGTH
```

```
  11 STOP
 100 FORMAT(BZ,A20,2X,A,2X,I3,2X,A20)
 200 FORMAT(1H0,A20,' TO ENTER HOSPITAL ON ',A11/
    1  1H ,A20,' WILL BE PERFORMED BY MR. ',A9/
    2  1H ,'EXPECTED LENGTH OF STAY IS',I3,' DAYS')
     END
```

The main points to note about this program are: the way the first block IF successively eliminates groups of names; the use of the MOD function to calculate a remainder; and the call to the subroutine ADMIT with the three values required stored in the first three arguments and the two results of the subroutine's calculations being returned by means of the last two arguments. An example of the results produced by this program can be seen in Fig. 7.11.

```
JAMES SIDEBOTHAM      TO ENTER HOSPITAL ON 17 JUN 1982
BRAIN TRANSPLANT       WILL BE PERFORMED BY MR. CARELESS
EXPECTED LENGTH OF STAY IS 84 DAYS

PETER WORRIER         TO ENTER HOSPITAL ON 23 MAR 1982
TOE AMPUTATION         WILL BE PERFORMED BY MR. CARELESS
EXPECTED LENGTH OF STAY IS 5 DAYS

JANE BOSSIT           TO ENTER HOSPITAL ON 19 SEP 1982
APPENDECTOMY           WILL BE PERFORMED BY MR. DREADFUL
EXPECTED LENGTH OF STAY IS 7 DAYS

ARTHUR KNOWSALL       TO ENTER HOSPITAL ON 12 MAY 1982
GALL STONE REMOVAL     WILL BE PERFORMED BY MR. DREADFUL
EXPECTED LENGTH OF STAY IS 5 DAYS

SUSAN MCTAVISH        TO ENTER HOSPITAL ON 5 FEB 1983
FACELIFT               WILL BE PERFORMED BY MR. BRILLIANT
EXPECTED LENGTH OF STAY IS 12 DAYS
```

Fig. 7.11   Results produced by HOSP program

7.5   Character expressions as embedded formats

In Section 6.9 we saw that a format could be embedded in an input or output statement by expressing it as a character constant. A character constant is a special case of a character expression, and it should, therefore, come as no surprise to discover that a character expression can appear as an embedded format

```
READ (1,FORM) A,B,C
WRITE (2,FORM1//FORM2) X,Y,Z
PRINT FORM1(I:J)//FORM2//FORM3, P,Q,R
```

This can be a particularly useful feature in situations where the format of the output may differ slightly depending upon the values of the information being output (or some other criterion). A simple example of its use is given below; a more realistic and sophisticated example will be found in Chapter 9 (Example 9.4).

Example 7.4

Write a program which reads a name (from columns 1–20) followed by the number of boy and girl children the person has (in columns 23 and 25, respectively). Print the name and total number of children in an easily readable fashion.

The logic of this program is so simple that we do not need a structure plan. The only difficulty lies in arranging the output format

```
      PROGRAM FAMILY
      CHARACTER*35 NAME*20,F,F1
      F1 = '(1H0,A20,'' HAS '',I1,'' CHILDREN'')'
      DO 10, I=1,100
        READ (1,100) NAME,NBOYS,NGIRLS
        IF (NAME.EQ.'END') GOTO 11
        NCH = NBOYS + NGIRLS
        F = F1
        IF (NCH.EQ.0) THEN
          F(18:21) = ' ''NO'
        ELSE IF (NCH.EQ.1) THEN
          F(28:) = ''')'
        ELSE IF (NCH.GE.10) THEN
          F(19:19) = '2'
        END IF
        IF (NCH.GT.0) THEN
          PRINT F,NAME,NCH
        ELSE
          PRINT F,NAME
        END IF
   10   CONTINUE
   11 STOP
  100 FORMAT(A20,T23,I1,T25,I1)
      END
```

We can see (from the first block IF) that there are four cases

(a) If NCH = 0 the value of F is altered to

     '(1H0,A20,'' HAS '', ''NO CHILDREN'')'

(b) If NCH = 1 it is altered to

     '(1H0,A20,'' HAS '',I1,'' CHILD'')'

(c) If NCH $\geqslant$ 10 it is altered to

        `'(1HO,A20,'' HAS '',I2,'' CHILDREN'')'`

(d) Otherwise it is the original value of F1

        `'(1HO,A20,'' HAS '',I1,'' CHILDREN'')'`

Notice that when counting characters in a character string the representation of an apostrophe (`'`) occupies only *one* character position.

These will allow the results to be well-laid out with none of the bad grammer (e.g. 1 CHILDREN) that is seen far too often in computer-produced tables.

7.6 Intrinsic functions for character manipulation

Fortran 77 contains eight intrinsic functions for use in various types of character operations. We have met four of these (LGT, LGE, LLE and LLT) in Section 7.4, and seen that they are used to compare two character strings using the lexical collating sequence used by the ASCII coding system. The remaining functions are shown in Fig. 7.12.

ICHAR(C)	gives the integer equivalent of C
CHAR(I)	gives the character equivalent of I
LEN(C)	gives the length of C
INDEX(C1,C2)	gives the starting position of the sub-string C2 within C1

Fig. 7.12 Character manipulation functions

ICHAR(C) returns as its value an integer (almost certainly the internal code) which represents the *single* character C. This integer number will lie in the range 0 to n-1 inclusive (where 'n' is the number of different characters that can be represented by the particular computer being used) and is the position of the character in the collating sequence (where the first character in the sequence has position 0). Thus if ICHAR(C1).LT.ICHAR(C2) is true, then C1 must come before C2 in the collating sequence.

CHAR(I) is the inverse of ICHAR and returns the character corresponding to the number I, where $0 \leqslant I \leqslant$ n-1. Thus

        CHAR(ICHAR(C)) is the same as C
        ICHAR(CHAR(I)) is the same as I, for $0 \leqslant I \leqslant$ n-1

LEN(C) returns, as its value, the length of the character variable or expression which is provided as its argument. It is primarily of use in subroutines (see Section 10.4).

INDEX(C1,C2) is used to search for the first occurrence of the string C2 in C1. If the *complete* string C2 does exist within C1 then the value returned is the starting position of C2 in C1. If it does not then the value zero is returned. Example 7.5 shows an interesting use of this function.

Example 7.5

Several pages of text have been punched onto 80-column cards for input to the computer; none of the words in the text is split between cards. The final card is blank. Write a program which counts the number of times the word THE occurs in the text.

We shall start with a structure plan

> *1* Initialise count
> *2* Repeat the following
>> *2.1* Read a card
>> *2.2* If it is empty then exit
>> *2.3* Repeat the following
>>> *2.3.1* If rest of card does not contain THE then exit
>>> *2.3.2* Add one to count of THEs
>>> *2.3.3* Adjust 'start' of card
> *3* Print result

Notice that we shall need to search through each card in turn, looking for the word THE. We can do this by repeatedly looking at the 'current' card, but starting each time from the position immediately *after* the end of the last THE. A further problem is to avoid treating THEM, THEIR, etc. as correct matches. The easiest way to do this is to search for the five character sequence ' THE '; the problem of words at the left and right-hand edges of a card can be dealt with by adding extra spaces.

```
      PROGRAM SEARCH
      CHARACTER CARD*82
      N = 0
      CARD = ' '
C ALLOW FOR UP TO 1000 CARDS
      DO 10, I=1,1000
         READ '(A80)',CARD(2:81)
         IF (CARD.EQ.' ') GOTO 11
         M1 = 1
         DO 5, J=1,20
           M = INDEX(CARD(M1:),' THE ')
           IF (M.EQ.0) GOTO 10
           N = N+1
           M1 = M1+M+3
    5    CONTINUE
   10    CONTINUE
   11 PRINT '(''THE WORD THE OCCURRED '',I4,'' TIMES'')',N
      STOP
      END
```

Notice that the 82-character variable CARD can be set to spaces by assigning a single space (which will be extended to 82 spaces) and can be compared with an all blank card by comparing it with a single space (which will also be extended to 82 spaces).

The READ statement (using the standard input unit and an embedded format) reads the 80 characters from the card into positions 2–81 of CARD, thus leaving a space at the beginning and end of the string. The search can now be made for ' THE ' with safety.

For each new card M1 is set to one and a match is sought in the substring from position M1 to the end of the card. If a match is made then the intrinsic function INDEX sets M to the position *within that substring* of the first character of ' THE '; this is used to increase M1 to point to the space immediately after 'THE', and the process is repeated. If no match is made then M is set to zero by INDEX and the next card is read. (Setting M1 to point to the space after ' THE ' avoids any problems when THE is in columns 78–80 of the card. If we set M1 to the character after the space it would cause an error in this situation unless CARD was given a length of 83.)

The final count is printed by a simple PRINT statement with an embedded format.

Summary

●   CHARACTER variables must be declared together with their length.

●   Character substrings may be referred to in place of character variables.

●   Character strings may be combined by use of the concatenation operator (//).

●   Character strings are ordered according to a defined collating sequence.

●   Character expressions may be used in embedded formats.

Character declaration	CHARACTER list of names
	CHARACTER*length list of names
	CHARACTER name1*len1,name2*len2,...
	CHARACTER*length name1,name2*len2,...
Character expressions	string//string
	where 'string' is character variable
	character constant
	character substring
Character substrings	character name(first:last)
	character name(first:)
	character name(:last)

Fig. 7.13   Fortran 77 statements introduced in Chapter 7

Exercises

7.1   Write a program to print a list of the characters in the Fortran character set followed by their internal representation on your computer.

7.2   Write a program to print a list of all the characters in the internal code used by your computer in order of their internal representation (i.e. from 0 to 63, or 0 to 127, etc.).

7.3   What will be printed by the following program?

```
PROGRAM TEST73
CHARACTER*25 A*44,B
A = 'THIS IS AN ODD EXAMPLE OF CHARACTER HANDLING'
B = A(:4)//A(31:)
B(11:) = B(3:10)
B(13:16) = A(37:)
A(8:8) = A(19:)
B(17:) = A(29:30)//A(42:)
B(3:4) = A(22:)
B(13:15) = B(4:5)
B(8:8) = A(24:)
B(23:) = A(8:)
WRITE (*,'(1H1,'//B(13:15)//')') B
STOP
END
```

7.4   Modify the program written in question 6.6 to analyse drinking habits so that it will produce
   (a)   The average number of visits to a pub per week (by sex) for those who drink mainly in a pub, for each social class (A, B, C1, C2, D, E).
   (b)   The most popular drink (by sex) for each social class.

7.5   Write a program which reads text data consisting of words of not more than 10 letters separated by one or more spaces. Produce a table showing the number of words of 1 letter, 2 letters, . . . , 10 letters. The data is terminated by a record beginning with ****.

7.6   A set of personal data consists of records in the following format

Columns 1–30 First name and surname (separated by a space)
Column   33   Sex (M or F)
Columns 36,37 Age
Column   40   Marital status (S, M, D or W, for Single, Married, Divorced, Widowed)

The data is terminated by a blank record.

Read the data and print it out in the form of a table in the following format
```
SURNAME, FIRSTNAME SINGLE(MALE) 37
```

7.7   Write a program which reads arithmetic questions in words (e.g FOUR TIMES SIX?) and prints both question and answer in numeric form (e.g. 4*6=24). Assume only single digits in the data and choose your own means of defining the end of the data.

8 Other Types of Variable

8.1 REAL and INTEGER declarations

We have seen that a character variable is 'declared' using a non-executable type *specification* statement of the form

    CHARACTER name*len,...

We may also declare real and integer variables in a similar way

    REAL name1,name2,...
    INTEGER name3, name4,...

For real and integer variables, of course, it is not usually necessary to include any declaration, as their type is defined by the initial letter of their name. The use of a type declaration, however, does enable us to avoid names such as NAGE or XMEAN which have an added letter at the beginning to define the type

    INTEGER AGE
    REAL MEAN

Such type specifications can make our programs more readable, but the major reason for using a REAL or INTEGER type specification statement is concerned with the use of *arrays* of variables (see Chapter 9).
    As well as these three types of variable, Fortran has facilities for a further three, all of which need to be declared (some programmers, therefore, prefer to declare *all* their variables for consistency). Some compilers have an option which will print a warning message (or even an error!) whenever a variable is referred to in a program without having first been declared. This can help to avoid any errors due to mistyping of variable names, and does, of course, require all real or integer variables to appear in an appropriate type specification statement. The Standard, however, does not require us to declare real or integer variables so this check should always be capable of being switched off.
    We shall only declare real or integer variables if it is more convenient to do so than to use an awkward name.

8.2 LOGICAL variables

Logical expressions have one of two values – *true* or *false* (see Chapter 5). We can store such a logical value in a *logical variable*, which we must first declare in a type specification statement

    LOGICAL name1,name2,...

A logical variable is stored in a numeric storage unit (as are integer and real variables) even though only two values are possible. Once we can store a logical value it becomes necessary to be able to define a logical constant and to read or write logical values.

The two possible logical values are written as

```
.TRUE. and .FALSE.
```

and may be used in an assignment statement in the usual way

```
PROGRAM LOGVAR
LOGICAL ERFLAG
ERFLAG = .FALSE.
    .
    .
    .
    .
```

A logical variable is normally used in three situations

- To save the result of evaluating a logical expression which would otherwise be evaluated in several different places.

- To enable the value of a logical expression to be saved for use at a later stage when it might no longer be possible to evaluate it.

- To clarify a program by use of a meaningful name.

We can illustrate the first and last of these by reference to Example 6.4 which produced some rather complicated statistics from a survey of people's occupations. One of the items of data in this example was a code (ISEX) which contained a 0 if the respondent was male, a 1 if she was female, and a 9 if this was the end of the data. In several places there was a test of the form

```
IF (ISEX.EQ.0)...
```

whose purpose is not immediately clear. If at the start of the program we had included the following declaration

```
LOGICAL MALE
```

and had added the statement

```
MALE = ISEX.EQ.0
```

after the test for a terminator, we could replace all the other tests by statements of the form

```
IF (MALE)...
```

which is very much clearer. The assignment statement may look a trifle odd at first, but the right-hand side is simply an assertion, or logical expression, which has the value true or false, and which can therefore be assigned to the logical variable MALE.

The evaluation of the expression ISEX.EQ.0 is therefore only carried out once, regardless of the number of times a decision is to be made on the basis of the sex of the respondent, and each subsequent use of this value is made much clearer by a suitable choice of name.

The other main use of a logical variable is to remember a condition for use later. A typical example is a program which reads its data and checks it for validity before proceeding to some analysis of that data. If there is an error in the validity of the data there is no point in carrying out the analysis.

Suppose, for example, that an accounting program is reading details of sales and performing certain operations as a result. As a rough check on the data the account number is checked to lie in the range 1–250 and the total value is checked to be less than £500. A program can be written to input the data in a loop and then carry out some analysis if, and only if, all the data was within the limits specified.

```
      PROGRAM ACCNTS
      LOGICAL DTAERR
      INTEGER ACCNUM
C SET DTAERR TO AN INITIAL VALUE OF FALSE
      DTAERR = .FALSE.
      DO 10, I=1,5
        READ *,ACCNUM,VALUE
C SET DTAERR TRUE IF DATA IS INVALID
        DTAERR = DTAERR
     1            .OR. ACCNUM.LT.1 .OR. ACCNUM.GT.250
     2            .OR. VALUE.GE.500.0
              .
              .
              .
   10 CONTINUE
      IF (.NOT.DTAERR) THEN
              .
              .
              .
      END IF
      STOP
      END
```

Notice here that the logical variable DTAERR is initially set false. Then, after each set of data has been read, it is set to its current value *or* ACCNUM outside its range *or* sales value too great. Thus, if either account number or sales value is outside its permitted range then DTAERR is set to *true*. Thereafter it is set true every time through the loop without the need to check the account number or sales value. At the end of the loop it will, therefore, be true if *any* data item was in error, and can be used in a block IF to determine what action (if any) should be taken.

Logical values may be input and output, with certain restrictions by use of the L edit descriptor (see Fig. 8.1).

Descriptor	Meaning
L*w*	(a) input *w* characters as a representation of a logical value
	(b) output *w* − 1 blanks followed by T or F to represent a logical value

Fig. 8.1 The L edit descriptor

On output the logical values true and false are represented by T and F, respectively, preceded by an appropriate number of spaces. On input there are several possible ways of representing true and false; however essentially there are two possible forms

        Tcccc... or Fcccc...
        .Tcccc... or .Fcccc...

where 'cccc...' represents *any* characters. In all cases there may be leading blanks. Thus, for example, all the following will be input by the edit descriptor L10 as true

        T
        TRUE
        .T
        .T.
        .TRUE.
        TRUTHFUL
        TREMENDOUS
              .TRUE.
                 T

while the following will all be input as false

        F
        FALSE
        .F
        .F.
        .FALSE.
        FUTILE
        FANCIFUL
              .FALSE.
                 F

If the first non-blank character(s) in an input field are not T, F, .T or .F an error will occur.

8.3 DOUBLE PRECISION variables

Remember that a real value is an approximation, accurate to a known number of significant figures. This accuracy is determined by the form of a floating point number which allocates a fixed number of 'bits' to the mantissa (thus defining the accuracy) and a fixed number to the exponent (thus defining the range of the numbers). For some types of calculation the accuracy of arithmetic using real values may not be enough and so a second form of number is available with a larger number of significant digits. This uses two consecutive numeric storage units and is called *double precision* (although it does not necessarily hold numbers to exactly twice as many significant digits). Like character and logical variables, a double precision variable must be declared in a type specification statement

> DOUBLE PRECISION name1,name2...

The input and output of double precision values is performed by F, E, D or G edit descriptors in exactly the same way as for real values.

Double precision constants are written in the exponent and mantissa form, but with a D to separate the two parts instead of an E as with real constants (see Section 5.2), thus

> 1D−7 is *double precision* 0.0000001
> 14713D−3 is *double precision* 14.713
> 12.7192D0 is *double precision* 12.7192
> 9.413D5 is *double precision* 941300.0

When using double precision values in a mixed-mode arithmetic expression a similar process occurs to that with which we are already familiar. The expression is evaluated in stages using the normal priority rules, and if one operand is double precision and the other is real or integer then the real or integer value is converted to double precision before the operation is carried out to give a double precision result.

For most purposes real arithmetic is quite accurate enough. If it is not then, for a particular application, double precision variables can be used either in critical areas or throughout the program, as appropriate.

One of the great benefits of the Fortran 77 intrinsic functions is that most of them have *generic* names (see Appendix A). This means that if, for example, SIN is called with a real argument then it is evaluated using real arithmetic to give a real result; if it is called with a double precision argument then it is evaluated using double precision arithmetic to give a double precision result. The same applies, of course, to operators $(+, -, $ etc.$)$ and so if all the real variables are declared as double precision this is normally all that is required to carry out all operations in double precision instead of real (single precision). When transferring a program from one computer to another with inherently less precision this can be extremely useful.

The use of double precision variables usually imposes a very significant overhead on the program, causing it to take considerably longer to run. Fig. 8.2 shows an example of some of the results produced by a program which evaluates the following expression for various values of N

$$\left(\sqrt{\frac{N}{N-1} \star \frac{N-2}{N-3} \star \ldots \star 1}\right)^2 \star \frac{N-1}{N} \star \frac{N-3}{N-2} \star \ldots \star 1$$

This expression should, of course, equal 1, but rounding errors will inevitably creep in.

	DOUBLE PRECISION		REAL ARITHMETIC	
N	VALUE	TIME	VALUE	TIME
1	1.000000000000000	121 USECS.	1.00000000	80 USECS.
2	0.999999999999993	134 USECS.	0.99999845	121 USECS.
3	0.999999999999972	188 USECS.	0.99997759	161 USECS.
4	0.999999999999986	215 USECS.	0.99998236	175 USECS.
5	0.999999999999886	256 USECS.	0.99966931	202 USECS.
10	0.999999999999957	445 USECS.	0.99935496	323 USECS.
25	0.999999999994621	998 USECS.	0.99784017	742 USECS.
50	0.999999999877943	1875 USECS.	0.99507058	1403 USECS.
75	0.999999999797680	2699 USECS.	0.99204040	2105 USECS.
100	0.999999999742911	3603 USECS.	0.98961556	2766 USECS.

Fig. 8.2   A comparison of real and double precision arithmetic

In this case it can be seen that even when $N = 100$ the double precision calculation is extremely accurate and would be printed as 1.0 if nine or fewer decimal places were specified. However when using ordinary real calculation even with $N = 2$ the result is only accurate to five places and with $N = 100$ the error comes in the second decimal place!

It must be emphasised that this is a totally artificial example but it does show that if a great deal of complicated calculation (especially including multiplication and/or division) is required then the use of double precision arithmetic may be highly desirable.

Fig. 8.2 also indicates the time overhead involved in using double precision. Even for $N = 1$ (which is essentially the calculation of $(\sqrt{1.0})^2$) the double precision version took 121μsecs compared with only 80μsecs for the real (or single precision one), while for $N = 100$ the times were 3603μsecs and 2766μsecs. (1μsec is 0.000001 seconds.)

8.4 COMPLEX **variables**

The sixth and last type of variable is somewhat esoteric and is used for certain specialist applications such as the calculations frequently carried out by electrical engineers. This type of variable is called *complex* and consists of two parts – a real part and an imaginary part. In Fortran such a number is stored in two consecutive numeric storage units as two separate real numbers – the first representing the real part and the second representing the imaginary part. A complex variable must be declared in a type specification statement

COMPLEX name1,name2,...

A complex constant is written as a pair of real numbers, separated by a comma and enclosed in parentheses

(1.5, 7.3)
(1.59E4, −12E−1)

In mathematical terms the complex number (X, Y) is written $X + jY$, where $j^2 = -1$. This leads to the rules for complex arithmetic which are shown in Fig. 8.3.

If $Z1 = (X1, Y1)$
$\quad\ Z2 = (X2, Y2)$

then $Z1 + Z2 = (X1 + X2, Y1 + Y2)$

$\quad Z1 - Z2 = (X1 - X2, Y1 - Y2)$

$\quad Z1 * Z2 = (X1 * X2 - Y1 * Y2, X1 * Y2 + Y1 * X2)$

$\quad Z1/Z2 = \left(\dfrac{X1 * X2 + Y1 * Y2}{X2^2 + Y2^2}, \dfrac{X2 * Y1 - Y2 * X1}{X2^2 + Y2^2} \right)$

Fig. 8.3 Complex arithmetic

Real or integer numbers may be combined with complex numbers to form a mixed-mode expression, but double precision numbers may not be. The evaluation of such a mixed-mode expression is achieved by first converting the real or integer number to a complex number with a zero imaginary part. Thus, if Z1 is the complex number (X1, Y1) then

    R*Z1

is converted to

    (R,0)*(X1,Y1)

which is evaluated as

    (R*X1,R*Y1)

Similarly

    I+Z1

is evaluated as

    (REAL(I)+X1,Y1)

Several special functions are available (see Appendix A) for use with complex numbers. For example

    AIMAG(Z)   obtains the imaginary part of Z

and

    CONJG(Z)   obtains the 'complex conjugate' (X,-Y)

Many of the generic functions such as SIN, LOG, etc. can also be used with complex arguments (full details can be found in Appendix A).

The input and output of complex numbers is achieved by reading or writing two real numbers (the real and imaginary parts), using any appropriate edit descriptor. Fig. 8.4 shows an example of both complex input and complex output.

```
      PROGRAM CMPLX
      COMPLEX A,B,C
C   READ TWO COMPLEX NUMBERS
      READ (1,'(BZ,2F10.3)') A,B
      C = A*B
C   PRINT DATA ITEMS AND THEIR PRODUCT
      WRITE (2,200) A,B,C
  200 FORMAT(1H0,'  A = (',F10.3,',',F10.3,')'/
     1        1H0,'  B = (',F10.3,',',F10.3,')'/
     2        1H0,'A*B = (',F10.3,',',F10.3,')')
      STOP
      END

  A = (     12.500,      8,400)

  B = (      6.500,      9.600)

A*B = (      0.610,    174.600)
```

Fig. 8.4   An example of complex arithmetic

8.5   The IMPLICIT statement

In the absence of any declaration a variable is assumed to be integer if the initial letter of its name begins with one of the six letters I–N, and real otherwise. Such undeclared variables are said to have an *implicit type* (which is implied by the initial letter of their name).

We can however alter this state of affairs by defining a new set of implicit types by means of a further specification statement

IMPLICIT type1(list1),type2(list2),...

where type1, etc. are types of variables (e.g. INTEGER, COMPLEX, CHARACTER* len) and list1, etc. define the initial letters which are to imply the corresponding type. The list of initial letters consists of a list of one or more letters and/or ranges of letters denoted by the first and last letters of the range separated by a minus sign (e.g. P–T).

Thus the statement

IMPLICIT DOUBLE PRECISION(A–H), LOGICAL(L)

will cause all undeclared variables starting with A, B, C, D, E, F, G or H to be double precision variables, all those starting with L to be logical, and, of course, those starting with I, J, K, M or N to be integer. All remaining undeclared variables (starting with letters in the range O–Z) will be real.

Because the IMPLICIT statement is defining default conditions it must appear *before* any other specification statements (except PARAMETER, see Section 8.7).

The IMPLICIT statement can be very useful when a program uses a large number of variables of a type other than real or integer, as it avoids the need to declare them all. However it must be used with care since it is easy to forget that some of the normal defaults are not being used. Thus, for example, it would be very easy to write a statement such as

```
DO 10, L=N1,N2
```

despite having already defined all variables beginning with L to be logical by means of an IMPLICIT statement such as the one above. This error would, presumably, be detected by the compiler and could be corrected by including the declaration

```
INTEGER L
```

at the start of the program (after the IMPLICIT statement!). However two statements such as

```
A = SQRT(X+Y)
Z = (A+Y)*P
```

would, with the same IMPLICIT statement, lead to a double precision version of $\sqrt{X+Y}$ being stored in A, which in turn would cause the expression in the second statement to be evaluated using double precision arithmetic before the result was stored in Z as a real value. In this case nothing would cause any error, and the correct answer would be obtained. However, no extra accuracy would be gained through the (inadvertent) use of double precision since all the values being used have been calculated using single precision arithmetic; the only effect will be a (marginal) amount of wasted time!

8.6   Defining initial values

In many of the programs that we have written so far there has been a need for some of the variables used to be assigned an initial value before the program really starts to do anything. When a program is loaded into the computer after it has been compiled, a substantial part of the memory it occupies is thereby set to some value (namely the machine-code instructions). On many systems, all the variable space will also be set to a predefined value (sometimes zero, sometimes an 'impossible' value that will cause an error if accessed before the program has given the variable a value).

In Fortran it is possible to instruct the compiler to arrange that, when the compiled program is loaded, certain defined variables are loaded with specific initial values, thus avoiding the wasted time associated with assigning these initial values (only to alter them). This is achieved with a **DATA** statement, which takes the form

> **DATA** nlist1/clist1/,nlist2/clist2/,...

or

> **DATA** nlist1/clist1/nlist2/clist2/...

where each 'nlist' is a list of variable names and each 'clist' is a list of constants. There must be exactly the same number of items in a 'clist' as in the corresponding 'nlist'. The effect of the statement is to ensure that each variable in 'nlist' is given the initial value specified by the corresponding constant in 'clist'. Thus

```
DATA A,B,N/1.0,2.0,17/,C/'FRED'/
```

will give the (presumably) real variables **A** and **B** initial values of **1.0** and **2.0**, the (presumably) integer variable **N** an initial value of **17**, and the (presumably) character variable **C** an initial value of **'FRED'**.

For numeric variables the normal rules of assignment apply and the constant will be converted to the appropriate type if necessary. The rules for assignment also apply to character variables, and a character constant will be extended with blanks on the right or truncated from the right, if necessary, in order to make it the same length as the character variable. It is also permitted to give an initial value to a character substring

```
DATA CHAR(7:10)/'FRED'/
```

It frequently happens that several variables are to be given the same initial value (e.g. 0) in which case it is possible to precede the constant with the number of repetitions required and an asterisk. Thus, the initialisation section of the golfing program written in Example 7.2 could be written as follows

```
PROGRAM GOLF
CHARACTER*12 PLAYER,FIRST,SECOND
DATA FIRST,SECOND/2*' '/,
*   N11,N12,N13,N14,N21,N22,N23,N24,NT1,NT2/10*0/
```

A **DATA** statement must appear after any specification statements. It is usual practice to place **DATA** statements at the beginning of the executable portion of the program, but this is not necessary. They could equally well be placed immediately before the **END** statement, although this does make their purpose, which is to provide initial values, slightly less apparent. Wherever a **DATA** statement is placed it will cause initialisation to be carried out when the program is loaded, i.e. just before the start of execution.

8.7 Giving names to constants

As well as giving initial values to variables, a `DATA` statement can be used to give a value to a variable which is never changed

```
DATA PI/3.1415926536/
```

This variable can then be used in place of the constant both to save writing (as here) and to improve the clarity of the program. However we are using a variable in place of a constant which is not a desirable course of action for several reasons – on aesthetic (or stylistic) grounds, because of practical considerations such as efficiency, and, most importantly, because of the possibility of the variable being (erroneously) assigned another value.

The `PARAMETER` statement allows us to give a name to a constant, and takes the form

```
PARAMETER (name1=const1,name2=const2,...)
```

where 'const1', etc. are constants or constant expressions and 'name1', etc. are the names which are to be associated with them. Notice that the part of the statement which defines the name and value looks exactly like an assignment statement, except that the expression on the right of the equals sign is composed only of constants. Thus a better way of giving a value to `PI` is to write

```
PARAMETER (PI=3.1415926536)
```

which defines `PI` as a constant with the required value. On every occasion in the program that `PI` is referred to the compiled program will, therefore, refer to `3.1415926536`.

A constant expression can be used to define constants which can be defined more accurately as an expression, for example

```
PARAMETER (THIRD=1.0/3.0)
```

or where the value is expressed more clearly by an expression, such as

```
PARAMETER (PI3BY4=3.0*PI/4.0)
```

When an expression is used in this way there are two restrictions

- Only the operators +, −, * and / may be used, except that ** may be used as long as the exponent is integer; parentheses may be used in the normal way.

- If a named (or *symbolic*) constant appears in a constant expression it must have been defined in an earlier `PARAMETER` statement, or in an earlier part of this statement.

The latter rule means that the following is allowed

```
PARAMETER (PI=3.1415926536,PI3BY4=3.0*PI/4.0)
```

If the implied type of the constant name is not suitable then it must appear in a type or IMPLICIT statement to define the correct type. Such a type or IMPLICIT statement must come *before* the PARAMETER statement in the program. Apart from this a PARAMETER statement may appear anywhere after the initial (PROGRAM) statement and before the first DATA or executable statement. It is the only kind of statement which may come before an IMPLICIT statement, as long as the latter does not alter the implied type of any name in the PARAMETER statement.

The normal rules for mixed-mode expressions and assignments apply, and therefore the following statement

```
PARAMETER (ICON=3.0/4*5,CON=3/4*5)
```

will result in the constant ICON having a value of 3 (3.0/4*5→3.0/ 4.0*5→0.75*5→3.75→3), while CON will have a value of 0.0 (3/4*5→ 0*5→0→0.0).

A named constant which has been defined in a PARAMETER statement may appear in any subsequent statement as part of an arithmetic expression, or may appear as a value in a DATA statement.

Example 8.1

As part of a larger project, it is required to write a program which will input data relating to sales made in a large department store during the previous day. The data has been transcribed from records produced by each cash-till and consists of the following items

Columns 1–4   department code
Columns 11–14   goods code
Columns 21–26   price
Columns 31–36   amount tendered by customer
Columns 41–46   change given

The last three items all take the same format – LLL.PP, where LLL is the number of pounds and PP is the number of pence.

The departments are in four groups (Hardware, Electrical, Furnishing and Clothing) with the first letter of the department code being H, E, F or C as appropriate.

The data is terminated by a record consisting of the word END in columns 1–3 and otherwise blank.

The program is to read each input record and check that the three figures (price, amount tendered and change given) are consistent with each other. If they are then the data is to be passed to a subroutine called FILE which takes three arguments, the department code, the goods code and the price, in that order. If there is an error then a message should be printed.

When all the data has been input the total sales for each group of departments should be printed, unless there was an error in some data for that group.

We shall start, of course, with a structure plan.

1   Initialise departmental sums
2   Repeat the following
    2.1   Read next set of data
    2.2   If it is 'END' then exit
    2.3   If data is valid then
        2.3.1   Send data to FILE
        2.3.2   Update group total
    otherwise
        2.3.3   Print error message
        2.3.4   Set group error flag
3   Repeat for each department group
    3.1   If no data errors then
        3.1.1   Print total sales
    otherwise
        3.1.2   Print error message

The logic of this is quite straightforward and so we can proceed to our program

```
PROGRAM SALES
PARAMETER (MAX=10000)
CHARACTER*4 DEP,GOODS,GROUP*1
LOGICAL ERRC,ERRE,ERRF,ERRH
DATA SUMC,SUME,SUMF,SUMH/4*0.0/
DATA ERRC,ERRE,ERRF,ERRH/4*.FALSE./
DO 10, I=1,MAX
  READ (1,101) DEP,GOODS,PRICE,CASH,CHANGE
  IF (DEP.EQ.'END') GOTO 11
  GROUP = DEP
  IF (ABS(CASH-PRICE-CHANGE).LT.0.01) THEN
    CALL FILE(DEP,GOODS,PRICE)
    IF (GROUP.EQ.'C') THEN
      SUMC = SUMC+PRICE
    ELSE IF (GROUP.EQ.'E') THEN
      SUME = SUME+PRICE
    ELSE IF (GROUP.EQ.'F') THEN
      SUMF = SUMF+PRICE
    ELSE
      SUMH = SUMH+PRICE
    END IF
  ELSE
    WRITE (2,201) DEP,GOODS,PRICE,CASH,CHANGE
    IF (GROUP.EQ.'C') THEN
      ERRC = .TRUE.
    ELSE IF (GROUP.EQ.'E') THEN
      ERRE = .TRUE.
    ELSE IF (GROUP.EQ.'F') THEN
      ERRF = .TRUE.
```

```
          ELSE
             ERRH = .TRUE.
          END IF
        END IF
10    CONTINUE
11 IF (ERRC) THEN
        WRITE (2,202)  'CLOTHING'
      ELSE
        WRITE (2,203)  'CLOTHING',SUMC
      END IF
      IF (ERRE) THEN
        WRITE (2,202)  'ELECTRICAL'
      ELSE
        WRITE (2,203)  'ELECTRICAL',SUME
      END IF
      IF (ERRF) THEN
        WRITE (2,202)  'FURNISHING'
      ELSE
        WRITE (2,203)  'FURNISHING',SUMF
      END IF
      IF (ERRH) THEN
        WRITE (2,202)  'HARDWARE'
      ELSE
        WRITE (2,203)  'HARDWARE',SUMH
      END IF
      STOP
101 FORMAT(BZ,2(A4,6X),3(F6.2,4X))
201 FORMAT(1H0,'DATA ERROR IN FOLLOWING RECORD:'/
   * 1H ,2(A4,6X),3(F6.2,4X)/)
202 FORMAT(1H0,'ERROR(S) IN ',A,' DATA')
203 FORMAT(1H0,A,' SALES WORTH $',F9.2)
      END
```

The program uses a named constant **MAX** to define the 'fail-safe' value for the main input loop. This can be altered during testing to a much lower value. **DATA** statements are used to initialise four sums to zero, and four error flags to false. The main input loop then follows the structure plan very closely except that the group code is extracted first (from the first character of the department code).

Look carefully at the test for data validity. It would not be safe to write

```
IF (CHANGE.EQ.CASH-PRICE)...
```

owing to the problem of arithmetic error during real arithmetic. The program therefore calculates the absolute value of the difference between the cash tendered and the sum of the price and change; if this is less than 0.01 (i.e. one penny) then the data is taken to be correct.

It will be noticed that the repeated block **IF** statements look rather unwieldy. The next chapter will show how this can be avoided.

Summary

- Variables may be declared to be of type LOGICAL, DOUBLE PRECISION or COMPLEX.
- Default types may be altered by an IMPLICIT statement.
- The DATA statement provides initial values for variables.
- The PARAMETER statement is used to give a name to a constant.

Type declarations	REAL list of names
	INTEGER list of names
	LOGICAL list of names
	DOUBLE PRECISION list of names
	COMPLEX list of names
IMPLICIT *statement*	IMPLICIT type (range) ,...
	e.g. IMPLICIT COMPLEX(A–H) ,LOGICAL(L)
Initial values	DATA list of names / list of values /
PARAMETER *statement*	PARAMETER (name=value) ,...

Fig. 8.5   Fortran 77 statements introduced in Chapter 8

Exercises

8.1 Find out the range of values on your computer for values of integer, real and double precision types, and the accuracy to which values of the last two types are held.

8.2 Write appropriate declarations for this program.

```
      PROGRAM TEST82
      IMPLICIT DOUBLE PRECISION(A–H),LOGICAL(L)
      DATA ERR/.FALSE./,C1,C2/'A','Z'/
      READ 100,A,B,L,M,X,Y
      F = ABS(X)
      DO 10, I=L,M
        READ 101,N,P,Q,R
        IF (C1.LE.N .AND. N.LE.C2) THEN
          Z = CMPLX(P,Q)
          H = F*R+1D4
        ELSE
          ERR = .TRUE.
        END IF
        IF (INT(Z–X).GT.Y) GOTO 11
10    CONTINUE
```

```
 11 IF (.NOT.ERR) THEN
       PRINT *,B
    ELSE
       PRINT *,'FAILED!'
    END IF
    STOP
100 FORMAT(I5,3X,A6,2I8,2F10.2,I3)
101 FORMAT(A1,4X,2F10.4,F20.6)
    END
```

8.3 In Exercise 5.5 the value of sin X was calculated using an infinite series. Modify this program so that the value of π is stored as a named constant and the program can use either single precision (real) or double precision calculation, depending upon some extra item of data.

8.4 A racing tortoise trainer uses a computer to analyse the results of a season's racing. For each race he records the name of the tortoise (Percy, Quentin, Rudolph or Samantha), the length of the race (in feet), the time (in hours, minutes and seconds in the format hh.mm.ss) and the position in the race. He wishes to produce a table showing for each tortoise the number of races and the number of first, second and third places achieved. In addition, for any tortoise that managed an average speed in excess of 1 ft/min in any race, he requires the average speed for all that tortoise's races. Write a program to produce this information.

8.5 Write a program to process electricity accounts. Each set of data should consist of the customer's name, his address (3 lines) and the previous and current meter readings. The program should produce a quarterly account showing the customer's name and address followed by the two meter readings, the amount of electricity used at each of two rates and the consequent cost, and the total charge. The two rates and the number of units to be charged at the first (higher) rate should be read before any other data at the start of the program.

 **Arrays**

9.1 Arrays of variables

In all that we have said so far, and in all the programs we have written, we have used one name to refer to one location in the computer's memory. Sometimes, such as in Examples 7.2 and 8.1, this has meant that the same sequence of statements has been repeated several times but with different names for the variables. There are a great many situations when we should like to repeat a sequence of statements (e.g. in a loop) but instead of always using the same set of variables we should like to use a different set, and then another, and so on.

One way to do this would be to have a group or *array* of locations in the memory, all of which are identified by the same name but with an index or *subscript* to identify individual locations. Fig. 9.1 shows this concept, using the same types of boxes as were used in Chapter 1 to originally introduce the concept of named memory locations.

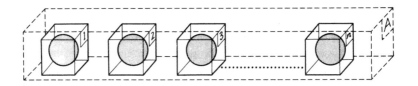

Fig. 9.1 An array of memory locations

Thus, the whole set of 'n' boxes is called A, but within the set we can identify individual boxes by their position within the set. Mathematicians are familiar with this concept and would refer to a set like this as the vector A and would refer to the individual elements by writing $A_1, A_2, \ldots A_n$.

In Fortran we call a set of related variables which have the same name an *array*, and we refer to the individual variables within the array as *array elements*. We cannot adopt the mathematical concept of a subscript to identify these array elements (although we do borrow the name); instead we follow the name of the array by an identifying integer value enclosed in parentheses – A(1), A(2),...A(n).

More precisely, an array element is defined by writing the name of the array followed by a subscript, where the subscript consists of an integer expression (known as the subscript expression) enclosed in parentheses. Thus if A, B and C are arrays the following are all valid ways of writing an array element

```
A(10)
B(I+4)
C(3*I+MAX(I,J,K))
A(INT(B(I)*C(J)+A(K)))
```

Notice that function references are allowed as part of the subscript expression, as are array elements (including elements of the same array).

9.2 Array declarations

When we refer to a variable for the first time, either in a specification statement, a DATA statement, or an executable statement, the compiler will allocate an appropriate storage unit (or units in the case of double precision, complex, or character variables). It is not always possible to tell from these statements how many storage units to allocate for an array, and never from just the first one. Since the compiler needs to know how many storage units are required so that it can allocate a contiguous area of the memory for the array, it is necessary to declare the size of the array at the start of the program.

The easiest way to do this is to follow the name of the array in an appropriate type declaration by the number of array elements enclosed in parentheses

```
REAL A(20), TABLE(35)
CHARACTER*20 NAME(100), CODE(100)*4
INTEGER AGE(100), NUM(25)
```

Notice that if a character array name includes a length specification then this comes after the size of the array, and specifies the length of each element of the array.

In this form of declaration the subscripts will run upwards from 1 to the size of the array, and thus the integer array AGE may have subscripts running from 1 to 100, inclusive.

If we wish to have subscripts which do not start at 1 we can use an extended form of declaration consisting of the minimum and maximum values of the subscript, separated by a colon, with the complete subscript specification being enclosed in parentheses

```
REAL C(0:20)
INTEGER ERROR(-10:10)
```

In this case the real array C can have subscripts in the range from 0 to 20, and therefore has a size of 21; while the integer array ERROR also has a size of 21, but has subscripts running from −10 up to +10.

We see, therefore, that the simple form of array declaration is the same as the more comprehensive one with a minimum subscript value of one

```
INTEGER AGE(1:100), NUM(1:25)
```

There is another way of declaring an array, although it is included in

Fortran 77 mainly for historical reasons and is not normally used. This is by use of a DIMENSION statement

```
DIMENSION NAME(100),ERROR(-10:10),AGE(100)
```

This performs exactly the same array declaration function as do the REAL, INTEGER and other type specification statements shown above, but does not specify any type. If the type of the array is not that implied by its initial letter then a separate type statement is required

```
INTEGER AGE,ERROR
CHARACTER*20 NAME
DIMENSION AGE(100),NAME(100),ERROR(-10:10)
```

Since the dimensions could have been included in the type statements there is little point in having a separate DIMENSION statement. If a DIMENSION statement is used then it must come with the other specification statements, after any IMPLICIT statements, and before any DATA or executable statements.

The specification of the maximum, and possibly minimum, subscript is called the *dimension declarator*. The array name followed by a dimension declarator in parentheses is called an *array declarator*.

The primary reason for declaring an array is to enable the compiler to allocate sufficient storage space. Another important reason is described in Chapter 10 when we learn how to write our own subroutines and functions. Fig. 9.2 shows a short extract from a program which does nothing in particular; however look at the three assignment statements. The first one is clearly intended to assign the Ith element of the array TOM to A; TOM appears in an array declaration at the start of the program. The second one has exactly the same structure, but this time it requires that the intrinsic function ABS be used to find the absolute value of J before assigning this value to B (after converting it to real). The third assignment statement also takes exactly the same form. However there is no array declaration and FRED is not the name of an intrinsic function. In this case, therefore, the compiler assumes that FRED is

---

```
PROGRAM FIG92
REAL TOM(10)
    .
    .
    .
A  =  TOM(I)
B  =  ABS(J)
C  =  FRED(K)
    .
    .
    .
END
```

Fig. 9.2   Array and function references

---

an *external function* subprogram which is being provided by the user and generates the necessary code to 'call' the function. The value of the function will then be assigned to C.

Thus we see that there are three different ways in which an expression of the form

name (expression)

can be interpreted. An intrinsic function is recognised by the compiler, but the distinction between an array element and a function reference can only be made because the array must have been declared.

9.3 Using arrays and array elements

An array element can be used anywhere that a variable can be used. In exactly the same way as a variable, it identifies a unique location in the memory to which a value can be assigned or input, and whose value may be used in an expression or output list, etc. The great advantage is that by altering the value of the subscript it can be made to refer to a different location.

The use of array variables within a loop therefore greatly increases the power and flexibility of a program. This can be seen in Fig. 9.3 where a short loop enables up to 100 sets of survey data to be input *and stored* for subsequent analysis in a way which is not otherwise possible. This program also illustrates how useful the PARAMETER statement can be when dealing with large numbers of arrays.

```
      PROGRAM SURVEY
      CHARACTER*20 NAME(100)
      INTEGER SEX(100),AGE(100)
      REAL HEIGHT(100),WEIGHT(100)
      DO 10, I=1,100
         READ (1,101) NAME(I),SEX(I),AGE(I),HEIGHT(I),WEIGHT(I)
      IF (NAME(I).EQ.'END') GOTO 11
  10  CONTINUE
  11     .
         .
         .
         .
      END
```

Fig. 9.3 Inputting data to an array

In the program each array has a maximum subscript of 100 and, thus, the program is suitable for up to 100 sets of data. The maximum value of the control variable for the conditional DO-loop is, therefore, also 100. There may be other uses of this same maximum value of 100 elsewhere in the program. If we wish to change this value either during testing or because there is more data than anticipated there will be a number of statements to change which is both time-consuming and a potential source of errors. We could, of course, read a maximum value for the DO-loop control variable, but the array dimension declarators must be constants or constant expressions, *not* variables. Fig. 9.4, however, shows the same program but using a named constant MAX.

```
      PROGRAM SURVEY
      PARAMETER (MAX=100)
      CHARACTER*20 NAME(MAX)
      INTEGER SEX(MAX),AGE(MAX)
      REAL HEIGHT(MAX),WEIGHT(MAX)
      DO 10, I=1,MAX
        READ (1,101) NAME(I),SEX(I),AGE(I),HEIGHT(I),WEIGHT(I)
        IF (NAME(I).EQ.'END') GOTO 11
   10 CONTINUE
   11    .
         .
         .
         .
      END
```

Fig. 9.4   Using a PARAMETER with arrays

In this case it is clear that by changing the single PARAMETER statement we can effect the required change throughout the program. There is no possibility of either forgetting to change one occurrence, or altering an occurrence of the constant 100 which has a different meaning and, therefore, should not be changed. Notice, incidentally, that no confusion occurs through the constant being called MAX (which is also the name of an intrinsic function) since the syntax of a statement will always show whether the constant MAX or the function MAX is being referred to. However, if an array was called MAX it would be impossible to distinguish any reference to the intrinsic function of the same name and so the function MAX would become inaccessible.

An array name, unlike an array element, can only be used in a limited number of situations. This is because the array name refers, in some sense, to the *whole* array, and therefore cannot be used in the same situations as can a variable or an array element. We have already seen that the array name can appear in a type-statement and in an array declarator. It can also be used as the argument to a subroutine or function, e.g.

```
      PROGRAM ARGS
      REAL A(100), B(50)
      CALL GETARR(A,B,N)
        .
        .
        .
        .
```

Other situations in which an array name can appear without any subscript are in a DATA statement, an input/output statement, and as a format identifier (we shall meet others in later chapters).

9.4   Giving initial values to an array

The elements of an array may be given initial values in three different ways. The first of these uses exactly the same form of DATA statement introduced in Section 8.6, except that array elements are included in the list of names. Thus the following statements will set the first four elements of the array A to zero, and the last one to -1.0. The other elements of A (A(5) to A(19)) are not given any initial value and are therefore initially undefined.

```
PROGRAM INIT1
REAL A(20)
DATA A(1),A(2),A(3),A(4)/4*0.0/,A(20)/-1.0/
    .
    .
    .
    .
```

If more than a few elements of an array are to be initialised it is not necessary to write out the names of all the individual array elements; instead we may use an *implied-DO list*. This takes the form

(dlist,int=m1,m2,m3)

or simply

(dlist,int=m1,m2)

where 'dlist' is a list of array element names and the expression 'int=m1,m2,m3' or 'int=m1,m2' is exactly similar to the corresponding expression in a DO-loop, except that 'int' (the *implied-DO-variable*) must be an integer variable and 'm1', 'm2' and 'm3' must be constants or constant expressions, and 'm3' must be positive (but see also Section 9.8). The implied-DO-variable only exists for the purpose of the DATA statement and does not affect the value of any other variable having the same name.

The effect of the implied-DO list is to repeat the list of array element names for each value of the implied-DO-variable. Thus the statements

```
PROGRAM INIT2
REAL A(20)
DATA (A(I),I=1,4)/4*0.0/,A(20))/-1.0/
    .
    .
    .
    .
```

have exactly the same effect as those in the previous example, in which A(1), A(2), A(3) and A(4) were all listed individually. The following statements show a more sophisticated use in which A(1), A(2), A(4), A(5), A(7),... are set to zero, while every third array element (A(3), A(6),...) is set to one

```
PROGRAM INIT3
REAL A(20)
DATA (A(I),A(I+1),I=1,19,3)/14*0.0/,
*     (A(I),I=3,18,3)/6*1.0/
      .
      .
      .
      .
```

The third and last way of initialising an array is to write the name of the array (without any subscripts) in the list of items to be initialised, and exactly the right number of values in the value list

```
PROGRAM INIT4
REAL A(20)
DATA A/20*0.0/
```

In this case, therefore, the array name represents a list of *all* its elements, in order, and requires the corresponding number of values.

Example 9.1
Rewrite the program for Example 8.1 (the analysis of sales in a department store) using arrays to simplify the code.

We noted in Example 8.1 that there were many repetitions of similar sequences of statements to deal with the four different groups of departments. We can now keep all the relevant items in arrays and use loops to repeat the sequences. The structure of the program will remain the same as before

1 Initialise departmental sums
2 Repeat the following
    2.1 Read next set of data
    2.2 If it is 'END' then exit
    2.3 If data is valid then
        2.3.1 Send data to FILE
        2.3.2 Update group total
    otherwise
        2.3.3 Print error message
        2.3.4 Set group error flag
3 Repeat for each department group
    3.1 If no data errors then
        3.1.1 Print total sales
    otherwise
        3.1.2 Print error message

Clearly we need to keep the group sums and error flags in arrays, but two other arrays will be required. The first of these (CODE) will contain the four group codes, while the second (NAME) will contain their names. We can now write the program

```
      PROGRAM SALES2
      PARAMETER (MAX=10000)
      CHARACTER*4 DEP,GOODS,CODE(4)*1,NAME(4)*10
      LOGICAL ERR(4)
      REAL SUM(4)
      DATA SUM/4*0.0/,ERR/4*.FALSE./
      DATA CODE/'C','E','F','H'/
      DATA NAME/'CLOTHING','ELECTRICAL','FURNISHING',
     *  'HARDWARE'/
      DO 10, I=1,MAX
        READ (1,101) DEP,GOODS,PRICE,CASH,CHANGE
        IF (DEP.EQ.'END') GOTO 11
        IF (ABS(CASH-PRICE-CHANGE).LT.0.01) THEN
          CALL FILE(DEP,GOODS,PRICE)
          DO 5, J=1,4
            IF (DEP(:1).EQ.CODE(J)) SUM(J) = SUM(J)+PRICE
    5     CONTINUE
        ELSE
          WRITE (2,201) DEP,GOODS,PRICE,CASH,CHANGE
          DO 6, J=1,4
            IF (DEP(:1).EQ.CODE(J)) ERR(J) = .TRUE.
    6     CONTINUE
        END IF
   10   CONTINUE
   11 DO 15, I=1,4
        IF (ERR(I)) THEN
          WRITE (2,202) NAME(I)
        ELSE
          WRITE (2,203) NAME(I),SUM(I)
        END IF
   15   CONTINUE
      STOP
  101 FORMAT(BZ,2(A4,6X),3(F6.2,4X))
  201 FORMAT(1H0,'DATA ERROR IN FOLLOWING RECORD:'/
     *  1H ,2(A4,6X),3(F6.2,4X)/)
  202 FORMAT(1H0,'ERROR(S) IN ',A,' DATA')
  203 FORMAT(1H0,A,' SALES WORTH $',F9.2)
      END
```

Notice how, in addition to shortening the program considerably, the use of arrays has meant that the overall program structure is more obvious and is not blurred by repeated sequences in block IF's.

An alternative approach to the decisions and actions in the main input loop would be first to set an integer (say N) to one of the values 1, 2, 3 or 4, depending upon the group code, and then to use this as a subscript to the arrays SUM and ERR. The main loop would then take the following form

```
      DO 10, I=1,MAX
        READ (1,101) DEP,GOODS,PRICE,CASH,CHANGE
        IF (DEP.EQ.'END') GOTO 11
        DO 5, N=1,4
          IF (DEP(:1).EQ.CODE(N)) GOTO 6
    5     CONTINUE
    6   IF (ABS(CASH-PRICE-CHANGE).LT.0.01) THEN
          CALL FILE(DEP,GOODS,PRICE)
          SUM(N) = SUM(N)+PRICE
        ELSE
          WRITE (2,201) DEP,GOODS,PRICE,CASH,CHANGE
          ERR(N) = .TRUE.
        END IF
   10   CONTINUE
```

9.5 Input and output of arrays

The situation with regard to the input and output of arrays is very similar to that which exists for DATA statements. Thus individual array elements may appear in an input or output list in the same way as variable names. An implied-DO list may appear to define a sequence of array elements, and an array name may appear (unsubscripted) in order to specify *all* the elements of the array. The major difference is that the restrictions on the implied-DO list in a DATA statement do not apply in an input/output statement and the rules are exactly the same as those which apply to a DO-statement. In particular, since the defining expressions for the implied-DO may be variables or variable expressions they may be dependent upon values input by the same statement (see Fig. 9.5).

```
      PROGRAM ARINPT
      REAL A(20)
      READ (1,101) N,(A(I),I=1,N)
  101 FORMAT(BZ,I2/(5F10.3))
          .
          .
          .
      END
```

Fig. 9.5 Input using an implied DO-list

This form of input statement must, however, be used with care for it opens the door to a frequent cause of errors. Consider, for example, what would happen if, by accident, the data started with a number larger than 20, say 25. The READ statement would input this value and then, under the control of the implied-DO list, would read sufficient data to occupy the array elements A(1) to A(25). However A was declared with a maximum subscript of only 20. Unfortunately, checking that the subscript value is within the defined bounds is a time-consuming task. Many compilers will only insert the code for such checking into the compiled program upon request, for example during testing. If such checking is absent or inactive the program will store the 25 values in 25 consecutive storage units starting at A(1). The last five of these are, however, not part of the array A and may be other variables, constant values or even, in some situations, part of the program!

The fact that these memory locations have been overwritten may not be immediately apparent, and the subsequent incorrect results and/or program failure can be very difficult to find. In order to guard against this possibility it is often preferable first to read the number of values, then to check that this is acceptable, and only then to read the full set of data. Fig. 9.6 shows a modified version of the program from Fig. 9.5.

```
PROGRAM ARINPT
REAL A(20)
READ (1,100) N
IF (N.GE.1 .AND. N.LE.20) THEN
   READ (1,101) (A(I),I=1,N)
ELSE
   PRINT *,'INVALID NUMBER:  ',N
END IF
   .
   .
   .
END
```

Fig. 9.6   Improved use of an implied DO-list for input

Example 9.2

Rewrite the program for Example 7.2 (the calculation of the prizewinners in a golf tournament) using arrays to simplify the code, and print the first *three* players.

This is very similar to the earlier program, but with slightly more involved comparisons and exchanges owing to the need to keep details of the leading three players. Our structure plan will be as follows

  1   Initialise details for first three places
  2   Repeat the following
    2.1   Read name and scores
    2.2   If name = 'END OF DATA' then exit
    2.3   Calculate total score
    2.4   If total < current leader then
        2.4.1.   Move current 1st and 2nd to 2nd and 3rd
        2.4.2   Insert this player as new leader
        but if total < current 2nd player then
        2.4.3   Move current 2nd to 3rd
        2.4.4   Insert this player as new 2nd player
        but if total < current 3rd player then
        2.4.5   Insert this player as new 3rd player
  3   Print details of first three players

We shall set up six arrays in which to store the names, four individual round scores and total scores for each of the top three players. We shall then be able to write a simple loop to carry out the checking for position and the moving of the details of the leaders.

```
      PROGRAM GOLF2
      PARAMETER (MAX=100)
      CHARACTER*12 PLAYER,LEADER(3)
      INTEGER T1(3),T2(3),T3(3),T4(3),T(3)
      DATA LEADER/3*' '/
      DATA T1,T2,T3,T4,T/12*500,3*2000/
      DO 10, I=1,MAX
        READ (1,101) PLAYER,N1,N2,N3,N4
        IF (PLAYER.EQ.'END OF DATA') GOTO 11
        NT = N1+N2+N3+N4
        DO 6, J=1,3
          IF (NT.LT.T(J)) THEN
            DO 5, K=2,J,-1
              LEADER(K+1) = LEADER(K)
              T1(K+1) = T1(K)
              T2(K+1) = T2(K)
              T3(K+1) = T3(K)
              T4(K+1) = T4(K)
5             T(K+1) = T(K)
            LEADER(J) = PLAYER
            T1(J) = N1
            T2(J) = N2
            T3(J) = N3
            T4(J) = N4
            T(J) = NT
            GOTO 10
          END IF
6       CONTINUE
10    CONTINUE
11    WRITE (2,201) (LEADER(I),T(I),T1(I),T2(I),T3(I),T4(I),
     *  I=1,3)
      STOP
101   FORMAT(BZ,A12,4(1X,I2))
201   FORMAT(1H1,'FORTRAN 77 GOLF TOURNAMENT'///
     1  1H ,'THE FIRST THREE PLAYERS (IN ORDER) WERE:'//
     2  (1H ,A12,2X,'TOTAL:',I4,'(',3(I2,','),I2')'))
      END
```

The major difference between this and the earlier version concerns the loop for checking and moving the leaders, and it is instructive to examine this closely.

First, the player's total is compared with each of the three leader's in turn. If it is less than one of them a second, nested, loop is started. This moves the leaders from 2 down to J one place downwards. Thus if J was 1 (i.e. the player is to be the new leader) the second player moves to third place, and the first player to second; if J was 2 (i.e. the player is to be in second place) the second player moves to third place; if J was 3 (i.e. the player is to be in third place) then no moves are made because the DO-statement (DO 5,K=2,3,−1) has a zero trip count and the loop is not obeyed. Finally, the player's details are inserted in jth place, as required.

The other major differences are that the arrays are initialised in DATA statements very succinctly, and the results are printed using an implied-DO list.

9.6 A method of sorting the contents of an array

In Example 9.2 we saw how the use of arrays could greatly simplify the ordering of the leading three players in a golf tournament. However the program did not preserve the other scores, and the method used only worked with the rather (artificial) assumption that all the total scores (or, at any rate, the leading three) were different.

A far more general problem is that of sorting a set of data into some order, while preserving it all for subsequent use. Sorting is a subject into which much research has been carried out; however, for our purposes a simple general-purpose sorting method will suffice. If small amounts of data are to be sorted it is perfectly adequate; but if large amounts are to be sorted one of the many specialist sorting methods (e.g. *Quicksort*) should be used.

We shall investigate the method of 'Straight Selection', because it is reasonably efficient and easy to understand. Essentially the method involves searching through all the items to be sorted and finding the one which is to go at the head of the sorted list. This is then exchanged with the item currently at the head of the list. The process is then repeated starting immediately after the item just sorted into its correct place, and so on. Each time one more item is moved to its correct place. Fig. 9.7 shows the progress of such a sort, in which eight numbers are sorted so that the lowest is on the left and the highest is on the right. The two numbers to be exchanged at each stage are shown circled.

Initial order	⑦	①	8	4	6	3	5	2
1st change	1	⑦	8	4	6	3	5	②
2nd change	1	2	⑧	4	6	③	5	7
3rd change	1	2	3	④	6	8	5	7
4th change (no move)	1	2	3	4	⑥	8	⑤	7
5th change	1	2	3	4	5	⑧	⑥	7
6th change	1	2	3	4	5	6	⑧	⑦
7th change	1	2	3	4	5	6	7	8

Fig. 9.7 Sorting by straight selection

This is quite a simple method to code in Fortran, as we shall see in Example 9.3.

Example 9.3

Write a program which prints all the players in the golf tournament described in Example 7.2 in their finishing order (i.e. lowest score first, highest score last), together with their position.

Essentially this program merely requires us to sort the data into order of increasing score. However with six variables for each player, moving these about will take a considerable time. A much better way, therefore is to leave the player's data where it is and to sort a *pointer* to the data. We can do this by keeping one extra item for each player – their position in the original data. We can use this as a subscript to the arrays for names and scores. Our structure plan is therefore as follows

    1   Repeat the following
         1.1   Read name and scores for next player
         1.2   If name = 'END OF DATA' then exit
         1.3   Calculate total score for this player
         1.4   Store player's number
    2   Repeat the following for all unsorted places
         2.1   Find lowest remaining score
         2.2   Exchange pointer to it with pointer to first unsorted place
    3   Use pointers to print players in their final order

There are no particular problems here and so we can proceed with the program

```
      PROGRAM GOLF3
C  MAX DEFINES MAXIMUM NUMBER OF PLAYERS ALLOWED
      PARAMETER (MAX=100)
      CHARACTER*12 PLAYER(MAX)
      INTEGER T1(MAX),T2(MAX),T3(MAX),T4(MAX),T(MAX),N(MAX)
C  READ DATA
      DO 10, I=1,MAX
        READ (1,101) PLAYER(I),T1(I),T2(I),T3(I),T4(I)
        IF (PLAYER(I).EQ.'END OF DATA') GOTO 11
        T(I) = T1(I)+T2(I)+T3(I)+T4(I)
10      N(I) = I
      PRINT *,MAX,' PLAYERS AND NO TERMINATOR!'
C  SET NUM TO NUMBER OF PLAYERS
11 NUM = I-1
C  SORT POINTER ARRAY IN ORDER OF SCORES
      DO 20, I=1,NUM-1
        I1 = I
        LEAST = T(N(I))
        DO 15, J=I+1,NUM
          IF (T(N(J)).LT.LEAST) THEN
            I1 = J
            LEAST = T(N(J))
          END IF
15        CONTINUE
```

```
C  EXCHANGE POINTERS IF NECESSARY
         IF (I1.NE.I) THEN
            NTEMP = N(I)
            N(I) = N(I1)
            N(I1) = NTEMP
         END IF
   20    CONTINUE
C  PRINT RESULTS
         WRITE (2,201) (I,PLAYER(N(I)),T(N(I)),T1(N(I)),T2(N(I)),
      *  T3(N(I)),T4(N(I)),I=1,NUM)
         STOP
  101 FORMAT(BZ,A12,4(1X,I2))
  201 FORMAT(1H1,'FORTRAN 77 GOLF TOURNAMENT'///
      1 1H ,'FINAL ORDER AFTER FOUR ROUNDS'//
      2 (1H ,I3,A16,2X,'TOTAL:',I4,' (',3(I2,',',),I2,')'))
      END
```

There are several points to note in this program. First, the number of players is checked and a warning printed if 100 are read without a terminator. The variable NUM is set to the number of players read for use in the sorting phase. The array N (which is initialised during input) is then sorted into the correct order.

Notice that it is permissible to have an array element as a subscript to an array. I1 is set to the position of the head of the list of items still to be sorted, and LEAST is set to the total score of the player in that position. A nested loop then looks at all total scores of players after this and if it finds a lower score alters I1 and LEAST accordingly. When all items have been inspected I1 will contain the subscript of the element of the array N which points to the lowest remaining score. If I1 is the same as I then this is already at the head of the remaining items; if it is not then the pointers are exchanged.

Finally, the results are printed by using N(I) as a subscript to the players' details in an implied-DO list. Notice that the value of the implied-DO-variable can also be output, thus providing the finishing position. Fig. 9.8 shows the beginning of the results produced by this program

---

FORTRAN 77 GOLF TOURNAMENT

FINAL ORDER AFTER FOUR ROUNDS

```
 1    NICKLAUS      TOTAL: 278 (71,69,68,70)
 2    PLAYER        TOTAL: 279 (73,66,71,69)
 3    JACKLIN       TOTAL: 281 (68,71,71,71)
 4    PALMER        TOTAL: 282 (72,70,70,70)
 5    BALLESTEROS   TOTAL: 282 (65,71,74,72)
 6    WATSON        TOTAL: 282 (72,70,68,72)
 7    JAMES         TOTAL: 283 (71,71,70,71)
 8    FALDO         TOTAL: 283 (72,69,71,71)
 9    COLES         TOTAL: 283 (68,74,73,68)
10    LANGER        TOTAL: 284 (71,71,69,73)
```

Fig. 9.8 Results produced by GOLF3 program

One minor improvement could be made to this program. As can be seen from Fig. 9.8, if two or more players have the same score they are listed in an apparently random order. It would be more pleasing, perhaps if, in this situation, they were listed in alphabetic order.

Sorting each set of players who have the same total score into alphabetic order would be awkward and inefficient. A better way would be first to sort all the data into alphabetic order, and then to ensure that the relative order of players having the same score is not subsequently altered. Unfortunately the program to sort the scores does so by exchanging the 'next' player with the one at the 'head' of the unsorted part of the data, thus causing the original ordering to be completely destroyed. However, we can avoid this problem if all the players from the 'head' to the one before the 'next' player are moved down by one position, and then the 'next' player is inserted in his correct position.

This method is considerably less efficient than the original one, since it involves many more moves, but it will achieve our desired aim. The initial alphabetic sort can use the more efficient method, and the following code, inserted in place of the original sorting loop, will achieve the required result (where NAME is a variable which is declared as CHARACTER*12).

```
C   SORT POINTER ARRAY INTO ALPHABETIC ORDER OF NAMES
        DO 13, I=1,NUM-1
          I1 = I
          NAME = PLAYER(N(I))
          DO 12, J=I+1,NUM
            IF (PLAYER(N(J)).LT.NAME) THEN
              I1 = J
              NAME = PLAYER(N(J))
            END IF
12        CONTINUE
C   EXCHANGE POINTERS IF NECESSARY
          IF (I1.NE.I) THEN
            NTEMP = N(I1)
            N(I1) = N(I)
            N(I) = NTEMP
          END IF
13      CONTINUE
C   SORT POINTER ARRAY IN ORDER OF SCORES
        DO 20, I=1,NUM-1
          I1 = I
          LEAST = T(N(I))
          DO 15, J=I+1,NUM
            IF (T(N(J)).LT.LEAST) THEN
              I1 = J
              LEAST = T(N(J))
            END IF
15        CONTINUE
```

```
C  MOVE POINTERS IF NECESSARY
         IF (I1.NE.I) THEN
            NTEMP = N(I1)
            DO 16, J=I1,I+1,-1
  16           N(J) = N(J-1)
            N(I) = NTEMP
         END IF
  20     CONTINUE
```

Fig. 9.9 shows the result of running this improved program with the same data as Fig. 9.8.

```
FORTRAN 77 GOLF TOURNAMENT


FINAL ORDER AFTER FOUR ROUNDS

    1     NICKLAUS      TOTAL: 278 (71,69,68,70)
    2     PLAYER        TOTAL: 279 (73,66,71,69)
    3     JACKLIN       TOTAL: 281 (68,71,71,71)
    4     BALLESTEROS   TOTAL: 282 (65,71,74,72)
    5     PALMER        TOTAL: 282 (72,70,70,70)
    6     WATSON        TOTAL: 282 (72,70,68,72)
    7     COLES         TOTAL: 283 (68,74,73,68)
    8     FALDO         TOTAL: 283 (72,69,71,71)
    9     JAMES         TOTAL: 283 (71,71,70,71)
   10     LANGER        TOTAL: 284 (71,71,69,73)
```

Fig. 9.9   Sorted results from GOLF3 program

9.7   Arrays as embedded formats

A character expression can be used as an embedded format (see Chapter 7). It is also possible to use an array for this purpose. In this case, however, the format is considered to be a concatenation of *all* the elements of the array. Thus the two PRINT statements in the following program will produce identical results

```
PROGRAM IOEX
CHARACTER*25 F(10)
F(1) = '('
F(2) = '1H1,'
F(3) = '''THE RESULT OF DIVIDING'','
F(4) = 'I4,'
F(5) = '''BY'','
F(6) = 'I4,'
F(7) = '''IS'','
F(8) = 'F9.3'
```

```
      F(9) = ')'
      READ *,I,J
      X = REAL(I)/J
      PRINT 201,I,J,X
  201 FORMAT(1H1,'THE RESULT OF DIVIDING',I4,' BY',I4,' IS',
     *  F9.3)
      PRINT F,I,J,X
      STOP
      END
```

The use of a complete array to build up a variable format can be useful in some circumstances, especially when, as in Example 9.4 it is required to build up a complex format during the execution of the program from a number of separate elements. Hence we shall write the program for the next example using an array; the reader may wish to rewrite it using substrings.

Example 9.4

A common problem with programs concerned with geometric definition is that of printing the mathematical formulae defining the various surfaces, since these have a very wide range of formats. Write a simplified version of the printing element of such a program which takes its data as a number of items on separate lines and prints their interpretation as defined below.

The data consists of

(a) A name of up to six characters.
(b) An integer code = 1 for a point
                    = 2 for a line
                    = 3 for a circle
(c) Three real numbers, as defined below.

The results should consist of a single printed line in one of the following forms

        'name is the point (A, B, C)'
        'name is the line $AX + BY + C = 0$'
        'name is the circle $(X - A)^2 + (Y - B)^2 - R^2 = 0$'

where A, B, C and R are the real numbers read as data. There should be no unnecessary space (e.g. after names) and no multiple signs (e.g. +−5.0Y). All data values lie in the range −100.0 to +100.0 and are accurate to two places of decimals. A 'name' of **** indicates the end of data.

This example is an exercise in formatting, but nevertheless a structure plan will be useful

    1 Repeat the following
       1.1 Read name
       1.2 If name is **** then exit
       1.3 Read code, A, B and C (or R)
       1.4 Find length of 'name' (say L)
       1.5 Print name in first L chars, followed by 'is the'

1.6 If code = 1 then
    1.6.1. Print 'point (A, B)'
    but if code = 2 then
    1.6.2 Print 'line $AX + BY + C = 0$'
    but if code = 3 then
    1.6.3 Print 'circle $(X - A)^2 + (Y - B)^2 - R^2 = 0$'

We shall need to establish a means of deciding in what format to print the numbers to avoid extra spaces and/or multiple signs.

The extra spaces can be dealt with by determining the size of each number and using an appropriate field width. The multiple signs can be dealt with in a similar manner by not printing a + sign if the number is negative; however, a more elegant method is to use the SP edit descriptor (see Section 6.7) to insert either plus or minus signs as appropriate.

We can now proceed with the program.

```
      PROGRAM GEODAT
      CHARACTER*12 FORM(13),F1(10),FN(6)*3,FNUM(6)*5,F2(3)*5
      CHARACTER NAME*8
      INTEGER TYPE
      REAL A(3)
      DATA FORM/'(1H0,', 'A6,', ''' IS THE '',', 10*''/
      DATA F1/''' CIRCLE '',', '''('',', '''X'',',
     1        'SP,', 'F7.2,', ''')**2+(Y'',',
     2        'F7.2,', ''')**2'',', 'F7.2', '''=0''')'/
      DATA FN/'A1,', 'A2,', 'A3,', 'A4,', 'A5,', 'A6,'/
      DATA FNUM/'F4.2,', 'F5.2,', 'F6.2,', 'F7.2,',
     1         'F8.2,', 'F9.2,'/
C ALLOW FOR 1000 SURFACES
      DO 50, I=1,1000
        READ '(A6)',NAME
        IF (NAME.EQ.'****') GOTO 55
        READ '(BZ,I1/(F7.2))',TYPE,A
C FIND NUMBER OF CHARACTERS IN NAME BY SEARCHING FOR
C TWO SPACES
        N = INDEX(NAME,'  ')-1
C STORE A "N" EDIT DESCRIPTOR
        FORM(2) = FN(N)
C COPY MASTER FORMAT
        DO 10, J=1,10
10        FORM(J+3) = F1(J)
        IF (TYPE.EQ.1) THEN
C POINT
          FORM(4) = '''POINT'','
          FORM(7) = ''',''','
          FORM(9) = ''',''','
          FORM(11) = ''')''')'
        ELSE IF (TYPE.EQ.2) THEN
```

```
C  LINE
          FORM(4) = '''LINE '','
          FORM(9) = '''Y'','
          FORM(11) = ' '
          FORM(12) = ' '
       ELSE
C  CIRCLE
          A(1) = -A(1)
          A(2) = -A(2)
          A(3) = -A(3)**2
       END IF
C  FIND SIZES OF NUMBERS
       DO 20, J=1,3
          X = ABS(A(J))
          IF (X.LT.10.0) THEN
            N = 1
          ELSE IF (X.LT.100.0) THEN
            N = 2
          ELSE IF (X.LT.1000.0) THEN
            N = 3
          ELSE IF (X.LT.10000.0) THEN
            N = 4
          ELSE
            N = 5
          END IF
C  ADD 1 TO N IF NUMBER NEEDS A SIGN
          IF (A(J).LT.0.0 .OR. TYPE.EQ.3
      *        .OR.(TYPE.EQ.2 .AND. J.NE.1)) N = N+1
   20     F2(J) = FNUM(N)
C  INSERT F EDIT DESCRIPTORS IN FORMAT
       IF (TYPE.EQ.1) THEN
          FORM(6) = F2(1)
          FORM(8) = F2(2)
          FORM(10) = F2(3)
       ELSE IF (TYPE.EQ.2) THEN
          FORM(5) = F2(1)
          FORM(8) = F2(2)
          FORM(10) = F2(3)
       ELSE
          FORM(8) = F2(1)
          FORM(10) = F2(2)
          FORM(12) = F2(3)
       END IF
   50  PRINT FORM,NAME,A
   55 STOP
      END
```

A careful analysis of this program will show that most of the logic is concerned with identifying the length of the name of the surface and the size of the three numbers, and then creating A and F edit descriptors of the correct field width. The length of the name (maximum 6) is found by storing it in a variable (NAME) of length 8 and then using the intrinsic function INDEX to find the first of two consecutive spaces. If the length is 6 then these will be the two extra spaces added to make the length 8; however, if the name read was less than six characters, the first space will come after the last character of the name. It is therefore an easy matter to determine how many characters there are in the name.

The numbers are dealt with more easily since they must lie in the range -100.0 to $+100.0$ (apart from the constant term for the circle (R^2) which lies in the range 0 to 10000.0). It is a trivial matter, therefore, to determine the number of digits (including a sign) and hence the field width required.

The method used is to base all three formats (for circle, line and point) on that for a circle, and replace appropriate elements. This will leave many extra spaces between edit descriptors, which will be ignored. It will also leave two array elements (FORM(12) and FORM(13)) containing non-blank characters after the final right parenthesis for a point; these characters will be ignored. Essentially, therefore the program generates a format in one of the following three forms

```
(a)  (1H0,A6,' IS THE ','POINT ','(',F7.2,',',F7.2,',',
     F7.2,')')
(b)  (1H0,A6,' IS THE ','LINE ',F7.2,'X',SP,F7.2,'Y',
     F7.2,' ',' ','=0')
(c)  (1H0,A6,' IS THE ','CIRCLE ',
     '(','X',SP,F7.2,')**2+(Y',F7.2,')**2',F7.2,'=0')
```

with appropriate field widths for the A and F edit descriptors.

9.8 Multi-dimensional arrays

We have, so far, only considered an array as having a single subscript. This is not sufficient for many purposes (e.g. HT(N,M) could identify the height at grid position (N,M) in a set of geographical data), and Fortran 77 allows us to have up to *seven* subscripts for a single array. The number of subscripts is defined in the array declaration, and thus

```
INTEGER MARK(6,50)
```

defines an array (MARK) with two subscripts – the first running from 1 to 6, the second from 1 to 50. This array could also be declared in any of the following ways

```
INTEGER MARK(1:6,1:50)
DIMENSION MARK(6,50)
DIMENSION MARK(6,1:50)
INTEGER MARK(1:6,50)
etc.
```

In a similar way the array declaration

```
REAL C(100,100,0:3,0:3)
```

defines a real array with four subscripts – the first two running from 1 to 100 and the second two from 0 to 3. Such an array might be used in a surface-fitting program, in which the surface is split into up to 100 sections in both X and Y directions, and the equation of the surface in the rectangular area which is the I th in the X direction and the J th in the Y direction is given by

$$\sum_{\substack{N=0,3 \\ M=0,3}} C\ (I, J, N, M)\ X^N Y^M = 0$$

Note, however, that a multi-subscripted (or multi-dimensional) array can very rapidly use up the available memory and must be used with care. The array C, above has a size of 100 by 100 by 4 by 4, that is 160000 numeric storage units – rather more than the total memory available on many computers!

An element of a multi-dimensional array must always be written with the correct number of subscripts, and can, of course, be used in exactly the same way as a variable or an element of a single-subscripted array. We saw in Sections 9.4 and 9.5 how an implied-DO may be used to initialise, input or output part of a single-subscripted array. The same is true of a multi-dimensional array.

When we defined an implied-DO list as

(dlist,int=m1,m2,m3)

we said that dlist was a list of array element names. We can now extend this definition to state that it is a list of array element names and/or implied-DO lists for DATA statements, and a list of *any* input or output list items for input or output statements. Thus we may read data into the array MARK (as declared above) by a statement such as

    READ 101,((MARK(I,J),I=1,N),J=1,M)

where N is 6 or less and M is no more than 50 in order to keep within the declared bounds of the array.

However if we wish to use the name of the array without any subscripts in an input/output or DATA statement there is a slight problem. With a single-dimensional array the order in which the array elements are stored is quite obvious, but this is not so with a multi-dimensional array. For example the array MARK could be stored in the order

    MARK(1,1) MARK(2,1)...MARK(6,1) MARK(1,2)...

or it could be stored in the order

    MARK(1,1) MARK(1,2)...MARK(1,50) MARK(2,1)...

Clearly it is vital that we know which order is used if any data or initial values are to be provided in the correct sequence. The rule used in Fortran is that

- A multi-dimensional array is stored in the computer's memory in such a way that the first subscript changes most rapidly, the second next most rapidly, and so on, with the last subscript changing most slowly.

In the case of the array MARK this means that the first of the two alternatives above is the correct one

```
MARK(1,1) MARK(2,1)...MARK(6,1) MARK(1,2)...
```

This means that if enough data were supplied completely to fill the array MARK it would be provided in the same order. Since it is probable that the first subscript (in the range 1–6) will correspond to the exam and the second (in the range 1–50) to the student this would mean that all the marks for one pupil (MARK(1,1)...MARK(6,1)) would be followed by all the marks for the next pupil. If the data was available more readily with all the marks for one exam followed by all the marks for the next exam then either the array should be dimensioned

```
INTEGER MARK(50,6)
```

or an implied-DO list should be used

```
((MARK(I,J),J=1,50),I=1,6)
```

Example 9.5
Students in a particular institution have to sit twelve papers in their final examination, each of which is marked out of 100. They are awarded degrees of varying classes depending upon the following rules

(a) A student who *averages* over 75 % and who never gets less than 60 % is awarded a 'First';

(b) A student who does not obtain a First but who averages over 50 % and who never gets less than 30 % is awarded a 'Second';

(c) A student who does not obtain a First or a Second but who averages over 30 % is awarded a 'Third';

(d) A student who is not classified as First, Second or Third but who averages over 20 % and achieves at least 35 % on three papers is awarded a 'Pass'.

The results of each paper are provided separately, in alphabetic order of the candidates, all of whom attempt all papers. Write a program to read the results for each paper (name in columns 1–20, mark in columns 23–25) and to print the final class lists with the names in each class being given in alphabetic order. No marks are to be shown, but any student who achieves over 75 % in every paper is 'starred' with an asterisk before his/her name. The number of candidates is supplied as the first item of data, and will not exceed 150.

The structure plan for this program is quite a simple one – the major difficulty being the logic associated with classifying the students.

1   Initialise classes to 9 (failed!)
2   Read number of candidates (N)
3   If N>150 then fail with an error message
4   Repeat for each exam
    4.1   Repeat for each candidate
        4.1.1   Read next name and mark
5   Repeat for each candidate
    5.1   Calculate average mark
    5.2   If average >75 then
        5.2.1   Set class to -1 (to represent 'starred' 1st)
        5.2.2   Repeat for each exam
            5.2.2.1   If mark <75 then set class positive
            5.2.2.2   If mark <60 then set class to 9
    5.5   If class >1 (i.e. not a 'first') then
        5.6   If average >50 then
            5.6.1   Set class to 2
            5.6.2   Repeat for each exam
                5.6.2.1   If mark <30 then set class to 3
            otherwise if average >30 then
            5.6.3   Set class to 3
            otherwise if average >20 then
            5.6.4   Set class to 4 (to represent a 'pass')
            5.6.5   Set count to 0
            5.6.6   Repeat for each exam
                5.6.6.1   If mark >35 then increment count
            5.6.7   If count <3 then set class to 9 (failed)
6   Print lists of students in each class

Notice that the logic required to test for Firsts, Seconds, Thirds and Passes is very similar but not quite the same. In the next chapter we shall see how we can write our own subroutines; a suitable subroutine could then deal with all four cases, thereby considerably simplifying the overall structure as well as the actual program.

The structure of the data does not show in the structure plan. In this case we shall need four arrays – one for the candidates' names, one (two-dimensional) for their individual marks, one for their total marks (or their average), and one for their class. In the problem, and also in the structure plan, we have referred to the average mark. However the average mark is simply the total divided by 12 and therefore the logic would work equally well with the total marks, but without the need for a lot of (unnecessary) division. We shall adopt this simplification

```
PROGRAM FINALS
CHARACTER NAME(150)*20
INTEGER MARK(150,12),TOTAL(150),CLASS(150)
DATA CLASS/150*9/,TOTAL/150*0/
READ *,N
IF (N.GT.150) THEN
   PRINT 200,N
```

```
  200 FORMAT(1H1,'ERROR — MAXIMUM NUMBER OF CANDIDATES IS 150,',
     *    'NOT',I4)
        STOP
      END IF
      READ 101,((NAME(I),MARK(I,J),I=1,N),J=1,12)
  101 FORMAT(BZ,A20,2X,I3)
      DO 50, I=1,N
        DO 5, J=1,12
    5     TOTAL(I) = TOTAL(I)+MARK(I,J)
        IF (TOTAL(I).GT.900) THEN
C  FIRSTS MUST HAVE A TOTAL OF MORE THAN 900
          CLASS(I) = -1
C  CHECK INDIVIDUAL MARKS
          DO 10, J=1,12
            IF (MARK(I,J).LT.75) CLASS(I) = ABS(CLASS(I))
            IF (MARK(I,J).LT.60) CLASS(I) = 9
   10       CONTINUE
        END IF
        IF (CLASS(I).GT.1) THEN
          IF (TOTAL(I).GT.600) THEN
C  SECONDS MUST HAVE A TOTAL OF MORE THAN 600
          CLASS(I) = 2
C  CHECK INDIVIDUAL MARKS
            DO 15, J=1,12
              IF (MARK(I,J).LT.30) CLASS(I) = 3
   15         CONTINUE
          ELSE IF (TOTAL(I).GT.360) THEN
C  THIRDS MUST HAVE A TOTAL OF MORE THAN 360
          CLASS(I) = 3
          ELSE IF (TOTAL(I).GT.240) THEN
C  PASSES MUST HAVE A TOTAL OF MORE THAN 240
          CLASS(I) = 4
          M = 0
C  CHECK INDIVIDUAL MARKS
            DO 20, J=1,12
              IF (MARK(I,J).GE.35) M = M+1
   20         CONTINUE
C  SET CLASS TO 9 IF NOT ENOUGH PAPERS WITH 35%
            IF (M.LT.3) CLASS(I) = 9
          END IF
        END IF
   50   CONTINUE
```

(continued)

```
C  PRINT CLASS LISTS
      PRINT 201
      DO 60, I=1,N
        IF (CLASS(I).LT.2) THEN
          PRINT 202,NAME(I)
          IF (CLASS(I).LT.0) PRINT 203
        END IF
  60  CONTINUE
      PRINT 204
      DO 70, I=1,N
        IF (CLASS(I).EQ.2) PRINT 202,NAME(I)
  70  CONTINUE
      PRINT 205
      DO 80, I=1,N
        IF (CLASS(I).EQ.3) PRINT 202,NAME(I)
  80  CONTINUE
      PRINT 206
      DO 90, I=1,N
        IF (CLASS(I).EQ.4) PRINT 202,NAME(I)
  90  CONTINUE
      STOP
 201  FORMAT(1H1,
     *  'THE FOLLOWING ARE AWARDED FIRST CLASS HONOURS:'//)
 202  FORMAT(1H ,10X,A20)
 203  FORMAT(1H+,9X,'*')
 204  FORMAT(1H0,
     *  'THE FOLLOWING ARE AWARDED SECOND CLASS HONOURS:'//)
 205  FORMAT(1H0,
     *  'THE FOLLOWING ARE AWARDED THIRD CLASS HONOURS:'//)
 206  FORMAT(1H0,
     *  'THE FOLLOWING ARE AWARDED UNCLASSIFIED DEGREES:'//)
      END
```

Summary

- An array is an ordered set of array elements stored in consecutive memory locations.

- An array and the range of its subscripts must be declared.

- Arrays may have up to seven subscripts and are stored so that the first subscript changes fastest, then the next, and so on.

- Array elements are used in the same way as variables.

- An implied–DO in both DATA statements and input/output lists to specify several consecutive array elements.

- An unsubscripted array name in a DATA statement or input/output list represents a list of all the elements of the array.

Array declarations	type name(declarator),...
	e.g. `REAL A(100),B(10:50),C(-5:5)`
	`DIMENSION` name(declarator)
Initialising arrays	`DATA` array name / list of values /
	`DATA` (name(int),int=e1,e2,e3) / list of values /
Input and output of arrays	`READ` (control information list) array name
	`PRINT *,`(array name(int),int=el,e2,e3)

Fig. 9.10   Fortran 77 statements introduced in Chapter 9

Exercises

9.1   Write declarations for suitable arrays in which to store the following sets of data
   (a)   The names of the teams in a league of 22 teams and the number of matches won, drawn and lost to date.
   (b)   The names, sexes, ages, heights and weights of a maximum of 1000 respondents to a survey.
   (c)   The number of people aged 21, 22, 23, ..., 45 responding to the survey in (b), above.
   (d)   The names and scores of the 11 members of a cricket team during a season of 17 two-innings matches.

9.2   Write suitable statements to initialise all the arrays defined in question 9.1.

9.3   A football league consists of 16 teams. After each match 3 points are awarded for a win and 1 point for a draw. Write a program to read the results of a number of matches and to print the number of matches won, drawn and lost by each team together with the number of points earned. The results should be read in a fixed format in the form

```
LIVERPOOL 0 SHEFFIELD UTD 6
```

9.4   Modify the program written in question 9.3 so that the results are sorted into order with the team having the most points at the top. If two teams have the same number of points their order is determined by the difference between goals scored and goals conceded.

9.5   A survey of wild-life in a particular area has divided the area into a grid of regions each $100\,m^2$, forming a rectangle 2 km × 3 km. The small regions are identified by a co-ordinate system in which they are numbered from 0 to 29 West–East and from 0 to 19 South–North; thus region (12,7) is the region whose South West corner is 1200m East of the 'origin' and 700m North of it (where the 'origin' is the South West corner of the larger area). For each region the number of fox-holes, badger-setts and squirrel-nests has been recorded in the form of the co-ordinates of the region (in columns 1,2 and 4,5) followed by three counts of the form

nn **BADGERS**   (or **FOXES** or **SQUIRRELS**)

where nn is in columns 11,12 (and 26,27 and 41,42), BADGERS, etc. is in columns 14–23 (and 29–38 and 44–53)
e.g.

12 14   11 FOXES   14 BADGERS   9 SQUIRRELS

Unfortunately not all the recorders put the animals in the same order. Write a program to read this data and to produce the following analyses.
(a) The total population of each type of animal (assuming one per nest, hole or sett).
(b) The region or regions with the highest population of each type of animal.
(c) The region or regions with the lowest population of each type of animal.

9.6 Students in an exam each sit 5 papers. There are no more than 100 students in all (the exact number will be provided as data) and the names and marks for each paper are provided in the same order. Write a program which reads the names and marks for each paper and then prints the results in order of their average mark for the five papers. Any student who obtains over 70% for each paper is awarded a distinction which should be shown on the list. Any student who averages less than 30% has failed and should be omitted from the list.

9.7 A class contains ten pupils called Alfred, Beatrice, Charles, Diana, Elizabeth, Fiona, George, Henry, Isobel and Jonathon. Each pupil sits exams in Arithmetic, Biology, Chemistry, Divinity, English, French, Geography and History. Mark sheets have been prepared in the following form

Columns   1–9   Name
Columns 11–20 Exam
Columns 22–24 Mark

This data is in a random order and is terminated by a record containing **END DATA** in columns 1–8. It has been decreed that all those with worse than the average mark for an exam will fail. Write a program to read the data and print a table showing which exams each pupil has passed.

Functions and Subroutines

10.1 Procedures, subprograms and their use

Many of our program examples have required some process to be carried out which we either did not wish to define in detail (such as the graph-plotting in Example 5.3), or which required some 'standard' procedures to be carried out (such as calculating a square root or finding the largest of a set of values). In these situations we have used *procedures* of two different types – subroutines and (intrinsic) functions.

A subroutine is accessed by means of a CALL statement which gives the name of the subroutine and a list of *arguments* which will be used to transmit information between the (main) program and the subroutine

        CALL name(arg1,arg2,...)

The CALL statement causes a *transfer of control* so that instead of obeying the next statement in the program, the computer obeys the statements contained within the subroutine 'name'. When the subroutine has completed its task it returns to the calling program ready to obey the next statement. Some of the arguments may be used to return 'results', where this is appropriate.

A function, however, operates rather differently. It is referenced in the same way as a variable or array element simply by writing its name, followed by any arguments it may have, enclosed in parentheses. The execution of the function differs markedly from that of a subroutine. It returns a value (the *function value*) which is available as the value of the function reference, just as writing the name of a variable or array element provides a value – the value stored in a particular memory location. A function reference, therefore, is not a complete statement like a subroutine CALL but is part of an expression, and may appear anywhere that an expression may appear (e.g. on the right-hand side of an assignment statement, in an output list, as an argument to a subroutine call or function reference, etc.). We have used a number of intrinsic functions, which are defined within the Fortran language, but we may also reference other functions in the same way

        var = funl(arg1,arg2,...)
        PRINT*,fun1(arg1,arg2,...)
        CALL sub1(fun1(arg1,arg2,...),a2,a3,...)
        var = fun2(fun1(arg1,arg2,...),a2,a3,...)

If a subroutine has no arguments then we simply give the subroutine name in the CALL statement

    CALL sub

However, if a function has no arguments (which is an unusual, though not impossible, situation) then we must include the parentheses

    var = fun()

This is because, as we discussed in Chapter 9, the Fortran compiler recognises that a name followed by a left parenthesis is either a reference to an array element or a function reference, and uses the presence or absence of an array declaration to decide which. If the parentheses were omitted it would require a completely different approach.

Subroutines and functions are the two main types of procedures that are available in Fortran. Functions are further subdivided into three different types – intrinsic functions, external functions and statement functions. A complete list of intrinsic functions and their use is found in Appendix A. The other two types will be discussed in some detail in Sections 10.6 and 10.7.

Subroutines and *external* functions are also known as *subprograms*, together with a third type (Block Data subprograms – see Chapter 11). The three types of subprogram, together with the *main program*, are known as *program units*.

10.2 Programs and program units

Up to this point we have not concerned ourselves with subprograms and have considered our programs to consist of a sequence of statements starting with an optional PROGRAM statement and finishing with an END statement, as shown in Fig. 10.1. More correctly, we should now define this as the *main program unit*. We can also have subprogram program units of the three types referred to in Section 10.1. A *subroutine program unit* (see Fig. 10.2) has exactly the same overall structure except that the first statement is a SUBROUTINE statement (see Section 10.3). Similarly an *external function program unit* (see Fig. 10.3) begins with a FUNCTION statement, as described in Section 10.6, but otherwise has the same structure as a main program or a subroutine. A *block data program unit* (see Fig. 10.4) is also essentially the same, except that it does not contain any executable statements (it is described in Section 11.5).

    PROGRAM name
         .
         .
         .
       Specification statements, etc.
         .
         .
         .
       Executable statements
         .
         .
         .
    END

Fig. 10.1 A main program unit

```
SUBROUTINE  name(arg,...)
        .
        .
    Specification statements, etc.
        .
        .
    Executable statements
        .
        .
END
```

Fig. 10.2   A subroutine program unit

```
FUNCTION  name(arg,...)
        .
        .
    Specification statements, etc.
        .
        .
    Executable statements
        .
        .
END
```

Fig. 10.3   An external function program unit

```
BLOCK DATA  name
        .
        .
    Specification statements, etc.
        .
        .
END
```

Fig. 10.4   A block data program unit

A program can, therefore, consist of a number of different program units, of which exactly one must be a main program unit. Execution of the program will start at the beginning of the main program unit.

There may be any number of subprogram units in a complete program and one of the most important concepts of Fortran is that one program unit is never aware of any other program unit. The only link between a 'calling program' and a subprogram is through the name of the subprogram and the arguments and/or function value, and this link is only completed (after compilation has finished) when the full program is loaded ready for execu-

204 FORTRAN 77 PROGRAMMING

tion. This very important principle means that it is possible to write subprograms totally independently of the main program, and so opens up the way for 'libraries' of subprograms.

10.3 Writing subroutines

In Fig. 10.2 we see that a subroutine subprogram (or simply a subroutine) starts with an initial SUBROUTINE statement, which consists of the word SUBROUTINE followed by the name of the subroutine, followed where appropriate by a list of names enclosed in parentheses

SUBROUTINE name(a1,a2,...)

These names are called *dummy arguments* and represent the *actual arguments* which will appear in a CALL statement.

If the subroutine has no arguments then the initial statement is simply

SUBROUTINE name

The rest of the subroutine is exactly the same as in the (main) programs we have been writing up to now, but with the addition of one new statement

RETURN

This statement does exactly what it says and causes a return to the calling program, enabling execution to continue at the statement immediately after the CALL statement which transferred control to the subroutine.

```
      SUBROUTINE SORT(NUM,N)
      INTEGER NUM(100)
      DO 10, I=1,N-1
        IMIN = I
        NMIN = NUM(I)
        DO 5, J=I+1,N
          IF (NUM(J).LT.NMIN) THEN
            IMIN = J
            NMIN = NUM(J)
          END IF
    5     CONTINUE
C EXCHANGE NUMBERS IF NECESSARY
        IF (IMIN.NE.I) THEN
          NUM(IMIN) = NUM(I)
          NUM(I) = NMIN
        END IF
   10   CONTINUE
C ARRAY NOW SORTED - SO RETURN
      RETURN
      END
```

Fig. 10.5 A subroutine to sort integers

Fig. 10.5 shows a complete subroutine which sorts an integer array into increasing order (i.e. with the lowest value in the first element and the highest value in the last).

There are several important points to be learned from an examination of this subroutine. The first of these concerns the names used for the variables and for the dummy arguments (NUM and N). These names are all *local* names and are meaningful only within the subroutine. Each subprogram is unaware of any others, and this locality of variable names is probably the most important consequence of this. More formally, the *scope* of the names of any such variables, arrays or dummy arguments in a program unit is the extent of that program unit, and no more. (We had a similar, though more restricted, example of the scope of a variable where the scope of the implied-DO-variable is the extent of the implied-DO only.)

This means that the variables I, J, IMIN and NMIN in the subroutine SORT, refer only to their use within that subroutine. We may (and probably do) have variables called I (or any of the others) in some, or all, of the other program units without the least confusion, because each other I has a different scope (i.e. it is only defined in some other program unit).

The dummy arguments NUM and N are slightly different because, although the names are defined only within the subroutine (just like I, J, IMIN and NMIN) the actual memory locations are also accessible from the calling program. We can illustrate this most easily by referring to Fig. 10.6, which shows a suitable test program for the subroutine SORT. In this program the array of integers is called A and the number of integers is called NUM, whereas in the subroutine they are called NUM and N, respectively. Thus in the subroutine SORT the array NUM is merely another (local) name for the array called A in the main program, and N is another (local) name for the integer called NUM in the main program. Within the subroutine the array NUM and the integer N can be used just as though they were purely local variables like I, J, IMIN and NMIN; however, on entry to the subroutine they contain the values set up in A and NUM by the main program, and on return to the main program their values are accessible by the main program in the same way. This relationship between actual arguments (A and NUM in this case) and dummy arguments (NUM and N in this case) is the key to writing and using subprograms and we shall examine it in more detail in the next section (10.4).

```
      PROGRAM SORTST
      INTEGER A(200)
      READ *,NUM,(A(I),I=1,NUM)
      CALL SORT(A,NUM)
      PRINT 201,(A(I),I=1,NUM)
  201 FORMAT(1H1,'SORTED NUMBERS:'//(1H ,10I10))
      STOP
      END
```

Fig. 10.6 A test program for subroutine SORT

There is one more interesting thing to note about the subroutine SORT, and this is the form of the array declaration. Since NUM is an array it must be declared; however, since it is only another name for the array **A** in the main program no space needs to be reserved for it in the memory. Nevertheless, the declaration is required so that **NUM** is recognised as an array and not thought to be an external function. There is, however, a conflict over the size of the array, for in Fig. 10.5 the array **NUM** is defined as having subscripts from 1 to 100, whereas in Fig. 10.6 the (same) array **A** is defined with subscripts up to 200. There are several solutions to this impasse which we shall discuss in Section 10.4; for the present we shall ignore this problem (which is, in fact, only a problem if the compiler inserts code to check for the subscript going 'out of bounds').

There are no restrictions on what may be done in a subroutine, and a subroutine can, therefore, carry out input or output or use other subroutines or functions in just the same way as can the main program. The only slight restriction is that a subroutine is not allowed to call itself, or to call another subroutine or function which (directly or indirectly) may cause a call to the calling subroutine. The calling of a subroutine by itself is called *recursion* and can be a useful facility in some situations. In Fortran, recursion is not allowed, and any recursive calls will lead to a failure of the program (often, if not detected, through the program going into an infinite loop in which it keeps 'returning' to itself).

It is important that we understand the implications of the relationship between the dummy arguments in the subroutine and the actual arguments in the **CALL** statement.

10.4   Actual arguments and dummy arguments

The initial **SUBROUTINE** statement normally contains a list of dummy arguments, enclosed in parentheses. A **CALL** to that subroutine contains a list of actual arguments which must agree, exactly, with the dummy arguments with respect to the number of arguments and their types. During the execution of a **CALL** statement the locations of the actual arguments in the memory will be passed to the subroutine in such a way as to enable the dummy arguments to refer to the same memory locations as did the actual arguments.

An actual argument may be any of the following

   (i)   a constant
  (ii)   a variable name
 (iii)   an array element name
 (iv)   a character substring
  (v)   an expression
 (vi)   an array name
(vii)   an intrinsic function name
(viii)   an external procedure name (subroutine or function)
 (ix)   a dummy procedure name
  (x)   an alternate return specifier (see below)

A dummy argument may be any of the following

(a)   a variable name (for types (i)–(v))
(b)   an array name (for types (vi) and (iii))
(c)   a dummy procedure name (for types (vii)–(ix))
(d)   an asterisk (for type (x))

If the dummy argument is a *variable name* then the actual argument may be a constant, a variable name, an array element name, a character substring or an expression, as long as it is of the correct type or delivers a result of the correct type. Thus if a subroutine is defined with the initial statement

```
SUBROUTINE EXAMPL(A,B,I,N)
```

then any of the following would be acceptable CALL statements (where IA is an integer array)

```
CALL EXAMPL(1.0,2.5,IA(5),0)
CALL EXAMPL(X,Y*SIN(Z),MAX(N1,N2,N3),N4)
CALL EXAMPL(P,Q,I,IA(I))
etc.
```

If the dummy argument is a *character variable* then it must, of course, be declared as such and must be given a length. This length must be less than or equal to the length of the actual argument; if it is less than the length of the actual argument then only the left-most 'len' characters will be treated as the dummy argument (where 'len' is the length of the dummy argument). This can cause problems in a general subroutine and a special form of character declaration is therefore available for dummy arguments, in which the length of the character variable is written as (*); this causes the length of the dummy argument to be defined as being the same as that of the actual argument

```
SUBROUTINE SUB(N,C,X)
CHARACTER C*(*)
        .
        .
        .
        .
```

As a general rule, unless the length of a dummy argument can never change (e.g. a code of fixed length) it is advisable to declare all character dummy arguments in this way to ensure that everything works correctly. If it is required to know the actual length then the intrinsic function LEN may be used.

If the dummy argument is an *array* then, as we have already seen, we have a potential problem over its size. We may deal with this in two ways. The first is to declare the dummy array with one or more of its dimensions containing a variable name, provided that any such variable name is also a dummy argument of the same subroutine (or appears in a COMMON block in that subroutine (see Chapter 11)). Thus we may write

```
SUBROUTINE DEMO(A,B,N)
REAL A(N),B(4,N)
        .
        .
        .
        .
```

This type of declaration is called an *adjustable array declaration*, because the size of the array is adjusted each time the subroutine is called.

The second way is to declare the dummy array with its *last* subscript defined by an asterisk

```
SUBROUTINE DEMO2(A,B,C)
REAL A(*),B(4,*),C(0:5,6,*)
    .
    .
    .
    .
```

This type of declaration is called an *assumed-size array declaration*, because the array is assumed to be large enough for all references that are made to it, and does not have any defined size. Because its size is unknown, an assumed-size dummy array name cannot be used as an item in an input/output list (where its unknown size should determine the number of items to be read or written) or as an embedded format (where its unknown number of elements should be concatenated to create the format).

It is important to understand that only the last dimension declarator of an assumed-size array declarator may be an asterisk. We can see why this is so by considering the storage of the array B, above. Since the first subscript changes fastest the order of storage is

```
B(1,1)  B(2,1)  B(3,1)  B(4,1)  B(1,2)  B(2,2)...
```

As long as it is only the last subscript whose maximum size is unknown there is no problem, but clearly if the limits for any other subscript were unknown it would be impossible to determine the location of any element of the array.

If a dummy argument is an array (with either constant, adjustable or assumed size) then the actual argument may be an array, an array element or an array element substring. If the actual argument is a non-character array name then, as long as it is not larger than the dummy array, everything is straightforward and the first element of the dummy array is the same as the first element of the actual array, and so on. This does not, however, mean that the subscripts need to be the same, or even that there need to be the same number of subscripts. Fig. 10.7 shows a program extract which contains several calls to the subroutine ARRARG. The dummy array A has two subscripts, whereas the actual array (X) in the first call has only one and the actual array (Y) in the second has two, but with very different ranges for its subscripts. The following correspondence, therefore, will exist between various elements of these arrays during the first two calls to the subroutine

```
A(1,1) and X(1)  or Y(0,-10) as appropriate
A(6,1) and X(6)  or Y(5,-10) as appropriate
A(7,1) and X(7)  or Y(0,-9) as appropriate
A(9,1) and X(9)  or Y(2,-9) as appropriate
A(1,2) and X(10) or Y(3,-9) as appropriate
A(5,4) and X(32) or Y(1,-5) as appropriate
A(9,6) and X(54) or Y(5,-2) as appropriate
```

```
PROGRAM MAIN
REAL X(100),Y(0:5,-10:10)
   .
   .
   .
CALL ARRARG(X)
CALL ARRARG(Y)
CALL ARRARG(X(15))
CALL ARRARG(Y(3,0))
   .
   .
   .
END

SUBROUTINE ARRARG(A)
REAL A(9,6)
   .
   .
   .
END
```

Fig. 10.7   Arrays as dummy arguments

If the actual argument is a non-character array element name then the dummy argument is associated with it in such a way that the first element of the dummy array is the same as the actual (array element) argument. The second two calls to the subroutine ARRARG in Fig. 10.7 use this form of actual argument with the following correspondences during the execution of the subroutine

A(1,1) and X(15) or Y(3,0) as appropriate
A(4,1) and X(18) or Y(0,1) as appropriate
A(9,1) and X(23) or Y(5,1) as appropriate
A(1,2) and X(24) or Y(0,2) as appropriate
A(5,4) and X(46) or Y(4,5) as appropriate
A(9,6) and X(68) or Y(2,9) as appropriate

If the dummy argument is a character array things get more complicated because as well as the array subscripts the length of the array elements must also be considered. In fact a slightly different arrangement holds here and can be best understood if we consider how a character array is stored in the memory. Fig. 10.8 shows part of an actual array (A) which consists of 10 elements, each of length 6; the total length of the array is thus 60 characters. It also shows a dummy array (D) which consists of 15 elements, each of length 4. If the array name A is the actual argument then the first *character* of the first element of A is the same as the first character of the first element of D (see Fig. 10.8). We can readily see that although there is a correspondence between characters there is no correspondence between array elements unless both arrays have the same length declared for their elements. If the actual argument is an array element or an array element substring, then the first character of the element or substring corresponds to the first character position of the dummy array. In all cases the dummy argument array must not extend beyond the end of the actual argument array.

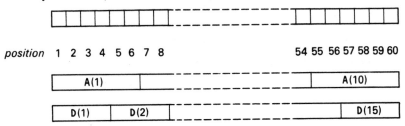

Fig. 10.8 Correspondence between character array arguments

If the length of the dummy array is declared as (∗) then each element of that array will have the same length as each element of the actual argument array. Notice that even in this case correspondence between array elements is not assured, for example when the actual argument is a substring of an array

```
      PROGRAM MAIN
         .
         .
         .
      CALL ALTRET(*10,X,Y,*20,*99,N)
    5 .....
         .
         .
   10 .....
         .
         .
   20 .....
         .
         .
   99 .....
         .
         .
      END

      SUBROUTINE ALTRET(*,A,B,*,*,N)
         .
         .
      RETURN J
         .
         .
      END
```

Fig. 10.9 Alternative return from a subroutine

element which does not start at the first character of that array element.

Most arguments to subroutines fall into one of the two broad categories above in which the dummy argument is either a variable or an array. However there are two other types of dummy argument possible – a dummy procedure and an asterisk.

A *dummy procedure* is a means whereby the name of an intrinsic function, a subroutine or an external function may be passed to a subroutine or function as an argument. This has one or two further implications which are described in Section 10.5.

Finally we may use an *asterisk* as a dummy argument in association with a special form of actual argument which allows alternative places for the subroutine to return to. These are specified in the list of actual arguments by writing *label, where 'label' is a statement label in the same program unit as the CALL statement. In the subroutine an extended form of the RETURN statement is used in which the word RETURN is followed by an integer expression

       RETURN intexp

```
      PROGRAM MAIN
         .
         .
         .
      CALL ALTRET(X,Y,N,IRET)
      GOTO (10,20,99),IRET
    5 .....
         .
         .
   10 .....
         .
         .
   20 .....
         .
         .
   99 .....
         .
         .
      END

      SUBROUTINE ALTRET(A,B,N,J)
         .
         .
      RETURN
         .
         .
      END
```

Fig. 10.10   An equally bad alternative to Fig. 10.9

If the value of the expression when the RETURN is obeyed is one, then a return is made to the statement labelled with the actual argument label which corresponds to the first asterisk dummy argument; if it is two a return to the second is made, and so on. If the value of the expression is less than one or greater than the number of asterisks in the dummy argument list, then a normal RETURN is made to the statement following the CALL statement. Fig. 10.9 illustrates this process, and it can be seen that if J has the value one then a 'return' will be made to the statement labelled 10, if it is 2 the return will be to label 20, and if it is 3 execution will continue from label 99. If J is less than 1 or greater than 3 then execution will continue from the next statement, i.e. the one labelled 5.

   In fact the use of this facility is normally to be deplored. It serves no particularly useful purpose since exactly the same effect can be obtained, with a greater degree of flexibility by returning the value of J through an additional argument

        SUBROUTINE ALTRET (A,B,N,J)

thus allowing the calling program to preserve a good, well-planned structure. The alternate return is essentially the same as returning the value J and using it in a computed GOTO (see Fig. 10.10) and is not recommended for precisely the same reasons as were given in Section 5.6 when the reader was advised against using that statement.

Example 10.1
As part of a research project, into various types of mental disorder, a psychiatrist wishes to analyse the frequency with which his patients repeat words. To this end he has recorded his consultations with his patients and has arranged to have these recordings transcribed onto 80-columns punched cards. Before starting to write the analysis part of his program he wishes to ensure that he can read these cards and split their contents into words. Assuming that no words are of more than twelve letters, that each word is separated from its neighbours by at least one space, and that words are not split between cards, write and test a subroutine which will read the data from cards and store it as individual, left-justified, words in an array. ('Left-justified' means that each word starts in position 1 of an element of the array, with extra spaces on the right if necessary.) There will never be more than 1500 words for one patient, and the data will be terminated by a blank card.

This is a good example of the step-by-step approach to program development and testing (and is based on a real project known to the author). In the Intermission (pages 130–134) we saw that this was a sensible way to develop a large program; however, the use of subroutines makes it very much easier. Our initial structure plan might look like this

   1 Repeat the following
      1.1 Read the next card
      1.2 If it is blank then exit
      1.3 Repeat up to 40 times

1.3.1 Extract the next word (if there is one)
1.3.2 If end of card reached then exit
1.3.3 Store word in next element of array
1.3.4 If 1500 words read then exit from *both* loops
2 Return array and number of words

This is fairly straightforward apart from steps 1.3 and 1.3.1. Step 1.3 says 'repeat up to 40 times' because there can be no more than 40 words separated by spaces on an 80-column card (and only then if they are all single-letter words!). Step 1.3.1 however is more complicated, although it is quite clear that this (extracting the next word) is what we want to do. Since it is more difficult we shall put it in another subroutine

1 Initialise a blank 12-character word and count of characters
2 Repeat the following from current position to 80
   2.1 Get next character
   2.2 If it is not blank then exit
3 Store character at beginning of word
4 If current position is 80 then
   4.1 Set end-of-card flag
   4.2 Return with word
   otherwise
   4.3 Repeat from current position to 80
      4.3.1 Get next character
      4.3.2 If it is blank then exit
      4.3.3 Store character in next position in word
      4.3.4 If 12 characters stored then exit
   4.4 If current position is 80 then set end-of-card flag
   4.5 Return with word

This subroutine will examine a single card from the current position to the end. It will first ignore any spaces until it finds a non-space character. It will then store successive characters until a blank is found to end the word. If at any stage the 80th column is processed in this way it is treated as the end of a word. The subroutine looks like this

```
      SUBROUTINE SPLIT(CARD,NPOS,WORD,END)
      CHARACTER CARD*80,WORD*12,CHAR
      LOGICAL END
      END = .FALSE.
      WORD = ' '
      DO 10, I=NPOS,80
         CHAR = CARD(I:I)
         IF (CHAR.NE.' ') GOTO 11
10    CONTINUE
11    WORD(1:1) = CHAR
      NC = 2
      IF (I.GE.80) THEN
         END = .TRUE.
         NPOS = 81
         RETURN
```

```
      ELSE
        DO 15, J=I+1,80
          CHAR = CARD(J:J)
          IF (CHAR.EQ.' ') GOTO 16
          WORD(NC:NC) = CHAR
          NC = NC+1
          IF (NC.GT.12) GOTO 16
  15      CONTINUE
  16    IF (J.GE.80) END = .TRUE.
        NPOS = J+1
        RETURN
      END IF
      END
```

We see that CARD and NPOS are used to give information to the subroutine, and WORD and END to return the next word and an indication of whether the card is fully examined yet. NPOS is also used to return the position of the *next* character in CARD. This subroutine is not yet foolproof, however the detail checks (e.g. to take some more definite action if a 12-letter word is read) woud merely hide the overall structure and ideally should not be necessary (which does not excuse their omission in real life). There is one point to note, namely that if the remainder of the card is blank then the subroutine will return a blank word. We must eliminate this in the calling routine.

We can test this very simply by use of the following test program

```
      PROGRAM TEST1
      CHARACTER CARD*80,WORD(40)*12
      LOGICAL END
C   READ CARDS UNTIL ONE IS BLANK
      DO 10, I=1,500
        READ '(A80)',CARD
        IF (CARD.EQ.' ') GOTO 11
        N = 1
        DO 5, J=1,40
          CALL SPLIT(CARD,N,WORD(J),END)
          IF (END) GOTO 6
  5       CONTINUE
  6     PRINT 201,CARD,(WORD(K),K=1,J)
  10    CONTINUE
  11 STOP
 201 FORMAT(1H0,'CARD READ WAS:'/1H ,A80/
     *  1H ,'WORDS ARE ',6A15/(1H ,10X,6A15))
      END
```

This program can be used to test SPLIT with various combinations of words and spaces. Once it is fully tested the main subroutine can be written and tested

```
      SUBROUTINE WORDS(WORD,N,MAXWDS)
      CHARACTER WORD(MAXWDS)*12,CARD*80
```

```
      LOGICAL END
      N = 1
      DO 50, I=1,MAXWDS
        READ '(A80)',CARD
        IF (CARD.EQ.' ') GOTO 60
        NPOS = 1
        DO 25, J=1,40
          CALL SPLIT(CARD,NPOS,WORD(N),END)
          IF (WORD(N).NE.' ') N = N+1
          IF (END) GOTO 50
          IF (N.GT.MAXWDS) GOTO 60
  25    CONTINUE
  50  CONTINUE
  60 N = N-1
      RETURN
      END
```

Note that SPLIT is called in such a way as to cause it to place the next word directly into the next element of the array WORD. However, the subscript to the array is only incremented if this word is not all blank, thus ensuring that the blank words returned at the end of a card are overwritten.

Once again, testing is simple now that SPLIT is known to work

```
      PROGRAM TEST2
      CHARACTER WORD(1500)*12
      CALL WORDS(WORD,N,1500)
      PRINT 201,N,(WORD(I),I=1,N)
 201 FORMAT(1H1,I4,' WORDS WERE READ AS FOLLOWS:'//
     *  (1H ,6A15))
      STOP
      END
```

10.5 Procedures as arguments

In addition to expressions (including variables, constants, etc.), array names and alternate return specifiers, Fortran 77 allows a calling program to pass the names of procedures to a subroutine by means of its arguments. Before this can be done the subroutine, external function or intrinsic function names must appear in one of two special specification statements which tell the compiler that the names are the names of procedures. The first of these statements declares a list of names to be those of external procedures (subroutines or functions) and takes the form

    EXTERNAL proc1,proc2,...

The second declares a list of names to be intrinsic functions

    INTRINSIC fun1,fun2,...

The latter declaration is necessary because, as we saw in Example 9.3, it is permissible to have a variable or array of the same name as an intrinsic function. Thus in the absence of an INTRINSIC statement declaring SIGN to be an intrinsic function, the statement

```
CALL SUB(A,B,SIGN)
```

will assume SIGN to be a real variable (unless it is declared to be something else). However, if the declaration

```
INTRINSIC SIGN
```

appears at the start of the program unit then the CALL statement will pass the name of the intrinsic function SIGN to the subroutine SUB. It follows that if a name appears in an INTRINSIC declaration it must not appear in any other specification statement in the same program unit, or be used in any way other than as an intrinsic function in that program unit.

The EXTERNAL statement is similar, and declares that the names given in the statement are those of external procedures. In this case the compiler, as we have seen, is not aware of their existence and the reason for the declaration is more obvious. If the name of an intrinsic function appears in an EXTERNAL statement it refers to an external procedure and the intrinsic function is not available in that program unit. Thus the declaration

```
EXTERNAL LOG
```

will mean that any reference to LOG (as a subroutine or as a function) will refer to an external procedure LOG and that the intrinsic function of the same name cannot be used. Thus if a library of subroutines contains a procedure called LOG then it can be used without any confusion; it also means that the programmer can provide his own LOG function (for example using a different method of evaluation or to a different base).

If an actual argument is a procedure name (which must appear in an EXTERNAL or INTRINSIC statement) then the corresponding dummy argument must be a dummy procedure. A dummy procedure is a name which either will be identified as a subroutine or function name because of its context (i.e. it appears after CALL or is followed by a left parenthesis when it has not been declared as an array) or which appears in an EXTERNAL statement. Thus the name of a procedure may be passed through several subroutines, as can be seen in Fig. 10.11. Notice that, although LOG and SQRT are intrinsic functions and are declared as such in the main program, once a procedure has been passed to one subroutine it is a dummy procedure so far as that subroutine is concerned and, if declared, must be declared as EXTERNAL. Thus in Fig. 10.11 we see that both SUB and FUN appear in an EXTERNAL statement in a subroutine SUB1. In subroutine SUB2, however, SUB appears in a CALL statement and F appears followed by a left parenthesis (and is not declared as an array); no EXTERNAL declaration is required therefore in subroutine SUB2.

There is one (small) restriction on the names of intrinsic functions which may appear as actual arguments, namely that the names of intrinsic functions for type conversion (INT, REAL, etc.), lexical comparison (LGE, LGT, etc.), or maximum and minimum (MAX, MIN, etc.) must not be passed to another

```
PROGRAM MAIN
EXTERNAL ANALYS
INTRINSIC SQRT,LOG
   .
   .
CALL SUB1(ANALYS,SQRT,A,B)
   .
   .
END

SUBROUTINE SUB1(SUB,FUN,X,Y)
EXTERNAL SUB,FUN
   .
   .
CALL SUB2(N,X,FUN,SUB)
   .
   .
END

SUBROUTINE SUB2(N,A,F,SUB)
   .
   .
CALL SUB(A,N,F(X+2))
   .
   .
END
```

Fig. 10.11   An example of procedures as arguments

subroutine in this way. In practice these are not the names one would be likely to want to use in this way, so the restriction is unlikely to cause any difficulty.

There are a number of situations in which it is useful to have procedure names as arguments, of which one of the most common arises when writing general purpose subroutines. Such subroutines may be stored in a 'library' on the backing store of a computer for general or for private use, and are a valuable aid to programming. Frequently large libraries are available in specialised areas such as numerical analysis or graphics and may be incorporated into any program that requires them. If a subroutine in such a library requires some special action to be carried out which is dependent upon the particular computer and/or program it can call a subroutine whose name has been passed to it as an argument.

Example 10.2
The intrinsic functions for trigonometrical functions (SIN, COS, ASIN, etc.) operate in radians. Write a general purpose subroutine which will calculate the sine (or cosine or tangent) of an angle whose value is given in degrees, minutes and seconds of arc and will give the arcsine (or arccos or arctangent) of a real value in the same way. (For non-mathematicians, 2π radians = 360

degrees, where $\pi = 3.1415926536$, and one degree = 60 minutes, 1 minute = 60 seconds.)

The subroutine will need to be in two parts, one to deal with SIN, COS and TAN, and the other to deal with ASIN, ACOS and ATAN. We can deal with this by adopting a convention that the angle supplied for SIN, COS and TAN will always lie in the range $-360°$ to $+360°$ (which is more than sufficient to cater for all angles), and stating that if the integer number of degrees is outside this range then the arcsine, etc. of the real value is required. The subroutine will have five dummy arguments – three integers for the angle, one real for the sine, etc., and a dummy procedure. The structure plan is quite straightforward

    1 If |degrees| >360 then
        1.1 Calculate 'fun (real value)'
        1.2 Convert angle in radians to one in degrees etc.
        otherwise
        1.3 Convert angle in degrees etc. to radians
        1.4 Calculate 'fun (angle)'
    2 Return

The subroutine can then be easily written.

```
      SUBROUTINE TRIG(D,M,S,X,F)
      INTEGER D,M,S
      PARAMETER (PI=3.1415926536,TWOPI=2.0*PI)
      IF (ABS(D).GT.360) THEN
C ARC-FUNCTION REQUIRED
      A = F(X)*360.0/TWOPI
      D = A
      RM = (A-D)*60.0
      M = RM
      S = (RM-M)*60.0+0.5
C ROUNDING COULD SET S TO 60. DEAL WITH THIS
      IF (S.EQ.60) THEN
        S = 0
        M = M+1
        IF (M.EQ.60) THEN
          M = 0
          D = D+1
        END IF
      END IF
      ELSE
C TRIG-FUNCTION REQUIRED
      A = (D+M/60.0+S/3600.0)*TWOPI/360.0
      X = F(A)
      END IF
      RETURN
      END
```

Fig. 10.12 shows an example of a suitable test-program for this subroutine.

```
      PROGRAM TEST
      INTRINSIC SIN,COS,TAN,ASIN,ACOS,ATAN
      INTEGER D,M,S
C   READ UP TO 50 ANGLES. A ZERO ANGLE ENDS THE DATA
      DO 10, I=1,50
        READ *,D,M,S
        IF (D.EQ.0 .AND. M.EQ.0 .AND.S.EQ.0) GOTO 20
        CALL TRIG(D,M,S,X,SIN)
        PRINT 201,'SIN',D,M,S,X
        CALL TRIG(D,M,S,Y,COS)
        PRINT 201,'COS',D,M,S,Y
        CALL TRIG(D,M,S,Z,TAN)
        PRINT 201,'TAN',D,M,S,Z
        D = 1000
        CALL TRIG(D,M,S,X,ASIN)
        PRINT 202,'ARCSIN',X,D,M,S
        D = 1000
        CALL TRIG(D,M,S,Y,ACOS)
        PRINT 202,'ARCCOS',Y,D,M,S
        D = 1000
        CALL TRIG(D,M,S,Z,ATAN)
   10   PRINT 202,'ARCTAN',Z,D,M,S
   20 STOP
  201 FORMAT(1H0,A,'(',2(I4,','),I4,') IS',F10.6)
  202 FORMAT(1H0,A,'(',F10.6,') IS',2(I4,','),I4)
      END
```

Fig. 10.12   A test program for subroutine TRIG (Example 10.2)

10.6   Writing external functions

An external function is, in most respects, very similar to a subroutine in its overall structure and in the facilities that are available; also, like a subroutine it may not reference itself either directly or indirectly since this would lead to recursion. The major differences are in the initial statement of the subprogram and in the way in which the value of the function is determined. We saw in Fig. 10.3 that the initial statement consists of the word FUNCTION followed by a list of dummy arguments enclosed in parentheses

FUNCTION name(a1,a2,...)

If the function has no arguments then, unlike a subroutine, the parentheses must still be included in both the FUNCTION statement and in any reference to that function

FUNCTION name()

Unlike a subroutine, however, the name of a function has a type in order that it may be used in an expression with other primary elements such as constants, variables, array elements or substrings. Since the various type specification statements only apply within one program unit and since they must come after the initial statement of a program unit it is clearly impossible for any IMPLICIT or type declaration statement to affect the FUNCTION statement. There is therefore an extended form of FUNCTION statement in which the word FUNCTION is preceded by a type declaration

type FUNCTION name(a1,a2,...)

If no 'type' is included then the usual default based on the initial letter of 'name' is used. Thus

FUNCTION NEXT(a1,a2,...)

is an integer function and will return an integer value. On the other hand

REAL FUNCTION NEXT(a1,a2,...)

is a real function and will return a real value. In this case any program unit which refers to the function NEXT must declare it to be REAL in the usual way

REAL NEXT

A function may be declared to be of any of the six data types we have already met – INTEGER, REAL, DOUBLE PRECISION, COMPLEX, LOGICAL and CHARACTER. In the case of a CHARACTER function there will normally also be a length specification. This must either be a constant or constant expression, or it may be written as (*); in the latter case, the function assumes a character length the same as that specified in the program unit from which it is referenced. Thus in the example shown in Fig. 10.13 the function CFUN is a character function of length 10 when it is referenced from the main program, but one of length 6 when it is referenced from the subroutine SUB.

The same types of dummy arguments may be used in a FUNCTION statement as in a SUBROUTINE statement except that an asterisk is not allowed in a FUNCTION statement. Similarly all the types of actual argument described for subroutines in Sections 10.4 and 10.5 may be used with a function except for alternate return specifiers.

However as well as, optionally, returning some value or values to the calling program through its arguments a function subprogram always returns a *function value*. This is achieved by use of a variable of the same name as the function.

This variable *must* appear in the body of the function and *must* be defined with some value during execution of the function. When a RETURN statement is obeyed to leave the function and return to the calling program, the value of this variable is returned as the function value. There are no restrictions on the way in which this variable is used and/or defined and it may, for example, appear in an input or output list, in an expression, as an argument in a subroutine call or function reference, etc. The type of the variable is, of

```
PROGRAM MAIN
CHARACTER*10 CFUN,CH
  .
  .
CH = CFUN(X,Y,Z)
  .
  .
END

SUBROUTINE SUB
CHARACTER*6 CFUN,CH
  .
  .
CH = CFUN(A,B,C)
  .
  .
END

CHARACTER*(*) FUNCTION CFUN(A,B,C)
  .
  .
  .
END
```

Fig. 10.13   An example of the use of a character function

course, the same as the type of the function and so no type declaration is needed, and none is allowed.

A simple example of a function subprogram is one which calculates the average (or mean) of an array of real numbers

```
   REAL FUNCTION MEAN(A,N)
   REAL A(N)
   SUM = 0.0
   DO 10, I=1,N
10   SUM = SUM+A(I)
   MEAN = SUM/N
   RETURN
   END
```

This is a real function and so the variable MEAN is also real. Notice that the dummy array A has been declared as an adjustable array of size N. It would have been equally acceptable to declare it as an assumed-size array

```
   REAL A(*)
```

but since the number of elements which are to be accessed is known we may as well use it in the declaration. Fig. 10.14 shows how the same process would be achieved in a subroutine, and we can see that the only difference is that in the subroutine an extra dummy argument (AV) is used to return the mean. A much greater difference is apparent when we examine how they are used. Fig. 10.15 and 10.16 show, respectively, how a main program unit would use the function and subroutine in order to read a series of numbers and print their average.

```
      SUBROUTINE MEAN(A,N,AV)
      REAL A(N)
      SUM = 0.0
      DO 10, I=1,N
  10  SUM = SUM+A(I)
      AV = SUM/N
      RETURN
      END
```

Fig. 10.14   A subroutine to calculate an average

```
      PROGRAM TEST
      REAL X(500),MEAN
      READ *,N,(X(I),I=1,N)
      PRINT 201,N,MEAN(X,N)
 201  FORMAT(1H1,'AVERAGE OF',I4,' DATA VALUES IS',F12.3)
      STOP
      END
```

Fig. 10.15   A test program for function MEAN

```
      PROGRAM STEST
      REAL X(500)
      READ *,N,(X(I),I=1,N)
      CALL MEAN(X,N,A)
      PRINT 201,N,A
 201  FORMAT(1H1,'AVERAGE OF',I4,' DATA VALUES IS',F12.3)
      STOP
      END
```

Fig. 10.16   A test program for subroutine MEAN

Note that in the program in Fig. 10.15 the function name MEAN appears in a REAL type declaration statement. This is necessary because the main program unit FTEST knows that MEAN is a function (from the context since it is not declared as an array), but will assume that it returns an integer value unless informed otherwise.

Example 10.3

Write a function program, and a test program for it, which could be used to code a message (or, to be technically accurate, to encrypt it) by replacing each letter in the message by the one following it in the alphabet (Z is replaced by A), leaving all other characters unaltered.

A suitable approach would be to define a character function with a single character as its argument which returns the 'coded' character as its value. The structure plan for such a function is

> *1* If char. is in the range A–Y then
>   *1.1* return next letter
>   but if it is Z then
>   *1.2* return A
>   otherwise
>   *1.3* return char.

The only difficulty appears to be how we find the next letter. The use of the intrinsic function ICHAR to obtain an integer representation of a character and CHAR to obtain a character representation of an integer will be satisfactory as long as the 26 letters are represented by 26 consecutive integers. This will usually be the case and we shall assume it is so for this example; some internal codes, however, are not contiguous (see, for example, Appendix D.2) and if such codes are used to provide the integer equivalents with CHAR and ICHAR then the following program will not work

```
CHARACTER FUNCTION CODE(C)
CHARACTER C
IF ('A'.LE.C .AND. C.LE.'Y') THEN
   CODE = CHAR(ICHAR(C)+1)
ELSE IF (C.EQ.'Z') THEN
   CODE = 'A'
ELSE
   CODE = C
END IF
RETURN
END
```

A suitable test program, or *driver* program (as these main program units are usually called) is as follows

```
    PROGRAM CODER
    CHARACTER MESSGE*50,C,CODE
    READ '(A)',MESSGE
    DO 10, I=1,50
       C = CODE(MESSGE(I:I))
10     MESSGE(I:I) = C
    PRINT *,MESSGE
    STOP
    END
```

Notice that the input message is limited to 50 characters – this should be quite enough to test the function. Also note that the function is called repeatedly with a one-character substring and that the coded version is stored in a one-character variable C before being stored in the original message. It would be illegal to write

```
MESSGE(I:I)=CODE(MESSGE(I:I))
```

because of the restriction on characters which forbids any character position appearing on both sides of the equals sign in an assignment statement.

Fig. 10.17 shows an alternative version of the function CODE which uses a logical function to determine whether a character is a letter. There is no advantage in doing this in this particular example; it merely illustrates what can be done, although it may be felt that the structure and logic of this version of the function CODE is marginally more obvious than in the earlier version.

```
CHARACTER FUNCTION CODE(C)
CHARACTER C
LOGICAL LETTER
IF (LETTER(C)) THEN
  IF (C.NE.'Z') THEN
    CODE = CHAR(ICHAR(C)+1)
  ELSE
    CODE = 'A'
  END IF
ELSE
  CODE = C
END IF
RETURN
END

LOGICAL FUNCTION LETTER(C)
CHARACTER C
LETTER = 'A'.LE.C .AND. C.LE.'Z'
RETURN
END
```

Fig. 10.17   An alternative encoding method

10.7   Statement functions

An external function is both a procedure and a subprogram; however another form of function exists which is not a subprogram but is defined only within one program unit. Such a function, which is called a *statement function*, is written in a special way and consists only of a single statement. It takes the form

name(arg1,arg2,...) = expression

and must be placed after all specification statements, but before any executable statements. The expression may include references to constants, the dummy arguments of the statement function, variables or array elements that are defined within the same program unit (other than any of the same name as one of the dummy arguments), other statement functions as long as they are defined before this one, intrinsic functions, and external functions (as long as they do not alter the value of any of the statement function's dummy arguments).

Thus the function LETTER in Fig. 10.7 could have been declared as a statement function within the function CODE as follows

```
LETTER(C)='A'.LE.C.AND.C.LE.'Z'
```

This definition must appear after the last specification statement (which happens to be the type declaration for LETTER) and before any executable statements.

In this case the dummy argument (C) has the same name as a variable (actually a dummy argument of the function CODE), and has already been declared to be of the correct type. If a dummy argument in a statement function has the same name as some other item in the same program unit then it must also be of the same type (whether implied or declared). If we did not want to use the same name we could have written

```
CHARACTER X
LETTER(X)='A'.LE.X.AND.X.LE.'Z'
```

The main advantage of a statement function over an external function is speed and efficiency. A statement function is normally dealt with by the compiler, which inserts the appropriate code directly into the statement which is referencing it; it can thus be considered as a form of shorthand for the programmer. An external function reference, on the other hand, involves a transfer of control and of arguments, which imposes a certain overhead.

Typical examples of statement functions are to clarify logical expressions such as LETTER (above) or the following

```
LOGICAL ODD
ODD(N)=MOD(N,2).NE.0
```

which returns the value true if its integer argument is odd and false if it is even. Another common use is to simplify repeated arithmetic expressions, such as

```
UT(X,Y,T)=-X*SIN(T)+Y*COS(T)
VT(X,Y,Z,T,P)=-(X*COS(T)+Y*SIN(T))*SIN(P)+Z*COS(P)
```

which are used to perform co-ordinate transformations, and use the intrinsic functions SIN and COS.

10.8   The ENTRY statement

Sometimes it is useful to combine two or more subroutines into a single subroutine, or two or more functions into a single function, in order to take advantage of a large amount of common code. We can define additional entry points to a subprogram by means of the ENTRY statement which takes the form

ENTRY ename(arg1,arg2,...)

An ENTRY statement may appear anywhere after the initial SUBROUTINE or FUNCTION statement except between a block IF statement and its corresponding END IF, and between a DO-statement and the terminal statement of the loop it controls. If the ENTRY statement is in a subroutine then 'ename' is the name of a subroutine, but if it appears in a function then 'ename' is also the name of a function. In the latter case any type declaration for 'ename' must take place in an ordinary type specification statement, and the variable called 'ename' must not appear (other than in a type specification statement) before the ENTRY statement. The dummy arguments specified in the ENTRY statement must not appear in any statements before the ENTRY statement unless they are also dummy arguments in the initial SUBROUTINE or FUNCTION statement of the subprogram, or in another ENTRY statement that precedes this one.

The subroutine or function defined by the ENTRY statement can be used by any other program unit in the normal way and, when it is called, execution will start at the first executable statement after the ENTRY. Thus, in the following example the subroutine TRANS expects the angles THETA and PHI to be in radians (as required by the intrinsic functions SIN, COS, etc.), while DTRANS expects them in degrees and carries out an appropriate conversion.

```
      SUBROUTINE TRANS(X,Y,Z,THETA,PHI,U,V)
      PARAMETER (PI=3.1415926536)
      T = THETA
      P = PHI
      GOTO 1
C   DTRANS ENTRY HAS THETA AND PHI IN DEGREES
      ENTRY DTRANS(X,Y,Z,THETA,PHI,U,V)
      T = THETA*PI/180.0
      P = PHI*PI/180.0
    1 Remainder of subroutine
         .
         .
         .
      END
```

Notice that this is frequently, as here, a situation which requires the use of a GOTO statement to avoid some initial statements associated with the ENTRY. It would be possible to avoid this by writing

```
      SUBROUTINE DTRANS(X,Y,Z,THETA,PHI,U,V)
      PARAMETER (PI=3.1415926536)
      THETA = THETA*PI/180.0
      PHI = PHI*PI/180.0
```

```
C  TRANS ENTRY HAS THETA AND PHI IN RADIANS
      ENTRY TRANS(X,Y,Z,THETA,PHI,U,V)
                 .
                 .
                 .
                 .
      END
```

However, in this case the actual arguments corresponding to THETA and PHI will always be in radians on exit from the subroutine, even if they were in degrees on entry!

In this example both subroutines have the same number and type of arguments (which in fact even have the same names), but this need not necessarily be so. Fig. 10.18 shows a function which has three other entries.

```
      REAL FUNCTION MEANMD(A,N,XMIN,XMAX)
      REAL A(N),MEAN,MEANHI,MEANLO
C  MEANMD CALCULATES AVERAGE OF A(I),
C  WHERE XMIN.LE.A(I).LE.XMAX, FOR I=1 TO N
      AMIN = XMIN
      AMAX = XMAX
      GOTO 1
      ENTRY MEANLO(A,N,XMAX)
C  MEANLO CALCULATES AVERAGE OF A(I),
C  WHERE A(I).LE.XMAX, FOR I=1 TO N
C  THEREFORE SET AMIN TO A VERY LARGE NEGATIVE NUMBER
      AMIN = −1E30
      AMIX = XMAX
      GOTO 1
      ENTRY MEANHI(A,N,XMIN)
C  MEANHI CALCULATES AVERAGE OF A(I),
C  WHERE A(I).GE.XMIN, FOR I=1 TO N
C  THEREFORE SET AMAX TO A VERY LARGE POSITIVE NUMBER
      AMIN = XMIN
      AMAX = 1E30
      GOTO 1
      ENTRY MEAN(A,N)
C  MEAN CALCULATES AVERAGE OF ALL NUMBERS
C  THEREFORE SET AMIN AND AMAX TO VERY LARGE NEGATIVE
C  AND POSITIVE NUMBERS
      AMIN = −1E30
      AMAX = 1E30
C  LIMITS SET − NOW CALCULATE AVERAGE OF NUMBERS BETWEEN
```

```
C  AMIN AND AMAX
   1 SUM = 0.0
     NUM = 0
     DO 10, I=1,N
       IF (A(I).GE.AMIN .AND. A(I).LE.AMAX) THEN
         SUM = SUM+A(I)
         NUM = NUM+1
       END IF
  10   CONTINUE
     MEAN = SUM/NUM
     MEANLO = MEAN
     MEANHI = MEAN
     MEANMD = MEAN
     RETURN
     END
```

Fig. 10.18   A multi-entried function

The four functions have specifications as follows

MEAN(A,N)	returns the average of the N values in the array A, ignoring any outside the range -10^{30} to $+10^{30}$
MEANLO(A,N,AMAX)	as for MEAN but also ignoring any numbers greater than AMAX
MEANHI(A,N,AMIN)	as for MEAN but also ignoring any numbers less than AMIN
MEANMD(A,N,AMIN,AMAX)	returns the average of those of the N numbers in the array A which lie between AMIN and AMAX, inclusive

The method used is to call the dummy arguments which specify the limits (if any) XMIN and XMAX, and to use two local variables AMIN and AMAX. If one, or both, of the limits is not supplied then AMIN or AMAX, as appropriate, is set to the value, or values, supplied. If one, or both, of the limits is not supplied then AMIN or AMAX, as appropriate, is set to a very large positive or negative number (e.g. $+10^{30}$ or -10^{30}). The four functions then follow a common path and find the average of all the numbers which lie between AMIN and AMAX. Once this has been done all four function names are set to the average since it is not known at this stage which function name was used for the entry.

Example 10.4
Modify the sorting subroutine shown in Fig. 10.5 so that it will use the name SORTUP if the numbers are to be sorted into increasing order, and SORTDN if they are to be sorted into decreasing order.

An examination of the sorting subroutine shows that the only change to the logic that is required to sort the array into decreasing order is to change the relational expression from NUM(J).LT.NMIN to NUM(J).GT.NMIN (although if we were writing a new subroutine we would also change IMIN and NMIN to

IMAX and NMAX). Fig. 10.19 shows a 'truth table' for the three possible relationships and the value needed in the block IF logical expression in order that the sorting operates in the correct order.

	SORTUP	SORTDN
NUM(J).LT.NMIN	true	false
NUM(J).EQ.NMIN	false	false
NUM(J).GT.NMIN	false	true

Fig. 10.19 A truth table for sorting up or down

In fact it does not really matter whether the value for NUM(J).EQ.NMIN is true or false, since if it is true the two equal numbers will be exchanged, if it is false they will not; in either event the result is the same.

If, therefore, we define a logical variable UP whose value is true if we are to sort in increasing order and false if decreasing order is required, the logical expression

NUM(J).LT.NMIN.EQV.UP

is true if NUM(J) is less than NMIN for SORTUP and if NUM(J) is greater than or equal to NMIN for SORTDN, which is what we require. (.EQV. gives the value true if both its operands are true or if they are both false, see Section 5.5.) We can therefore use this to modify the subroutine

```
      SUBROUTINE SORTUP(NUM,N)
      INTEGER NUM(N)
      LOGICAL UP
      UP = .TRUE.
      GOTO 1
      ENTRY SORTDN(NUM,N)
      UP = .FALSE.
    1 DO 10, I=1,N-1
        IMIN = I
        NMIN = NUM(I)
        DO 5, J=I+1,N
          IF (NUM(J).LT.NMIN.EQV. UP) THEN
            IMIN = J
            NMIN = NUM(J)
          END IF
    5     CONTINUE
C   EXCHANGE NUMBERS IF NECESSARY
        IF (IMIN.NE.I) THEN
          NUM(IMIN) = NUM(I)
          NUM(I) = NMIN
        END IF
   10   CONTINUE
C   ARRAY NOW SORTED - SO RETURN
      RETURN
      END
```

If we wished to avoid the unnecessary exchange of equal numbers we could extend the logical expression in the first block IF so that the statement reads

```
IF ((NUM(J).LT.NMIN.EQV.UP).AND.NUM(J).NE.NMIN) THEN
```

10.9 The SAVE statement

Each subprogram is, as we have seen, an independent program unit and its variables and arrays are local to that program unit and may only be accessed by another program unit if they are used as actual arguments in a call to a subroutine or function. Once a RETURN has been obeyed, to return from a subroutine or function to the program unit which 'called' it, then all the local variables and arrays in that subroutine or function become inaccessible, until the subroutine or function is 'called' once more. In Fortran 77 these local variables and arrays are said to become *undefined* when this happens, and the corresponding memory locations become available for use by other program units. If the subprogram is entered again then its local variables and arrays will once more be available for use by that subprogram.

The important effect of this is that when a subprogram is re-entered its local variables and arrays will have *undefined values*, even if they had been assigned particular values on the previous entry. There are, however, a number of occasions when it is highly desirable for the value of one or more items to be preserved between calls. This can be achieved by use of the SAVE statement which takes the form

SAVE name1,name2,...

```
CHARACTER FUNCTION NEXT()
CHARACTER RECORD(80)
INTEGER POS
LOGICAL NOMORE
SAVE
DATA POS/81/,NOMORE/.FALSE./
IF (NOMORE) THEN
  NEXT = '?'
ELSE
  IF (POS.GT.80) THEN
    READ (5,'(80A1)',END=10) RECORD
    POS = 1
  END IF
  NEXT = RECORD(POS)
  POS = POS+1
END IF
RETURN
10 NEXT = '?'
NOMORE = .TRUE.
RETURN
END
```

Fig. 10.20 Use of SAVE in a function subprogram

where each 'name' is the name of a local variable or array name. This is a specification statement, and must therefore appear before any statement functions, DATA statements or executable statements. As its name implies it causes all those items in the list to be saved on exit from the subprogram so that on a subsequent entry they have the value that they had before. If a save statement has no names following it

    SAVE

then it will cause the saving of *all* variables and arrays which could be saved. Fig. 10.20 shows a function subprogram which returns the next character from a set of input records, each of 80 characters, or a '?' if there is no more data. The data is assumed to be input in such a way that an end-of-file condition (see Section 6.3) is established when there is no more data.

The function preserves all its local variables, namely the contents of the current record, the position of the next character within the record and a logical flag to indicate whether there is any more data, and uses these to return a suitable character. Notice, incidentally, that this function has no arguments. It will be used in a statement such as

    CHAR=NEXT()

10.10 Modular program development

One of the great advantages of subprograms is that they enable us to break a program design into several smaller, more manageable sections, and to then write and test each of these sections independently of the rest of the program.

In the Intermission (pages 130–134) we saw how even a very simple program could benefit from being developed in stages. In this chapter we have seen how we can test a subroutine or function by writing a simple 'driver' program which calls the subprogram with suitable arguments. The combination of these two concepts provides us with all we need for *modular program development*.

This approach breaks the problem down into its major functions, each of which can then be developed independently of the others. In a large project these functions or *modules* may be developed by different people. If necessary a module itself may be sub-divided into further modules. All that is necessary is that the *interface* between a module and the rest of the program is well-defined.

This interface consists of two parts. The first, the interface proper, is the list of arguments supplied to the module (or rather to the subprogram which is, in effect, the main program unit of the module). The second is the specification of the action of the module.

A structure plan gives very great assistance in modular development as it identifies, in a natural way, the major functions of the program. Rather than expanding these functions within a single structure plan, as we have been doing up to now, we can treat each of these major functions as a separate module to be developed independently. Once developed they can be integrated to form the complete program according to the top-level structure plan. We used this approach in a limited way in Example 10.1, but the following gives a more comprehensive illustration of the technique.

Example 10.5
Modify the golfing program (pages 145, 183, 186) so that the data can be typed in a completely free format as the player's name, followed by the scores for each of the four rounds of golf. The names may be typed in any way but will not exceed 30 characters, including any embedded spaces, and the scores will consist of digits without any embedded spaces. There will be at least one space between each item and the full line of input will never exceed 60 characters, including all spaces (both before the name, within the name and between the various items). A list of players is required in finishing order with their four round totals. Players with the same score should be in alphabetic order with the score only printed for the first one.

We have already done most of this apart from the absence of any defined input layout and a slight improvement to the format of the results. It is, however, a good vehicle with which to illustrate the modular approach. Our first structure plan is very simple

> *1* Read players names and scores
> *2* Sort into alphabetic order
> *3* Sort into finishing order
> *4* Print results

Each of these steps is independent of the others, but is quite a substantial problem. We can therefore treat each of them as an independent module. The common information which will be required by steps *2*, *3* and *4*, and which will be produced by step *1* is an array of names, an array of scores, and the number of players. To this we can add an array of pointers which will be sorted in steps *2* and *3* to simplify the process.
  We can now proceed to refine each of these steps starting with step *1*

> *1.1* Repeat the following
> > *1.1.1* Read the next record
> > *1.1.2* Extract name
> > *1.1.3* If name = 'END OF DATA' then exit
> > *1.1.4* Extract scores
> > *1.1.5* Calculate this player's total score
> > *1.1.6* Store pointer (i.e. index to arrays of players' names and scores)

Once again we have left two steps still undefined, namely steps *1.1.2* and *1.1.4* which 'extract' the name and scores from the input record. We can write these as further subprograms and suitable structure plans (with simplified numbering!) are as follows

> (a) *1* Repeat up to 60 times
> > *1.1* If next character is not a blank then exit
> >
> *2* Set up a blank name
> *3* Repeat up to 60 times
> > *3.1* If next character is a digit then
> > > *3.1.1* Store character position and exit
> > > otherwise
> > > *3.1.2* Insert character in next position of name

This will ignore leading blanks and then create a name consisting of all characters up to first digit.

    (b)   *1* Set score to zero
          2 Repeat from current position up to 60
          2.1 If next character is a digit then exit
          3 Repeat from current position up to 60
          3.1 If next character is not a digit then exit
          3.2 Multiply score by 10 and add digit

This will ignore characters which are not digits until a digit is found. It will then accumulate the number from successive digits until a non-digit character is found.

We could test each of these two (function) subprograms independently and then incorporate them with the main input module. At the first stage suitable driver programs can be written which simply read or otherwise set up suitable records and print the values provided by the function being tested. The full module might look like this

```
      SUBROUTINE INPUT(NAME,SCORE,P,N,MAX)
      CHARACTER*30 NAME(*),PLAYER,RECORD(60)*1
      INTEGER SCORE(*),P(*),ROUND,POS
      DO 20, I=1,MAX
        READ '(60A1)',RECORD
        NAME(I) = PLAYER(RECORD,POS)
        IF (NAME(I).EQ.'END OF DATA') GOTO 25
        SCORE(I) = 0
        DO 10, J=1,4
10      SCORE(I) = SCORE(I)+ROUND(RECORD,POS)
20    P(I) = I
25 N = I-1
      RETURN
      END

      CHARACTER*30 FUNCTION PLAYER(REC,N)
      CHARACTER REC(60),C,NAME*30
      LOGICAL DIGIT
      DIGIT(C) = '0'.LE.C .AND. C.LE.'9'
      DO 10, I=1,60
        IF (REC(I).NE.' ' GOTO 11
10    CONTINUE
11 NAME = ' '
      DO 20, J=I,I+29
        IF (DIGIT(REC(J))) THEN
          N = J
          GOTO 21
        ELSE
          K = J+1-I
          NAME(K:K) = REC(J)
        END IF
```

```
20   CONTINUE
21 PLAYER = NAME
   RETURN
   END

   INTEGER FUNCTION ROUND(REC,N)
   CHARACTER REC(60),D(0:9),C
   LOGICAL DIGIT
   DATA D/'0','1','2','3','4','5','6','7','8','9'/
   DIGIT(C) = '0'.LE.C .AND. C.LE.'9'
   ROUND = 0
   DO 10, I=N,60
     IF (DIGIT(REC(I))) GOTO 15
10   CONTINUE
15 DO 25, J=I,60
     IF (DIGIT(REC(J))) THEN
        DO 20, K=0,9
          IF (REC(J).EQ.D(K)) GOTO 21
20      CONTINUE
21      ROUND = 10*ROUND+K
     ELSE
        N = J
        GOTO 26
     END IF
25   CONTINUE
26 RETURN
   END
```

Notice that the two statement functions (DIGIT) in the functions PLAYER and ROUND assume that the characters 0–9 are consecutive characters. This will almost always be the case but is not laid down in the standard. All three subprograms have omitted to include checks for invalid data such as no 'END OF DATA', more than 30 characters in a name, more than 60 characters in a record (leading to incorrect or missing scores); these omissions are purely in the interests of space in this book and checks should be included in real-life.

The two sorting stages are simply subroutines using the same logic which has been used several times already. We shall merely give their specifications

> SUBROUTINE ASORT(NAME,PN)
>> sorts the *pointer* array P so that it points to the N names in the array NAME in alphabetic order

> SUBROUTINE SORT(NUM,P,N)
>> sorts the *pointer* array P so that it points to the N numbers in the array NUM in increasing order, and does not alter the sequence of identical numbers

Finally we come to the results. The only difficulty here is that the format is different depending upon whether the player's total score is the same as the previous player's, or not. A structure plan might be

1   Set 'last score' to an impossible value
2   Repeat N times
> *2.1*   If next player's score is not 'last score' then
>> *2.1.1*   Print a blank line followed by score
>>   and name
>
>   otherwise
>> *2.1.2*   Print name on next line

This can be coded quite easily

```
      SUBROUTINE PRINT(NAME,SCORE,P,N)
      CHARACTER*30 NAME(N)
      INTEGER SCORE(N),P(N)
      DATA LAST/-1/
      PRINT 200
      DO 10, I=1,N
        J = P(I)
        IF (SCORE(J).NE.LAST) THEN
          PRINT 201,SCORE(J),NAME(J)
          LAST = SCORE(J)
        ELSE
          PRINT 202,NAME(J)
        END IF
   10   CONTINUE
      RETURN
  200 FORMAT(1H1,'FORTRAN 77 GOLF TOURNAMENT'///
     *  1H ,'FINAL SCORES AFTER FOUR ROUNDS'//)
  201 FORMAT(1H0,I3,4X,A30)
  202 FORMAT(1H ,7X,A30)
      END
```

This subroutine, also, can easily be tested independently of all the others.

Finally the four modules can be gathered together with a simple main program unit to produce a complete program, *all of whose parts are known to work*

```
      PROGRAM GOLF
      PARAMETER (MAX=150)
      CHARACTER*30 NAME(MAX)
      INTEGER SCORE(MAX),INDEX(MAX)
      CALL INPUT(NAME,SCORE,INDEX,N,MAX)
      CALL ASORT(NAME,INDEX,N)
      CALL SORT(SCORE,INDEX,N)
      CALL PRINT(NAME,SCORE,INDEX,N)
      STOP
      END
```

Summary

- Fortran programs consist of a main program unit and optionally any number of subprogram program units.

- Subprograms may be subroutines or functions.

- Subprogram names are global.

- Every program unit has its own set of *local variables*.

- Communication between program units is achieved by *arguments*.

- Every *external function* has a *type*, which may be declared in the initial FUNCTION statement.

- Every function returns a value (the *function value*) as the function.

- A *statement function* is local to the program unit in which it is declared.

- The ENTRY statement enables a program unit to have two or more names and entry points.

- Variables which are local to a program unit become *undefined* when a RETURN is made from the program unit, unless they appear in a SAVE statement.

- Subroutines provide the means for *modular program development*.

Initial statements	SUBROUTINE name(list of dummy arguments) SUBROUTINE name FUNCTION name(list of dummy arguments) FUNCTION name() type FUNCTION name(list of dummy arguments) type FUNCTION name()
RETURN *statement*	RETURN
Statement function	name(list of dummy arguments) = expression
Alternate entry	ENTRY name(list of dummy arguments) ENTRY name ENTRY name()
Saving local variables	SAVE list of local variable names SAVE

Fig. 10.21   Fortran 77 statements introduced in Chapter 10

Exercises

10.1 Write appropriate initial statements and declarations for any dummy arguments (if necessary) for subprograms to carry out the following actions
   (a) Print an error message based upon an error indicator which may be −1 or an integer in the range 1–10.
   (b) Find the number of occurrences of one string within another string.

(c) Find the position of a name in a list of names.

(d) Find the roots (if any) of a quadratic equation ($ax^2 + bx + c = 0$).

(e) Read and check for validity the results of matches played in a league of 22 teams.

(f) Obtain the next word from data which is input as a stream of words separated by spaces.

10.2 Write statement functions to evaluate the following functions

(a) The Centigrade equivalent of a Fahrenheit temperature ($F = \dfrac{9C}{5} + 32$).

(b) The metric equivalent of a distance in feet and inches ($1\,\text{in} = 2.54\,\text{cm}$).

(c) The truth or otherwise of the assertion that a real value is an exact whole number.

(d) The truth or otherwise of the assertion that one real number is an integral factor of another.

10.3 Write a subprogram which reads data from the standard input unit consisting of words separated by spaces or the end of a record. Each 'call' to the subprogram should provide the calling program with the next word. Choose your own terminator for the data and action when all the data has been read. Write a suitable test program for your subroutine.

10.4 A set of survey data has been prepared as follows

Columns 1–30	First name and surname (separated by a space)
Column 33	Sex (M or F)
Columns 36, 37	Age
Column 40	Marital status (S = Single, M = Married, D = Divorced, W = Widowed)
Column 43	Housing (O = Owner-occupier, C = Council house tenant, P = Private house tenant, R = tenant with 2 or more rooms, B = tenant with one room)
Columns 46–50	Monthly income.

The data is terminated by a blank record.

(a) Write a subroutine to read the data and sort it into alphabetic order of *surname*.

(b) Write a subroutine to produce an array of pointers to all old-age pensioners (male aged 65 or over, female aged 60 or over) living on their own in a defined type of housing.

(c) Write a subroutine to produce an array of pointers to all single girls living in a single room.

(d) Write a subroutine to print a list of names (surname followed by first name) followed by sex and age based on a list of pointers to the names.

(e) Write a program to read data in the above format and to print lists of old-age pensioners living alone in council houses, single girls living in single rooms and married owner-occupiers under 40 years old with a monthly income of less than £500. Each list should be in alphabetic order of surnames with sex and age also given.

10.5 Write a program which can be used to code or decode a message in the following manner.

A keyword of up to 10 letters is read and used to encode the message by allocating each letter in the keyword its numeric position in the alphabet and replacing each letter of the message by the letter 'n' later in the alphabet, where 'n' is the value of the next letter of the keyword. The keyword is repeated as often as necessary and the alphabet is considered to be circular (i.e. A follows Z). A space is replaced by the next letter of the keyword. The coded message is written in groups of the same length as the keyword. Thus, if the keyword is FORTRAN (6, 15, 18, 20, 18, 1, 14) the message 'THIS EXERCISE IS FUN' is coded as follows

$T \rightarrow T + 6 = Z$
$H \rightarrow H + 15 = W$
$I \rightarrow I + 18 = A$
$S \rightarrow S + 20 = M$
$\triangledown \rightarrow \triangledown + 18 = R$
$E \rightarrow E + 1 = F$
$X \rightarrow X + 14 = L$
$E \rightarrow E + 6 = K$
$R \rightarrow R + 15 = G$
etc.

leading to the message

FORTRAN ZWAMRFL KGUCKFN OHRZMOI

where an extra letter (or letters in most cases) has been added at the end to fill the group.

(Hint: First write the encode part and test it, this can then be used to test the decoding part.)

10.6

PXAJQS	CMESWR	PRIOQI	HMHBRF
PWPEQA	QTFJAN	IRAGIB	JRFXQL
EXURRM	PGOCKX	QBAYWS	KQJXXS
JFFJBX	OUPBUS	VMSJVG	SMESEZ
PYONQW	UAPNZG	WXFKTA	PZMYTD
PGUJZL	PMOVPS	KQFNQY	EPADYX
PDJBJM	PZMYTD	PXURVK	UYGDVK
PRIOQI	HCWSFN	IXCVFV	AXJCQN
ICEJKH	PCOMFW	UXPBQW	UAPNVS
JFFJEX	NRAYEX		

RJXDL	APXCA	VPFDW	APJIZ	PTOMZ
JBXFZ	CWAIE	VPGDQ	HOGCF	CGGSX
RNYTK	RCAPT	GXTBS	GUITD	ZUIQI
LGIUX	ZLIDT			

(Hint: See Exercise 10.5)

# More Flexible Use of Storage

11.1 Local storage

Variables and arrays in a program unit are local to that program unit, and are not accessible by any other program units unless they appear as arguments in a 'call' to a subprogram. This has very important implications because it enables a subroutine or function subprogram to be written without any knowledge of the program unit from which it will be called, or indeed of any subprograms which it may use itself. All that is required is that the number and the type of the arguments is known.

The values of any local variables or arrays become undefined when a RETURN is made from a subprogram, unless either they appear in a list of names in a SAVE statement or there is a SAVE statement without any list (which saves everything that can be saved).

Frequently situations arise when the desire to develop a program in a modular fashion results in several subprograms having a very large number of arguments in order to access a large number of variables and/or arrays. In these situations the fact that storage is local to a program unit can be a great hindrance, and there is a requirement for a controlled form of *global* storage which can be accessed directly by more than one program unit.

11.2 Global storage

Remember that, in Fortran 77, the memory of a computer consists of a (large) number of storage units of two types. The first type is a *numeric* storage unit, and is used to store integers, real numbers, logical values, double precision numbers and complex numbers – the last two each requiring two consecutive storage units. The other type is a *character* storage unit which is used to store a single character; a character string of length 'len' requires 'len' consecutive storage units.

In a program unit we use a *name* to identify a storage unit of an appropriate type or, in the case of an array name or a character name, a block of consecutive storage units. These names, as we have seen, are *local* to the program unit and are for our convenience only. The compiler will refer to storage units by their *addresses* within the memory and will keep a list of names and their corresponding addresses only while it is compiling the program unit. (This is a slight over-simplification, but is sufficient for our present purpose.)

However, some names are preserved and have a *global* significance, for example the names of any subprograms that are defined or called.

To provide a global storage facility, Fortran allows blocks of the memory (consisting of one or more consecutive storage units of the same type) to be identified by a global name, and for the storage units contained within that block to be made available to any program unit that refers to the *block* by its global name. Such a block of consecutive storage units is called a COMMON block.

It is important to realise that the names of the individual storage units are not global names – the whole block is made available, not individual storage units. This means that a program unit may call the items in a COMMON block by any name that it wishes (just as it can use any name for its dummy arguments); the type and order of the items within the block are fixed, not their names.

11.3 Named COMMON blocks

A named block of storage is defined by a statement of the form

```
COMMON /name/nlist
```

where 'name' is the *global* name of the COMMON block and 'nlist' is a list of *local* variable names, array names or array declarators. Thus the statements

```
INTEGER AGE(50)
REAL MARK(50,6)
COMMON /EXAM/NUM,MARK,AV(50),AGE,AVAGE
```

define a COMMON block (EXAM) which consists of 402 numeric storage units. In this particular program unit the first of these is an integer (NUM), the next 300 a 2-dimensional real array (MARK), the next 50 a real array (AV), the next 50 an integer array (AGE), and the last a real number (AVAGE).

The COMMON statement is a specification statement and must, therefore, follow any IMPLICIT statements and precede any DATA, statement function or executable statements. Although not essential, it is good practice to precede

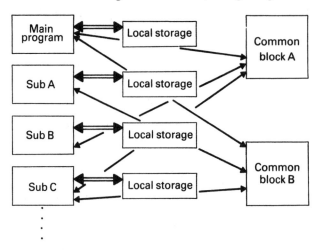

Fig. 11.1 Local and COMMON storage

it immediately by any type or array declaration statements which refer to items within the COMMON block, as has been done above.

Notice that because the name of a COMMON block is a global name it must be different from the names of any other COMMON blocks *or program units*. It can be the same as the local name of a variable or array (but not a constant), but as a general rule it is preferable not to use the same name in a single program unit for both a global and a local entity.

Fig. 11.1 illustrates this structure in graphic form, and also shows how the various COMMON blocks may be accessed by different program units.

One consequence of the fact that only the COMMON block name is global is that different program units may refer to the individual storage units within a COMMON block in different ways. For example, the COMMON block EXAM referred to above could be defined in another program unit as

        COMMON/EXAM/N,TOTAL(50,6),AV(50),NYRS(50),AVYRS

where different names have been used for two of the arrays and for both variables, or even as

        COMMON/EXAM/N,SCORE(50,7),NAGE(50),AVAGE

where the two real arrays have been declared as a single array. The order of storage of array elements (see section 9.8) means that those elements of SCORE whose second subscript is 7 occupy the last 50 storage units and thus correspond exactly to the array AV in the earlier COMMON block specifications.

In fact it is not necessary to specify all the items in a COMMON block but only those that are required in the program unit in which the COMMON statement occurs. Thus if the ages were not required we could write

        COMMON/EXAM/N,SCORE(50,7),DUMMY(51)

while if only the ages were wanted we could write

        COMMON/EXAM/DUMMY(351),NAGE(50),AV

In each case a 'dummy' array (DUMMY) has been included in the list of items forming the COMMON block. In the first case this serves to ensure that the total length of the COMMON block is correct, while in the second case it ensures that the array NAGE starts (correctly) at the 352nd storage unit of the block. (In practice most implementations will not bother if the same COMMON block has different lengths in different program units, and will allocate enough space for the largest length specified. The standard. however, states that all COMMON blocks of the same name must have the same length in all program units in which they appear – hence the extra array in the first case above.)

There is one important restriction concerning COMMON blocks. There are two types of storage unit (see section 11.2), one for characters and one for everything else. The effect of this is that if a COMMON block contains any character variables or character arrays then it cannot contain any variables or arrays or any other type.

As we would expect, we can declare several COMMON blocks in a single statement; however, because of the format of the statement there are two ways of doing this

```
COMMON /name1/list1,/name2/list2, . . .
COMMON /name1/list1/name2/list2/name3/ . . .
```

The second version (without any separating commas) is possible because of the 'slashes' which surround the names of the COMMON blocks. Thus we may write either

```
COMMON/EXAM/N,MARK,AV,AGE,AVAGE,/PUPILS/NAME
```

or

```
COMMON/EXAM/N,MARK,AV,AGE,AVAGE/PUPILS/NAME
```

In general a COMMON block will be specified in a single statement. This is not obligatory, however, and if the same COMMON block name appears in two (or more) COMMON statements in the same program unit then they are treated as though the two (or more) lists were combined into a single list. Thus the statements

```
COMMON/EXAM/NUM
COMMON/PUPILS/NAME,/EXAM/SCORE(50,6),AV(50)
COMMON/EXAM/NAGE(50),AVAGE
```

will have the same effect for the COMMON block EXAM as the statement

```
COMMON/EXAM/NUM,SCORE(50,6),AV(50),NAGE(50),AVAGE
```

Example 11.1
Rewrite Example 10.5 so that the subroutines used do not have any arguments.

The program for Example 10.5 is a good example of the type of situation in which COMMON blocks can be very useful. The main program (see Fig. 11.2) calls four subroutines, each of which operates on a substantial part of the

```
PROGRAM GOLF
PARAMETER (MAX=150)
CHARACTER*30 NAME(MAX)
INTEGER SCORE(MAX),INDEX(MAX)
CALL INPUT(NAME,SCORE,INDEX,N,MAX)
CALL ASORT(NAME,INDEX,N)
CALL SORT(SCORE,INDEX,N)
CALL PRINT(NAME,SCORE,INDEX,N)
STOP
END
```

Fig. 11.2 The main program unit for Example 10.5

same 'data base'. This consists of a character array (NAME) and two integer arrays (SCORE and INDEX) together with the number of players (N). In addition the subroutine INPUT requires the maximum number of players, which is also used as the dimension of the arrays by being declared as the constant MAX.

Constants may not appear in a COMMON block; however, we find on examining the subroutine INPUT that it is necessary to limit the number of players whose details are read and also (by implication) to provide dimensions for the arrays. Since the use of COMMON blocks means that the size of the arrays must be declared explicitly we can declare a constant (MAX) in each of the subroutines. Our main program will therefore be as follows

```
PROGRAM GOLF
PARAMETER (MAX=150)
CHARACTER*30 NAME(MAX)
INTEGER SCORE(MAX),INDEX(MAX)
COMMON /NAMES/NAME
COMMON /SCORES/N,SCORE,INDEX
CALL INPUT
CALL ASORT
CALL SORT
CALL PRINT
STOP
END
```

When we examine the subroutines we see that we can simply include the same five lines at the start of each one. Thus INPUT will start as follows

```
SUBROUTINE INPUT
PARAMETER (MAX=150)
CHARACTER*30 NAME(MAX)
INTEGER SCORE(MAX),INDEX(MAX)
COMMON /NAMES/NAME
COMMON /SCORES/N,SCORE,INDEX
CHARACTER PLAYER*30,RECORD(60)
INTEGER ROUND,POS
DO 20, I=1,MAX
    .
    .
    .
    .
```

The only other change is that the array INDEX was called P in the earlier version. We could, of course, alter the COMMON specification to use the name P. The advantage of having the identical specification in each subprogram is that these five lines can probably be stored in a file, within the computer system, and inserted directly into each program unit without the need for any retyping. This depends upon the particular computer system being used, but some way of inserting a block of statements will always be possible.

Exactly the same modifications will need to be made to the remaining three subroutines – ASORT, SORT and PRINT – thus giving all four modules access to any part of the data base that they require.

11.4 Blank COMMON

The COMMON statement, as we have seen, allows us to define a block of storage of a fixed size and to identify it by means of a global name. Fortran also allows us to have one further block of storage that is available to any program unit that requires it and that has neither a name nor a fixed size. This is known as *blank* COMMON and is declared in a similar way to that used for named COMMON blocks. If there are no preceding (named) blocks in the COMMON statement then we simply follow the word COMMON with a list of variables, array names or array declarators

```
COMMON X,Y,Z(-10:10)
```

Alternatively, or if there is a preceding COMMON block declaration in the same statement, we omit any name from the earlier form

```
COMMON/PLAYER/NAME,//X,Y,Z(-10:10)
```

There are three main differences between named COMMON blocks and blank COMMON (apart from the absence of a name for blank COMMON). The first is that, unlike a named COMMON block, the size of blank COMMON need not be the same in different program units. Thus if the COMMON block SCORES in Example 11.1 was placed in blank COMMON the subroutine ASORT could include the statement

```
COMMON N,INDEX(MAX)
```

while the main program unit and the other subroutines would contain

```
INTEGER SCORE(MAX),INDEX(MAX)
COMMON N,INDEX,SCORE
```

We shall meet the other two differences in the next two sections of this chapter.

Blank COMMON is usually appropriate where a number of variables and/or arrays are to be made available to all (or nearly all) of the program units in a program, and where they do not include both characters and other types of information. Named blocks are more appropriate where such COMMON storage is only required by a few of the subprograms, or where it is more convenient to split the COMMON storage into several smaller units. Fig. 11.3 illustrates this in graphic form.

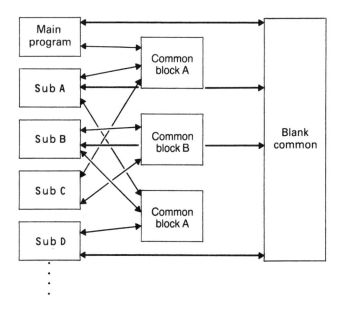

Fig. 11.3   Blank and named COMMON

11.5   Initialising COMMON blocks

We have seen that DATA statements can be used to give initial values to variables and array elements (Chapters 8 and 9). These are, of course, local variables and the DATA statements therefore provide initial values for storage locations which can only be accessed by name from the program units in which the DATA statements occur. The situation is rather different with COMMON blocks since the same storage locations are accessible from several different program units; that, after all, is the purpose of COMMON. This means that if a variable or array element was given an initial value by a DATA statement in one program unit then it could also be given a different initial value (presumably by accident) in another, which would lead to confusion and error. (It would also cause extra problems for the compiler which does not really know where the variables, etc., in a COMMON block are situated in the memory, but merely where they are relative to the start of the block. This is satisfactory for most purposes, but not, usually, for setting initial values.)

To get round these problems, the use of DATA statements to initialise variables and array elements in COMMON blocks is forbidden, except in a special type of subprogram which is called a *block data program unit*. We mentioned this very briefly in Chapter 10 (section 10.2) and Fig. 11.4 shows its overall structure (as already shown in Fig. 10.4). Note that it contains *no executable statements*.

A block data subprogram exists for the sole purpose of giving initial values to items contained in COMMON blocks. It cannot be obeyed by means of a CALL or other reference, and any attempt to do so will cause an error. Similarly the presence of any type of statement other than a specification statement, a DATA statement, or a comment, between the initial BLOCK DATA and the final END statements will lead to an error. The name of a block data

```
BLOCK DATA name
       .
       .
   Specification statements
       .
       .
   DATA  statements
       .
       .
   END
```

Fig. 11.4 A block data program unit

---

subprogram is a global name, like that of all other program units; however, there may be one un-named block data program unit. Since in many programs there is no need for more than one block data program unit the need for a name is frequently absent.

Block data program units also lead us to the second difference between blank COMMON and named COMMON blocks—blank COMMON cannot be initialised and thus cannot appear in a block data program unit. Any COMMON variables or arrays which require initial values must therefore be placed in named COMMON blocks.

11.6   Preserving values in COMMON blocks

In general, when a RETURN is made from a subroutine or function to its calling program unit the local variables and arrays in that subroutine or function become undefined and do not retain their values for a subsequent entry (see section 10.9). The SAVE statement enables us to save some, or all, of these values so that they are available for subsequent use.

A similar situation exists with COMMON blocks. A COMMON block enables two or more program units to share a block of memory. It would clearly be nonsense if an exit from a subroutine always caused any COMMON blocks to which it referred to become undefined. However there is one situation, which is somewhat analogous to the case of local variables in a single subprogram, in which there would be no such conflict. Fig. 11.5 illustrates this situation diagrammatically. The program consists of five program units and three COMMON blocks; furthermore, the subroutines are called in a hierarchical way (for ease of explanation) such that the main program calls SUBA, which calls SUBB, which calls SUBC, which calls SUBD. The diagram also indicates which COMMON blocks each program unit refers to.

If we examine this diagram carefully we see that, as control RETURNs from SUBD back up to the main program, at certain stages there will no longer be any reference to some of the COMMON blocks. Thus when a RETURN is made to SUBB we find that COMMON block C is no longer accessible as it is only referred to by SUBC and SUBD. Similarly, COMMON block B is no longer referred to once a RETURN has been made to SUBA. The third COMMON block (A) is referred to in the main program and will, therefore, always be required.

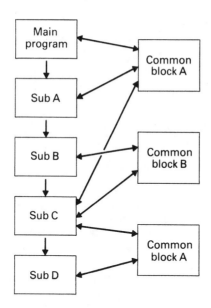

Fig. 11.5   Defined and undefined COMMON blocks

At those stages where a RETURN means that a COMMON block is no longer referred to by either the program unit currently being executed or by any 'higher level' program units the contents of the COMMON block become undefined in exactly the same way as do local variables on exit from a subprogram. If we do not wish this to happen, for example if we want to keep some or all of the COMMON values for use on the next entry to a subprogram (or group of subprograms), then we have two options.

The first is to use the SAVE statement. In Section 10.9 we stated that this took the form

SAVE name1, name2 . . .

where 'name1' etc. were the names of local variables or arrays. We can now extend this to include the global names of COMMON blocks (which are declared in the same program unit) enclosed in 'slashes'. Thus the statement

SAVE NAME,POS,/CB1/,SCORE

will save the three local variables NAME, POS and SCORE and *all* the contents of the COMMON block CB1.

If a COMMON block name appears in a SAVE statement in one subprogram, then it must appear in *every* subprogram which refers to that COMMON block.

The other way of preserving the values in a COMMON block (and probably the best way in many cases) is to declare the COMMON block in the main program. It is not necessary to use it there, but simply to include its name in a COMMON statement. As we saw in Fig. 11.5 this will mean that there is always a program unit which refers to the COMMON block and it will never become undefined.

In a large program with several named COMMON blocks it is, in any event, good practice to declare *all* the COMMON blocks in the main program unit so that it is possible to see the whole global storage at one time. This will also have the effect of preserving the values of all items in these blocks for the duration of the program.

This leads to the third difference between blank COMMON and COMMON blocks. Blank COMMON *never* becomes undefined; it is truly global and is always preserved throughout the entire execution of the program.

11.7 Sharing storage locations

In the foregoing we have assumed that a COMMON block is being used to enable several program units to access a common set of variables and arrays, to provide a common data base on which the program units may all operate. However, sometimes we may use a COMMON block for a very different reason, namely to reduce the amount of storage required by providing a common storage area which is used by different subprograms (or groups of subprograms) for completely different purposes. Thus one group of subprograms may contain a declaration such as

```
COMMON/SHARE/TABLE(4,25),MARK(50),N,X,P
```

while another might contain the declaration

```
COMMON/SHARE/A,B,C,AV(9,4,4),D(6)
```

Notice that both declarations lead to a size of 153 storage units, although the arrangement and type of value stored in those storage units is totally different.

Presumably the two groups of subroutines will not call each other, as this would destroy the contents of 'their' COMMON block, but they will be used in a sequential fashion. It would therefore be possible to have different COMMON blocks and to rely on the system to release the space used by one block when it becomes undefined. This is not always possible, however, and in any case many implementations will not re-use the storage space used by a COMMON block which has become undefined.

A more powerful way of sharing storage (or of referring to the same storage unit by two or more names, which comes to the same thing) is by means of the EQUIVALENCE statement. This allows the programmer to instruct the compiler to arrange for two or more variables or array elements to occupy the same storage unit, and takes the form

```
EQUIVALENCE (nlist1), (nlist2), . . .
```

where each 'nlist' is a list of variable names, array element names, array names and character substring names. If one of the names is of type CHARACTER then all the names in that list must also be of type CHARACTER.

The statement specifies that storage of all the items whose names appear in a list must start at the same storage unit. In this statement, *and in no other*, an array name is taken to refer to the first element of that array. Apart from the restriction regarding CHARACTER items there are no restrictions on the type of the names in a list and, for example, the statements

```
REAL R(2),RL,IM
COMPLEX C
EQUIVALENCE (R,RL,C),(R(2),IM)
```

will cause the real array R, the real variable RL and the complex variable C all to start at the same place, and will cause the real variable IM to start at the same place as R(2). Fig. 11.6 shows that this has the effect of making RL occupy the same storage unit as the real part of C, and IM the same storage unit as the imaginary part of C.

	real (C)	imag (C)
Complex C:		
Real array R:	R(1)	R(2)
Real variable R L:	RL	
Real variable I M:		IM

Fig. 11.6   Effect of equivalencing REAL and COMPLEX

It is not necessary for arrays or character strings to match and it is possible to arrange for them to overlap as is shown in Figs. 11.7 and 11.8. In the first of these the array elements X(50) and Y(100) are equivalenced, leading to the relationship shown in Fig. 11.7. This could equally well have been achieved by writing

```
EQUIVALENCE (X,Y(51))
```

or a number of other variations. The second example shows a similar situation with characters, where we can refer to substrings as well as variable names, array names and array elements. Once again there are a number of ways of expressing the relationship, and, for example, the shorter statement

```
EQUIVALENCE (A(6:),B,C(1)(3:))
```

would have done equally well, although reference to a substring of an array element should be avoided where possible, as it is slightly confusing at first sight.

					X(1)	X(2)		X(49)	X(50)
Y(1)	Y(2)		Y(49)	Y(50)	Y(51)	Y(52)		Y(99)	Y(100)

```
REAL X(50), Y(100)
EQUIVALENCE (X(50), Y(100))
```

Fig. 11.7   Equivalencing arrays

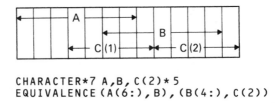

```
CHARACTER*7 A,B,C(2)*5
EQUIVALENCE (A(6:),B),(B(4:),C(2))
```

Fig. 11.8   Equivalencing character strings

EQUIVALENCE is usually used in large programs in association with **COMMON** blocks since it provides an easy way of identifying only those parts of the block which are relevant to a particular subprogram. For example if a **COMMON** block contains 10 variables A0 to A9 and ten arrays, each of a different size, B0 to B9 such that the total size of the block is 210 storage units it could be defined as follows

```
    COMMON/BLK/A0,A1,A2,A3,A4,A5,A6,A7,A8,A9,
   1  B0(5),B1(10),B2(7),B3(4,5),B4(8),B5(20),B6(4,6),
   2  B7(25),B8(7,9),B9(6,3)
```

However if a particular subprogram needed to access only A0, A7 and B4 we could write

```
    COMMON/BLK/BLK(210)
    EQUIVALENCE(A0,BLK),(A7,BLK(8)),(B4,BLK(53))
```

thereby avoiding the declaration of unnecessary variables and arrays. The next section shows the use of this technique in an extract from a very large real-life program.

In general these techniques are only applicable to large programs, and indeed **COMMON** is not usually required for small or medium-sized programs. In large programs, however, the ability to exercise a substantial degree of control over the layout of storage and its accessibility to different parts of the program can be absolutely invaluable.

11.8   An example from real-life

The real benefits of **COMMON** and **EQUIVALENCE** (especially the latter) cannot easily be demonstrated in a book such as this because they do not become apparent in programs of the size that we can include as examples. This section, therefore, shows a (very) short extract from a real-life program as an illustration of how they can be used in practice.

The program concerned is called APT IV, where APT stands for Automatically Programmed Tools, and was developed under sponsorship from over 100 organisations (including Rolls-Royce, ICL, IBM, Boeing, General Motors, the U.S. Air Force, etc.) at the Illinois Institute of Technology Research Institute in Chicago. The program, in fact, had its origins at M.I.T. in the late 1950's and was under continuous development for over 20 years, first at M.I.T., then at I.I.T.R.I., and finally at CAM-I (Computer Aided Manufacturing-International) at Arlington, Texas. The extract shown below dates from the central period of that development and was written in 1968. It predates Fortran 77 by some 10 years and yet, apart from some slight differences of style, is perfectly acceptable over a decade later – an eloquent tribute to the longevity of Fortran programs.

APT is a program which processes a high-level language so as to produce a control tape to drive a numerically controlled machine-tool, and has been used in the manufacture of almost all modern airliners, motor cars, spacecraft and innumerable artifacts which require high-precision machining of some or all of their parts. One part of the program is a 'library' of subroutines which are used in the analysis of the geometric surfaces defined by the user and in the calculation of the required motion on the machine-tool. In 1968, at the time of the first release of APT IV, this library contained 78 geometric definition routines, 92 tool motion routines, and 75 other routines – a total of 245 subroutines! (This was by no means the whole program – merely a part of one of four major phases.)

Due to the nature of the problem a very considerable number of these subroutines need access to global information and the layout of the storage is of vital importance. There are, in fact, twelve named **COMMON** blocks, of which one is conceptually divided into 18 different areas, several of which overlap.

Fig. 11.9 shows the first 70 or so lines of one subroutine from the library, **APT030**.

```
C
C.....FORTRAN SUBROUTINE              APT030...            3/1/68   GK
C
C              FORTRAN SUBROUTINE APT030
C
C PURPOSE       TO GENERATE THE CANONICAL FORM OF A CIRCLE DEFINED
C               AS TANGENT TO EACH OF TWO GIVEN LINES AND HAVING
C               A GIVEN RADIUS BY THE FOLLOWING APT STATEMENT
C               RESULT = CIRCLE/****, L1, ****, L2, RADIUS, RAD
C                 **** = XLARGE, YLARGE, XSMALL, YSMALL
C
C LINKAGE       CALL APT030 (RESULT, M1, L1, M2, L2, RAD)
C
C ARGUMENTS     RESULT  ARRAY TO CONTAIN THE CANONICAL FORM OF
C                       THE RESULTING CIRCLE
C               M1      INTEGER EQUIVALENT OF THE FIRST MODIFIER
C                           1 = XLARGE      2 = YLARGE
C                           4 = XSMALL      5 = YSMALL
C               L1      ARRAY CONTAINING THE CANONICAL FORM OF
C                       THE FIRST INPUT LINE
C               M2      INTEGER EQUIVALENT OF THE SECOND MODIFIER
C                           1 = XLARGE      2 = YLARGE
C                           4 = XSMALL      5 = YSMALL
C               L2      ARRAY CONTAINING THE CANONICAL FORM OF
C                       THE SECOND INPUT LINE
C               RAD     REAL VARIABLE CONTAINING THE VALUE OF THE
C                       DESIRED RADIUS
C
C SUBSIDIARIES TYPE                  ENTRY
C              SUBROUTINE            APT003
```

```
C              SUBROUTINE        APTO20
C              SUBROUTINE        APTO78
C
      SUBROUTINE APTO30 (RESULT,M1,L1,M2,L2,RAD)
      REAL L1,L2
      DIMENSION RESULT(7),L1(4),L2(4)
C
C
C
C...  1.MAIN CDE PACKAGE. INCLUDED IN EVERY PROGRAM IN THE SUBROUTINE
C...     LIBRARY.
C
      LOGICAL LDEF
      DIMENSION DEF(75),DSHARE(100),FXCOR(170),HOLRTH(20),SV(442),
     1          ZNUMBR(30),LDEF(15),ISV(379)
      DIMENSION IBRKPT(51),IDEF(20),IFXCOR(60),ISHARE(31),KNUMBR(51)
      COMMON/TOTAL/DEF,DSHARE,FXCOR,HOLRTH,SV,ZNUMBR,LDEF,ISV
      EQUIVALENCE(ISV(30),IBRKPT(1)),(ISV(110),KNUMBR(1)),
     1           (ISV(190),IDEF(1)),(ISV(210),ISHARE(1)),
     2           (ISV(279),IFXCOR(1))
C
C
C
C...  2.DEF BLOCK. REAL VARIABLES USED BY DEF. RED. ROUTINES WHICH MUST
C...     REMAIN INVIOLATE.
C
      REAL LN1
      DIMENSION        A(12,2),  AHOLD(2,4),    C1( 8),
     1                 LN1( 5),       R(10),   REF(2,4)
C
      EQUIVALENCE (DEF(1),A(1,1)),(DEF(25),AHOLD(1,1)),(DEF(33),C(1)),
     +            (DEF(41),LN1(1)), (DEF(46),R(1)), (DEF(56),REF(1,1))
C
C
C...  3. DSHARE DEF. RED. BLOCK. USED FOR REAL VARIABLES AND SHARED WITH
C...     ARELEM
C
      REAL L
      DIMENSION                   C(100),  G(93),  L(83),
     +           P(79), SC(63),  T(47), T1(35),  V(23)
C
      EQUIVALENCE  (DSHARE(100),  C(100),  G(93),  L(83),
     +           P(79), SC(63),  T(47), T1(35),  V(23))
C
C...  10. ZNUMBR BLOCK. REAL LITERALS.
C
      EQUIVALENCE (ZNUMBR(1),Z0), (ZNUMBR(2),Z1) , (ZNUMBR( 3),Z2)   ,
     1    (ZNUMBR( 4),Z3)   , (ZNUMBR( 5),Z5)   , (ZNUMBR( 6),Z10)   ,
     2    (ZNUMBR( 7),Z90)  , (ZNUMBR( 8),Z1E6) , (ZNUMBR( 9),Z1E38) ,
     3    (ZNUMBR(10),Z5EM1) , (ZNUMBR(11),Z6EM1) , (ZNUMBR(12),Z9EM1) ,
     4    (ZNUMBR(13),Z11EM1), (ZNUMBR(14),Z12EM1), (ZNUMBR(15),Z1EM2) ,
     4    (ZNUMBR(16),Z1EM3) , (ZNUMBR(17),Z1EM5) , (ZNUMBR(18),Z5EM6) ,
     5    (ZNUMBR(19),Z1EM6) , (ZNUMBR(20),Z1EM7) , (ZNUMBR(21),Z1EM9) ,
     6    (ZNUMBR(22),Z1EM1) , (ZNUMBR(23),ZM1)   , (ZNUMBR(24),DEGRAD),
     7    (ZNUMBR(25),PI)
C
```

Fig. 11.9   An example of the use of **COMMON** and **EQUIVALENCE** in **APT IV**

Notice that most of the lines are comments. In a large program it is essential to document fully every aspect of the program, and the inclusion of detailed comments and a specification of each subprogram within that subprogram is a sure way of doing this. This subroutine is used in the definition of a circle given two tangent lines and its radius.

The subroutine starts with a definition of the COMMON block TOTAL, which is 'included in every program in the subroutine library'. This block consists of 8 arrays, each of which will be equivalenced to other variables and/or arrays as appropriate for the particular subroutine.

'Block' 2 then contains a definition of arrays which are equivalenced to the array DEF.

'Block' 3 is a shared block, and in other routines 'blocks' 4, 5 and 6 are also equivalenced to the array DSHARE in completely different ways. Thus, different groups of subroutines will use this part of the COMMON block TOTAL for their own purposes in a well-planned and consistent way.

This subroutine does not use those parts of the COMMON block which correspond to the arrays FXCOR, HOLRTH or SV, and the next set of statements define 'block' 10, which consists of a set of real variables equivalenced to the array ZNUMBR.

Subsequent 'blocks' in this subroutine also define parts of the array ISV, which is actually defined in no less than 8 ways, not all of which define the whole array.

Thus each of the 245 subroutines in the library defines only those parts of the total data base which are relevant to its particular needs.

APT is a particularly good example of the use of COMMON and EQUIVA-LENCE due to the combination of its size and complexity with the overall modular structure of the program. However any large program can frequently benefit from an analysis of its global storage requirements, followed by the design of a suitable global data base with local entities equivalenced to the appropriate parts.

Summary

- A COMMON block is a contiguous block of memory in which the individual items are identified by their position within the block.

- A COMMON block may have a global name.

- There may be at most one (unnamed) blank COMMON block.

- Initial values can only be given to items in a named COMMON block, and then only in a special, non-executable, BLOCK DATA program unit.

- Named COMMON blocks become *undefined* when no currently active program units refer to them, unless referred to in a SAVE statement.

- The EQUIVALENCE statement instructs the compiler to arrange the program's storage so that two or more items share the same location(s).

COMMON *block declarations*	COMMON /name/list of local names
	COMMON list of local names
Initial statement	BLOCK DATA name
	BLOCK DATA
Saving COMMON *blocks*	SAVE /COMMON block name/,...
Sharing storage	EQUIVALENCE (name1,name2,...),...

Fig. 11.10   Fortran 77 statements introduced in Chapter 11

Exercises

11.1 Write the necessary specification statements to create a COMMON data base for
  (a) An accounting program which needs details of customers' names and account numbers, credit limits, outstanding balances and any other relevant items.
  (b) A payroll program which needs details for each employee of name, works number, hourly rate of pay, nominal hours worked per week, overtime rate of pay, weekly tax-free allowance, weekly superannuation payments, etc.
  (c) A program to analyse exam results.

11.2 Rewrite the program written in exercise 10.4 (e) to use COMMON blocks whenever possible.

11.3 Rewrite the program extract shown in Fig. 11.9 in a style more consistent with Fortran 77.

12 File Handling

12.1 Files and records

We have now met almost all the features of Fortran 77 and are well equipped to tackle problems of widely varying complexity. There is, however, one class of problems which we cannot even begin to deal with; namely, those problems in which the result of one run of the program are used as (part of) the input for a subsequent run. All our programming to date has been based on the assumption that when the program is run it reads some data, processes it, produces some results, and finishes. The results, it has been tacitly assumed, are produced in printed (or in graphical) form, while the data is typed directly into the computer (or punched onto cards for input). Once the program has finished nothing is left within the computer system.

This is, in fact, all that is required of a large proportion of programs; however, a significant number need to preserve some of the results produced for use on a subsequent occasion. Examples of this range from data processing activities such as payroll calculation or financial accounting, where past records are essential, to analysis of scientific experiments over a period of time, control of airline reservations, scheduling of production, or any other activity which requires knowledge of some past events of the same or similar type.

The backing store or *file store* of the computer system is used for this purpose. This consists of special input/output units usually, though not always, based on either magnetic tape and/or rapidly rotating magnetic disks. Information may be transferred to and from these units by using READ and WRITE statements in a similar manner to that used for data and results transferred via the standard input and output units. However, before we examine this in more detail, we must first define two important concepts – a record and a file.

We have referred to *records* informally when discussing input and output in the previous chapters, and have understood it to refer to a sequence of characters such as a line of type, a punched card, or a printed line of results. However, a record does not necessarily correspond in this way to some physical entity, but refers to some defined sequence of characters *or of values*. There are three types of records in Fortran 77 – formatted, unformatted and endfile records – and we shall discuss these in some detail in the next two sections.

A sequence of records forms a *file*, and the two main types are internal files (see section 12.4) and external files. We shall investigate external files in more detail before we start to examine the records of which they are comprised.

An *external file* is an identifiable sequence of records which is stored on some external medium. Thus a deck of punched cards is a file, as is a sheet of printed results. However, regardless of this strict definition, when we refer to a file we normally mean a file which is kept on backing store. There are two main types of backing store (magnetic tape and magnetic disk) and they have one very important difference.

A magnetic tape is essentially a *sequential* storage medium – in other words each record written to such a tape will normally be written after the previously written record, so that the normal way of reading the records is in the same order as they were written. A typical magnetic tape is over 2000 ft long (or almost 0.75 km) and may contain as many as 50 million characters or their equivalent. It would be extremely time-consuming to search for individual records in a random order. A magnetic disk on the other hand not only contains a considerably larger amount of information (perhaps as many as 500 million characters) but can access any of it in a fraction of a second since, at worst, the read head only needs to travel a few inches to position itself on the required part of the disk. Such a storage unit can therefore be used for *direct access* of information as well as sequential access, although the information in the file may need to contain some extra identifying information if this is to work correctly. Because the information anywhere on a magnetic disk (or other similar device) can be accessed so rapidly, and because a disk can hold so much information, a single disk will usually store a large number of separate files of information, frequently belonging to a number of different users of the computer. It is the job of the computer's operating system to keep a catalogue of all the files so that they can be made available to a program when required.

Because of the problems of sequential access, a magnetic tape usually consists of a single file, but the computer's operating system will catalogue this so that a record is kept of which file is stored on which physical magnetic tape. Thus the operating system will, usually, be able to request that the appropriate tape be loaded by a (human) computer operator whenever a program wishes to use a file which is stored on that tape.

For most purposes we may ignore the differences between the various types of backing store units and simply consider their mode of access –sequential or direct. However before we start to use either type of file we must investigate in more detail the three types of record which may make up a file.

12.2   Formatted and unformatted records

The first type is called a *formatted record*. Such a record consists of a sequence of *characters* selected from those which can be represented by the processor being used – that is the 49 characters in the Fortran character set plus any other special characters which may be permitted. (See Appendix D for details of two common character sets.) A formatted record is written by a formatted output statement such as we have been using since Chapter 6

```
WRITE(3,200) A,B,N,M
```

or by an output statement which uses list-directed formatting

```
WRITE(4,*) P,Q,X,Y
```

It may also be created by some means other than a Fortran program; for example it may be typed at a terminal or punched on a card. It is read, in a similar fashion, by a formatted input statement (including one which uses list-directed formatting).

An aspect of input or output records with which we have not concerned ourselves until now is their *length*. This is important in some situations, especially when using direct-access files (see Section 12.7), and for a formated record is measured in characters. Thus if the first statement above has an associated format

```
200 FORMAT (2F10.3,2I6)
```

then the length of the record(s) produced will be 32 characters. The second, list-directed, output statement is more awkward, since an understanding of the formats used (which may depend upon the size of the numbers and/or strings) is necessary before the length of the record produced can be determined. However list-directed formatting will not normally be used in situations where the length of the record(s) needs to be known. The length of a record may also depend upon the processor and the external medium (for example consider what happens with printer control characters when output is sent to the printer) and may be zero in some circumstances.

A formatted record is formatted so that it can be represented in a form that human beings (or another computer) can understand. The work involved in converting values from their internal (binary) representation into character form, or vice-versa, imposes a considerable overhead. If the information is being written to a file so that the same program, or another one, can subsequently read it back there is clearly no need to convert it to character form. (Indeed, where numbers are concerned, the process of converting to character form and then converting back to internal form will probably introduce errors due to the difference in precision of the internal and character representations.) For this purpose there exists in Fortran 77 a second type of record – an *unformatted record*.

An unformatted record consists of a sequence of *values* (in a processor-dependent form) and is, essentially, a copy of some part, or parts of the memory. An unformatted record can only be produced by an unformatted output statement, which is the same as a formatted WRITE statement but without any format specifier

```
WRITE(6) A,B,N,M
WRITE(UNIT=5,ERR=99) X,Y,Z
```

Similarly, an unformatted record can only be read by an unformatted input statement

```
READ(6) A,B,N,M
READ(UNIT=5,END=98,ERR=99) X,Y,Z
```

The length of an unformatted record is measured in computer dependent terms, and will depend primarily upon the output list used when it was written. The two most common units of measurement are 'bytes' or 'words' (see Appendix D for a definition of these). It is essential that, where the length is important, the programmer is aware of the units used on his computer and the relationship between these units and the various types of information. Thus, for example, a computer system which uses 'bytes' as a unit of measurement will typically use one byte for a character storage unit and four bytes for a numeric storage unit, whereas one which uses 'words' as a unit of measurement might use one word for a character storage unit and two for a numeric one, or even one word for both types of storage unit.

One important difference between the input/output of formatted and unformatted records is that whereas a formatted input or output statement may read or write more than one record by use of a suitable format, e.g.

```
     WRITE(5,500)N,M,(A(I),I=1,100)
 500 FORMAT(2I8/(4F12.4))
```

an unformatted input or output statement will always read or write exactly *one* record. The length of the input list in an unformatted read statement must therefore be the same length as the output list that wrote it, or less (in which case the last few items will remain unread).

12.3 Endfile records

As well as formatted and unformatted records there is a third type of record which is particularly important for files which are to be accessed sequentially; this is the *endfile record*. An endfile record is a special type of record which can only occur as the last record of a file and is written by a special statement

```
     ENDFILE u
```

or

```
     ENDFILE (auxlist)
```

In the first case 'u' is the unit number to which an endfile record is to be written, while in the second case 'auxlist' may contain any of the specifiers shown in Fig. 12.1 (which are the same as the corresponding specifiers for use with a WRITE statement introduced in Chapter 6).

UNIT = u (or u)
ERR = s
IOSTAT = *ios*

Fig. 12.1 Specifiers for use with ENDFILE

The ENDFILE statement writes a special endfile record to the specified file and leaves the file positioned after that record. It is not possible to subsequently write to, or read from, that file without first repositioning it using a REWIND or BACKSPACE statement (see section 12.6).

An endfile record has no defined length, but if it is read by an input statement it will cause an 'end-of-file condition' which can be detected by an END or IOSTAT specifier in a READ statement (see section 6.3). If it is not specifically detected in this way an error will occur and the program will fail.

It is good practice to place an endfile record at the end of all sequential files. In this way a program which is subsequently reading the file can detect the end of the file very easily without the need for any other special records or counts. It also acts as a safeguard against an error which might cause the program not to detect the end of the information in the file. We shall see an example of its use in Example 12.3, when we discuss in detail how we may use sequential files to store information between program runs.

12.4   Internal files

An internal file is not really a file at all but behaves like one, and can be used to great advantage in particular situations; we shall therefore describe its features and its use before discussing (real) external files.

An internal file is actually a means whereby the power and flexibility of the Fortran 77 formatting process can be used to convert information in the memory from one format to another. Such a file is a character variable, character array element, character array, or character substring.

If the file is a character variable, array element or substring then it consists of a single record, while if it is a character array it consists of a sequence of records, each of which corresponds to one element of the array. In the latter case the whole file must be input or output by means of a single statement since a READ or WRITE statement on an internal file *always* starts at the beginning of the file.

An internal file can only be read by a (sequential) formatted READ statement that does not specify list-directed formatting. It can only be written by a (sequential) formatted WRITE statement that does not specify list-directed formatting, or it can be created by any other appropriate means – for example by an assignment statement or by input from some other source.

We specify an internal file by using the name of the character variable (or other item) in a READ or WRITE statement in place of the unit identifier. Thus if LINE is a character variable we may write

```
WRITE(LINE,201) X,Y,Z
READ(UNIT=LINE,FMT=150) A,B,C
etc.
```

The following two examples illustrate two typical situations in which an internal file can be useful.

Example 12.1
Write a function subprogram which takes a real number (X) and an integer (N) and returns as its value the value of X rounded to N significant digits.

This is an artificial example since it is difficult to see why we should wish to reduce the accuracy to which numbers are held internally, but it does give a simple illustration of how an internal file can be used. To carry out this function by some other means would involve a complicated sequence of arithmetic operations and tests; however, the E edit descriptor automatically produces a number rounded to a given number of significant digits. All the function needs to do therefore is to choose an appropriate format, depending on the value of N. We shall assume that N must lie within the range 1–9 (i.e. that numbers cannot be held to more than 9 digits of accuracy) and will treat numbers outside this range as 1 or 9, as appropriate.

```
      REAL FUNCTION ROUND(X,N)
      CHARACTER D(9),NUM*20
      DATA D/'1','2','3','4','5','6','7','8','9'/
C CHECK VALUE OF N AND SET I TO VALID N
      IF (N.LT.1) THEN
        I = 1
      ELSE IF (N.GT.9) THEN
        I = 9
      ELSE
        I = N
      END IF
C USE CHARACTER EXPRESSION AS FORMAT FOR OUTPUT
      WRITE (NUM,'(E20.'//D(I)//')') X
C INPUT FORMAT CAN BE STANDARD
      READ (NUM,'(F20.0)') ROUND
      RETURN
      END
```

The function first sets I to the number of significant digits and then 'writes' X to the 20-character internal file NUM using a format of E20.d, where d is the character representation of I. This number will occupy a maximum of 16 characters and so a field width of 20 is more than sufficient. The subsequent input is easier since the form of the character representation (including an exponent) means that only the field width is necessary for an F edit descriptor.

Example 12.2

A survey has been carried out to obtain statistics concerning the occupation of people in a certain area. The results of the survey are available for input to the computer in the following format

columns 1–20   name
column 23   sex (M/F)
column 25   job status = 1 if in full-time education
                          = 2 if in full-time employment
                          = 3 if in part-time employment
                          = 4 if temporarily unemployed
                          = 5 if not working or seeking a job

This is followed by one or more items depending upon the job status of the respondent

job status	= 1	columns 28,29	age
	= 2	columns 28–31	monthly salary (in pounds)
	= 3	columns 28–31	monthly salary (in pounds)
		columns 34–37	other monthly income (in pounds)
	= 4	columns 28,29	age
		columns 32–34	no. of months unemployed
	= 5	columns 28,29	age
		column 31	code = 1 if looking after children
			= 2 if looking after any other relatives
			= 3 for any other reason

The data is terminated by a record which contains the characters *END* in columns 1–5 and is otherwise blank.

Write an input subprogram which will read a maximum of 1000 records and store the relevant details in suitable arrays for subsequent use by other subprograms.

This data is very similar to that used in Example 6.4. In that case the data was read and re-read by use of T edit descriptors with unspecified fields being assumed to be blank. A far better way is to read each record into a character variable and then to treat this as an internal file which can be read by an appropriate format.

We shall need the following arrays for the data

NAME	CHARACTER*20	name of respondent
MALE	LOGICAL	*true* if male, *false* otherwise
STATUS	INTEGER	job status
AGE	INTEGER	age (where appropriate)
SALARY	INTEGER	monthly salary (where appropriate)
EXTRA	INTEGER	other monthly income (where appropriate)
JOBLES	INTEGER	no. of months unemployed (where appropriate)
HOME	INTEGER	code for those not working (where appropriate)

Since there are eight of these, and they will be required by other subprograms, we shall place them in two COMMON blocks, one (NAMES) for the CHARACTER array NAME and the other (SURVEY) for the remaining seven arrays. We also notice that, of these eight potential data items, all respondents will have entries in the first three, but none will have entries in more than two of the others. A further examination shows that no respondent is required to give both age and salary, and that no respondent gives more than one of the other three. We may therefore save considerable memory space by use of EQUIVALENCE to enable these two groups to share the same storage.

A structure plan for the subroutine can now be drawn up

   1 Repeat the following up to 1000 times
      1.1 Read next record into an internal file
      1.2 If name is *END* then exit
      1.3 Read name, sex, and job status from file

> *1.4* If job status is 1 then
>   *1.4.1* read age
>   otherwise if job status is 2 then
>   *1.4.2* read salary

.
.
.

2 Return with count of people

The subroutine is then quite straightforward

```
      SUBROUTINE INPUT(NP)
      PARAMETER (MAX=1000)
      CHARACTER NAME(MAX)*20,SEX,REC*40
      LOGICAL MALE(MAX)
      INTEGER STATUS(MAX),AGE(MAX),SALARY(MAX),EXTRA(MAX),
     *         JOBLES(MAX),HOME(MAX)
      COMMON /SURVEY/MALE,STATUS,AGE,EXTRA
      COMMON /NAMES/NAME
      EQUIVALENCE (AGE,SALARY),(EXTRA,JOBLES,HOME)
      DO 10, I=1,MAX
        READ 100,REC
100     FORMAT(A40)
        IF (REC(1:5).EQ.'*END*') GOTO 11
        READ (REC,150) NAME(I),SEX,JSTAT
150     FORMAT(A20,2X,A1,1X,I1)
        MALE(I) = SEX.EQ.'M'
        STATUS(I) = JSTAT
        IF (JSTAT.EQ.1) THEN
          READ REC,'(27X,I2)') AGE(I)
        ELSE IF (JSTAT.EQ.2) THEN
          READ (REC,'(27X,I4)') SALARY(I)
        ELSE IF (JSTAT.EQ.3) THEN
          READ (REC,'(27X,I4,2X,I4)') SALARY(I),EXTRA(I)
        ELSE IF (JSTAT.EQ.4) THEN
          READ (REC,'(27X,I2,2X,I3)') AGE(I),JOBLES(I)
        ELSE IF (JSTAT.EQ.5) THEN
          READ (REC,'(27X,I2,1X,I1)') AGE(I),HOME(I)
        END IF
10    CONTINUE
11 NP = I-1
      RETURN
      END
```

Notice that the original data is read using an A40 edit descriptor thus creating an all character representation of the data in the internal file REC. This may be dealt with in the usual way as a character variable, or it may be read as an internal file. Thus, for example, the first input from the file and the following statement could be replaced by

```
      NAME(I) = REC(1:20)
      MALE(I) = REC(23:23).EQ.'M'
```

However the job status code will still need to be converted to integer form and the READ statement is the easiest way to do this. Notice also that the job status has been placed in a variable as well as in the array for ease of writing (and comprehension) in the block IF.

12.5   Connecting an external file to your program

Before an input/output *unit* can be used it has to be *connected* to the program, although certain peripheral units (such as the standard input unit and the standard output unit) will always be *preconnected* (see sections 6.1 and 6.3). We need to examine how we can connect a particular file to our program and what implications this has.

Every computer system normally has a very large number of files which, in some sense or other 'belong' to that computer. Some, such as a lineprinter listing, do not belong to it for very long while others, such as files on backing store, may belong to it for a considerable period of time. These files have been created by the various users of the computer, or by those who are responsible for its operation, or even by the computer's operating system, and have various levels of accessibility. For example, a file containing a library of widely used subroutines, or a Fortran 77 compiler, will probably be available to all users of the computer; a file created by a user to contain his own, private, research data, on the other hand, will almost certainly only be accessible by the user himself. At any given time, therefore, a particular program will only be allowed to access a certain number of the files held by the computer; only these files are said to *exist* for that program.

Before a file can exist it must be created, and therefore *creating* a file means causing a file to exist that did not previously exist. Notice that this does not necessarily have any effect on the total number of files known to the whole computer system – the act of creating a file simply means that the file exists for the program that creates it. For example, a program may wish to access a file belonging to another user; the act of creating the file in this case merely means granting access to it, whereupon it will exist for this program. In a similar way, *deleting* a file means terminating the existence of a file; once again it does not necessarily mean that the file is removed from the computer system. One effect of this is that a file may exist and yet not contain any records, for example when it has just been created but not yet written to.

For any information to be transferred between a file and a program the file must be *connected* to a unit, in other words a logical connection (or relationship) must be established between the file and a unit number (as used in a READ or WRITE statement); in some cases a physical connection must also be established (e.g. a particular magnetic tape must be loaded on a tape deck). Some units will be preconnected to a program, but all others must be specifically connected, before being used, by means of an OPEN statement. This takes the form

    OPEN (olist)

where 'olist' is a list of open specifiers, as shown in Fig. 12.2.

```
UNIT = u (or u)
FILE = fn
STATUS = st
ACCESS = acc
FORM = fm
RECL = len
BLANK = bl
ERR = s
IOSTAT = ios
```

Fig. 12.2   Specifiers for use with OPEN

The first of these, UNIT, must be present, while the others are all optional.

The UNIT specifier takes the same form as in the READ, WRITE and ENDFILE statements, and, as in those cases, the 'UNIT=' may be omitted if this is the first specifier.

If we are concerned with files on backing store they will normally have a name by which they are known to the computer system. This name is specified by using the FILE specifier which takes the form

```
FILE=fn
```

where 'fn' is a character expression which, after the removal of any trailing blanks, takes the form of a file name for the particular computer system. Thus if a file name may consist of up to 12 characters we could read the name of a file as data and then connect the file of that name to our program as follows

```
        .
        .
        .
CHARACTER*12,FNAME
READ '(A12)',FNAME
OPEN (9,FILE=FNAME)
        .
        .
        .
```

This will connect unit 9 to the file whose name was input, and thereafter any input or output using unit 9 will read from or write to that file.

We sometimes wish to define certain restrictions on our use of the file; for example we may wish to ensure that we do not overwrite an existing file by accident. We may use the STATUS specifier for this purpose by writing

```
STATUS = st
```

where 'st' is a character expression which, after removing any trailing blanks, is one of OLD, NEW, SCRATCH or UNKNOWN. Note that 'st' is a character *expression* and therefore, in practice, we write

```
STATUS  =  'OLD'
STATUS  =  'NEW'
```
etc.

If 'st' is OLD then the file must already exist, whereas if it is NEW then it must not already exist. If a file whose status is specified as NEW is successfully opened then its status is changed to OLD and any subsequent attempt to OPEN the file as NEW will fail.

If 'st' is SCRATCH then a special un-named file is created for use by the program; when the program ceases execution the file will be deleted and will cease to exist. Such a file can therefore be used as a temporary file for the duration of execution only. It is not permitted, for obvious reasons, to specify that the status of a named file (i.e. one with a FILE specifier) is SCRATCH.

Finally, if 'st' is UNKNOWN, or if no STATUS specifier is included, the status of the file is dependent upon the particular implementation. In most cases if the file exists it will be treated as OLD, if it does not exist it will be treated as NEW. Some implementations have different UNKNOWN conditions and so no assumptions should be made without checking on the exact situation for the computer being used.

The next two specifiers define what type of file we require, in terms of its mode of access and whether or not it is formatted. The first of these

```
ACCESS=acc
```

specifies the mode of access which is to be used; 'acc' is a character expression which, ignoring any trailing blanks, is either SEQUENTIAL or DIRECT. If this specifier is omitted then SEQUENTIAL is assumed; in general, therefore, an ACCESS specifier is only used to define DIRECT access.

Because of the different ways in which they are written and read, the records in a file must either all be formatted or all be unformatted, and the specifier

```
FORM=fm
```

is used to specify which is required. The character expression 'fm' must take one of the two values FORMATTED or UNFORMATTED, after the removal of any trailing blanks. If this specifier is omitted then the file is assumed to be formatted if it is connected for sequential access, but unformatted if it is connected for direct access. Thus

```
OPEN (9,FILE='DATAFILE')
```

will connect the file DATAFILE to unit 9 as a formatted, sequential access file. On the other hand

```
OPEN (8,FILE='DATA2',ACCESS='DIRECT')
```

will connect the file DATA2 to unit 8 as an unformatted, direct access file, and

```
OPEN (7,STATUS='SCRATCH',FORM='UNFORMATTED')
```

will create a temporary 'scratch file' and connect it to unit 7 as an unformatted, sequential access file.

The next specifier, RECL, is only used with direct access files and will be discussed in Section 12.7.

The final aspect of a file which may need specifying concerns the interpretation of blank characters in formatted numeric fields. Normally, when reading a formatted file that has been connected to the program by means of an OPEN statement, any blank characters which are read as part of a number are ignored. Since, in general, such a file will have been created by another program (or by the same one) any blanks will normally be either leading or trailing and should be ignored. We may, however, specify that blanks are not to be ignored by means of a specifier of the form

```
BLANK=bl
```

where 'bl' is, ignoring any trailing blanks, either NULL or ZERO. If it is NULL, or if the specifier is omitted, then any blanks will be ignored in formatted numeric fields; if it is ZERO they will be treated as zeros. Note that this only applies to files that are explicitly connected to the program; the interpretation of such blanks in preconnected files is processor dependent (see Section 6.8). In this connection, we saw how we could use the BN or BZ edit specifiers to define *for a particular format* what interpretation was to be placed on blanks. Such an edit descriptor will always over-ride the effect of any BLANK specifier for input using that format. A BLANK specifier is not allowed with an unformatted file.

The final two specifiers are concerned with recognising when an error occurs during the connection process (e.g. if the named file does not exist or is of the wrong type). In the event of an error the execution of the program will be terminated unless either an ERR or IOSTAT specifier is present (or both); these are similar in effect to those used with READ, WRITE and ENDFILE. If the specifier

```
ERR=s
```

is present and an error occurs then processing will continue from the statement with label 's'. If the specifier

```
IOSTAT=ios
```

is present then the integer variable 'ios' will be set to zero if no error occurs and to a computer-dependent positive value if some error has occurred. Examination of 'ios' may indicate the cause of the error and, in some circumstances, may enable the program to take remedial action.

In certain circumstances it is permitted to obey an OPEN statement which refers to a unit already connected to a file. There are essentially three cases here

- If the file in the OPEN statement is not the same as that currently connected then the currently connected file is 'disconnected' (see the description of CLOSE below) and the specified, new, file connected.

- If the file in the OPEN statement is the same as that currently connected then the only other specifier that is allowed is BLANK, to alter the interpretation of blanks thereafter.

- If the unit is preconnected then the OPEN statement may be used to define additional properties (e.g. BLANK='ZERO').

It is never permitted to attempt to connect a unit to a file if that file is already connected to a different unit.

Sometimes it is useful to be able to 'disconnect' a file, although this will be done automatically when the program's execution is finished. This can be achieved by use of the statement

CLOSE (auxlist)

where 'auxlist' is a list of one or more of the specifiers shown in Fig. 12.3. There must be a UNIT specifier, and the ERR and IOSTAT specifiers take the usual form. The STATUS specifier, however, is used to define what is to happen to the file after it has been disconnected. If the character expression 'st' has the value KEEP, after the removal of any trailing blanks, then the file will continue to exist; however, if it has the value DELETE then the file will cease to exist and cannot be accessed again by the program. (Note that the use of STATUS='DELETE' does not necessarily mean that the file is removed from the computer's file store, but merely that it no longer exists as far as this program is concerned.) If no STATUS specifier is given then KEEP is assumed, unless the file was opened with a STATUS='SCRATCH' specifier, in which case DELETE is assumed.

UNIT $= u$ (or u)
STATUS $= st$
ERR $= s$
IOSTAT $= ios$

Fig. 12.3 Specifiers for use with CLOSE

12.6   File positioning statements

As well as opening and closing a file and writing or reading records in the file there are two further statements which enable us to 'position' a file. The first of these

BACKSPACE u

or

BACKSPACE (auxlist)

causes the file to be positioned just before the *preceding* record (i.e. it enables the program to read the last record again.) 'auxlist' is a list of UNIT, ERR or IOSTAT specifiers as shown in Fig. 12.4.

UNIT $= u$ (or u)
ERR $= s$
IOSTAT $= ios$

Fig. 12.4 Specifiers for use with BACKSPACE and REWIND

The other file positioning statement is

    REWIND u

or

    REWIND (auxlist)

which causes the file to be positioned just before the *first* record so that a subsequent input statement will start reading the file from the beginning.

These two statements are particularly important when we are dealing with endfile records because if a program has either read or written an endfile record it cannot read or write any more records until either a BACKSPACE or REWIND statement has positioned the file before the endfile record (Section 12.3).

One further important point about the positioning of a file particularly concerns the writing of information to a file in a sequential manner. The rule in Fortran is that *writing a record to a sequential file destroys all information in the file after that record*. This is, in part, a reminder of the days when all sequential files were on magnetic tape and the physical characteristics of a magnetic tape unit had exactly this effect.

Thus it is not possible to use BACKSPACE and/or REWIND in order to position a file so that a particular record can be overwritten by a new one, but only so that the rest of the file can be overwritten or a particular record or records can be read. (Selective overwriting of individual records is possible with direct access files, see Section 12.7.)

A common use of BACKSPACE in conjunction with ENDFILE is to add information at the end of a previously written file, e.g.

```
             .
             .
             .
C   READ UP TO END OF FILE
    20 READ (5,END=21) N
       GOTO 20
    21 BACKSPACE 5
C   NOW ADD NEW INFORMATION
       WRITE (5) . . . . .
             .
             .
             .
```

```
C  FINISH FILE WITH AN END-OF-FILE FOR NEXT TIME
      ENDFILE 5
          .
          .
          .
```

We are now in a position to illustrate the use of files in a real example.

Example 12.3

The weekly paid employees in a certain organisation have their pay determined in the following way

(a) The gross pay consists of N hours at a basic rate of pay plus a higher rate for all subsequent hours. Both rates of pay and the number of basic hours (N) are fixed on an individual basis.
(b) Tax is a fixed percentage of the gross pay less a tax free allowance.
(c) Health insurance is a fixed percentage of that part of the gross pay which falls below a fixed limit.
(d) The nett pay is the gross pay less tax and health insurance deductions.

A file is kept which contains details of all weekly paid employees in increasing order of their staff numbers.

Each week, a file of data is prepared containing, for each employee, their staff number and the hours worked (in hours and minutes) during the previous week. This data is sorted into increasing order of staff numbers before input to the computer.

Write a program to update the master file and to produce weekly payslips showing name, staff number, gross pay, deductions and nett pay.

This is a slightly simplified version of one of the classic data processing applications. One of the major problems in this type of application is the matching of new data to that on file. We have eliminated this by requiring the data to be pre-sorted; in real-life an initial (input) phase will produce a suitably sorted file. We have also ignored such matters as the addition of new employees and the deletion of those who have left. The simplified problem nevertheless is a realistic one.

We shall assume that the calculation of deductions follows the normal (British) practice, and that a change in the rate of tax applies to the whole year, whereas a change in insurance contributions only applies from the date of the change. This means that tax must be calculated by first calculating the tax due on the total gross pay to date in the current year (at the current rate) and subtracting from this the tax already paid.

In addition to the name, staff number, basic weekly hours, both basic and overtime rates of pay and weekly tax free pay, it will be necessary to keep the gross pay earned to date, the gross tax-free pay to date and the tax paid to date. Also for completeness it would seem advisable to keep the insurance contributions paid to date and the total nett pay earned to date, although this last can easily be calculated from the other items.

The basic method of operation will be to copy the file, updating each record with new weekly data before producing a payslip. If there are no details for an employee it will be assumed that no hours were worked – this will normally generate a tax refund because of the increase in the total tax-free pay to date. To avoid difficulties, an employee who has not worked should have a record with zero hours; however, we shall endeavour to deal with missing employees correctly.

The current rates of tax and insurance and the maximum pay on which insurance contributions are based will be read before reading the employee data.

We are now ready to write a structure plan

1   Open old and new files
2   Read fixed rates etc.
3   Repeat the following until the end of the master file
    3.1   Read next employee record
    3.2   Read next data record
    3.3   If they match then
          3.3.1   Calculate gross weekly pay
          3.3.2   Calculate deductions
          3.3.3   Calculate nett pay
          3.3.4   Write updated record to new file
          3.3.5   Print payslip
          otherwise
          3.3.6   Print warning message
          3.3.7   Update tax details
          3.3.8   Write updated record to new file
          3.3.9   Print payslip
          3.3.10 'Backspace' file of data records
4   Put endfile on new file

Notice particularly step *3.3.10*. If the employee record on file does not match that submitted as data then we are assuming that no hours have been worked by the employee on file. We therefore update his record on file and calculate any tax refund due before printing a payslip (having already printed a warning of possible errors). We now need to compare the next record on file with the same input data and the easiest way to do this is simply to read the same input data again; this can be achieved by 'backspacing' the input file (even if it is the standard input unit).

Note that steps *3.3.2–3.3.5* are essentially the same as steps *3.3.7–3.3.9* apart from the fact that the gross pay in the latter case is zero. We can, therefore, put these steps into a subroutine.

One final point before we write the program, concerns the names of the two files. We shall read these as data; clearly the old file must already exist, however, it does not matter whether the new one exists already (in which case it will be overwritten) or whether it does not (in which case it will be created). The program now follows from the structure plan

```
      PROGRAM PAYROL
      CHARACTER*12 NEWFIL,OLDFIL,NAME*20
      REAL  INSRTE,INSMAX
      INTEGER STFNUM,HRS
      COMMON /STAFF/NAME
      COMMON /PAYDTA/STFNUM,HOURS,HRATE,ORATE,ALLOW,CUMGRS,
     *        CUMALL,CUMTAX,CUMINS,CUMNET,TAXRTE,INSRTE,INSMAX
```

```
C
C  INITIAL DATA IS READ FROM THE STANDARD INPUT UNIT
C  ERRORS ARE PRINTED ON THE STANDARD OUTPUT UNIT
C  UNIT 5 IS PAYROLL DATA (PRE-CONNECTED)
C  UNIT 6 IS PAYSLIPS (PRE-CONNECTED)
C  UNIT 7 IS OLD FILE
C  UNIT 8 IS NEW (UPDATED) FILE
C
C  FORMAT 101 IS FOR NAMES OF FILES (OLD,NEW)
C
   101 FORMAT(A12,8X,A12)
C
C  FORMAT 102 IS FOR TAX RATE, INSURANCE RATE, AND
C                      MAXIMUM SALARY FOR INSURANCE DEDUCTIONS
C
   102 FORMAT(BZ,2F10.2,F10.0)
C
C  FORMAT      103 IS FOR EMPLOYEE NUMBER AND TIME WORKED (HRS,MINS)
C
   103 FORMAT(BZ,I4,2X,I3,1X,I2)
C
C  READ FILE NAMES AND OPEN THEM
       READ 101,OLDFIL,NEWFIL
       OPEN (7,FILE=OLDFIL,STATUS='OLD',FORM='UNFORMATTED',
     *  ERR=93)
       OPEN (8,FILE=NEWFIL,FORM='UNFORMATTED',ERR=94)
C  READ TAX RATES ETC.
       READ 102,TAXRTE,INSRTE,INSMAX
C  CONVERT PERCENTAGE RATES TO FRACTIONS
       TAXRTE = 0.01*TAXRTE
       INSRTE = 0.01*INSRTE
C  MAIN LOOP TO UPDATE FILE AND PRINT PAYSLIPS
       DO 10,I=1,10000
         READ (7,END=15) NAME,STFNUM,HOURS,HRATE,ORATE,ALLOW,
     *     CUMGRS,CUMALL,CUMTAX,CUMINS,CUMNET
         READ (5,103) NUM,HRS,MINS
         IF (NUM.EQ.STFNUM) THEN
C  CALCULATE GROSS PAY
           TIME = HRS+MINS/60.0
           IF (TIME.GT.HOURS) THEN
             GROSS = HRATE*HOURS+ORATE*(TIME-HOURS)
           ELSE
             GROSS = HRATE*TIME
           END IF
```

(continued)

```
C  UPDATE FILE AND PRINT PAYSLIP
         CALL UPDATE(GROSS)
       ELSE
C  NO DATA FOR EMPLOYEE ON FILE
         PRINT '(1H ,''WARNING - NO DATA FOR '',A20,
     *       '' STAFF NUMBER:'',I6)', NAME,STFNUM
C  UPDATE FILE AND PRINT PAYSLIP FOR ZERO GROSS PAY
         CALL UPDATE(0.0)
C  BACKSPACE PAYROLL DATA AND TRY AGAIN
         BACKSPACE 5
       END IF
   10    CONTINUE
C  ALL EMPLOYEE RECORDS UPDATED
   15 ENDFILE 8
      STOP
C  ERRORS DURING OPENING FILES
   93 PRINT 290,OLDFIL
      STOP
   94 PRINT 290,NEWFIL
      STOP
  290 FORMAT(1H1,'*** ERROR DURING OPENING OF ',A12,
     * 'PROCESSING TERMINATED ***')
      END

      SUBROUTINE UPDATE(GROSS)
      CHARACTER*20 NAME
      REAL INSRTE,INSMAX,INSDED
      INTEGER STFNUM
      COMMON /STAFF/NAME
      COMMON /PAYDTA/STFNUM,HOURS,HRATE,ORATE,ALLOW,CUMGRS,
     *        CUMALL,CUMTAX,CUMINS,CUMNET,TAXRTE,INSRTE,INSMAX
C  CALCULATE TAX DUE
      CUMGRS = CUMGRS+GROSS
      CUMALL = CUMALL+ALLOW
      TAX = TAXRTE*(CUMGRS-CUMALL)
      TAXDED = TAX-CUMTAX
C  CALCULATE INSURANCE DEDUCTION
      IF (GROSS.GT.INSMAX) THEN
        INSDED = INSRTE*INSMAX
      ELSE
        INSDED = INSRTE*GROSS
      END IF
C  CALCULATE NETT PAY
      PAY = GROSS-(TAXDED+INSDED)
C  WRITE UPDATED FILE
      WRITE (8) NAME,STFNUM,HOURS,HRATE,ORATE,ALLOW,CUMGRS,
     * CUMALL,TAX,CUMINS+INSDED,CUMNET+PAY
C  PRINT PAYSLIP
      WRITE (6,200) NAME,STFNUM,GROSS,TAXDED,INSDED,PAY
      RETURN
  200 FORMAT(1H1,A20,4X,I6/1H0,F8.2,2(5X,F8.2)/1H0,10X,F8.2)
      END
```

12.7   Direct access files

One of the problems with magnetic tapes (or any other sequential storage medium) is that it is grossly inefficient to read the information in any order other than sequential, and it is impossible to write information to them other than sequentially. One of the consequences of this is that data processing applications which use this form of backing store spend a large part of their time sorting information into the correct order for the next stage. Thus, in Example 12.3 we assumed that the weekly data was already in the correct order. In real life an earlier stage would have read the data and stored it in a file, having first sorted it into order of staff numbers as required by the next part of the program. Many applications, especially those which run in 'real-time' such as reservation or enquiry systems, are not practical with this restriction on their access to backing store.

A later form of magnetic storage, which has now largely replaced magnetic tape for all purposes other than archiving, is the magnetic disk. This consists of one or more rapidly rotating disks on which information is written in a series of concentric bands. In systems which have several, parallel, disks rotating on the same axis (see Fig. 12.5), each disk has its own read/write head and information is written on a series of parallel bands (forming a *cylinder*) in order to minimise the movement of the heads.

Fig. 12.5   Single and multiple-disk drives

In the worst case the time it takes to access a particular record on a disk is the time taken to move the read/write head from the outermost to the innermost band (or *track*), or vice-versa, plus the time of one complete revolution. This will only be a fraction of a second, and in general the access time is considerably less than this.

A disk unit is, therefore, known as a *direct access* (or sometimes *random access*) device because, for most practical purposes, it can directly access any information stored on it. There are other types of direct access device, but their use is negligible compared with the almost universal use of disks.

The widespread availability of direct access devices was the major factor in the development of sophisticated filing systems on computers. As long as all files were sequential it was impossible to allow large numbers of users to have large numbers of files without the system becoming completely overloaded, with filestore overheads consuming most of the computing power available. A filestore kept on direct access devices, however, does not carry the same overhead, and so the arrival of direct access backing storage led to the development of comprehensive and sophisticated file-store systems.

A file that is kept on a direct access device does not need to be accessed in a direct access fashion. Many applications are perfectly suited to sequential access and this is the default form of access to a file in Fortran 77. Direct access files are, however, particularly useful in two related situations. The first of these is when the problem requires the use of direct access in order to read or write the records in the file in a random order, while the second is when the problem requires the selective over-writing (or updating) of some individual records in the file. This is not possible with a sequential file since writing a record causes it to become the *last* record in the file (Section 12.6).

If we wish to use a direct access file we must include the specifier

```
ACCESS='DIRECT'
```

in the OPEN statement for the file (see Section 12.5). This is not all that is required, however, since if a file is to be read, and more especially, written in a random order there are certain 'housekeeping' matters that must be attended to.

The first of these concerns the length of the records in the file. In order to allow the flexibility of being able to read and write records in any order it is necessary for all records to have the same length. This is specified in the OPEN statement for the file by the inclusion of the specifier

```
RECL=len
```

where 'len' is the length of each record in the file. Formatted record lengths are measured in characters, whereas unformatted record lengths are measured in some unit which depends upon the particular computer system being used (Section 12.2). If a file is connected for direct access it is assumed to be unformatted unless specifically stated to be formatted by means of a FORM specifier (Section 12.5). The nature of direct access devices means that it is rarely possible to transfer a file directly to another type of computer, and it is usually first copied onto a sequential medium such as magnetic tape, or transmitted (sequentially) along a direct connection between the computers. Direct access files are, therefore, almost invariably unformatted and the record length is computer dependent.

In order to write to, or read from, a direct access file it is necessary to define which record is to be written or read. In Chapter 6 we mentioned an additional specifier

```
REC=rn
```

which is used for direct-access input/output and, indeed, it is the presence (or absence) of this specifier that determines whether a READ or WRITE statement is a direct-access input/output statement, or a sequential one; 'rn' is the *record number* of the record to be read or written and takes the form of an integer expression with a positive value. Thus the statement

```
WRITE (7,REC=20) A,B,C,D
```

will write the values of A,B,C,D as an unformatted record to record 20 of the direct-access file connected to unit 7, and

```
READ (7,REC=I) W,X,Y,Z
```

will read the record number I from the same file.

We said that every record must have the same length in a direct access file, namely that defined in the OPEN statement. However, to a large extent, Fortran 77 enables us to ignore this restriction.

When writing an unformatted record to a direct-access file, the length of the record must not exceed the record length specified for the file. If it is less than the specified record length then the rest of the record in the file will be filled with undefined values in order to make it the correct length. As long as we do not attempt to read more than was written there is, therefore, no problem.

A similar situation exists with formatted records except that the record will be filled out with trailing blanks to make it the correct length. If a format used to write (or read) a direct access file specifies more than one record, then each successive record will be given a number one greater than the previous one. Thus the statements

```
    WRITE (8,200,REC=75) (A(I),I=1,100)
200 FORMAT (10F12.2)
```

will cause ten records to be written, since the format specifies that each record contains ten real numbers; these records will be numbered from 75 to 84, inclusive.

Example 12.4

Modify the program written for Example 12.3 so that the weekly data does not need to be sorted into order.

If the data is not to be sorted before input then, clearly, the master file will need to be capable of being accessed in a random fashion. The simplest way to deal with the problem is to use the staff number as the record number and to use it to access directly each employee's cumulative data, update it and produce the payslips. It is essential to have an input record for every employee as the absence of an employee would not be recognised. An altered version of the earlier program is then easily written

```
      PROGRAM PAYROL
      CHARACTER*12 FILNAM
      REAL INSRTE,INSMAX
      INTEGER STFNUM,HRS
      COMMON /TAXINS/TAXRTE,INSRTE,INSMAX
C
C   INITIAL DATA IS READ FROM THE STANDARD INPUT UNIT
C   ERRORS ARE PRINTED ON THE STANDARD OUTPUT UNIT
C   UNIT 5 IS PAYROLL DATA (PRE-CONNECTED)
C   UNIT 6 IS PAYSLIPS (PRE-CONNECTED)
C   UNIT 7 IS MASTER FILE
C
C   FORMAT 101 IS FOR MASTER FILE NAME
C
  101 FORMAT(A12)
C
```

```
C  FORMAT 102 IS FOR TAX RATE, INSURANCE RATE, AND
C                   MAXIMUM SALARY FOR INSURANCE DEDUCTIONS
C
  102 FORMAT(BZ,2F10.2,F10.0)
C
C  FORMAT      103 IS FOR EMPLOYEE NUMBER AND TIME WORKED (HRS,MINS)
C
  103 FORMAT(BZ,I4,2X,I3,1X,I2)
C
C  READ MASTER FILE NAME AND OPEN IT
C  PROGRAM ASSUMES 1 UNIT PER CHARACTER STORAGE UNIT
C  AND 4 UNITS PER NUMERIC STORAGE UNIT
      READ 101,FILNAM
      OPEN (7,FILE=FILNAM,STATUS='OLD',ACCESS='DIRECT',
     *  RECL=56,ERR=93)
C  READ TAX RATES ETC.
      READ 102,TAXRTE,INSRTE,INSMAX
C  CONVERT PERCENTAGE RATES TO FRACTIONS
      TAXRTE = 0.01*TAXRTE
      INSRTE = 0.01*INSRTE
C  MAIN LOOP TO UPDATE FILE AND PRINT PAYSLIPS
      DO 10, I=1,10000
         READ (5,103) STFNUM,HRS,MINS
C  ZERO STFNUM INDICATES THE END OF DATA
         IF (STFNUM.EQ.0) GOTO 15
C  UPDATE FILE AND PRINT PAYSLIP
         CALL UPDATE(STFNUM,HRS+MINS/60.0)
   10    CONTINUE
C  ALL PAYROLL DATA PROCESSED
   15 STOP
C  ERROR DURING OPENING
   93 PRINT 290,FILNAM
      STOP
  290 FORMAT(1H1,'*** ERROR DURING OPENING OF ',A12,
     *  'PROCESSING TERMINATED ***')
      END

      SUBROUTINE UPDATE(NUM,TIME)
      CHARACTER*20 NAME
      REAL INSRTE,INSMAX,INSDED
      COMMON /TAXINS/TAXRTE,INSRTE,INSMAX
C  GET EMPLOYEE'S RECORD
      READ (7,REC=NUM) NAME,HOURS,HRATE,ORATE,ALLOW,CUMGRS,
     *  CUMALL,CUMTAX,CUMINS,CUMNET
C  CALCULATE GROSS PAY
      IF (TIME.GT.HOURS) THEN
         GROSS = HRATE*HOURS+ORATE*(TIME-HOURS)
      ELSE
         GROSS = HRATE*TIME
      END IF
```

```
C   CALCULATE TAX DUE
        CUMGRS = CUMGRS+GROSS
        CUMALL = CUMALL+ALLOW
        TAX = TAXRTE*(CUMGRS-CUMALL)
        TAXDED = TAX-CUMTAX
C   CALCULATE INSURANCE DEDUCTION
        IF (GROSS.GT.INSMAX) THEN
           INSDED = INSRTE*INSMAX
        ELSE
           INSDED = INSRTE*GROSS
        END IF
C   CALCULATE NETT PAY
        PAY = GROSS-(TAXDED+INSDED)
C   WRITE UPDATED RECORD
        WRITE (7,REC=NUM) NAME,HOURS,HRATE,ORATE,ALLOW,CUMGRS,
      *    CUMALL,TAX,CUMINS+INSDED,CUMNET+PAY
C   PRINT PAYSLIP
        WRITE (6,200) NAME,NUM,GROSS,TAXDED,INSDED,PAY
        RETURN
    200 FORMAT(1H1,A20,4X,I6/1H0,F8.2,2(5X,F8.2)/1H0,10X,F8.2)
        END
```

The main points to notice in this program are that the subroutine UPDATE now reads the employee's record and that a record length of 56 has been defined for the master file. Each record consists of the 20-character name and nine real items; a comment at the start of the program states that the units of length are *assumed* to be 1 and 4 for the two types of storage unit. Thus NAME requires 20 'units' and each of the other nine items requires 4 'units', giving a total of 56.

The other point is that we now need a terminator for the data; the program assumes a zero staff number, which can be provided by a blank terminator card.

This program works correctly but it does have two deficiencies – one major and the other minor. The first is that the same file is used throughout and is updated record by record. If an error should occur (for example due to a data error or even a machine breakdown) the file will be left in a partially updated state. This is not good practice, and it is always advisable to keep the original version of the file unaltered. We could adopt a similar approach to that used earlier and read records from one file and write the updated records to a new file but this also has a disadvantage.

Previously, if an employee was omitted from the input file he was paid as though he had worked zero hours and his record updated accordingly. With the new direct access version he will not be paid in this situation, and furthermore, if records were copied from an old file to a new one for each employee then in this case his record would not be copied and he would disappear from the master file! The solution is either to keep an index of all employees on file and to read each employee who is paid, and then to copy any unpaid employees' records at the end, or to copy the complete file at the start of the program and update this copy.

The second deficiency concerns the record numbers. The standard merely states that these must be positive integers; however, many implementations assume that they will run upwards from 1 to a 'reasonable' number. If this is the case then a system based on arbitrary numbers may cause problems and we shall need to use a different value for the record number – based, presumably, on the staff number, since this is the only identifying item in the weekly input data.

There are a number of ways of doing this but all will essentially involve producing a table containing staff numbers and corresponding record numbers. The most efficient form of creating such a table is to use a *hashing* technique to create a *hash table*. This is a means whereby an identifier is converted into an integer in a given range (i.e. the size of the table). The algorithm used to carry out this conversion will vary depending upon the type of problem, but for our purposes a simple algorithm will serve to demonstrate the principle.

We shall define a table of size MAXEMP and use the *remainder* after dividing the staff number by MAXEMP as a subscript to the table. If this element is already occupied we shall increase the subscript by one and try again. The process is repeated until a vacant element is found; if the end of the table is reached then the search continues from the beginning. A hash table is ideally suited for both the insertion and retrieval of information, but not for its deletion since the appearance of blank elements could upset any subsequent use of the table unless it is completely recreated. In our case the insertion (and if necessary any deletion and reconstruction) will be done by whatever program is used to add employees to the file, and the table will only be used in this program to obtain the record number for a particular employee.

Our table will contain a zero for every element which is unoccupied and the staff number for every element that is occupied. By negating the value of the staff number when the employee's record is updated we can also use the same table at the end of the program to deal with any employees who were not paid because no details of their hours worked were submitted. The table will, of course, be stored in a file and read from there at the start of processing.

Fig. 12.6 shows the revised program.

```
      PROGRAM PAYROL
      PARAMETER (MAXEMP=1000)
      CHARACTER*12 OLDFIL,NEWFIL
      REAL INSRTE,INSMAX
      INTEGER STFNUM,HRS
      COMMON /TAXINS/TAXRTE,INSRTE,INSMAX
      INTEGER RECNUM(MAXEMP)
      COMMON /HASH/RECNUM
C
C INITIAL DATA IS READ FROM THE STANDARD INPUT UNIT
C ERRORS ARE PRINTED ON THE STANDARD OUTPUT UNIT
C UNIT 5 IS PAYROLL DATA (PRE-CONNECTED)
C UNIT 6 IS PAYSLIPS (PRE-CONNECTED)
C UNIT 7 IS OLD MASTER FILE
C UNIT 8 IS NEW MASTER FILE
C UNIT 9 IS HASH TABLE FILE
```

```
C
C   FORMAT 101 IS FOR NAMES OF OLD AND NEW MASTER FILES
C
  101 FORMAT(A12,8X,A12)
C
C   FORMAT 102 IS FOR TAX RATE, INSURANCE RATE, AND
C                      MAXIMUM SALARY FOR INSURANCE DEDUCTIONS
C
  102 FORMAT(BZ,2F10.2,F10.0)
C
C   FORMAT      103 IS FOR EMPLOYEE NUMBER AND TIME WORKED (HRS,MINS)
C
  103 FORMAT(BZ,I4,2X,I3,1X,I2)
C
C   READ MASTER FILE NAMES AND OPEN THEM
C   PROGRAM ASSUMES 1 UNIT PER CHARACTER STORAGE UNIT
C   AND 4 UNITS PER NUMERIC STORAGE UNIT
        READ 101,OLDFIL,NEWFIL
        OPEN (7,FILE=OLDFIL,STATUS='OLD',ACCESS='DIRECT',
     *  RECL=56,ERR=93)
        OPEN (8,FILE=NEWFIL,ACCESS='DIRECT',RECL=56,ERR=94)
C   OPEN HASH TABLE FILE AND READ HASH TABLE
        OPEN (9,FILE='HASHFILE',STATUS='OLD',FORM='FORMATTED',
     *  ERR=95)
        READ (9) RECNUM
C   READ TAX RATES ETC.
        READ 102,TAXRTE,INSRTE,INSMAX
C   CONVERT PERCENTAGE RATES TO FRACTIONS
        TAXRTE = 0.01*TAXRTE
        INSRTE = 0.01*INSRTE
C   MAIN LOOP TO UPDATE FILE AND PRINT PAYSLIPS
        DO 10, I=1,MAXEMP
          READ (5,103) STFNUM,HRS,MINS
C   ZERO STFNUM INDICATES THE END OF DATA
          IF (STFNUM.EQ.0) GOTO 15
C   UPDATE FILE AND PRINT PAYSLIP
          CALL UPDATE(STFNUM,HRS+MINS/60.0)
   10   CONTINUE
C   ALL PAYROLL DATA PROCESSED
C   CHECK FOR ANY UNPAID EMPLOYEES
   15 DO 20, I=1,MAXEMP
          IF (RECNUM(I).GT.0) CALL UPDATE(RECNUM(I),0.0)
   20   CONTINUE
      STOP
```

(continued)

```
C  ERROR DURING FILE OPENING
   93 PRINT 290,OLDFIL
      STOP
   94 PRINT 290,NEWFIL
      STOP
   95 PRINT 290,'HASHFILE'
      STOP
  290 FORMAT(1H1,'*** ERROR DURING OPENING OF ',A12,
      *  ' - PROCESSING TERMINATED ***')
      END


      SUBROUTINE UPDATE(NUM,TIME)
      PARAMETER (MAXEMP=1000)
      CHARACTER*20 NAME
      REAL INSRTE,INSMAX,INSDED
      COMMON /TAXINS/TAXRTE,INSRTE,INSMAX
      INTEGER RECNUM(MAXEMP)
      COMMON /HASH/RECNUM
C  FIND EMPLOYEE'S RECORD NUMBER
      I = MOD(NUM,MAXEMP)+1
      DO 5, J=I,MAXEMP
        IF (RECNUM(J).EQ.NUM) THEN
C  SET NUM TO RECORD NUMBER
          NREC = J
          GOTO 10
        ELSE IF (RECNUM(J).EQ.0) THEN
C  NO ENTRY FOR THIS EMPLOYEE
          GOTO 99
        END IF
    5   CONTINUE
C  NOT YET FOUND - SEARCH FROM BEGINNING OF TABLE
      DO 6, J=1,I-1
        IF (RECNUM(J).EQ.NUM) THEN
          NREC = J
          GOTO 10
        ELSE IF (RECNUM(J).EQ.0) THEN
          GOTO 99
        END IF
    6   CONTINUE
C  EMPLOYEE'S STAFF NUMBER NOT FOUND - PRINT ERROR
   99 PRINT 299,NUM
  299 FORMAT(1H0,'*** ERROR - STAFF NUMBER',I4,
      *  ' NOT ON FILE')
      STOP
C  STAFF NUMBER FOUND - SET ENTRY NEGATIVE
   10 RECNUM(NREC) = -RECNUM(NREC)
C  GET EMPLOYEE'S RECORD
      READ (7,REC=NREC) NAME,HOURS,HRATE,ORATE,ALLOW,
      *  CUMGRS,CUMALL,CUMTAX,CUMINS,CUMNET
```

```
C  CALCULATE GROSS PAY
      IF (TIME.GT.HOURS) THEN
        GROSS = HRATE*HOURS+ORATE*(TIME-HOURS)
      ELSE
        GROSS = HRATE*TIME
      END IF
C  CALCULATE TAX DUE
      CUMGRS = CUMGRS+GROSS
      CUMALL = CUMALL+ALLOW
      TAX = TAXRTE*(CUMGRS-CUMALL)
      TAXDED = TAX-CUMTAX
C  CALCULATE INSURANCE DEDUCTION
      IF (GROSS.GT.INSMAX) THEN
        INSDED = INSRTE*INSMAX
      ELSE
        INSDED = INSRTE*GROSS
      END IF
C  CALCULATE NETT PAY
      PAY = GROSS-(TAXDED+INSDED)
C  WRITE UPDATED RECORD
      WRITE (8,REC=NREC) NAME,HOURS,HRATE,ORATE,ALLOW,CUMGRS,
     *  CUMALL,TAX,CUMINS+INSDED,CUMNET+PAY
C  PRINT PAYSLIP
      WRITE (6,200) NAME,NUM,GROSS,TAXDED,INSDED,PAY
      RETURN
  200 FORMAT(1H1,A20,4X,I6/1H0,F8.2,2(5X,F8.2)/1H0,10X,F8.2)
      END
```

Fig. 12.6 Revised payroll program using a hash table

Notice that the hash table searching starts from the initial guess and searches to the end of the array. If a zero is found then it means that the employee cannot be on file. In a full hash table system, with both entry and retrieval the employee would be entered in the table at this point. If neither the correct number or a blank is found then the table is searched from the beginning up to the start point.

When a match is made the index to the array is kept as the record number and the entry in the table is negated. Finally when all the data has been read the hash table should consist of zeros and negated staff numbers. Any positive entries have not been paid and so UPDATE is called to calculate their pay (i.e. tax refund) on the basis of zero hours worked.

Since the program copies all the records from the old file (7) to the new file (8), any failure can be dealt with by re-running the complete job from the old file.

12.8 The INQUIRE statement

For most purposes the statements described above will enable a program to carry out any file operations it requires. There are, however, occasions, especially when writing a general purpose subroutine, when it would be useful to find out, or check up on, the various details which are applicable to files (e.g. whether it is formatted, connected for direct access, etc.). This can be achieved by means of a special statement which can provide any required information of this nature about a file

INQUIRE (list)

This statement (note the spelling!) allows the program to enquire about a file which is defined by name or to enquire about a file which is connected to a given unit. In the first case the list (see Fig. 12.7) must contain a FILE specifier and no UNIT specifier, while in the second case there must be a UNIT specifier and no FILE specifier. Any of the other specifiers may appear at most once.

UNIT = u (or u)
FILE = fn } one only

EXIST = lex
OPENED = lop
NUMBER = num
NAMED = lnm
NAME = fn
ACCESS = acc
SEQUENTIAL = seq
DIRECT = dir
FORM = fm
FORMATTED = fmt
UNFORMATTED = unf
RECL = len
NEXTREC = nr
BLANK = bl
ERR = s
IOSTAT = ios

Fig. 12.7   Specifiers for use with INQUIRE

Several of these specifiers (ACCESS, FORM, RECL, BLANK) are similar to those used in an OPEN statement but have the reverse effect. Thus

ACCESS=acc

will cause the character variable 'acc' to be assigned the value 'SEQUENTIAL' or 'DIRECT' as appropriate. If no file is connected than 'acc' becomes undefined.

Similarly

FORM=fm

causes the character variable 'fm' to be assigned the value 'FORMATTED' or 'UNFORMATTED', or to become undefined

RECL=len

causes the integer variable 'len' to be assigned the record length of the file if it is connected for direct access, or to become undefined otherwise; and

BLANK=bl

causes the character variable 'bl' to be assigned the value `'ZERO'` if blanks are to be treated as zeros and `'NULL'` if they are to be ignored; if there is no connection, or if the file is not formatted then 'bl' becomes undefined.

The SEQUENTIAL, DIRECT, FORMATTED and UNFORMATTED specifiers provide a way of determining what is *allowed* with a file, regardless of whether it is connected. In each case the character variable is assigned the value `'YES'`, `'NO'` or `'UNKNOWN'`. Thus

DIRECT=dir

will cause the character variable 'dir' to be assigned the value `'YES'` if direct access is allowed on this file, `'NO'` if it is not allowed, and `'UNKNOWN'` if the processor cannot determine whether it is allowed or not.

The EXIST specifier allows a program to determine if a file (or unit) exists. If it does then the logical variable 'lex' is set true, if it does not then it is set false.

OPENED is somewhat similar and sets the logical variable 'lop' to true if the specified file is connected to some unit, or if the specified unit is connected to some file; otherwise it is set false.

NAMED also assigns a value to a logical variable; in this case 'lnm' is set true if the file has a name, otherwise it is set false.

Closely related to these specifiers are NUMBER and NAME. NUMBER causes the integer variable 'num' to be assigned the number of the unit currently connected to the specified file, while NAME causes the character variable 'fn' to be assigned the name of the file currently connected to the specified unit. In both cases if no unit or file is connected (or in the latter case if the file has no name) then the variable becomes undefined. Thus we may write

```
      .
      .
      .
      INQUIRE (FILE='MYFILE',OPENED=LOP,NUMBER=N)
      IF (LOP) THEN
C  MYFILE IS ON UNIT N
      .
      .
      .
      ELSE
        OPEN (7,FILE='MYFILE')
        N = 7
      END IF
      .
```

Finally the NEXTREC specifier sets the integer variable 'nr' to the value 'n+1' where 'n' is the record number of the last record read or written to the file, if it is connected for direct access; if no records have yet been written or read then 'nr' is set to 1. If the file is not connected for direct access, or if its position is indeterminate because of an error, then 'nr' is undefined.

INQUIRE will normally only be used in certain specialised situations, where it can be extremely useful. One more general situation, however, could be to avoid the necessity of reading the file names in a program such as the payroll program developed in Examples 12.3 and 12.4. For example, a cycle of three files could be used in such a way that the oldest was deleted at the end of each run. At the beginning of execution therefore only two of the three files will exist. INQUIRE can be used to establish which two exist and then use this knowledge to open the correct files. The following subroutine will do this

```
      SUBROUTINE OPNFIL
C
C  THIS SUBROUTINE OPENS THREE FILES
C  UNIT 7 IS THE OLD MASTER FILE
C  UNIT 8 IS THE NEW MASTER FILE AND DOES NOT YET EXIST
C  UNIT 10 IS NOT USED, BUT SHOULD BE DELETED
C          AT THE END OF AN ERROR-FREE PROGRAM EXECUTION
C
      INTEGER U(5)
      LOGICAL F(3)
      CHARACTER*12 FILE(3)
      DATA FILE/'FILE1','FILE2','FILE3'/,U/10,7,8,10,7/
C  ESTABLISH WHICH FILE DOES NOT EXIST
      DO 5, I=1,3
         INQUIRE (FILE=FILE(I),EXIST=F(I))
    5    CONTINUE
C  SET J TO INDICATE UNIT NUMBERS FOR THE THREE FILES
      IF (F(1).AND.F(2)) THEN
         IF (F(3)) GOTO 99
         J = 0
      ELSE IF (F(2).AND.F(3)) THEN
         IF (F(1)) GOTO 99
         J = 2
      ELSE IF (F(3).AND.F(1)) THEN
         IF (F(2)) GOTO 99
         J = 1
      ELSE
         GOTO 99
      END IF
C  OPEN ALL THREE FILES
      DO 10, I=1,3
         OPEN (UNIT=U(I+J),FILE=FILE(I),ACCESS='DIRECT',
     *   RECL=56,ERR=98)
   10    CONTINUE
      RETURN
```

```
C  ERROR DURING FILE OPENING
   98 PRINT 298,FILE(I)
  298 FORMAT(1H1,'*** ERROR DURING DURING OPENING OF ',A12,
     * ' - PROCESSING TERMINATED ***')
      STOP
C  WRONG NUMBER OF FILES EXIST
   99 PRINT 299,(FILE(I),F(I), I=1,3)
  299 FORMAT(1H1,'*** INVALID FILE COMBINATION:'//
     1  1H ,'  FILE NAME    EXISTS'/
     2  3(1H ,A12,5X,L1/)/
     3  1H ,'PROCESSING TERMINATED')
      STOP
      END
```

This subroutine opens all three files so that unit 8 is the one which did not previously exist, unit 7 is the more recent of the other two (in cyclic order) and unit 10 is the remaining one. At the end of the program, after a successful execution, there should be the additional statement

```
      CLOSE(10,STATUS='DELETE')
```

If there are not exactly two existing files an error will be produced in the form of a truth table, see Fig. 12.8.

```
*** INVALID FILE COMBINATION:

   FILE NAME    EXISTS
FILE1           T
FILE2           F
FILE3           F

PROCESSING TERMINATED
```

Fig. 12.8 Error table produced by subroutine OPNFIL

Each time the program is run the updated master file created by the last run will be used as the old master file and a new one will be created. Thus the program itself will ensure that an orderly cycle is maintained. In the event of an error all three files will remain and the programmer can delete the appropriate one. If there is no error then the oldest of the three files is deleted at the end of the program.

Summary

- A record is a formatted sequence of characters or an unformatted sequence of values.

- A file is a sequence of records.

- Files may be sequential, direct-access or internal.

- An internal file is a character variable or array.

- An internal file enables the edit descriptors used in formatting to be used to convert an item in memory into another format.

- The OPEN statement connects a file to a specified input or output unit.

- The INQUIRE statement enables a program to establish details about files at execution time.

Input/output statements	READ (unformatted cilist) input list e.g. READ (7,END=99) A,B,C WRITE (direct-access cilist) output list e.g. WRITE (8,REC=N) X,Y,Z ENDFILE unit number ENDFILE (auxiliary information list)
File connection	OPEN (open information list)
File disconnection	CLOSE (close information list)
File positioning	BACKSPACE unit number BACKSPACE (auxiliary information list) REWIND unit number REWIND (auxiliary information list)
File enquiry	INQUIRE (enquiry list)

Fig. 12.9 Fortran 77 statements introduced in Chapter 12

Exercises

12.1 Find out what conventions exist regarding file names in your computer, and any special features concerning the OPENing of files (e.g. some systems have added extra STATUS specifiers to accord with particular operating system facilities).

12.2 Modify the program written for question 9.4 so that the football results to date are stored on a file. Each run of the program should update this 'master file' and print a new league table based on all the results so far.

12.3 A class of less than 100 pupils has a test each week whose results are provided to the computer as the student's name (surname only) followed by the mark which is separated from the name by at least one space. After the 10th (and final) test the term's results should be printed in order of total marks.

12.4 Write a program or programs which will carry out the following activities

(a) Read survey data in the form defined below and store it in a suitable file:

Columns 1–30 First name and surname, separated by one space
Column 33 Sex (M or F)
Columns 36,37 Age
Column 40 Status = 1 if in full-time education
 = 2 if in full-time employment
 = 3 if in part-time employment
 = 4 if temporarily unemployed
 = 5 if not working or seeking a job

This is followed by further information, depending upon status
= 1 column 43 = 1 if at school
 = 2 if at University or Polytechnic
 = 3 if elsewhere
= 2 columns 43–46 monthly salary
 column 49 marital status (S=Single, M=Married, D=Divorced, W=Widowed)
 columns 52,53 no. of children
= 3 columns 43–46 monthly salary
 columns 49–52 additional income
 column 55 marital status
 columns 58,59 no. of children
= 4 columns 43–45 no. of months unemployed
 column 48 marital status
 columns 51,52 no. of children
= 5 column 43 marital status
 columns 46,47 no. of children
 column 50 = 1 if looking after children
 = 2 if looking after other relatives
 = 3 for any other reason

(b) Read survey data in the above format and add the information to the existing file.

(c) Sort the survey file so that it (or some part of it) is in alphabetic order of surnames.

(d) Print names of people in the file who satisfy certain conditions such as
 (i) over 18 and at school
 (ii) at University or Polytechnic
 (iii) earning over £1000 per month
 (iv) male and unemployed for over 10 weeks
 (v) single with more than one child
 (vi) earning less than £500 per month and having more than two children
 (vii) widowed, under 55 and looking after relatives
 etc.

Afterword-Seven Golden Rules

This book has attempted to teach the reader both the techniques of Fortran 77 programming and an approach to designing those programs. This approach can be summarised in the *Seven Golden Rules of Programming*

1 *Always plan ahead*
   It is invariably a mistake to start to write a program without having first drawn up a program design plan which shows the structure of the program and the various levels of detail.

2 *Develop in stages*
   In a program of any size it is essential to tackle a part of the program at a time, so that the scale and scope of each new part of the program is of manageable proportions.

3 *Modularise*
   The use of subroutines, or groups of subroutines, which can be written and tested independently is a major factor in the successful development of large programs, and is closely related to the staged development of the programs.

4 *Keep it simple*
   A complicated program is usually both inefficient and error-prone. Fortran 77 contains features which can greatly simplify complex program structures; modularisation can also usually be of assistance here.

5 *Test thoroughly*
   Always test your programs thoroughly at every stage, and try to cater for as many situations (both correct and incorrect) as possible. The best method, if it can be arranged, is to ask a colleague to provide some test data, given only the specification of what the program (or module) is supposed to do.

6 *Document all programs*
   There is nothing worse than returning to an undocumented program after an absence of any significant time. Most programs can be adequately documented by the use of meaningful names, and by the inclusion of plenty of comments. A program has only to be written once but it will be read many times, so effort expended on self-documenting comments will be more than repayed later.

7   *Enjoy your programming*
Writing computer programs, and getting them to work correctly, are challenging and intellectually stimulating activities. They should also be enjoyable. There is an enormous satisfaction to be obtained from getting a well-designed program to perform the activities that it is supposed to perform. It is not always easy, but it should be fun!

Appendix A Intrinsic Functions

The Fortran 77 language contains a considerable number of built-in functions, formally known as intrinsic functions. These functions are automatically available to any program that requires them, and do not need to be declared or otherwise identified other than by means of a function reference.

Most of the functions have a *generic* name which avoids the necessity of a different name depending on the type of the arguments. Section A.1 gives a list of all these generic functions together with a specification of the types of their arguments and results and a definition of their action.

There are a smaller number of intrinsic functions which can only take a single type of argument, and these functions are listed in the same way in Section A.2.

Finally Section A.3 lists the *specific names* of the various generic functions. Thus, for example, the generic function **ABS** may be used with an integer, real, double-precision or complex argument. In earlier versions of Fortran there were four separate functions corresponding to the four types of argument, namely **IABS**, **ABS**, **DABS** and **CABS** respectively. These four names may also be used in Fortran 77 in this way (primarily for reasons of compatibility) and are known as the specific names of the generic functions.

In the following lists the types of the arguments are indicated by the following symbols

I	integer
R	real
C	character
D	double precision
X	complex

In the case of the generic functions, which can all accept arguments of more than one type, a composite type is used – thus, IRD means that the argument may be Integer, Real, or Double precision.

A.1   Generic names of functions

Name and specification	Type of results	Definition
ABS(IRD)	same as argument	absolute value $\lvert IRD \rvert$
ABS(X)	real	$\sqrt{\text{REAL}(X)^2 + \text{AIMAG}(X)^2}$
ACOS(RD)	same as argument(s)	arccos(RD)
AINT(RD)	same as argument(s)	truncation: REAL(INT(RD))
ANINT(RD)	same as argument(s)	nearest whole number: REAL(INT(RD + 0.5)) if RD $\geq$ 0, REAL(INT(RD $-$ 0.5)) if RD $<$ 0
ASIN(RD)	same as argument(s)	arcsin(RD)
ATAN(RD)	same as argument(s)	arctan(RD)
ATAN2(RD1,RD2)	same as argument(s)	arctan(RD1/RD2)
CMPLX(IRD)	complex	complex number:(REAL(IRD),0)
CMPLX(IRD1,IRD2)	complex	complex number:(REAL(IRD1),REAL(IRD2))
CMPLX(X)	complex	complex number X
COS(RDX)	same as argument	cos(RDX)
COSH(RD)	same as argument	cosh(RD)
DBLE(IRX)	double precision	double precision version of REAL(IRX)
DBLE(D)	double precision	double precision number D
DIM(IRD1,IRD2)	same as argument(s)	positive difference: MAX(IRD1−IRD2,0)
EXP(RDX)	same as argument(s)	e^{RDX}
INT(RDX)	integer	integer equivalent of REAL(RDX)
INT(I)	integer	integer I
LOG(RDX)	same as argument(s)	natural logarithm $\log_e$(RDX)
LOG10(RD)	same as argument(s)	common logarithm $\log_{10}$(RD)
MAX(IRD1,IRD2, . . .)	same as argument(s)	largest value of IRD1,IRD2, . . .
MIN(IRD1,IRD2, . . .)	same as argument(s)	smallest value of IRD1,IRD2, . . .
MOD(IRD1,IRD2)	same as argument(s)	remaindering: IRD1 − INT(IRD1/IRD2)∗IRD2
NINT(RD)	integer	nearest integer: INT(ANINT(RD))
REAL(ID)	real	real equivalent of ID

REAL(R)	real	real number R
REAL(X)	real	real part of X
SIGN(IRD1,IRD2)	same as argument(s)	transfer of sign: $|IRD1|$ if $IRD2 > 0$, $-|IRD1|$ if $IRD2 < 0$
SIN(RDX)	same as argument(s)	$\sin(RDX)$
SINH(RD)	same as argument(s)	$\sinh(RD)$
SQRT(RDX)	same as argument(s)	$\sqrt{RDX}$
TAN(RD)	same as argument(s)	$\tan(RD)$
TANH(RD)	same as argument(s)	$\tanh(RD)$

A.2 Names of non-generic functions

Name and specification	Type of results	Definition
AIMAG(X)	real	imaginary part of X
AMAX0(I1,I2, …)	real	REAL(MAX(I1,I2, …))
AMIN0(I1,I2, …)	real	REAL(MIN(I1,I2, …))
CHAR(I)	character	processor dependent character equivalent of I
CONJG(X)	complex	complex conjugate: (REAL(X), $-$ AIMAG(X))
DPROD(R1,R2)	double precision	double precision product R1*R2
ICHAR(C)	integer	processor dependent integer equivalent of single character C
INDEX(C1,C2)	integer	position of first character of C2 in C1; if C2 does not appear in C1 then zero
LEN(C)	integer	length of C
LGE(C1,C2)	logical	true if C1 = C2 or C1 follows C2 in the lexical collating sequence, otherwise false
LGT(C1,C2)	logical	true if C1 follows C2 in the lexical collating sequence, otherwise false
LLE(C1,C2)	logical	true if C1 = C2 or C1 precedes C2 in the lexical collating sequence, otherwise false
LLT(C1,C2)	logical	true if C1 precedes C2 in the lexical collating sequence, otherwise false
MAX1(R1,R2 …)	integer	INT(MAX(R1,R2, …))
MIN1(R1,R2, …)	integer	INT(MIN(R1,R2, …))

A.3   Specific names of generic functions

Name and specification	Type of results	Definition
ABS(R)	real	ABS(R)
ACOS(R)	real	ACOS(R)
AINT(R)	real	AINT(R)
ALOG(R)	real	LOG(R)
ALOG10(R)	real	LOG10(R)
AMAX1(R1,R2, . . .)	real	MAX(R1,R2, . . .)
AMIN1(R1,R2, . . .)	real	MIN(R1,R2, . . .)
AMOD(R1,R2)	real	MOD(R1,R2)
ANINT(R)	real	ANINT(R)
ASIN(R)	real	ASIN(R)
ATAN(R)	real	ATAN(R)
ATAN2(R1,R2)	real	ATAN2(R1,R2)
CABS(X)	real	ABS(X)
CCOS(X)	complex	COS(X)
CEXP(X)	complex	EXP(X)
CLOG(X)	complex	LOG(X)
CMPLX(R1,R2)	complex	CMPLX(R1,R2)
COS(R)	real	COS(R)
COSH(R)	real	COSH(R)
CSIN(X)	complex	SIN(X)
CSQRT(X)	complex	SQRT(X)
DABS(D)	double precision	ABS(D)
DACOS(D)	double precision	ACOS(D)
DASIN(D)	double precision	ASIN(D)
DATAN(D)	double precision	ATAN(D)
DATAN2(D1,D2)	double precision	ATAN2(D1,D2)
DBLE(R)	double precision	DBLE(R)
DCOS(D)	double precision	COS(D)
DCOSH(D)	double precision	COSH(D)
DDIM(D)	double precision	DIM(D)
DEXP(D)	double precision	EXP(D)
DIM(R)	real	DIM(R)
DINT(D)	double precision	AINT(D)
DLOG(D)	double precision	LOG(D)
DLOG10(D)	double precision	LOG10(D)
DMAX1(D1,D2, . . .)	double precision	MAX(D1,D2, . . .)
DMIN1(D1,D2, . . .)	double precision	MIN(D1,D2, . . .)
DMOD(D1,D2)	double precision	MOD(D1,D2)
DNINT(D)	double precision	ANINT(D)
DSIGN(D1,D2)	double precision	SIGN(D1,D2)
DSIN(D)	double precision	SIN(D)
DSINH(D)	double precision	SINH(D)
DSQRT(D)	double precision	SQRT(D)
DTAN(D)	double precision	TAN(D)
DTANH(D)	double precision	TANH(D)

Name and specification	Type of results	Definition
EXP(R)	real	EXP(R)
FLOAT(I)	real	REAL(I)
IABS(I)	integer	ABS(I)
IDIM(I1,I2)	integer	DIM(I1,I2)
IDINT(D)	integer	INT(D)
IDNINT(D)	integer	NINT(D)
IFIX(R)	integer	INT(R)
INT(R)	integer	INT(R)
ISIGN(I1,I2)	integer	SIGN(I1,I2)
MAXO(I1,I2, . . .)	integer	MAX(I1,I2, . . .)
MINO(I1,I2, . . .)	integer	MIN(I1,I2, . . .)
MOD(I1,I2)	integer	MOD(I1,I2)
NINT(R)	integer	NINT(R)
REAL(I)	real	REAL(I)
SIGN(R)	real	SIGN(R)
SIN(R)	real	SIN(R)
SINH(R)	real	SINH(R)
SNGL(D)	real	REAL(D)
SQRT(R)	real	SQRT(R)
TAN(R)	real	TAN(R)
TANH(R)	real	TANH(R)

Appendix B The Syntax of Fortran 77

This appendix is provided to give a complete reference guide to the syntax of Fortran 77 in a form which is quite easy for the non-specialist to understand. It consists of a set of charts (B.1) and a cross-reference index (B.2), together with an initial explanation of how to use the charts. The material contained in both the charts and the cross-reference index is taken from Appendix F of the Fortran 77 standard. It is reproduced, with permission, from American National Standard Programming Language FORTRAN (ANSI X3.9–1978), copyright 1978 by the American National Standards Institute. Copies of this standard may be purchased from the American National Standards Institute at 1430 Broadway, New York, N.Y. 10018.

The charts themselves are in what has come to be called 'railroad normal form' because, as we shall see, they are designed to be followed in a manner similar to a train travelling along a railway (or 'railroad') track. They have been designed for ease of human readability and not as a formal language definition suitable for the writer of a compiler. Thus, for example, they do not reflect certain features such as

- the precedence of operators
- the use of blanks to improve layout
- the use of continuation lines
- comment lines
- context dependent aspects such as data type requirements, uniqueness of labels, actual and dummy argument matching, etc.

In the charts upper case letters and special characters must be used exactly as written (e.g. READ), whereas lower case letters are used to represent syntactic entities (e.g. label). In order to avoid any confusion over the meaning of spaces, where the name of a syntactic entity would normally consist of two or more words the spaces are replaced by underline characters (e.g. array_element_name).

The charts themselves, as has been mentioned above, are in the form of 'railroad tracks' and alternative paths are indicated by 'points' (or 'switches') in the track. Just as a train can only follow certain paths in this situation, so the syntax can only develop in certain ways. In many cases the chart includes some form of loop, and in order to limit the number of times the loop may be repeated (where this is appropriate) two conventions are adopted

- If a stretch of track contains a number (n) enclosed in a circle then this means that this section of track must be traversed *exactly n times*.
- On the other hand if it contains a number (n) enclosed in a half-circle then the meaning is that this section of track may be traversed *a maximum of n times*.

A simple example of this is the definition of a symbolic name (chart 99), which must take the form of a maximum of six letters or digits, of which the first must be a letter. The chart for this is

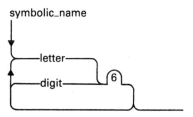

The charts themselves (B.1) start at the highest level – an executable program – and gradually increase in detail until the final charts (111–116) define the various characters which may be used in Fortran programs, and which are thus used to form the other syntactic items. In general they need no further explanation, but occasionally some explanatory information does follow the charts in the form of a 'pseudo-footnote' preceded by the chart number enclosed in parentheses.

The cross-reference index (B.2) lists all the syntactic entities which appear in the charts together with the number(s) of the chart(s) in which they are referenced. The two together thus provide a quick and easy way of checking the exact format of any particular type of statement.

B.1 Fortran 77 syntax charts

F2 <u>Charts</u>

1 executable_program:

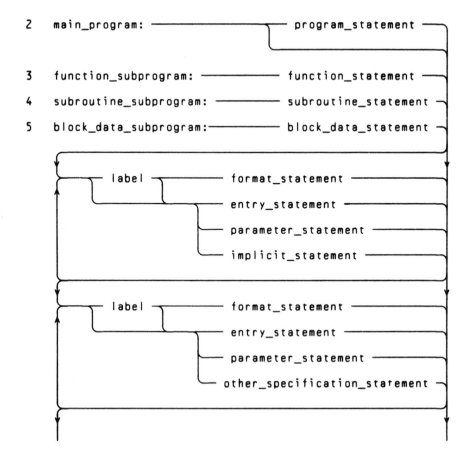

(1) An executable program must contain one and only one main program.

An executable program may contain external procedures specified by means other than FORTRAN.

2 main_program: program_statement

3 function_subprogram: function_statement

4 subroutine_subprogram: subroutine_statement

5 block_data_subprogram: block_data_statement

       label   format_statement
                      entry_statement
                      parameter_statement
                      implicit_statement

       label   format_statement
                      entry_statement
                      parameter_statement
                      other_specification_statement

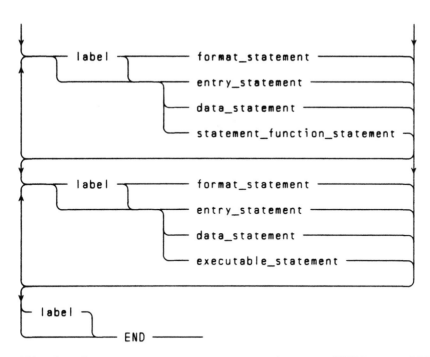

(2) A main program may not contain an ENTRY or RETURN statement.

(5) A block data subprogram may contain only BLOCK DATA, IMPLICIT, PARAMETER, DIMENSION, COMMON, SAVE, EQUIVALENCE, DATA, END, and type-statements.

6   other_specification_statement:

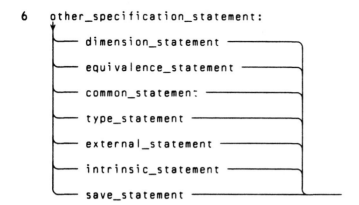

executable_statement:

- assignment_statement
- goto_statement
- arithmetic_if_statement
- logical_if_statement
- block_if_statement
- else_if_statement
- else_statement
- end_if_statement
- do_statement
- continue_statement
- stop_statement
- pause_statement
- read_statement
- write_statement
- print_statement
- rewind_statement
- backspace_statement
- endfile_statement
- open_statement
- close_statement
- inquire_statement
- call_statement
- return_statement

(7) An END statement is also an executable statement and must appear as the last statement of a program unit.

8   program_statement: ─────── PROGRAM program_name ───

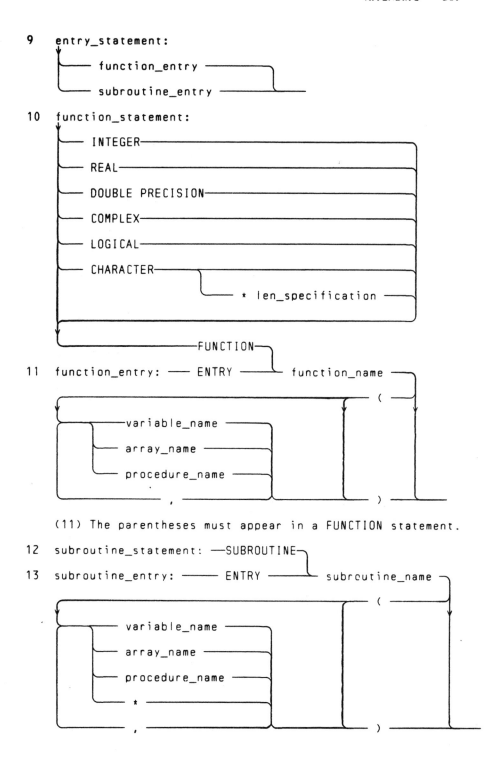

9   entry_statement:

    function_entry
    subroutine_entry

10 function_statement:

    INTEGER
    REAL
    DOUBLE PRECISION
    COMPLEX
    LOGICAL
    CHARACTER
                    * len_specification

    FUNCTION

11 function_entry: ─── ENTRY ─────── function_name

    variable_name
    array_name
    procedure_name
                ,
    (
)

(11) The parentheses must appear in a FUNCTION statement.

12 subroutine_statement: ─SUBROUTINE─

13 subroutine_entry: ─────── ENTRY ─────── subroutine_name

    variable_name
    array_name
    procedure_name
    *
                ,
    (
)

14 block_data_statement:

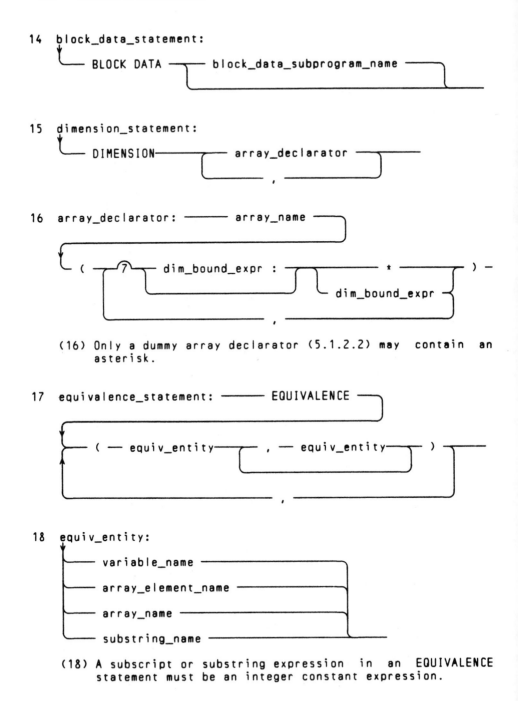

    BLOCK DATA ——— block_data_subprogram_name ———

15 dimension_statement:

    DIMENSION——— array_declarator ———
                        ,

16 array_declarator: ——— array_name ———

    (——⑦——— dim_bound_expr : ———— * ————) –
                                    dim_bound_expr
                        ,

(16) Only a dummy array declarator (5.1.2.2) may contain an asterisk.

17 equivalence_statement: ——— EQUIVALENCE ———

    (— equiv_entity——— , — equiv_entity———)
                        ,

18 equiv_entity:

    —— variable_name ———
    —— array_element_name ———
    —— array_name ———
    —— substring_name ———

(18) A subscript or substring expression in an EQUIVALENCE statement must be an integer constant expression.

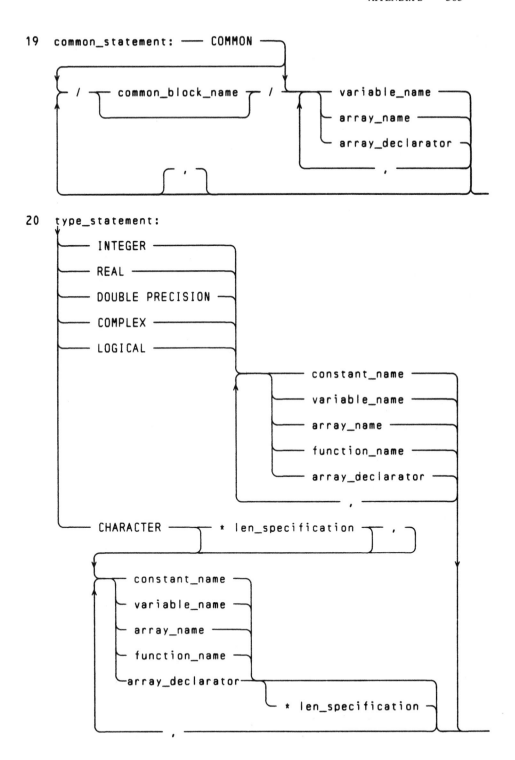

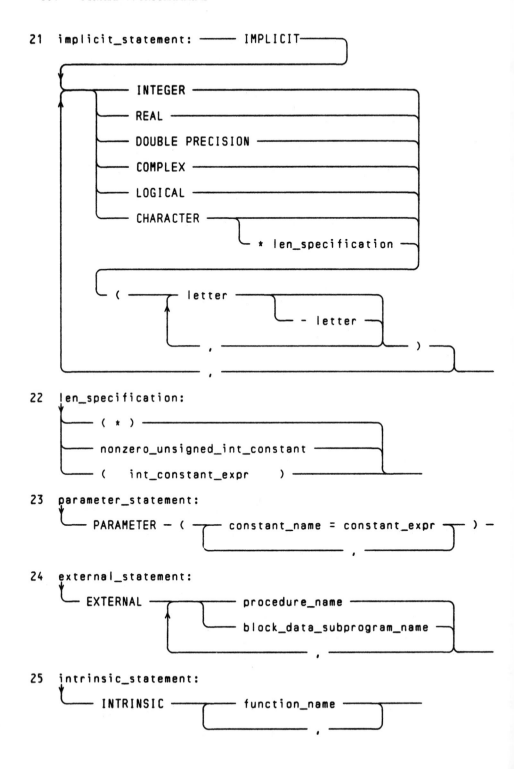

21 implicit_statement:

22 len_specification:

23 parameter_statement:

24 external_statement:

25 intrinsic_statement:

26 save_statement:

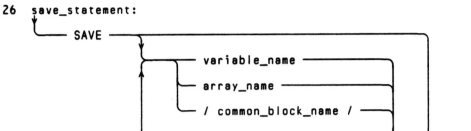

27 data_statement:

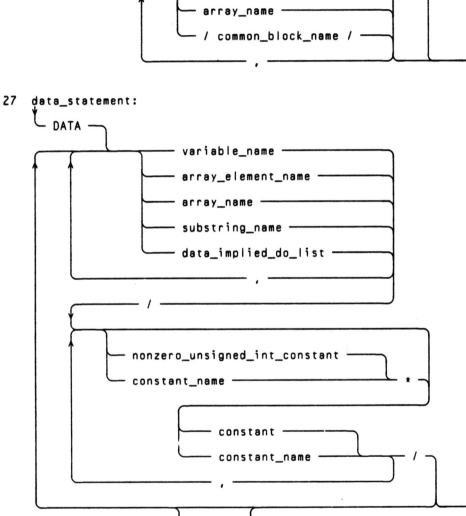

28 data_implied_do_list:

(diagram)

- array_element_name
- data_implied_do_list
- ,
- variable_name =
- int_constant_expr , int_constant_expr) 1

29 assignment_statement:

(diagram)

- variable_name
- array_element_name
- substring_name = expression
- ASSIGN label TO variable_name

30 goto_statement:

(diagram)

- unconditional_goto
- computed_goto
- assigned_goto

31 unconditional_goto: —— GO TO —— label ——

32 computed_goto:

GO TO (label ,) , integer_expr

33 assigned_goto:

GO TO variable_name , (label ,)

34 arithmetic_if_statement:

IF (int_real_dp_expr) label , label , label

35 logical_if_statement:

         IF (logical_expression) executable_statement

(35) The executable statement contained in a logical IF
     statement must not be a DO, block IF, ELSE IF, ELSE,
     END IF, END, or another logical IF statement.

36 block_if_statement:

         IF (logical_expression) THEN

37 else_if_statement:

         ELSE IF (logical_expression) THEN

38 else_statement: ——— ELSE ———

39 end_if_statement: — END IF ———

40 do_statement:

         DO label ———————— ,

         variable_name = int_real_dp_expr —— , int_real_dp_expr
                                                    1

41 continue_statement: ——— CONTINUE ———

42 stop_statement: ——— STOP

43 pause_statement: — PAUSE

                  digit   5

                  character_constant

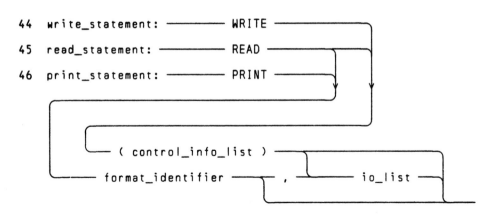

44 write_statement: ────── WRITE ──────

45 read_statement: ────── READ ──────

46 print_statement: ────── PRINT ──────

(control_info_list)

format_identifier ─── , ─── io_list ───

47 control_info_list:

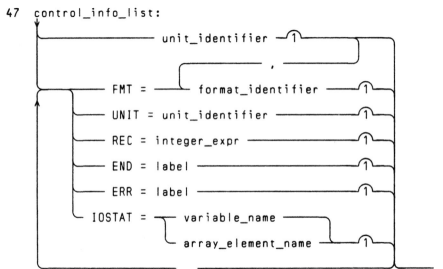

unit_identifier

,

FMT = ── format_identifier
UNIT = unit_identifier
REC = integer_expr
END = label
ERR = label
IOSTAT = ┬─ variable_name
         └─ array_element_name

,

(47) A control_info_list must contain exactly one unit_identifier. An END= specifier must not appear in a WRITE statement.

48 io_list:

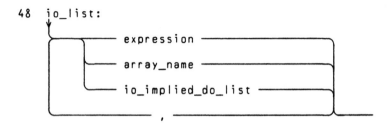

expression
array_name
io_implied_do_list

,

(48) In a READ statement, an input/output list expression must be a variable name, array element name, or substring name.

49 io_implied_do_list:

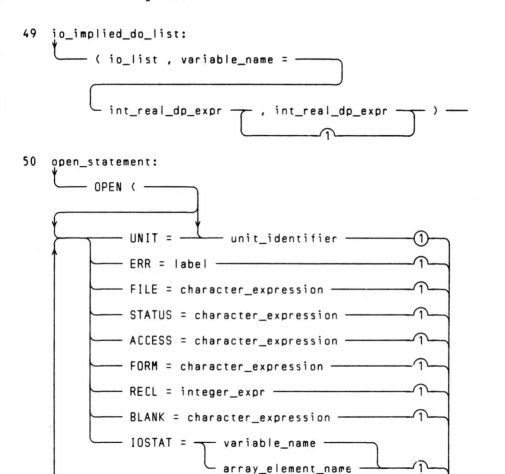

50 open_statement:

51   close_statement:

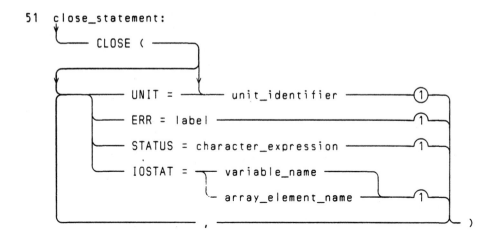

52 inquire_statement:

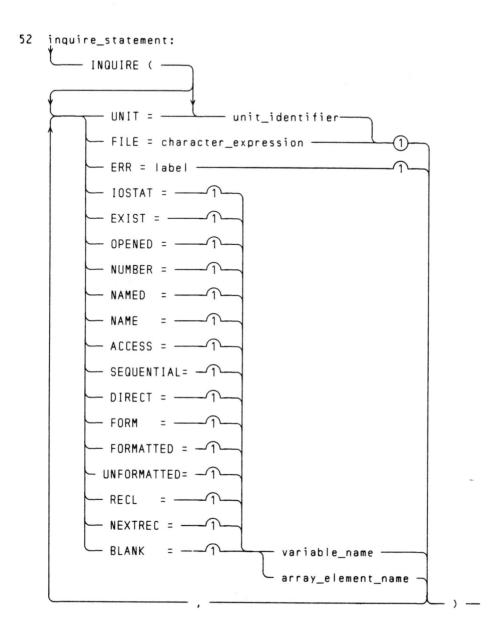

53 backspace_statement:

54 endfile_statement:

55 rewind_statement:

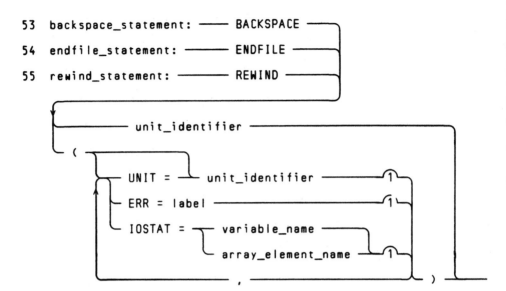

(53,54,55) BACKSPACE, ENDFILE, and REWIND statements must contain a unit identifier.

56 unit_identifier:

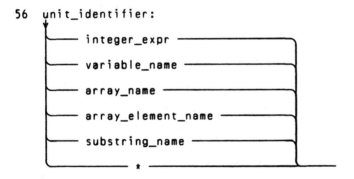

(56) An unit identifier must be of type integer or character, or be an asterisk.

57 format_identifier:

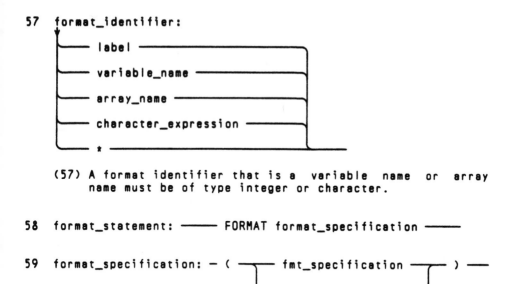

   label

   variable_name

   array_name

   character_expression

   *

(57) A format identifier that is a variable name or array name must be of type integer or character.

58 format_statement: ——— FORMAT format_specification ———

59 format_specification: — (——┬—— fmt_specification ——┬—) —

60   fmt_specification:

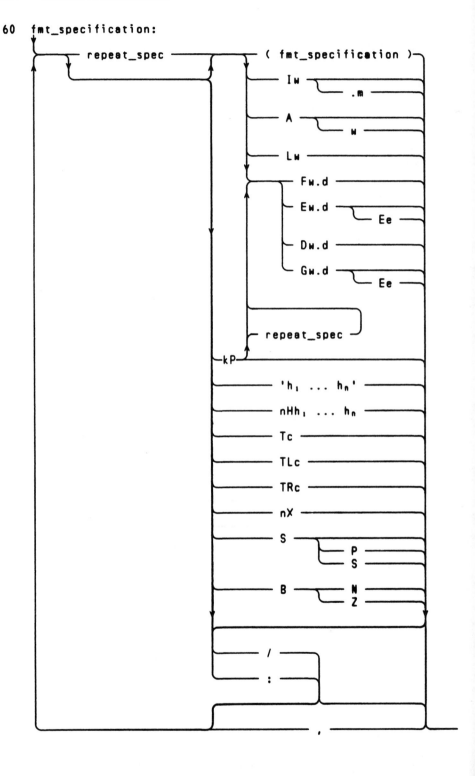

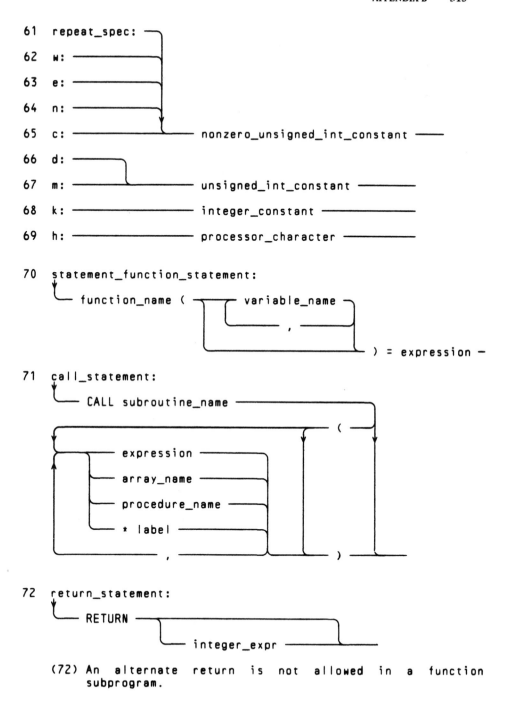

61 repeat_spec:
62 w:
63 e:
64 n:
65 c: ——— nonzero_unsigned_int_constant ———
66 d:
67 m: ——— unsigned_int_constant ———
68 k: ——— integer_constant ———
69 h: ——— processor_character ———

70 statement_function_statement:
function_name (variable_name ,) = expression —

71 call_statement:
CALL subroutine_name
expression
array_name
procedure_name
* label
(,)

72 return_statement:
RETURN
integer_expr

(72) An alternate return is not allowed in a function subprogram.

73 function_reference:

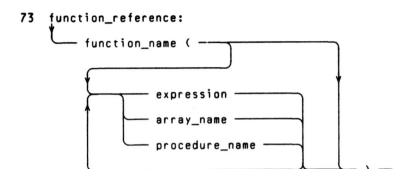

74 expression:

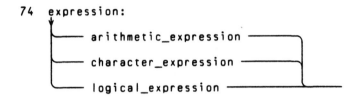

75 constant_expr:

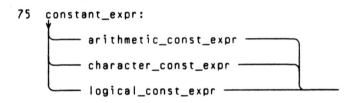

76 arithmetic_expression:

77 integer expr:

78 int_real_dp_expr:

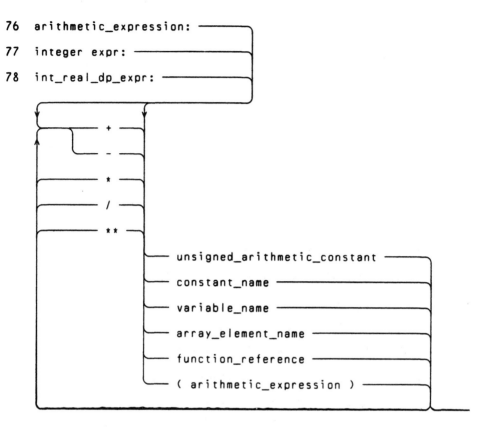

(76) A constant name, variable name, array element name, or
     function reference in an arithmetic expression must be
     of type integer, real, double precision, or complex.
     Tables 2 and 3 (6.1.4) list prohibited combinations
     involving operands of type complex.

(77) An integer expression is an arithmetic expression of
     type integer.

(78) An int_real_dp_expression is an arithmetic expression of
     type integer, real, or double precision.

79 arithmetic_const_expr:

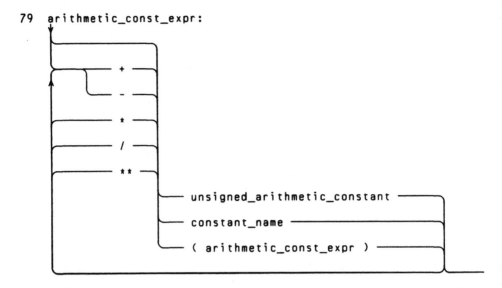

(79) A constant name in an arithmetic constant expression must be of type integer, real, double precision, or complex. Tables 2 and 3 (6.1.4) list prohibited combinations involving operands of type complex. The right hand operand (the exponent) of the ** operator must be of type integer.

80 int_constant_expr:

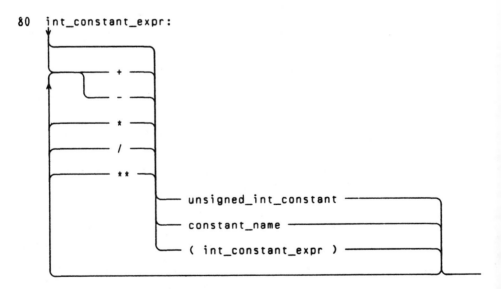

(80) A constant name in an integer constant expression must be of type integer.

81 dim_bound_expr:

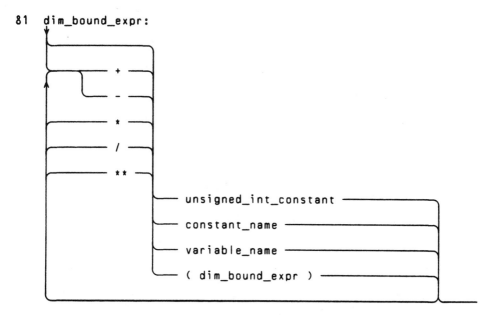

(81) Each variable name in a dimension bound expression must be of type integer and must be a dummy argument or in a common block.

82 character_expression:

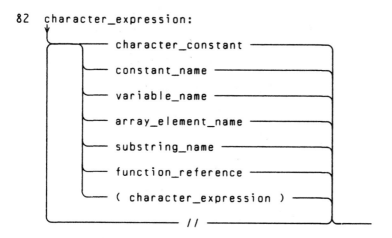

(82) A constant name, variable name, array element name, or function reference must be of type character in a character expression.

83   character_const_expr:

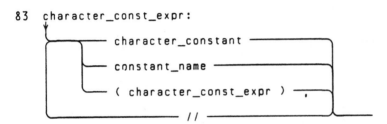

(83) A constant name must be of type character in a character
     constant expression.

84   logical_expression:

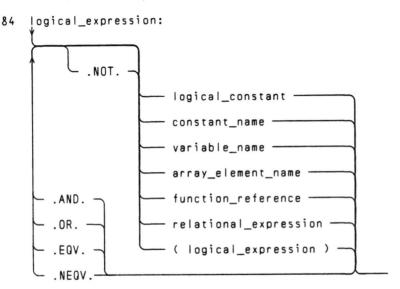

(84) A constant name, variable name, array element name, or
     function reference must be of type logical in a logical
     expression.

85   logical_const_expr:

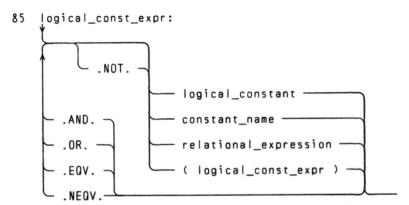

(85) A constant name must be of type logical in a logical constant expression. Also, each primary in the relational expression must be a constant expression.

86 relational_expression:

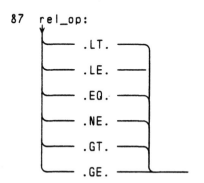

- arithmetic_expression   rel_op   arithmetic_expression
- character_expression   rel_op   character_expression

(86) An arithmetic expression of type complex is permitted only when the relational operator is .EQ. or .NE.

87 rel_op:

```
.LT.
.LE.
.EQ.
.NE.
.GT.
.GE.
```

88 array_element_name:

array_name (integer_expr 7)

89 substring_name:

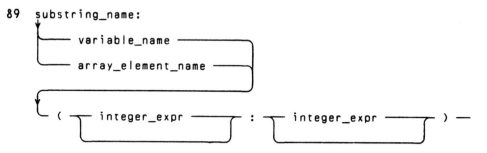

variable_name

array_element_name

(integer_expr : integer_expr)

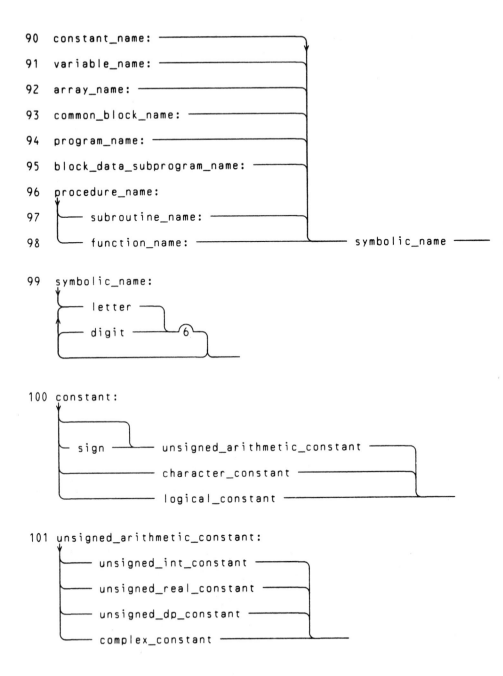

```
90   constant_name:
91   variable_name:
92   array_name:
93   common_block_name:
94   program_name:
95   block_data_subprogram_name:
96   procedure_name:
97        subroutine_name:
98        function_name:                              symbolic_name

99   symbolic_name:
          letter
          digit         6

100  constant:
          sign       unsigned_arithmetic_constant
                     character_constant
                     logical_constant

101  unsigned_arithmetic_constant:
                     unsigned_int_constant
                     unsigned_real_constant
                     unsigned_dp_constant
                     complex_constant
```

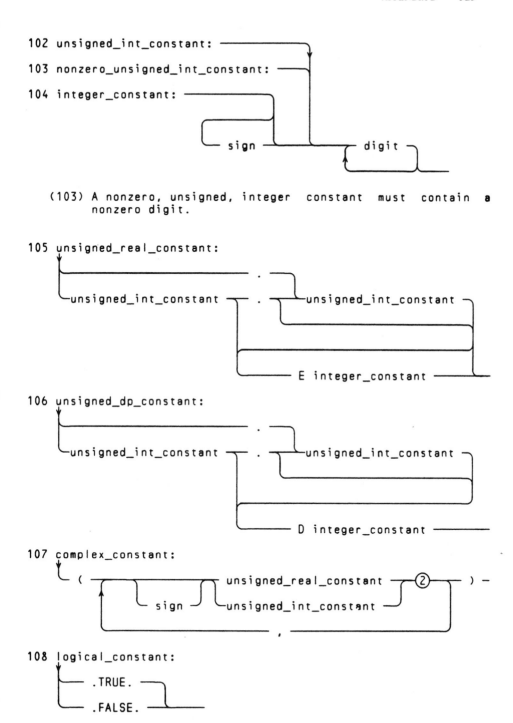

102 unsigned_int_constant:

103 nonzero_unsigned_int_constant:

104 integer_constant:

sign

digit

(103) A nonzero, unsigned, integer constant must contain a nonzero digit.

105 unsigned_real_constant:

unsigned_int_constant   .   unsigned_int_constant

E integer_constant

106 unsigned_dp_constant:

unsigned_int_constant   .   unsigned_int_constant

D integer_constant

107 complex_constant:

(sign unsigned_real_constant ②) –
unsigned_int_constant

108 logical_constant:

.TRUE.
.FALSE.

109 character_constant:

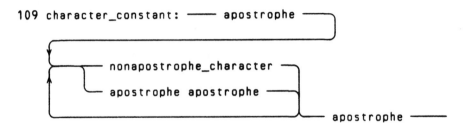

(109) An apostrophe within a data string is represented by two
      consecutive apostrophes with no intervening blanks.

110 label:

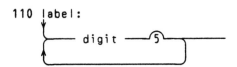

(110) A label must contain a nonzero digit.

111 processor_character:

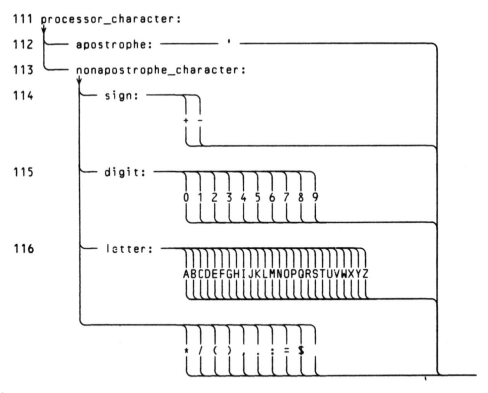

(111) A blank is a processor character. The set of processor
      characters may include additional characters recognized
      by the processor.

B.2   Cross-reference index to the syntax charts

F3   <u>Cross-Reference Index to Syntax Charts</u>

Def. Item: Reference

```
112   apostrophe: 109
 79   arithmetic_const_expr: 75, 79
 76   arithmetic_expression: 74, 78, 86
 34   arithmetic_if_statement: 7
 16   array_declarator: 15, 19, 20
 88   array_element_name: 18, 27, 28, 29, 47, 50, 51, 52, 55, 56,
          78, 82, 84, 89
 92   array_name: 11, 13, 16, 18, 19, 20, 26, 27, 48, 56, 57, 71,
          73, 88
 33   assigned_goto: 30
 29   assignment_statement: 7

 53   backspace_statement: 7
 14   block_data_statement: 5
 95   block_data_subprogram_name: 14, 24
  5   block_data_subprogram: 1
 36   block_if_statement: 7

 65   c: 60
 71   call_statement: 7
 83   character_const_expr: 75, 83
109   character constant: 43, 82, 83, 100
 82   character_expression: 50, 51, 52, 57, 74, 82, 86
 51   close_statement: 7
 93   common_block_name: 19, 26
 19   common_statement: 6
107   complex constant: 101
 32   computed_goto: 30
 75   constant_expr: 23
 90   constant_name: 20, 23, 27, 78, 79, 80, 81, 82, 83, 84, 85
100   constant: 27
 41   continue_statement: 7
 47   control_info_list: 46

 66   d: 60
 28   data_implied_do_list: 27, 28
 27   data_statement: 5
115   digit: 43, 99, 110
 81   dim_bound_expr: 16, 81
 15   dimension_statement: 6
 40   do_statement: 7

 63   e: 60
 37   else_if_statement: 7
 38   else_statement: 7
 39   end_if_statement: 7
 54   endfile_statement: 7
  9   entry_statement: 5
 18   equiv_entity: 17
 17   equivalence_statement: 6
  7   executable_statement: 5, 35
 74   expression: 29, 48, 70, 71, 73
```

Def. Item: Reference

 24   external_statement: 6

 60   fmt_specification: 59, 60
 57   format_identifier: 46, 47
 59   format_specification: 58
 58   format_statement: 5
 11   function_entry: 9
 98   function_name: 11, 20, 25, 70, 73
 73   function_reference: 78, 82, 84
 10   function_statement: 3
  3   function_subprogram: 1

 30   goto_statement: 7

 69   h: 60

 21   implicit_statement: 5
 52   inquire_statement: 7
 80   int_constant_expr: 22, 28, 80
 78   int_real_dp_expr: 34, 40, 49
104   integer constant: 68, 105, 106
 77   integer_expr: 32, 47, 50, 56, 72, 88, 89
 25   intrinsic_statement: 6
 49   io_implied_do_list: 48
 48   io_list: 46, 49

 68   k: 60

110   label: 5, 29, 31, 32, 33, 34, 40, 47, 50, 51, 52, 55, 57, 71
 22   len_specification: 10, 20, 21
116   letter: 21, 99
 85   logical_const_expr: 75, 85
108   logical constant: 84, 85, 100
 84   logical_expression: 35, 36, 37, 74, 84
 35   logical_if_statement: 7

 67   m: 60
  2   main_program: 1

 64   n: 60
113   nonapostrophe character: 109
103   nonzero unsigned int constant: 22, 27, 65

 50   open_statement: 7
  6   other_specification_statement: 5

 23   parameter_statement: 5
 43   pause_statement: 7
 46   print_statement: 7
 96   procedure_name: 11, 13, 24, 71, 73
111   processor character: 69
 94   program_name: 8
  8   program_statement: 2

Appendix C Statement Order in Fortran 77

We can identify eleven major types of statement in Fortran 77 and, as we have seen when introducing the various individual statements, there are certain restrictions on the order of statements of different types within a single program unit. The eleven major types are as follows

(a) Initial statements – PROGRAM (2.1)
    FUNCTION (10.6)
    SUBROUTINE (10.3)
    BLOCK DATA (11.5)
(b) Comment lines (2.1)
(c) IMPLICIT statements (8.5)
(d) PARAMETER statements (8.7)
(e) Other specification statements –

INTEGER	(8.1)
REAL	(8.1)
DOUBLE PRECISION	(8.3)
COMPLEX	(8.4)
LOGICAL	(8.2)
CHARACTER	(7.2)
DIMENSION	(9.2)
EQUIVALENCE	(11.7)
COMMON	(11.2)
EXTERNAL	(10.5)
INTRINSIC	(10.5)
SAVE	(10.9)

(f) DATA statements (8.6)
(g) Statements function statements (10.7)
(h) ENTRY statements (10.8)
(i) FORMAT statements (6.5)
(j) Executable statements
(k) END statements (2.1)

The first line of a program unit must be an initial statement (a); a PROGRAM statement may only appear as the first line of the main program unit and indicates the starting point of the whole program.

The last line of a program unit must be an END statement (k).

Within a program unit in which they are allowed

(i) Any PARAMETER statements (d) must precede any DATA statements (f), statement function statements (g) or executable statements (j), and must follow any IMPLICIT (c) or other specification statements (e) which define the type of a symbolic constant name defined in a particular PARAMETER statement.

(ii)   Any **IMPLICIT** statements (c) must precede all other specification statements (e).

(iii)   All specification statements (c,d,e) must precede all **DATA** statements (f), statement function statements (g) and executable statements (j).

(iv)   **DATA** statements (f) may appear anywhere after the specification statements (c,d,e).

(v)   any statement function statements (g) must precede all executable statements (j).

(vi)   **FORMAT** statements (i) and comment lines (b) may appear anywhere.

(vii)   **ENTRY** statements (h) may appear anywhere except between a block **IF** statement and the corresponding **END IF** statement, and between a **DO**-statement and the terminal statement of the **DO**-loop which it controls.

These rules are shown pictorially in Figure C.1, in which the horizontal lines indicate groups of statements which cannot be mixed and the vertical lines indicate groups of statements between which mixing can occur.

Comment lines	PROGRAM, FUNCTION, SUBROUTINE or BLOCK DATA statement		
	FORMAT and ENTRY statements	PARAMETER statements	IMPLICIT statements
			Other specification statements
		DATA statements	Statement function statements
			Executable statements
END statement			

Fig. C.1   Statement order within a program unit

Appendix D Two Common Character Codes

Character information which is stored in the memory of a computer must first be converted into a coded form. This coded form will almost always consist of 6, 7 or 8 *bits* (0's or 1's), giving a total of 64, 128 or 256 possible characters. Each character will, as we saw in Chapter 7, be stored in a single character storage unit. The compiler writer is free to choose whatever size of storage unit he wishes (as long as it can hold one character), but typically this will be either 8 bits (commonly referred to as a *byte*), or, where this is not possible, the smallest easily addressable unit of memory (commonly referred to as a *word*) – which may be 24, 36 or even more bits in length.

The actual coding system used does not matter as a general rule, although it may affect the range of characters available. However a program which has extensive character comparisons and/or manipulation may cause problems when transferred to another computer which uses a different character code. This problem can be largely alleviated by use of the LGT, LGE, LLE and LLT intrinsic functions for character comparisons (see Section 7.4), since these will always compare characters according to their order in the ASCII code; this code is given in Section D.1.

D.1 ASCII code

The ASCII code uses 7 bits to define each character, giving a total of 128 in all. Codes 0–31 are used for special, non-printing, 'control' characters, as is code 127; the remaining codes are shown below

32	space	64	@	96	
33	!	65	A	97	a
34	"	66	B	98	b
35	#	67	C	99	c
36	$	68	D	100	d
37	%	69	E	101	e
38	&	70	F	102	f
39	'	71	G	103	g
40	(	72	H	104	h
41	)	73	I	105	i
42	*	74	J	106	j
43	+	75	K	107	k
44	,	76	L	108	l
45	-	77	M	109	m
46	.	78	N	110	n
47	/	79	O	111	o

48	0	80	P	112	p
49	1	81	Q	113	q
50	2	82	R	114	r
51	3	83	S	115	s
52	4	84	T	116	t
53	5	85	U	117	u
54	6	86	V	118	v
55	7	87	W	119	w
56	8	88	X	120	x
57	9	89	Y	121	y
58	:	90	Z	122	z
59	;	91	[	123	{
60	<	92	\	124	|
61	=	93	]	125	}
62	>	94	^	126	~
63	?	95	_		

D.2 EBCDIC code

The EBCDIC code (Extended Binary Coded Decimal Interchange Code) is a widely-used 8-bit code, and is thus capable of defining 256 different characters. In practice, however, there are not that many characters available and, apart from a few extra non-printing control characters, EBCDIC contains the same characters as does ASCII, but coded in a rather more scattered way, and in a different order

64	space	128	not used	192	not used
65–74	not used	129	a	193	A
75	.	130	b	194	B
76	not used	131	c	195	C
77	(	132	d	196	D
78	+	133	e	197	E
79	|	134	f	198	F
80	&	135	g	199	G
81–89	not used	136	h	200	H
90	!	137	i	201	I
91	$	138–144	not used	202–208	not used
92	*	145	j	209	J
93	)	146	k	210	K
94	;	147	l	211	L
95	not used	148	m	212	M
96	–	149	n	213	N
97	/	150	o	214	O
98–106	not used	151	p	215	P
107	,	152	q	216	Q
108	%	153	r	217	R
109	_	154–160	not used	218–224	not used
110	>	161	~	225	not used
111	?	162	s	226	S

112–120	not used	163	t	227	T
121		164	u	228	U
122	not used	165	v	229	V
123	#	166	w	230	W
124	@	167	x	231	X
125	'	168	y	232	Y
126	=	169	z	233	Z
127	"	170–191	not used	234–239	not used

240	0	241	1	242	2
243	3	244	4	245	5
246	6	247	7	248	8
249	9	250–255	not used		

Answers to Selected Exercises

Chapter 2

2.1   RC = real constant, IC = integer constant, CC = character constant,
        − = something else.

IC	RC	CC	IC
—	—	—	CC
RC	RC	—	RC
—	IC	RC	IC
RC	RC	—	CC

2.2

valid	valid	valid	illegal
valid	illegal	valid	illegal
illegal	illegal	valid	illegal
illegal	illegal	illegal	valid

2.3   0.9 8.00 76.00 1.23 2.00 345.60 9.80 4.56 7.00
        (Each READ starts a new record; / terminates input)

2.4

real	real	integer	integer
—	integer	integer	real
real	integer	real	integer
real	real	—	—

2.8
```
     PROGRAM TEST28
     READ *,I,J,K,L
     IPLUSJ = I+J
     KPLUSL = K+L
     NDIFF = IPLUSJ-KPLUSL
     PRINT *,NDIFF
     STOP
     END
```

Chapter 3

3.1

−31	20.5
0.0	21.0
0.0	44
17	21
3.0	

3.2   LOG has one argument, MAX can have any number greater than one.

3.3 *1* Read number of apples per box and total number of apples
     2 Calculate number of full boxes
     3 Calculate number of apples left over
     4 Print results

3.4 *1* Read total distance, number of stops and amount of petrol needed to top up the tank
     2 Calculate average fuel consumption
     3 Print results

3.5

```
      PROGRAM TEST35
C  READ NUMBER OF MARKS
      READ *,N
C  SET MARKS TO ZERO INITIALLY
      M1 = 0
      M2 = 0
      M3 = 0
      M4 = 0
      M5 = 0
      M6 = 0
      M7 = 0
      M8 = 0
      M9 = 0
      M10 = 0
C  DATA MUST HAVE A / AFTER LAST MARK
      READ *,M1,M2,M3,M4,M5,M6,M7,M8,M9,M10
      AV = REAL(M1+M2+M3+M4+M5+M6+M7+M8+M9+M10)/N
      PRINT *,'AVERAGE OF',N,' MARKS IS',AV
      STOP
      END
```

(The / in the data means that the remaining input list variables will be unaltered, i.e. zero. Adding these extra values will not, therefore, affect the average.)

3.6 (a) 4.8333
     (b) 4.8333
     (c) 5.0
     (d) 17.8333

3.7 A suitable structure plan is

     1 Read height of wall and its length
     2 Convert to half-inches (i.e. a whole number)
     3 Calculate number of bricks for length using integer division
     4 Calculate number of rows of bricks for height similarly
     5 Calculate and print total number of bricks

3.8

```
        PROGRAM TEST38
        READ *,PAY
C   TAKE OUT $1-25
        PAY = PAY-1.25
C   CONVERT PAY TO INTEGER PENCE
C   (ALLOWING FOR TRUNCATION ERRORS)
        NPAY = (PAY+0.005)*100
C   RESET PAY TO ITS ORIGINAL VALUE
        PAY = PAY+1.25
C   CALCULATE NUMBER OF $10 NOTES
        L10 = NPAY/1000
        NPAY = NPAY-1000*L10
C   SIMILARLY FOR OTHER NOTES AND COINS
        L5 = NPAY/500
        NPAY = NPAY-500*L5
        L1 = NPAY/100
        NPAY = NPAY-100*L1
C   ADD $1 TAKEN OUT EARLIER
        L1 = L1+1
        NP50 = NPAY/50
        NPAY = NPAY-50*NP50
        NP10 = NPAY/10
        NPAY = NPAY-10*NP10
C   ADD 20 PENCE TAKEN OUT EARLIER
        NP10 = NP10+2
        NP5 = NPAY/5
        NPAY = NPAY-5*NP5
C   ADD 5 PENCE TAKEN OUT EARLIER
        NP5 = NP5+1
        NP2 = NPAY/2
        NP1 = NPAY-2*NP2
C   PRINT CASH BREAKDOWN
        PRINT *,'TOTAL PAY IS $',PAY
        PRINT *,'THIS NEEDS',L10,' $10 NOTES'
        PRINT *,'            ',L5,' $5 NOTES
        PRINT *,'            ',L1,' $1 NOTES'
        PRINT *,'            ',NP50,' 50p COINS'
        PRINT *,'            ',NP10,' 10P COINS'
        PRINT *,'            ',NP5,' 5P COINS'
        PRINT *,'            ',NP2,' 2P COINS'
        PRINT *,'            ',NP1,' 1P COINS'
        STOP
        END
```

Chapter 4

4.1 (a) 11 times   (d) 3 times
(b) 3 times   (e) 0 times
(c) 4 times   (f) 9 times

4.2
```
        PROGRAM TEST43
        THIRD = 1.0/3.0
        DO 10, I=1,100
          X = I
          PRINT *,I,I*I,I**3,SQRT(X),X**THIRD
  10    CONTINUE
        STOP
        END
```

4.3 Use a / in the data to terminate input (see exercise 3.5).

4.5
```
        PROGRAM TEST45
        READ *,NPL
        DO 10, I=1,NPL
          READ *,NINGS
          NTOT = 0
          NNOT = 0
          DO 5, J=1,NINGS
            READ *,NRUNS
C  USE SIGN TO SET N TO -1 IF NOT OUT, +1 OTHERWISE
            N = SIGN(1,NRUNS)
C  NOW USE MIN TO ADD 1 TO NNOT IF N=-1, 0 OTHERWISE
            NNOT = NNOT-MIN(N,0)
C  ADD ABSOLUTE VALUE OF NRUNS TO TOTAL RUNS
  5         NTOT = NTOT+ABS(NRUNS)
C  CALCULATE AVERAGE AND PRINT DETAILS
          AV = REAL(NTOT)/(NINGS-NNOT)
          PRINT *,'PLAYER:',I,'  INNINGS:',NINGS,
     *    ' NOT OUT:',NNOT, '   TOTAL:',NTOT,' AVERAGE:',AV
  10    CONTINUE
        STOP
        END
```

Chapter 5

5.1
(a)	false	(e)	false
(b)	true	(f)	true
(c)	true	(g)	true
(d)	true	(h)	true

5.3 A suitable structure plan is

  1 Initialise sums of all marks, all distinctions, all passes and counts of distinctions and passes to zero
  2 Repeat the following
    2.1 Read three marks
    2.2 If first mark is negative then exit
    2.3 Form sum of marks and add to sum of all marks
    2.4 If sum > 225 then
      2.4.1 Print 'student n has passed with distinction'

2.4.2 Add sum to sum of distinctions
2.4.3 Add 1 to count of distinctions
but if sum > 150 then
2.4.4 Print 'student n has passed'
2.4.5 Add sum to sum of passes
2.4.6 Add 1 to count of passes
otherwise
2.4.7 Print 'student n has failed'
3 Calculate sum of fails from other sums and number of fails from other counts
4 Calculate and print averages (if they exist)

5.6

```
      PROGRAM TEST56
      PI = 3.1415926536
      DO 10, NDEG=0,90
        A = NDEG*PI/180.0
        A2 = A*A
C  T IS THE LAST TERM, SGN IS ITS SIGN
        T = A
        SGN = 1.0
        S = T
        DO 5, J=3,10000,2
C  STOP IF LAST TERM WAS LESS THAN 0.000001
          IF (T.LT.1E-6) GOTO 6
          T = T*A2/(J*(J-1))
          SGN = -SGN
    5     S = S+SGN*T
    6   PRINT *,NDEG,S,SIN(A)
   10   CONTINUE
      STOP
      END
```

Chapter 6

6.1   0.6   811.1   1155.66   344
at the top of a new page.

6.2 (a)   `100 FORMAT (3(F4.2,3X))`
               `READ 100,A,B,C`
         (b)   `101 FORMAT (3(I2,3X,I2,7X))`
               `READ 101,IF,II,JF,JI,KF,KI`
         (c)   `200 FORMAT (1H ,2(F4.2,' * '),F4.2,`
               `*   '(',F6.2,' CUBIC FEET)')`
               `PRINT 200,A,B,C,A*B*C`

6.5
```
        PROGRAM TEST65
        PRINT 200
200 FORMAT(1H1, 5X,
   *   '1    2    3    4    5    6    7    8    9   10   11   12'/)
        DO 10, I=1,12
          PRINT 201,I,I,2*I,3*I,4*I,5*I,6*I,7*I,8*I,9*I,10*I,
   *    11*I,12*I
   10   CONTINUE
        STOP
201 FORMAT(1H ,I2,12I4)
        END
```

Note that this cannot be done using nested DO-loops as each PRINT will start a new record. The use of a '+' printer control character would not help either as it would not be possible to have a variable number of spaces at the start. In Chapter 9 we shall meet an 'implied-DO' which will greatly simplify this problem.

Chapter 7

7.1
```
        PROGRAM TEST71
        CHARACTER C,CSET*49
        CSET = 'ABCDEFGHIJKLMNOPQRSTUVWXYZ'
        CSET(27:) = '0123456789 =+-*/(),.$'':'
        PRINT '(1H1,''INTERNAL CODES FOR FORTRAN'',
   *   ''CHARACTERS'' /)'
        DO 10, I=1,49
          C = CSET(I:I)
          PRINT '(1H ,10X,A1,I6)',C,ICHAR(C)
   10   CONTINUE
        STOP
        END
```

7.3 THE ACTOR IS A DARING MAN
at the top of a new page.

7.6
```
        PROGRAM TEST76
        CHARACTER*30 NAME,FNAME,SNAME
        CHARACTER SEX,STATUS,SEXX*8,STAT*8
        DO 10, I=1,1000
          READ 100,NAME,SEX,NAGE,STATUS
          IF (NAME.EQ.' ' .AND . SEX.EQ.' ' .AND. NAGE.EQ.0
   *        .AND. STATUS.EQ.' ') GOTO 11
C   FIND END OF EACH NAME
          N = INDEX(NAME,' ')
          FNAME = NAME(:N)
          LF = N-1
          SNAME = NAME(N+1:)
          LS = INDEX(SNAME,' ')-1
```

```
C   SET SEXX TO SEX AND LSX TO ITS LENGTH
        IF (SEX.EQ.'M') THEN
          SEXX = 'MALE'
          LSX = 4
        ELSE
          SEXX = 'FEMALE'
          LSX = 6
        END IF
C   SET STAT TO STATUS AND LST TO ITS LENGTH
        IF (STATUS.EQ.'S') THEN
          STAT = 'SINGLE'
          LST = 6
        ELSE IF (STATUS.EQ.'M') THEN
          STAT = 'MARRIED'
          LST = 7
        ELSE IF (STATUS.EQ.'D') THEN
          STAT = 'DIVORCED'
          LST = 8
        ELSE
          STAT = 'WIDOWED'
          LST = 7
        END IF
C   PRINT DETAILS IN REQUIRED FORMAT
        PRINT 200,SNAME(:LS),FNAME(:LF),STAT(:LST),
     *      SEXX(:LSX),NAGE
   10   CONTINUE
   11 STOP
  100 FORMAT(A30,2X,A1,2X,I2,2X,A1)
  200 FORMAT(1H ,A,',  ',A,3X,A,'(',A,')',I5)
        END
```

Note the use of substrings and A formats to print exactly the right number of characters.

Chapter 8

8.2
```
        LOGICAL ERR
        CHARACTER C1,C2,B*6,N
        INTEGER A,L,Y
        REAL F
        COMPLEX X,Y
        DOUBLE PRECISION R
```

Chapter 9

9.1 (a)
```
CHARACTER*30 TEAM(22)
INTEGER WON(22),DRAWN(22),LOST(22)
```
(b)
```
CHARACTER*20 NAME(1000)
LOGICAL MALE(1000)
INTEGER AGE(1000)
REAL HEIGHT(1000),WEIGHT(1000)
```
(c)
```
INTEGER NRESP(21:45)
```
(d)
```
CHARACTER*20 PLAYER(11)
INTEGER SCORE(11,17,2)
```

9.2 (a)
```
DATA TEAM/22*' '/,WON,DRAWN,LOST/66*0/
```
(b)
```
DATA NAME/1000*' '/,MALE/1000*.FALSE./,
* AGE/1000*0/,HEIGHT,WEIGHT/2000*0.0/
```
(c)
```
DATA NRESP/25*0/
```
(d)
```
DATA PLAYER/11*' '/,SCORE'374*0/
```

9.7
```
      PROGRAM TEST97
      CHARACTER*9 PUPIL(10),NAME,EXAM(8)*10,EX*10,PASS(8)*4
      REAL MARK(10,8),AV(8)
      DATA PUPIL/
     1 'ALFRED','BEATRICE','CHARLES','DIANA',
     * 'ELIZABETH',
     2 'FIONA','GEORGE','HENRY','ISOBEL','JONATHON'/,
     3 EXAM/
     4 'ARITHMETIC','BIOLOGY','CHEMISTRY','DIVINITY',
     5 'ENGLISH','FRENCH','GEOGRAPHY','HISTORY'/,
     6 MARK/80*0/
        DO 10, I=1,100
          READ 100,NAME,EX,SCORE
          IF (NAME.EQ.'END DATA') GOTO 11
          DO 5, J=1,10
            IF (NAME.EQ.PUPIL(J)) GOTO 6
     5      CONTINUE
C INVALID NAME - PRINT ERROR AND IGNORE
          PRINT 201,NAME
          GOTO 10
     6    DO 7, K=1,8
            IF (EX.EQ.EXAM(K)) GOTO 8
     7      CONTINUE
C INVALID EXAM
          PRINT 202,EX
          GOTO 10
     8    MARK(J,K) = SCORE
     10   CONTINUE
```

```
C   ALL DATA READ - CALCULATE AVERAGES FOR EACH EXAM
    11 DO 15, I=1,8
          SUM = 0.0
          DO 14, J=1,10
    14      SUM = SUM+MARK(J,I)
    15    AV(I) = SUM/10.0
C   PRINT RESULTS
        PRINT 210
        DO 20, I=1,10
          DO 17, J=1,8
            IF (MARK(I,J).GE.AV(J)) THEN
              PASS(J) = 'PASS'
            ELSE
              PASS(J) = 'FAIL'
            END IF
    17      CONTINUE
          PRINT 211,PUPIL(I),PASS
    20    CONTINUE
        STOP
   100 FORMAT(A9,T11,A10,T22,F3.0)
   201 FORMAT(1H0,A9,' IS AN INCORRECT NAME')
   202 FORMAT(1H0,A10,' IS AN INCORRECT EXAM')
   210 FORMAT(1H1,T25,'EXAM RESULTS'//1H ,T14,
     *  'ARITH BIOL CHEM DIV. ENG.  FR. GEOG HIST'/)
   211 FORMAT(1H ,A9,4X,8A5)
        END
```

Chapter 10

10.1 (a)
```
        SUBROUTINE ERROR(N)
```
(b)
```
        INTEGER FUNCTION MATCH(C1,C2)
        CHARACTER*(*) C1,C2
```
(c)
```
        INTEGER FUNCTION POS(C1,C2)
        CHARACTER*(*) C1(*),C2
```
(d)
```
        SUBROUTINE ROOTS(A,B,C,X1,X2,EXIST)
        LOGICAL EXIST
```
(e)
```
        SUBROUTINE INPUT(TEAM,WON,DRAWN,LOST,ERR)
        CHARACTER*(*) TEAM(22)
        INTEGER WON(22),DRAWN(22),LOST(22)
        LOGICAL ERR
```
(f)
```
        CHARACTER*(*) FUNCTION NEXTWD()
```

10.2 (a)
```
        CENT(F) = 5.0*(F-32.0)/9.0
```
(b)
```
        REAL METRIC
        METRIC(NF,IN) = 2.54*(12*NF+IN)
```
(c)
```
        LOGICAL WHOLE
        WHOLE = ABS(MOD(X,1.0)).LE.1E-6
```
(d)
```
        LOGICAL FACTOR
        FACTOR(X,Y) = WHOLE(X/Y)
```
    placed after the specification in (c), above.

10.5 A suitable structure plan is

1 Read initial `ENCODE` or `DECODE` message
2 If `ENCODE` then read keyword
3 If `ENCODE` then
    3.1 Call subroutine `ENCODE` to encode message
    otherwise
    3.2 Call subroutine `DECODE` to decode message
4 Print encoded or decoded message

Subroutine `ENCODE`

1 Convert keyword to corresponding integers (`NADD`$(1:n)$)
2 Set `NBLOCK` to length (n) of keyword and `NCNT` to zero
3 Repeat the following
    3.1 Read next record
    3.2 If it is terminator then exit
    3.3 Find position of last non-space character (`NLAST`)
    3.4 Repeat for I=1 to `NLAST`
        3.4.1 Convert I'th character to its integer equivalent (1–26) or zero if it is a space
        3.4.2 Add code factor from `NADD`
        3.4.3 If integer is more than 26, subtract 26
        3.4.4 Store character equivalent as next char
        3.4.5 Add one to `NCNT`
        3.4.6 If `NCNT`=`NBLOCK` (i.e. this block is full) store block and reset variables
4 If necessary add extra characters at end of last block
5 Return with count of letter blocks in coded message (and coded message!)

Subroutine DECODE

1 Read first record
2 Extract first block. This is the keyword
3 Set `NBLOCK` to length of keyword
4 Move record `NBLOCK`+1 characters to left (i.e. remove keyword and following space)
5 Convert keyword to corresponding integers
6 Repeat the following
    6.1 Find last non-space character in record
    6.2 Calculate number of blocks (`NB`) in record
    6.3 Repeat `NB` times
        6.3.1 Convert next character
        6.3.2 Append it to current decoded message
    6.4 Read next record
    6.5 If it is the terminator then exit
7 Return with message and its length

Notice that with some care steps 3.4.1 to 3.4.4 of `ENCODE` can be placed in a subprogram which can also be used by step 6.3.1 of `DECODE`.

Chapter 11

11.1 (a)
```
          CHARACTER*30 NAME(1000)
          INTEGER ACCNUM(1000),INVDTE(1000)
          REAL LIMIT(1000),BALNCE(1000)
          COMMON/CUST/NAME,ACCNUM,LIMIT,BALNCE,INVDTE
```
where INVDTE contains the date of last invoice as an integral number of days from some fixed date.

(b)
```
          CHARACTER*20 NAME(1000)
          INTEGER WKSNUM(1000),HOURS(1000)
          REAL HRATE(1000),ORATE(1000),ALL(1000),
     *    SUPER(1000)
     1    CUMGRS(1000),CUMALL(1000),CUMTAX(1000),
     2    CUMINS(1000)
          COMMON/PAYROL/NAME,WKSNUM,HRATE,
     1    HOURS,ORATE,CUMGRS,ALL,CUMALL,CUMTAX,
     2    SUPER,CUMINS
```
(c)
```
          CHARACTER*20 NAME(100)
          INTEGER MARK(100,10)
          LOGICAL PASS(100,10)
          COMMON/EXAMS/NAME,MARK,PASS
```

Note that the above specifications assume a maximum of 1000 customers, 1000 employees and 100 students respectively. It would be preferable to use a PARAMETER statement at the start of the program unit to define a symbolic name for the appropriate (constant) maximum value.

Index